The Dictionary of

ITALIAN FOOD
AND DRINK

The Dictionary of

ITALIAN FOOD
AND DRINK

An A-to-Z Guide

with 2,300 Authentic Definitions

and 50 Classic Recipes

JOHN MARIANI

BROADWAY BOOKS
NEW YORK

BROADWAY

THE DICTIONARY OF ITALIAN FOOD AND DRINK.
Copyright © 1998 by John Mariani. All rights reserved. Printed in the United
States of America. No part of this book may be reproduced or transmitted in
any form or by any means, electronic or mechanical, including photocopying,
recording, or by any information storage and retrieval system, without written
permission from the publisher. For information, address Broadway Books, a
division of Bantam Doubleday Dell Publishing Group, Inc., 1540 Broadway,
New York, NY 10036.

Broadway Books titles may be purchased for business or promotional use or
for special sales. For information, please write to: Special Markets Department,
Bantam Doubleday Dell Publishing Group, Inc., 1540 Broadway,
New York, NY 10036.

BROADWAY BOOKS and its logo, a letter B bisected on the diagonal, are
trademarks of Broadway Books, a division of Bantam Doubleday Dell
Publishing Group, Inc.

Library of Congress Cataloging-in-Publication Data

Mariani, John F.
The dictionary of Italian food and drink : an A-to-Z guide with 2,300
authentic definitions and 50 classic recipes / John Mariani. —1st ed.
p.   cm.
Includes bibliographical references.
ISBN 0-7679-0129-0 (pbk.)
1. Food—Dictionaries.   2. Cookery, Italian—Dictionaries.
3. Beverages—Italy—Dictionaries.   I. Title.
TX349.M265   1998
641.5945′03—dc21   97-29229
CIP

FIRST EDITION

Designed by Judith Stagnitto Abbate

03   04   05   06   14   13   12   11   10   9   8   7   6   5

Acknowledgments

Alifetime goes into every book, and along the way an author meets so many people he wants to thank for their contribution to his work. A dictionary of any kind is a pastiche of fond memories and times spent speaking with people in their regional tongues. In Italy, conversation always turns to food, and that turns into debate, out of which comes first confusion, then enlightenment. There are so many memories I have like that of people who at the turn of a phrase brought to light a piece of information that had long eluded me. I am very grateful to all of them.

I must begin by thanking those people who made this book possible, beginning with my editor Harriet Bell, whose idea it was, and my agent Heide Lange, who helped make the idea workable.

I owe a special thank-you to Tony May, a restaurateur whose dedication to raising American consciousness about Italian food and drink is inexhaustible. Without his help in so many ways, I would still be trying to puzzle out the origin of a dialect term or the correct way to prepare a dish. Were it not for Anna Teresa Callan's careful reading of the manuscript and generous advice on how to improve it, this book would be rife with errors. Whatever remain, they fall wholly on my head.

To many others, my gratitude for help in so many ways. They include Paolo Alavina, Lidia Bastianich, Guido Bellanca, Edward Brivio, Arrigo Cipriani, Anna and Tony Cortese, Romeo De Gobbi, Lynn DiMenna, Tarcisio Fava, Filippo Il Grande, Sirio Maccioni, Laura Maioglio, Tonino Manca, Augusto Marchini, Nicola Marzovila, Bill Pèpe, Tom Passavant, Francesco Rabellino, Michele Sammarone, Piero Selvaggio, and Alan Tardi.

And, as always, thanks to my wife Galina and sons Misha and Christopher for never letting me get ahead of myself.

—JOHN MARIANI

Introduction

While the cuisine of most countries is the result of centuries of adapting to the influences of other, sometimes invasive food cultures, the gastronomy of Italy has always been an amalgam of myriad influences from around and beyond the Mediterranean.

Italy's location squarely within the Mediterranean basin and its own regional resources have always made it ripe for conquest. The Greek and Arab influence on the food culture of southern Italy, particularly Sicily, was tremendous from the very beginning of the region's history, and after Rome's conquest of what was then the known western world, Italy drew to it an amazing diversity of foods and culinary ideas from Gaul, Britain, Germany, Iberia, and Byzantium while at the same time exporting Roman foods, wines, and manners.

With the fall of the Roman Empire in the Middle Ages, Italy was divided into three large regions: The north was dominated by the German rulers of the Holy Roman Empire, the middle by the Papacy, and the south by a succession of Norman, German, French, and Spanish rulers, all bringing strong culinary influences to bear on those regions.

By the end of the Crusades, the European appetite for eastern spices was insatiable, and much of the supply came from the Middle East through Venice, one of the powerful new city-states that had thrown off foreign domination. So strong and wealthy did the Italian city-states become by the height of the Renaissance that the Italian royal courts, particularly those of the Florentine de'Medicis, became the tastemakers of their day, having enormous impact on the tastes and manners of France. When Caterina de'Medici moved to France upon marrying Henri II, she brought with her fifty chefs, waiters, and household personnel who helped introduce a new refinement to French cooking; she also brought the two sexes together in one dining room, which had hitherto been segregated.

Later, Spain, France, and the Austro-Hungarian Empire invaded or appropriated various Italian territories, adding their own culinary touches to what had previously been regional fare, so that it is debatable as to which came first—Vienna's *Wienerschnitzel* or Milan's *costoletta alla milanese*. Also at this time, an extraordinary array of exotic foods, including tomatoes, potatoes, and chile peppers, was introduced from the New World, further enriching the Italian larder.

Given all these culinary influences and imports, it is not until the Unification of Italy in 1861 that one can even begin to speak of an Italian national cuisine, although even then the food culture of Italy was perhaps more varied than any in Europe. After Unification and through increasing industrialization, the general outlines of what might be characterized as indigenous Italian cookery began to emerge as more and more Italians gained access to the same kinds of ingredients once available only in the north or south. While many people erroneously think that Italian food might be defined by the seemingly ubiquitous tomato sauce, for example, most Italians did not use tomatoes at all until well into the 19th century, and then only after the canning of southern tomatoes made widespread distribution throughout Italy possible.

Prior to the Unification there had, of course, been cookbooks detailing what people ate in Italy. Roman authors such as Apicius, a gourmet during the reign of Tiberius, wrote down recipes, but the first attempt at a true cookbook on Italian cuisine did not appear until 1475, when the librarian of the Vatican, Bartolomeo Sacchi, published *De honestate voluptate et valetudine vulgare* in Cremona (Concerning Honest Pleasure and Physical Well-Being). Sacchi, who later became known simply as Platina, drew mainly from Roman sources for his recipes and advocated a less contrived, more healthful kind of cooking than the extravagant cuisines of the Renaissance courts. His work was widely disseminated, appearing in a French edition in 1505. In 1570, Bartolomeo de'Scappi published *Cuoco secreto di Papa Pio Quinto* (The Secret Cooking of Pope Pius V), which also earned an international reputation for its dissertations on table service. It included the first picture of a new invention—the fork.

But there was little in print that could be made use of by the Italian home cook, who in any case had no use for a cookbook because he or she probably could not read or write.

The publication of Pellegrino Artusi's *La Scienza in cucina e l'arte di mangiar bene* (The Science of Cookery and the Art of Eating Well) in 1891—thirty years after the Unification—had an importance that went beyond being the first cookbook to bring together many of the strains of Italian cookery into one volume: Artusi's book, written in formal Italian, also spread the Italian language among a growing class of people who had learned to both read and write Italian, though they might still speak their local dialect at home.

Artusi's work did not delve deeply into regional Italian cookery, nor did he show much interest in the humblest of foods prepared by the majority of Italians of his day, who were extremely poor and who had to make something palatable from very meager supplies. Artusi's understandable pride in the food of his own region (Tuscany) favored the cooking of the north, but he did not intend to set down a strict, classical recipe for a dish, as did Auguste Escoffier when he wrote his text on French classic cuisine, *Le Guide culinaire* (1903), which was itself preceded by Carême's authoritative *L'Art de la cuisine française au dix-neuvième siècle* (1835).

France's gastronomy had certainly developed along similar provincial lines to Italy's, though the country itself was far more unified early on than was Italy, and France developed a far more sophisticated gastronomy both at home and in the new taverns, bistros, brasseries, and restaurants that blossomed after the Revolution of 1789. It was really not until the 20th century that full-fledged restaurants appeared in Italy, nor was there a population large enough to support them. Osterias and trattorias mainly serviced travelers, for few Italians had the means to eat out. Not unreasonably, Italians also regarded the food at restaurants as inferior to what could be made at home, and the true repository of regional cooking is still today in the homes.

After World War II, restaurants grew in number and importance in the large cities, and by that time it was possible to speak of widely accepted dishes, ingredients, and techniques that seemed fairly common and well known to Italian cooks, even while regional distinctions remained, and continue to remain, strong. The migration of southerners to northern cities increased the availability of southern-style dishes, while northerners introduced their foods to the south, so that it is now as easy to find *spaghetti alla Norma* in Turin as it is to find *ossobuco* in Palermo. Pizza, once a Neapolitan snack, is now on every corner in the Veneto, Umbria, Tuscany, Liguria, Sicily, and Sardinia.

Still, the people of even the smallest villages take enormous pride in their indigenous cooking, and there are dishes that are made one way in one town and in a slightly different way in another. As with all home cooking, individual cooks put their own mark on a traditional dish while respecting the essentials of what makes that dish unique to the region. And few Italian cooks would ever agree on anything like an exact recipe even for a dish that has achieved a kind of classic status. It is interesting to note, therefore, that an association of Neapolitan pizza makers have called for an official *denominzaione d'origine controllata* appellation for pizzas that require them to be made according to a fairly strict formula in order to earn the legal title of "pizza."

The task of making sense of Italian food and drink in all its diversity might seem impossible, and as one who has traveled for over thirty years in Italy, I am still amazed and delighted at the number of unfamiliar local delicacies and specialties I still find every time I go. But I have also found that despite having a different name and perhaps a slightly different seasoning, many dishes share a common taste and technique of preparation. And many dishes are only slight variations on a dish made more or less the same way in three neighboring regions. While it would be impossible to list, for instance, every local variation on braised hare *(lepre)*, I have tried in this volume to note enough variations that are either significantly different from others or seem wholly unique to a region.

In the case of "classic" dishes such as *ossobuco, saltimbocca,* and *trenette al pesto,* I have endeavored to obtain a recipe that most reasonable Italian cooks would agree on as being authoritative. In the case of dishes that were created in specific kitchens, especially those popularized since World War II, like *carpaccio, tirami sù,* and *fettuccine all'Alfredo,* I have gone as much as possible to the original source for the recipe. I claim absolutely no originality on my part for any recipe in this book, for creating something new would be antithetical to the aim of this book.

I have pored over scores of regional Italian cookbooks in order to determine which dishes are truly indigenous and not just renditions of dishes better known by other names; I have tried to note such variations in the text under a main entry. I might have come across dozens of recipes for stuffed artichokes, but I mentioned only those that have either widespread acceptance or are interesting variations of a regional recipe. When it comes to the amazing number of Italian cookies—many of which are no more than a mixture of flour, butter, and nuts—I am reminded of what Waverley Root wrote in his comprehensive volume *The Food of Italy* (1971): "You will excuse me, I trust, for not describing the other desserts listed in a Trieste cookbook I have before my eyes; there are 285 of them."

As with any dictionary, this one is set up alphabetically. Main entries are followed by a phonetic spelling of the word (see below for notes on Italian pronunciation). A literal translation is given whenever possible—but it is not always possible with dialect words whose origins are lost in ancient history or are no more translatable into English than *snickerdoodle* and *chug-a-lug* are into Italian. The definition is followed by other names by which the main entry might be called either within the same region or elsewhere; these are in italics. Some entries have cross-references in bold-face italics. The entry for *funghi,* for example, has cross-references to individual mushrooms. In those cases where I have been able to puzzle out the origin or derivation of the word, I have done so, which I hope helps to indicate the numerous sources from which Italian cuisine is drawn.

Variations on a dish or ingredient are in italics within the text of a main entry. These are repeated in the index. For instance, **aragosta** (spiny lobster) is a main entry, but the larger species, called *astaco* or *astice,* and the smaller species, called *pregadio,* are found within the text of the main entry, not as separate entries. If you come across a term and don't find it as a main entry, look it up in the index.

For seafood, I have given the taxonomic name for the wide array of species that would probably cause confusion for the American reader who would never find such species in American waters. In some cases, there is no English equivalent, so I thought it best to fall back on Linnaeus and the ichthyologists to pinpoint the precise species.

If this book helps the reader to understand both the breadth and depth of Italian food and drink while at the same time alerting him to why a dish is made a certain way and why it should not be altered on a whim or a fashion, then I feel I have succeeded in doing what I set out to do. Behind every dish in Italy there is a story, sometimes a legend, often a superstition; such considerations are inextricable from a true appreciation of why a dish or a drink is made and tastes the way it does. In trying to clear away some of the embellishments and misguided allowances that have confused good cooks as to exactly what a dish should be, I have tried to counter the absurd idea that Italian food may be interpreted in any way any cook wishes. Such a cavalier, modern attitude toward such an ancient and honorable cuisine is the reason Italian food is so often misunderstood and, too often, regarded as infinitely adaptable. It is not, and no one who has ever tasted a true *pesto* sauce made in Genoa when the basil is precisely at its peak, or the spring lamb known in Rome as *abbacchio,* which feeds upon the grasses and flowers growing outside of the city, or a *bellini* made at Harry's Bar when the white peaches of summer are at their sweetest and ripest will ever argue that such dishes can be altered without changing the exquisite flavor of such glorious examples of Italian food culture.

Italian Pronunciation

The pronunciation of Italian words is relatively easy, for every syllable is sounded and most words are accented on the next-to-last syllable. Even in dialects the pronunciation of words more or less follows common Italian patterns, with the exception of sounds that are clearly not of Italian origin, as with many German words used in Trentino and other northern regions. Italians sound out each syllable, though there are a few elisions of consonant sounds. As in any regional language, pronunciation of words will differ. When it comes to dialects, even the most well-educated Italian will have trouble understanding any that are not his.

Here is a list of standard Italian pronunciations of vowels, consonants, and syllables.

VOWELS

a	*ah,* as in *father*
e	*eh,* as in *met*
i	*ee,* as in *machine*
o	*oh,* as in *host,* or *o,* as in *pot*
u	*oo,* as in *cool*

CONSONANTS

b	As in English
c	Before *e* and *i*, like *ch* in *church*
	Before *a, o, u*, like *k* or *c* in *coat*
ch	Before *e* or *i*, like *ch* in *chemical*
d	As in English
f	As in English
g	Before *e* and *i*, like *g* in *general*
	Before *a, o, u*, like *g* in *goat*
gh	Before *e* or *i*, as *g* in *get* or *gill*
gl	Before *i*, elided as in *billiard*
gn	Before *n*, elided as in *onion*
h	Always mute
j	Rarely used, but as *j* in *jazz* or *y* in *Yugoslavia* if sounded
k	As *k* in *speck*. Used in northern Italy in words from German
l	As in English
m	As in English
n	As in English
p	As in English
q	Always combined with *u*, *qu-*, as in *quick*
r	As in English, but trilled
s	As *s* in *safe*, or as *z*, as in *vase*
sci	As *sh*
t	As in English
v	As in English
z	As *z* in *zoo*, or as *ds*, as in *maids*

A Note on Italian Usage

Though basic Italian is used throughout Italian cookery to describe its methods, food terms are so regional that conventional usage may vary from one dialect to another, and many dialect words or terms bear little resemblance to formal Italian. What most Italians call *maiale* (pork), a Piedmont native might call *crin*. Throughout Italy cooked cornmeal is called *polenta;* in Calabria, it is called *frascàtula.*

As in English, the language of Italian food is full of colorful colloquialisms. The dessert *tirami sù* is a Venetian colloquialism meaning "pick me up," much the same as an American may refer to a cocktail as a "pick-me-up." In Abruzzo, a simple dish of pork and chile peppers is called *'ndocca 'ndocca,* which translates inexplicably as something like "tap lightly, tap lightly," while the Calabrian sausage known as *'ndugghia* probably derives from the French term for sausage, *andouille,* a word picked up by the Calabrians during the time of France's occupation of their territory.

In many cases, the same food may take many regional names. Pasta shapes, especially, can have several regional names. For instance, *fettuccine* is used in Rome to describe the flat noodles more commonly known elsewhere in Italy as *tagliatelle.* And the ridged macaroni tubes known in one region as *cannolicchi rigati* are elsewhere found under the names *sciviotti ziti rigati, denti di cavallo rigati, fischiotti rigati, denti di pecora rigati,* and *canneroni rigati,* with only the word *rigati* (ridged) remaining the same.

Even within a region spellings differ for the same words, often the result of a linguistic attempt to turn a dialect sound into phonetic Italian. Even authoritative books on Italian cookery differ on the way to spell the name of a regional dish.

Pellegrino Artusi (1820–1911) has been credited as the first modern Italian author to attempt to set down hundreds of recipes prepared by the common people when he published *La Scienza in cucina e l'arte di mangiar bene* in 1891. But he is also credited with spreading the Italian language following Italy's Unification. As Kyle M. Phillips III, who translated Artusi's work into English in 1996, notes, "Over the years, Artusi's influence on Italian cuisine, and, for that matter, the Italian language, has been profound. When he published the book in 1891, only a small fraction of the Italian population even spoke Italian, and almost all lived in abject poverty." By appealing to the newly emerging middle class, Artusi's book helped codify Italian cookery while at the same time spreading the Italian language itself.

Since then Italians have become increasingly familiar with their own regional cooking, so that culinary terms that were once dialect have been absorbed into and standardized as part of the Italian language. Today a visitor from Genoa would have no trouble ordering his dinner at a restaurant in Palermo, and vice versa.

Italian is an inflected language and the standard rules for singular and plural forms are based on gender. While Italian does make distinctions between male and female animals of the same species *(bufalo* for a male buffalo, *bufala* for a female), it is impossible to know why some words are masculine and others feminine. In general, masculine nouns in the singular end in *-o* and feminine nouns in *-a.* Masculine nouns in the plural end in *-i* and feminine nouns in *-e.* Here are some examples:

Masculine

SINGULAR	PLURAL
piatto	*piatti*
scampo	*scampi*
sorbetto	*sorbetti*

Feminine

SINGULAR	PLURAL
galantina	*galantine*
melanzana	*melanzane*
quaglia	*quaglie*

There are exceptions to these rules, especially those singular nouns ending in *-e* that might be either masculine or feminine, e.g., *il padre* (the father) and *la madre* (the mother), which in both cases take the plural ending *-i.* There are even Italian masculine nouns that end in *-o* that become feminine in the plural, e.g., *l'uovo* (the egg), which becomes *le uova* in the plural. These and other exceptions fall well beyond the scope of this book, but the reader should be alert to them as he comes upon them.

The Italian definite article for the English word *the* agrees in gender and number with the noun it modifies. The most common form for the masculine singular noun is *il,* as in *il piatto* and *il sorbetto;* for the plural, *i,* as in *i piatti* and *i sorbetti. Lo* (singular) and *gli* (plural) are also used in some cases, as in *lo scampo, gli scampi.*

The form for feminine singular nouns is *la,* as in *la quaglia;* for the plural, *le,* as in *le quaglie.*

Usage referring to a food item in the singular or plural is, as in English, very much a matter of custom. For instance, in English, *oats* and *french fries* are never used in the singular; so, too, in Italian *spaghetti, gnocchi,* and *fagioli* are always used in the plural, a usage that is reflected in this book. As long as the reader recognizes the rationale for these plural spellings, I cannot imagine any confusion on the matter.

A

abbacchio (ah-BAH-k'yoh)   Milk-fed baby lamb. Also *agnellino di latte.* Principally a Roman term for spring lamb (now available year-round) whose special flavor derives from the local herbs it consumes. Ideally, between 30 and 60 days old, from 14 to 20 pounds in weight, and without baby fat. Usually roasted, if possible on a spit.

The word *abbacchio* may derive from *abbacchiare,* to beat down, as with a club *(bacchio)* used to kill the lambs, or to sell cheaply, as lamb would be sold when abundant each spring. See also *agnello* and *scottadito.*

abboccato (ah-bo-KAH-toh)   "Mouth filling." Descriptive term for a slightly sweet wine, such as **Orvieto,** which is also vinified in a dry version.

abbuoti (ah-BWOH-tee)   Molise dish of baked *involtini* of lamb intestines filled with sweetbreads, liver, and hard-boiled eggs. Also *torcinelli.*

abruzzese, all' (ahl-ah-broo-t'ZAY-zeh)   "In the style of *Abruzzo."* Term refers to the region's ample use of chile pepper, called **diavolicchio** or **peperoncino,** in various dishes, such as *lasagne all'abruzzese, cosciotto d'agnello all'abruzzese, frittata con acciughe all'abruzzese, brodetto delle coste abruzzese, fagioli cannellini all'abruzzese,* and *cardoni fritti all'abruzzese.*

Abruzzo (ah-BROO-t'zoh)   A region east of Rome located on the Adriatic Sea. It was historically linked with the region of Molise, so the two regions were referred to in the plural as *Abruzzi,* which is still sometimes heard, but in 1963 Molise seceded from the union, so that today Abruzzo is the correct name for the region.

Mountainous, but with grand valleys and a long shoreline, Abruzzo has access to good game, excellent seafood, and good grazing land. Though it is not a region of great wealth, the people eat well and abundantly, especially at lavish celebrations where the number of dishes can run into the dozens, including the famous **panarda,** which involves up to 60 dishes spread out over an entire day's eating and drinking. The region is known for the high caliber of its professional chefs, many of whom work in restaurants throughout Italy and abroad.

When a dish is prepared *all' Abruzzese,* it usually includes small hot chile peppers called **diavolicchi,** and high seasoning is a facet of the region's gastronomy. Tomatoes are also a prominent feature in the Abruzzo kitchen. Thus, *polpi in purgatorio* (octopus in Purgatory, though actually made with **seppie**) is so called because of the heat of the chiles and the redness of the tomatoes.

The most famous **pasta** of the region is **spaghetti** or **maccheroni alla chitarra,** cut on a stringed instrument into squared-off strands of pasta.

Le virtù is an ancient soup built around the legend of seven maidens who contributed pork, peas, herbs, pasta, carrots, and other ingredients.

The Abruzzese eat a great deal of seafood, usually simply prepared grilled fish and shellfish. Lamb is the most popular meat. A pork stew takes the euphonious name **'ndocca 'ndocca.**

Confetti are Abruzzese candies, sugar-coated almonds tossed at festivals and weddings for good luck.

The wines of Abruzzo, with just two **DOC** zones, are mostly workaday whites and reds, though some producers have had excellent results with the red **Montepulciano d'Abruzzo** and the white **Trebbiano** d'Abruzzo.

accarrexiau   (ah-kah-resh-ee-AU)   "Caressed." Lavish dish from Sardinia, made with a whole sheep stuffed with a suckling pig and cooked either over a pit of embers with aromatic herbs or buried in the ground and cooked over hot stones. Also *caraxiu.*

acceglio   (ah-CHEH-l'yoh)   Cow's milk cheese made in summer in Piedmont's Val Maira. It has a slightly acidic flavor.

acciuga   (ah-CHOO-gah)   The Mediterranean anchovy, *Engraulis encrasicholus.* Also *alice* and *anciova.* Eaten fresh (the season is from March through September), although pollution has destroyed much of the harvest in the Mediterranean. Anchovies are sometimes marinated in olive oil and lemon juice and eaten raw *(acciugata),* though most of the time the fish are salted *(acciughe sotto sale)* and sold from barrels or, as is more usual today, filleted and canned *(filetti d'acciuga).* Anchovy paste is called *pasta d'acciuga.* Anchovies are often mashed and added to a dish as a flavoring or used as a garnish for pizza and marinated red peppers.

In ancient Rome, anchovies were the basis for the highly prized, very expensive condiment called *garum,* a seasoning liquid made from salted anchovies left to ferment for up to three months.

accosciare   (ah-koh-SH'YAH-reh)   To truss, as meat or poultry.

aceto   (ah-CHEH-toh)   Vinegar, which in Italy is always made from wine. From the Latin *acetum*.

Aceto ordinario is fermented and produced in less than six months. *A. decolorato* is ordinary vinegar with its color and tannin removed, used primarily for pickling vegetables. *A. di vino* (wine vinegar) is made from high-quality vintage wines and takes about a year and a half to produce. **Balsamico** is a special vinegar of Modena made from the boiled-down must of **trebbiano** grapes.

acetosa   (ah-cheh-TOH-sah)   Sorrel, also known as *erba brusca,* commonly used in salads and soups.

acqua   (AH-kwah)   Water. From the Latin *aqua.*

Acqua del rubinetto is tap water, but most Italians drink bottled mineral water, *acqua minerale,* principally because in the past water from local sources was often not fit to drink and because Italians believe the minerals contained in the water, like iron, calcium, chloride, strontium, magnesium, potassium, and others, have health benefits. By law, to be called *acqua minerale* the bottled water must be determined to have some therapeutic value. Most mineral waters are from approved sources, usually underground springs, and may be bottled either still or with gas *(gassata),* which may occur naturally or be added. **Gazzosa** indicates lemon-flavored, sweetened carbonated water.

acquacotta   (AH-kwah-KOH-tah)   "Cooked water." A vegetable soup of the Tuscany countryside. Garlic is sautéed in olive oil, then various vegetables, such as sweet or hot peppers, celery, and tomato, are added. *Acquacotta* never contains meat. The reference to cooked water means that water, rather than broth, is used to make the soup. It is customarily a *zuppa di pane,* poured over a slice of crusty bread. In Maremma, the bread is sometimes topped with an egg yolk cooked by the hot soup.

acqua di fiori d'arancia   (AH-kwah dee fee-OHR-ee dee ah-RAHN-chah)   "Orange flower water." Flavoring made from water and the essence of orange blossoms.

acqua pazza, in   (een AH-kwah PAH-t'zah)   "Crazy water." Term for dishes cooked in seawater or in salted water, from southern Italy.

affettato   (ah-feh-TAH-toh)   Sliced, as cold meats. By tradition, a plate of such meats includes **prosciutto, coppa,** and **mortadella** and is served as an **antipasto,** never as part of a formal dinner.

affogato   (ah-foh-GAH-toh)   Poached.

affumicato   (ah-foom-ee-KAH-toh)   Smoked, as fish or meat, principally pork. Smoking is not a significant part of Italian food preparation. From the Latin *fumare* (to smoke).

africani   (ah-free-KAH-nee)   "Africans." Crisp light cookies made from egg yolks and sugar, so called because of their dark brown exterior. A specialty of the Tuscan town of Greve.

afrodisiaci   (ah-froh-dee-zee-AH-chee)   Aphrodisiacs. From the Greek *aphrodisiakos.*

Long a part of Roman and Italian legend, aphrodisiacs are mentioned in *De honesta voluptate et valetudine vulgare* (1475) (Concerning Honest Pleasure and Physical Well-Being) by Bartolomeo Sacchi (afterwards known as Platina). The more exotic the food, the more likely it is said to have an effect on the libido. Oysters, caviar, truffles, testicles, brains, and offal are commonly considered to have aphrodisiac qualities.

agglassato   (ah-glah-SAH-toh)   "Glazed food." Sicilian dish of braised beef, so called because of the glazed appearance of the dish caused by caramelization. From the Middle English *glasen.*

aglianico   (ah-L'YAH-nee-coh)   A red wine grape of Greek origin, widely planted in southern Italy. In Basilicata, wine made from this grape, *Aglianico del Vulture,* has a **DOC.** From the Italian word *ellenico* (Hellenic).

agliata, all'   (ahl-L'YAH-tah)   Any of several dishes made with a sauce of pressed garlic, bread, and vinegar. Called *aggiadda* in Liguria. From *aglio.*

aglio   (AH-l'yoh)   Garlic, *Allium sativum.* One of the basic seasonings of Italian food. Imperial Rome's export of the bulb led to the expression, *Ubi Roma ibi allium* (Where there is Rome, there is garlic).

Garlic has been credited with remarkable powers, from an antidote for dog bite to a protection against vampires, but in contemporary Italian cooking, it is used with discretion in the north and with gusto in the south.

Code d'aglio are the green sprouts of the garlic bulb. *Vestito* (clothed) refers to including the garlic skin with the garlic clove in a recipe.

aglio e olio   (AH-l'yoh eh OH-l'yoh)   "Garlic and oil." A pasta sauce made by frying chopped garlic in olive oil. The garlic must not be allowed to burn and blacken, or it will take on a bitter taste that also affects the taste of the oil.

agnello   (ah-N'YEH-loh)   Lamb. *Agnello da latte* is baby lamb still suckling, weighing about 20 to 25 pounds, slaughtered at one to three months old. From the Latin *agnus.*

After pork, lamb is the Italians' favorite meat. It is usually roasted, preferably on a spit over an open fire, most commonly flavored with garlic and rosemary. Lamb is also grilled as chops called **scottaditi,** and made into stews. In Abruzzo, it is boiled for two hours, then cooked in wine with vegetables and **peperoncino,** in a dish called *pecora a lu cutturu* in dialect. See also **abbacchio.**

agnolotti (ah-n'yoh-LOH-tee) Piedmont-style *ravioli*. Recipes date back to at least 1798. Though originally stuffed with cheese or herbs, most *agnolotti* today are stuffed with meat. The name would seem to mean "big lambs," but it is believed to come from a dialect word, *anolòt* (a cutting instrument), though one legend credits the creation of the dish to a chef named Angeloto in the kitchen of the Marchese of Monferrato. Called *agnolini* in Lombardy; *agnoli* in Mantua.

agone (ah-GOH-neh) Freshwater shad, *Alosa fallax nilotica*. Also *alosa* and *cheppia*. A bony fish of the herring family. The prized shad from Lake Como, fished in May and June, is often dried, pressed with bay leaves, grilled, and marinated in vinegar. When cured, shad is called **missoltit,** referring to the barrels in which the fish is packed, called *missolte,* though it is mostly eaten grilled, or cold. In Sicily, the fish is called *saracca*.

agresto (ah-GRESS-toh) Verjuice. A fairly sour flavoring made from the unfermented juice of unripe grapes. Used as a condiment or sauce with meat and seafood, though no longer as popular as simple oil and lemon juice or vinegar. The word may derive from Latin *agrestis* (relating to the country) or *acer* (sharp). See also **pollo ripieno alla lunigianese.**

agretto (ah-GREH-oh) Grass-like spring vegetable of northern Italy, *Salsola soda*. From Latin *acer* (sharp).

agriturismo (ah-gree-too-REEZ-moh) "Tourist farm." A farm that serves meals to travelers. Called a *maso* in Alto Adige and Trentino.

agro, all' (ahl-AH-groh) A lemon-juice dressing for boiled vegetables, such as asparagus and broccoli. From Latin *acer* (sharp).

agrodolce (ah-groh-DOHL-cheh) A sweet-and-sour flavor, usually referring to sauces or marinades containing vinegar and sugar, often with the addition of flavorings like bay leaf and garlic. From the Latin *acer* (sharp) and *dulcis* (sweet).

Sweet-and-sour sauces were probably brought back from the Middle East during the Crusades, for they became very popular during the Renaissance. They are still widely used in southern Italy, with vegetables and both meat and fish.

agrumi (ah-GROO-mee) General term for citrus fruits. Lemons and oranges were brought to southern Italy by the Arabs, then propagated throughout the south for distribution throughout Italy and Europe.

aguglia (ah-GOO-l'yah) Needlefish, *Belone belone*. A long, spear-nosed fish (*aguglia* means "needle" in Italian) with a purple or greenish backbone that turns bright green when cooked. Most often fried, grilled, or stewed.

ai ferri   (aye FEH-ree)   Cooked over an open fire. Includes meat, seafood, and vegetables, done in an open hearth, on a spit, or outdoors.

alaccia africana   (ah-lah-CHEE-yah ah-free-KAH-nah)   Southern Mediterranean fish in the sardine family, *Sardinella aurita. Alaccia* is a southern Italian term for *alice* (anchovy).

alalonga   (ah-lah-LOHN-gah)   Albacore tuna, *Thunnus alalunga.* The name refers to the fish's long pectoral fins. *Alalunga in agrodolce* is a dish of young tuna cooked with a sweet-and-sour onion sauce, from Calabria.

albana   (ahl-BAH-nah)   White wine grape of Emilia-Romagna. Also *greco* and *greco di Ancona.* The varietal called *albana di Romagna,* which some experts believe to be a separate grape, makes a dry **DOCG** white wine, which is also made in a *dolce* and *amabile* style.

albanesi   (ahl-bah-NAY-zee)   Ring-shaped cookies made with white wine and olive oil. The reference to Albanians is not clear.

albergo   (ahl-BEHR-goh)   Hotel or inn.

albesi al barolo   (ahl-BAY-see ahl bah-ROH-lo)   "Little Albans in *Barolo.*" Piedmontese chocolate and hazelnut cookies made with *Barolo* wine. The name refers to the town of Alba in Piedmont.

albicocca   (ahl-bee-KOH-kah)   Apricot. Also *baracoccu* and *piricocca.* The fruit may have been propagated by the Romans after Pompey's campaign in Armenia in the first century B.C. It disappeared from Italy and Europe with the breakdown of the Roman Empire, only to reappear when the Crusaders brought back plantings from the Middle East.

alborella   (ahl-boh-REH-lah)   "Bright fish." Also *avole.* A small white-fish, *Alburnus alborella,* of the Alpine lakes, particularly Lake Maggiore. Eaten fried, whole.

Alcamo   (al-KAH-moh)   **DOC** white wine of Sicily made from *catar-ratto bianco* grapes grown around the town of Alcamo. Also *bianco Alcamo.*

alchermes   (al-KEHR-mess)   A crimson-colored liqueur made from rose petals, iris, jasmine, and spices. Its color comes from cochineal, an insect, which prevents it from being imported into the United States. It is one of the essential ingredients in *zuppa inglese.* The word probably derives from the Arabic *al-kimiya* (alchemy).

alcool   (AHL-kool)   Alcohol. A word derived from the New Latin *alcohol,* originally from the Arabic *al-kuhul* (powdered antimony). Also *alcole.* Something containing alcohol is termed *alcolico.*

al dente   (ahl DEHN-teh)   "To the tooth." Term referring to the proper degree of doneness for **pasta** or **risotto,** denoting that it should still be somewhat chewy, neither hard nor mushy.

aleatico   (ah-leh-AH-tee-koh)   A red wine grape of Latium, Tuscany, Apulia, and Umbria, used in making **DOC** dessert wines. The name dates at least to the 14th century in reference to a *livatica* vine. Its muscatlike flavor makes some experts believe it is a mutation of *muscat blanc à petits grains.*

alezio   (ah-LEH-t'zee-yoh)   A **DOC** red or rosé wine of Apulia, made from **negroamaro** and **malvasia** grapes grown around Salento.

alfabeto   (ahl-fah-BEH-toh)   Tiny pasta shaped like alphabet letters, usually added to soup for children. From the Late Latin *alphabetum.*

al forno   (ahl FOHR-noh)   Baked or roasted in an oven. *Forno* is from the Latin *furnus.*

al fresco   (ahl FREH-skoh)   "In the fresh air," as a table at a restaurant, cafe, bar, or on a picnic. From the Latin *frigidus* (cool).

alice   See *acciuga.*

alimentari   (ah-lee-mehn-TAH-ree)   Grocery store. Usually small and family-owned, stocked with basic everyday foods and some regional specialties. From the Latin *alimentarius* (relating to food).

alionza   (ah-lee-OHN-zah)   A *frizzante* white **vino da tavola** made in Emilia.

allodola   (ah-LOH-doh-lah)   Lark. A tiny bird, roasted and eaten with the fingers. The best species for eating is considered to be the skylark, *Alauda arvensis.*

alloro   (ah-LOH-roh)   Laurel bay leaf. From the Latin *laurus.* The Romans believed the plant to be a noble one. Roman generals as well as Greek athletes were crowned with laurel. It was regarded as a medicinal aid as well as a protection against lightning, witches, and catastrophe.

Used as a seasoning herb in a wide variety of dishes and sauces. It is best used fresh.

al sangue   (ahl SAHN-g'weh)   "Bloody." Degree of doneness for meat, very rare with a warm center. *Molto al sangue* is extremely rare, barely cooked. From the Latin *sanguineus.*

Alto Adige   (AHL-toh AH-dee-jeh)   See ***Trentino–Alto Adige.***

alzavola   (ahl-ZAH-voh-lah)   Teal. Also *zarzegna.* A small wild duck, usually roasted or grilled. The name seems to refer to the bird's "lift into flight."

amabile   (ah-MAH-bee-leh)   "Lovable." Semisweet wine, slightly sweeter than ***abboccato.*** From the Latin for loving.

amarena   (ah-mah-REH-nah)   Sour cherry. The best are grown around Bologna and Modena. Often preserved in alcohol or sugar syrup, the cherries are served as a condiment or dessert sauce. From the Latin *amarus* (bitter). See also ***marasca.***

amaretti   (ah-mah-REH-tee)   "Little bitter (cookies)." Almond cookies. *Amaretti di Saronno* are the crisp almond macaroons created by Francesco Moriondo, pastry chef at the court of Savoy in the mid-17th century. They are eaten as cookies but are also often added to savory dishes, such as the yellow squash puree that is stuffed into ***tortelli.***

amaretto   (ah-mah-REH-toh)   With almond flavor. *Amaretto di Saronno* is a cordial with almond flavor (which actually comes from apricot pits). It is named after the town of Saronno. A wholly uncredited legend has it that the 16th-century artist Bernardo Luini was given the liqueur by his model. It has been commercially produced since the 19th century. See ***amaretti.***

amaro   (ah-MAH-roh)   "Bitter." A digestive spirit or wine with a characteristically bitter or bittersweet taste. Bitters are made from various herbs, spices, and alcohol, and originally were prepared by monks as medicinal aids. From the Latin *amarus* (bitter).
    Cynar, Punt e Mes, and *Ramazzotti* are well-known brands of *amari,* all with a slightly sweet flavor. But the *amaro* most distinguished by its bitterness is *Fernet,* believed to have been created in 1836 by Bernardo Branca, although some credit it to the physician to France's Henri II in the 15th century. It has been suggested that the name *Fernet* refers to a legendary inventor named Fernetius; others believe it is a contraction of the word *ferro* (iron) and *pulito* (clean) because a red-hot iron was plunged into the mixture to purify it.

amarone   (ah-mah-ROH-neh)   "Big bitter (wine)." An unusually strong high-alcohol (14 percent minimum) red wine from the Veneto, made from ***valpolicella*** grapes. Also *amarone della valpolicella.* The grapes are dried on mats to a near-raisin state, usually infected by ***muffa nobile*** to concentrate the sugars before pressing and fermentation, a process known as ***recioto.*** Before World War II, *amarone* was held in low regard as a tannic, oxidized sweet wine, but it is now vinified in a drier style.

amatriciana, all'   (ahl-ah-mah-tree-chee-AH-nah)   "Amatrice style." A pasta sauce made with *guanciale,* onion, chile peppers, tomato, and cheese. It is usually combined with *bucatini* or *spaghetti.* Also *alla matriciana.* The name refers to the town of Amatrice on the border of Latium and Abruzzo, and the dish is traditionally prepared on the first Sunday after the Italian public holiday of August 15.

SALSA ALL'AMATRICIANA

2 tablespoons olive oil
7 ounces guanciale or pancetta, thinly
  sliced
1 onion, chopped

1 pound tomatoes, peeled, seeded, and
  chopped
1 piece peperoncino
Salt and pepper

Heat the olive oil in a saucepan, add the *guanciale,* and brown lightly. Add the onion and cook until wilted. Drain off excess oil and add the tomatoes and *peperoncino.* Add salt and pepper to taste. Cook over low heat for about 40 minutes. Serve with *bucatini.* Makes 6 servings.

Americano   (ah-meh-ree-KAH-noh)   Aperitif made with *Campari,* sweet vermouth, sparkling water, and an orange slice. The drink is said to have been created by Domenico Marenco of Cùneo in 1880. It is not clear why it was called *Americano,* although it is possible the name is a corruption of Marenco.

AMERICANO

1 part Campari
2 parts sweet vermouth
Sparkling water
Slice of orange

Combine the *Campari* and vermouth on ice in a shaker and shake until very cold. Pour into a cocktail glass, add a splash of sparkling water, and garnish with an orange slice. Serves 1.

ammogghio   (ah-MOH-gee-yoh)   "Wrapping." Sicilian herb mixture of garlic, olive oil, and herbs spread on top of cooked fish.

amoretti   (ah-moh-REH-tee)   "Little loves." Very tiny specks of pasta cooked in soups. Such soups and pastas are easily digestible and are served to the sick, infirm, and young. From the Latin *amor* (love).

amor polenta   (ah-MOHR po-LEHN-tah)   "Love *polenta*." Cornmeal cake of Varese made with maraschino liqueur.

analcolico   (ah-nahl-KOH-lee-koh)   Nonalcoholic, as a drink.

ananasso   (ah-nah-NAH-soh)   Pineapple. Also *ananas*. From a Brazilian Guarani word *nana,* later adapted into botanical Latin, *Ananas comusus.* The pineapple is native to the New World, discovered by Columbus in 1493 on Guadeloupe. Upon its import to Europe, it was an immediate success; within half a century of its arrival, it was grown throughout the world's tropics. It is believed to have been first propagated, though unsuccessfully, in Italian hothouses in 1616.

The pineapple is not among the most popular of fruits in Italy. It is usually served fresh and simply when seasonally available.

anchellini   (ahn-keh-LEE-nee)   "Maidservants." Sicilian fried pasta pockets similar to *ravioli,* stuffed with chopped meat and fried, from Sicily. From the Latin *ancilla.*

anello   (ah-NEH-loh)   Ring, as in pastries or molded dishes. In Sicily, *anelletti* may refer to small rings of cuttlefish or to ring-shape pasta, also called *anellini.* From the Latin *ancus* (curved).

aneto   (ah-NEH-toh)   Dill. Though not among the more popular seasonings in contemporary Italian cookery, dill was popular in ancient Rome, where it was mixed into gladiators' meals as a tonic. From the Latin *anetheum.*

anguilla   (ahn-GWEE-lah)   Eel, *Anguilla anguilla.* This remarkable fish spawns in the Sargasso Sea and swims back to Europe two to three years later, then swims into rivers, where it becomes known as an elver. After about twelve years in the rivers, it returns to the sea.

The large *capitone* are traditionally prepared on Christmas Eve and Christmas, usually on a spit, in central and southern Italy. The eels from the Comacchio lagoon at the mouth of the Po River are considered a great delicacy; a favorite dish of the region is called *anguilla alla comacchiese,* done with garlic and tomato. *A. alla fiorentina* is marinated in oil, then baked with garlic and sage. *Bisato* is a Venetian word for eel. See also *capitone.*

anguria   (ahn-GOO-ree-yah)   Watermelon. Also *cocomero* and *melone.* Native to Africa but known early on to Mediterranean people, including the ancient Greeks, who may have had it as early as the fifth century B.C., and the Romans. Watermelon is usually consumed fresh, though the Sicilians make *gelo di melone* with it. It is sold on street corners in Italy.

anice (AH-nee-cheh) Anise. A plant native to the Mediterranean. The seed (aniseed) also provides anise oil. Anise has been considered a digestive aid since the days of ancient Rome. *Anicini* are anise-flavored biscuits of both Piedmont and Sardinia. (Anise is not related to the Asian star anise.) From the Greek *anison.*

animelle (ah-nee-MEH-leh) Sweetbreads. Though not as popular as a main dish in Italy as they are in France, sweetbreads are commonly fried or added to stews and, especially, to stuffed pastas and pasta sauces. The word may derive from the Latin *animula* (little soul).

anitra (AH-nee-trah) Duck. *Anitra selvatica* (also *masaro)* is a wild duck, of which there are many varieties, including *moretta, moriglione, quattr'occhi,* and others. Also *anatra.* The best time to catch wild ducks is in the fall, when they are fat from feeding. Wild duck is best roasted or braised. From the Latin *anas.*

Anitra col pien is a Veneto dish of roasted or boiled stuffed duck. In the Marches, duck is stuffed with salt pork, wild fennel, and garlic and roasted. *A. alla vallegiana* (duck valley-style) is another Veneto dish; the duck is stuffed with the bird's innards and **pancetta,** then boiled.

Papero is duckling.

anolini (ah-noh-LEE-nee) Small **ravioli** in a half-moon shape with ruffled edges, usually served in a chicken broth. A specialty of Emilia-Romagna, where they are also called *anolen* or *anulin.* The first mention of *anolini* in Italian print was in 1570, referring to a version stuffed with spices, raisins, and meats, served with a sweetened cheese sauce. *Anolini* today are commonly made with a filling of **stracotto,** bread crumbs, **parmigiano,** and nutmeg. *Anolini* are also made into a pastry **timballo** with meat juices and **parmigiano.**

ansonica (ahn-SOH-nee-kah) A white wine grape of Tuscany, used in making a dry amber wine. The grape is grown predominantly on the Argentario promontory and the island of Giglio.

antipasto (ahn-tee-PAH-stoh) "Before the meal." An appetizer. Also *apristomaco* (stomach opener). *Antipasti* have tremendous range and regional variety, from cold vegetables dressed in olive oil, slices of cheese, **prosciutto,** and other meats to hot foods like fried vegetables and fish. When several of these are assembled, it is called *antipasto misto. Antipasto affettato* is a combination of sliced cold meats, **salame,** and **prosciutto.**

A large *antipasto* may consist of plates of olives, **prosciutto, salame,** eggs, salads, pickled or braised onions, stuffed tomatoes and peppers, sweet and hot peppers, beans, beets, **vitello tonnato,** cold fish, marinated **calamari,** anchovies, sardines, **frittata,** and other dishes.

In Sicily, appetizers are called *grape 'u pitittu* (mouth openers).

aperitivo (ah-peh-ree-TEE-voh)   Aperitif. In addition to wine and *vermouth*, includes cocktails like the Martini, *Negroni, Americano*, and many *Campari*-based drinks enjoyed before a meal. An *aperitivo della casa* is a special cocktail of the house. From the French *apéritif*.

Apfelküchel (AHP-fell-koo-kell)   Apple fritters from Trentino–Alto Adige. The word is from the German.

apparecchio (ah-pah-REH-k'yoh)   "Apparatus." Blender or coffee grinder. Also, a batter for coating food or for making crêpes, pancakes, and similar items. From the Latin *apparare* (to prepare).

appassire (ah-pah-SEE-reh)   To sauté vegetables over low heat.

appiattire (ah-p'yah-TEE-reh)   To flatten a piece of meat with a mallet to make it tender by breaking down the meat fibers. From the Latin *patella* (clay plate).

apribottiglia (ah-pree-boh-TEEL-yah)   Bottle opener.

Aprilia (ah-PREEL-yah)   Three *DOC* grape varietals in Latium, named after the town of Aprilia near Rome. *Merlot, sangiovese*, and *trebbiano* are made under this name.

Aquileia (ah-kwee-LAY-ah)   A *DOC* zone of Friuli-Venezia Giulia. The name derives from the Roman city of Aquileia. There are 13 varietals included on the *DOC* list, ranging from white wines such as *chardonnay* and *pinot grigio* to red wines like *cabernet franc* and *merlot*. Also *Aquileia del Friuli*.

arachide (ah-RAH-kee-deh)   Peanut. Not much used in Italian cookery but eaten as a snack. From the Greek *arakos* (a legume).

aragosta (ah-rah-GOH-stah)   Spiny or rock lobster, *Palinurus elephas*. Also *alaustra*. Probably from the Greek *arachne* (spider), referring to the spiderlike appearance of the creature. Clawless and smaller than the American lobster (*Homarus americanus*), the *aragosta* is found in the Adriatic and around Sardinia in the Mediterranean. A larger species similar to the American lobster is called *astice, astaco*, or *elefante di mare* (*Homarus gammarus*). A small species is called *pregadio* (*Squilla mantis*).

The tail is usually simply grilled or steamed and eaten cold with lemon and olive oil, but *aragosta* may be prepared in a number of ways, including *fra diavolo*, or mixed with freshly cooked pasta.

arancia (ah-RAHN-ch'yah)   Orange. From the Arabic *naranj*. The fruit was known in ancient Rome as of the first century A.D., brought through the trade routes by the Arabs, who shipped it from India to Egypt, then to Ostia. The orange then disappeared for the most part after the fall of the Roman

Empire, until the Saracens brought the *arancia amara,* or bitter orange (*Citrus aurantum*) to Sicily around 1000 A.D. By the 13th century, it was cultivated throughout Italy. It was not eaten on its own but used as a flavoring agent. *A. dolce,* or sweet orange (*C. sinensis*) was brought to Italy by Portuguese traders from India in the 17th century.

A. rossa, the blood orange, probably grew by spontaneous mutation in Sicily, where varieties include the *nioco,* the *sanguinello,* the *sanguinello moscato,* and the widely propagated *tarocco.*

Oranges are generally eaten fresh, though their rind may be dried or candied, and they are used in **gelato, granita,** and **sorbetto.** They are also used in salads dressed with onions and vinegar and olive oil. A few preparations may use them in a sauce, but this is unusual.

Aranciata is orangeade or orange soda.

arancine   (ah-rahn-CHEE-neh)   "Little oranges." A specialty of Sicily, where they are also called *badduzzi di risu.* They are rice balls flavored with saffron, stuffed with vegetables, cheese, or meat, then breaded and fried. Sometimes they are served with a tomato sauce. Similar rice balls in Rome are called **suppli.**

Arborea   (ahr-BOH-ree-yah)   **DOC** wines of Sardinia, made from either **sangiovese** or **trebbiano** grapes grown around the Arborea plains.

arbufas   (ahr-BOO-fahs)   Gingerbread flavored with raisins, nuts, cinnamon, and honey, from Sardinia.

arca di Noe   (AHR-kah dee NOH-eh)   "Noah's ark." A mollusk, *Arca noae,* whose shell supposedly resembles Noah's ark. It is usually eaten raw, but it is also a prime ingredient in Liguria's *pasta con le zampe* (the local dialect word for the mollusk), in which it is cooked with garlic and oil.

arengo   (ah-REHN-goh)   Modest red wine of Piedmont, made in large quantities from **barbera** grapes.

aringa   (ah-REEN-gah)   Herring, *Clupea harengus.* Less popular as a food fish in Italy than in northern Europe, herring is usually smoked and filleted and served as a first course.

arista   (ah-REE-stah)   Boneless roast pork, larded with rosemary or wild fennel and garlic, brushed with olive oil, and roasted on a spit, from Tuscany.

Legend has it that the name was given to the dish after it was served to Greek bishops visiting Florence for the Ecumenical Council of 1450 and they pronounced it *"Aristos!"* ("the best" in Greek).

Arneis di Roero   (ahr-NAYS dee roh-EH-roh)   A wine grape. Regaining popularity after years of neglect, *arneis* is now used to make a **DOC** white wine in Piedmont. The word *arneis* is Piedmontese dialect for "little rascal," suggesting that the grape was not easy to grow from one year to the other. *Roero* refers to the zone where the grapes are grown. Also *Roero/Arneis.*

aromi   (ah-ROH-mee)   Herbs. From the Latin *aroma* (spice).

arrabbiata, all'   (ahl-ahr-rah-bee-AH-tah)   "Angry style." A spicy pasta sauce, usually served with **penne,** made with **pancetta,** tomato, and chile peppers. It is a specialty of the mid-south, especially Abruzzo, Molise, and Latium. From the Latin *iratus* (angry), referring to the hot peppers that give the dish its vibrant character.

arrosto   (ah-ROH-stoh)   Roasted. From the Old French *rostir.*

arsella   (ahr-SEH-lah)   Small clam called a wedge shell, *Donax trunculus,* eaten raw.

arsumà   (ahr-soo-MAH)   A wine-flavored custard, similar to **zabaione,** that originated in the town of Biella in Piedmont.

arugula   See *rucola.*

asciutto   (ah-SHOO-toh)   "Dry." The term usually refers to pasta that is not in broth but has been drained and sauced.

Asiago   (ah-see-AH-goh)   Sharp cow's milk cheese from the Veneto. Named after the area of Asiago, the cheese has been made from cow's milk since the 16th century, though originally it was made from ewe's milk. *Asiago d'allevo* is a young version, aged three ways: *fresco,* two months' aging; *mezzano,* three to five months; and *vecchio,* nine months or longer. *Pressato,* a milder, fattier version, is a commercial product made in the Po Valley by pressing the cheese to hasten ripening, then aging it only briefly.

asino   (AH-see-noh)   Donkey. Rarely eaten today in Italy. From the Latin *asina.*

asparago   (ah-SPAH-rah-goh)   Asparagus. In Milan, *asparagi alla milanese* is boiled asparagus served with a fried egg, butter, and **parmigiano.** *A. alla Cornaro* (named after Caterina Cornaro, a 16th-century Venetian heroine about whom Donizetti wrote an opera) is white asparagus dressed with a sauce of egg yolks, chopped walnuts, and orange peel. From the Latin.

asprinio   (ah-SPREE-n'yoh)   A white wine grape of Campania and Basilicata, used in making a light white table wine. Also *asprino.* The name may derive from the Italian *aspro* (acidic).

assaggio   (ah-SAH-j'yoh)   A taste of something, a morsel or little bit.

assortito   (ah-sohr-TEE-toh)   "Assorted." As in a platter of meats, fish, or vegetables.

astice   (ah-STEE-cheh)   Large lobster *(Homarus gammarus)* caught off the coast of Sardinia. Also *astaco* and *elefante di mare.* It is usually served grilled with olive oil and lemon or steamed; it may also be cooked with tomatoes and chile peppers to make *astice alla diavolo.*

Asti Spumante   (AH-stee spoo-MAHN-teh)   "Sparkling [wine] of Asti." Sweet **DOCG** sparkling wine of Piedmont, made from **moscato** *bianco* or *moscato di Canelli* grapes grown around the town of Canelli in Asti. Sparkling *moscato* was developed in the 1860s by Carlo Gancia.

attorta   (ah-TOHR-tah)   "Twisted." Cake shaped like a coiled snake, from Umbria. It is made with flour, almonds, and lemon peel. Also *serpe* (snake). From the Latin *torqueo* (to twist).

avanzi   (ah-VAHN-zee)   Leftovers. From the Latin *abante* (in front).

avemarie   (AH-vay-mah-REE-eh)   "Hail, Marys." Short, tube-shaped *maccheroni.* The reason for the name, after the prayer to the Virgin Mary, is not clear.

azienda agricola   (ah-t'zee-EHN-dah ah-GREE-koh-lah)   Term for a wine estate or farm. From the Middle Latin *agent* (agent) and *agricultura* (agri-culture).

B

babà (bah-BAH)   A cake made of sweet yeast dough with golden raisins. Baked in a tube pan, the cake is soaked in sugar syrup and rum and usually topped with a sugar icing and chopped almonds. *Babà* is also made in individual portions.

Though long associated with Naples, *baba* has Polish origins, supposedly when Stanislas Leczinsky, the deposed king of Poland who resettled in Lorraine in 1737, poured rum on his traditional *Gugelhopf* to moisten it and made the cake popular. Leczinsky thereupon named the cake after Ali Baba, hero of *The Thousand and One Nights*. Others believe the name is from the Polish word *baba* (old woman).

BABÀ AL RHUM

¹/₃ cup raisins
1¹/₂ ounces fresh compressed yeast
¹/₂ cup warm milk
1¹/₂ cups flour
1 tablespoon sugar
3 eggs
¹/₂ cup butter, melted and cooled

Pinch of salt

SYRUP:
3 tablespoons sugar
¹/₂ cup water
4 tablespoons rum

Soak the raisins in warm water for 30 minutes. Dissolve the yeast in the warm milk, add 4 tablespoons of the flour, and mix until blended. Cover and let the dough stand in a warm place for 30 minutes or until it doubles in size. On a pastry board, make a well with the rest of the flour. Add the risen dough, the sugar, the eggs, the butter, and salt into the center of the well and start mixing carefully, incorporating some of the flour into the mixture until all is well mixed. Knead until the dough is smooth and add the raisins, which have been drained and patted dry. Put the dough into a large buttered, sugar-dusted ring mold and let rise again, in a warm place, until double in size, approximately 1 hour. Then bake in a preheated 375° F oven for 45 minutes. Let cool for 20 minutes. Boil the sugar and the water for 5 minutes and add the rum. Unmold the baba and drizzle the syrup over the cake until absorbed.

---

babbaluci (bah-bah-LOO-chee)   Small snails, *Helix aspera.* They are usually cooked with garlic or in tomato sauce. *Babbaluci d'u festinu* or *b. del festino* are sold by vendors during *il festino,* the weeklong celebration of the feast of *Santa Rosalia,* the patron saint of Palermo, in July.

baccalà (bah-kah-LAH)   Dried salted cod. From the Dutch word *kabeljauw,* which became *bacalhau* among Portuguese sailors of the 16th century, who developed the technique later adapted by the Italians.

Chunks of freshly caught fish are salted on board fishing boats, then dried when the boats return to port. When readied for cooking, the cod is refreshed in several changes of water for 24 hours or longer, then cooked with many different ingredients.

Baccalà alla livornese, Livorno style, is braised with olive oil, white wine, and tripe. In Milan, *baccalà* is first boiled, then battered and fried. In Veneto, it is prepared with onions, milk, anchovies, and **parmigiano,** and served with **polenta.** In Friuli, *b. alla cappuccina* is made with anchovies, pine nuts, raisins, and spices. In Florence, *b. alla fiorentina* is fried, then cooked in tomato sauce. In Abruzzo and Molise, *b. alla cantalupese* is *baccalà* with black olives, tomatoes, pine nuts, celery, and golden raisins. *B. in zimino* is a Ligurian specialty of *baccalà* cooked with spinach. *B. alla vicentina* is an old dish of Vicenza made with *baccalà* simmered in milk until extremely tender and almost creamy. See also **stoccafisso.**

BACCALÀ ALLA FIORENTINA

2 pounds dried cod, soaked for 24
   hours in several changes of water
Salt and pepper
1 cup flour

¹/₄ cup olive oil
3 garlic cloves, crushed
2 cups tomato sauce

Trim and dry the cod and cut it into 2-inch pieces. Add salt and pepper to taste to the flour, then dredge the cod in the mixture, shaking off the excess. Heat the olive oil in a sauté pan over medium heat. Add the garlic and cook for 1 minute. Add the pieces of cod and cook for 5 minutes on each side, or until golden brown. Add the tomato sauce, correct the seasoning if necessary, and bring to a boil. Reduce to a simmer and cook for 10 minutes. Serves 6.

baccellone (ba-cheh-LOH-neh) "Big pod." Soft ewe's milk cheese from around Livorno, usually eaten with fava beans.

baci (BAH-chee) "Kisses." Round chocolate-and-hazelnut candies created by the Perugina candy company of Umbria in 1922. Each one is wrapped in foil within which is a paper imprinted with a romantic saying or piece of poetry.

baci di dama (BAH-chee dee DAH-mah) "Lady's kisses." Chocolate-covered almond cookies, a specialty of Piedmont.

baggiano (bah-J'YAH-noh) Fava bean. Tuscans use the term *baccello.* Both words derive from *baccello* (bean). The word *baggiana* is also used for a beef stew with fava beans, artichokes, and peas, a specialty of Rimini in Emilia-Romagna.

bagna caôda (BAH-n'yah KOW-dah) "Hot bath." A Piedmontese sauce of garlic, olive oil, and anchovy. The sauce is kept over a flame and raw or cooked vegetables are dipped into it. When most of the sauce is used up, eggs are cooked in the remaining oil. Also *bagna cauda.*
   Bagna caôda is a very old dish in Piedmont. Once considered poor people's food, it has become one of the most popular dishes of the region. Several other dishes in Piedmont take the word *bagna,* such as *b. dell inferno* and *b. del diavolo,* both made with tomatoes, oil, butter, milk, and anchovies, and served with **polenta.** *B. brusca* is a sauce or seasoning made from lemon, garlic, and anchovies, said to be brought to Modena and Ferrara during the Middle Ages

by emigrating Jews. *Bagnèt d'tomatiche* or *bagnèt ross* is a tomato-based sauce served with the **gran bui;** if made with herbs, it is called *bagnèt verd.*

BAGNA CAÔDA

6 tablespoons butter
¹/₂ cup olive oil
3 garlic cloves, crushed

4 anchovy fillets, rinsed and mashed
1 white truffle, chopped

Combine the butter, olive oil, garlic, and anchovies in a heavy saucepan over medium heat and cook until well blended. Add the truffle, warm it through, and serve in a ramekin. Select raw or cooked vegetables like cardoons, celery, and artichoke hearts for dipping. Serves 6.

bagnomaria   (BAH-n'yoh-mah-REE-yah)   "Mary's   bath."   Double boiler. Used to cook ingredients in one pot by immersing it in another pot full of simmering water. Also used to keep foods, especially sauces, warm. The term is also used to refer to the technique.

The origin of the term is from alchemy and refers both to Moses's sister Mary, said to be an alchemist, and the Virgin Mary, whose virtue of gentleness is part of the cooking process.

bagnun   (BAH-n'yoon)   Fresh anchovies cooked in tomato sauce, from Liguria, a specialty of fishermen of the Gulf of Tigullio. The word may refer to *bagno* (bath) because the fish is cooked as in a bath.

bagoss   (BAH-gohs)   Hard, grainy grating cheese of Lombardy, made in the Alpine Valle di Sabbia around Brescia. Also *bagozzo, gran bagozzo,* and *bresciano.*

baicoli   (bah-ee-KOH-lee)   "Little jokes." Cookies flavored with orange and baked twice for crispness, traditionally dipped in wine, from the Veneto.

ballotte   (bah-LOH-teh)   "Little balls." Chestnuts boiled and flavored with fennel or bay leaves, eaten as a snack.

balsamella   (bahl-sah-MEH-lah)   Also *besciamella.* An Italian version of the French *béchamel,* a thick white sauce made by stirring milk into butter and flour, to which other flavorings may be added.

The sauce is said to have been created in 1654 by French financier Louis de Béchamel (or Béchamiel), Lord Steward of the Royal Household of Louis XIV, although the town of Cesana in Emilia-Romagna claims the Italian version is named after Count Alessandro di Cagliostro, whose real name was Giuseppe Balsamo, born in the following century.

balsamico,   aceto (ah-CHEH-toh   bahl-SAH-mee-koh) Balsamic vinegar. A special condiment of Modena and Reggio Emilia made from the boiled-down grape must to one-half or one-third its original volume. This cooked must is known as *saba;* it is poured into barrels to ferment and to go through acetic oxidation. The liquid is then poured into a set of at least five barrels, called a *batteria,* made of different woods like juniper, oak, chestnut, ash, cherry, or mulberry, to age in attics called *acetaia* for several years after the "mother" forms on the top. Vinegars are replenished and topped off with new must each year. Some *balsamico* vinegars are aged a hundred years or longer.

Only five grape varieties may be used to make *balsamico—**trebbiano, lambrusco,** occhio di gatto, spergola,* and *berzemino.* Bottles of *balsamico* are submitted to the *Consorteria dell'Aceto Balsamico* for a **DOC** designation. Quality ranges from *tradizionale* to *qualità superiore* to *riserva* (which must be at least 12 years old) to the highest, *extra vecchia* (at least 25 years old). The very best vinegars are described as *da bere* (for drinking), although their cost makes more than a few drops prohibitive to drink; lesser varieties are referred to as *da condire* (for dressing). The *Consorteria* also stipulates that only about 8,000 bottles of 3.36 ounces each be offered for sale annually.

The name *balsamico* refers to the balsamlike aroma of the vinegars made around Modena for a thousand years, and unknown outside of that region until recently, and also to its balmlike effect. For centuries, *balsamico* was used primarily for medicinal purposes and as a sweetener. It was much prized and very expensive and was given as gifts among families, particularly among the nobility, who believed it could ward off plague. Mere drops would be used to add flavor to a sauce or to dress fruit. Only in the last decade has *balsamico* become a popular item in the kitchen—ironically, only after American entrepreneur Chuck Williams brought some from Modena for sale at his Williams-Sonoma kitchen specialty store in San Francisco in 1976; it was offered for sale in the store's national catalog a year later. Interest in the new product among Italian restaurateurs in the United States sparked an interest among cooks in Italy; balsamic vinegar has become as much a staple of American kitchens and restaurants as it is of those in Italy, France, Great Britain, and other countries. *Balsamico* is now used liberally in salads, on grilled meats and fish, and in ways wine vinegar might be. It is added in droplets to orange slices or strawberries.

Four types of balsamic vinegar are currently made in Italy: 1) the traditional vinegar made according to historic methods in Modena; 2) commercially produced vinegar in the style of Modena vinegars; 3) younger versions of Modena-style vinegar; and 4) imitation balsamic vinegar, primarily made in the south.

bamborino   (bahm-boh-REE-noh)   Beef flank. The word may refer to a chubby child.

bambuzene di Santa Caterina   (bahm-boo-T'ZEH-neh dee SAHN-tah kah-teh-REE-nah)   "St. Catherine's dolls." Doll-shaped cookies eaten to celebrate the feast of *Santa Catarina* (November 25), from Ravenna.

banana   (bah-NAH-nah)   Banana. The word *banana* derives from a West Indian word for the fruit. Though found growing wild in the tropics of Africa, Asia, and the Americas and perhaps cultivated as long ago as 1000 B.C. in Assyria, the banana does not seem to have reached ancient Greece or Rome, mainly because of its perishability in transport and the lack of seeds to plant. It was only after World War I that the banana was to be found readily in European markets. It has never made a significant contribution to Italian food culture.

In Italian the term *banana* also refers to a long, banana-shape bread used for sandwiches and is the name of a pasta shaped like chunks of cut-up bananas.

bandiera, la   (lah bahn-dee-YEH-rah)   Dish made with ingredients in the colors of the Italian flag called *la bandiera*—green (arugula and basil), white (potatoes and pasta), and red (tomato). The arugula and tomato are cooked together with garlic and olive oil, then combined with boiled potatoes and pasta, usually **ditalini.** A specialty of Apulia.

bar   (bahr)   As in English, a place to enjoy spirits and wine. In Italy, the variety of foods and the service of coffee may be more extensive than at a typical American or English bar. The term "American bar" in Italy refers more specifically to a place with a stand-up counter as well as chairs and tables where one may have mixed drinks and cocktails. A bartender is a *gestore di bar.*

barbabietola   (bahr-bah-B'YEH-toh-lah)   Beet. Thought to be native to Italy, it is far from Italians' favorite vegetable. The ancient Romans probably ate only the leaves, though by the Christian era the root seems to have come into some favor as a comestible.

Usually purchased already cooked, beets are dressed with olive oil, vinegar, and oil; if bought fresh they must be boiled or baked in an oven, then peeled before serving.

barba di frate   (BAHR-bah dee FRA-teh)   "Monk's beard." A thin wild grass with a slightly bitter, acidic taste. It is eaten raw or sautéed in olive oil. Also *barba di cappuccino.*

barbagliata   (bahr-bah-L'YAH-tah)   Also *barbarìa.* Drink of **espresso** and cocoa, served warm or cold, from Milan.

Barbaresco (bahr–bah–RES–koh)   Famed **DOCG** red wine of Piedmont, made from **nebbiolo** grapes grown around the town of Barbaresco. Similar to **Barolo,** it usually has a more refined "feminine" character. *Barbaresco* was first vinified in the 1890s by Domizio Cavazza of Alba's Oenological School, but was not held in high regard until the 1960s, when Bruno Giacosa and Angelo Gaja showed how refined the wine could be. Since then, the wine is often made in small barrels and as single estate bottlings. The use of new oak, pioneered by Angelo Gaja, has given the wine more finesse and enhanced its reputation.

barbera (bahr–BEH–rah)   The second most widely planted red grape variety in Italy, after **sangiovese.** *Barbera,* sometimes blended with **nebbiolo,** produces a **DOC** medium–bodied red in Piedmont, Emilia–Romagna, and Lombardy. *Barbera d'Alba,* made around Alba, is a rich, more complex wine with aging potential, while *Barbera d'Asti,* made around Asti, is generally softer and more acidic, meant to be drunk fairly young. Lighter still is *Barbera del Monferrato* from the hills of the same name, often containing other grapes like **grignolino** and **dolcetto.**

Bardolino (bahr–doh–LEE–noh)   **DOC** light red or rosé wine from Veneto, made from **corvina veronese,** *rondinella, molinara,* and *negrara* grapes grown around Lake Garda. A **classico** version is made around the town of Bardolino. It is sometimes made into a sparkling wine, and the rosé version is called **chiaretto.** There has even been an attempt to market a not–fully–aged *Bardolino Novello* as a competitor to France's *Beaujolais Nouveau.*

barile (bah–REE–leh)   Barrel. The term also refers to a bread loaf with a thick crust, made of hard durum wheat and weighing up to 4 pounds, from Apulia.

Barolo (bah–ROH–loh)   **DOCG** red wine of Piedmont, made from the **nebbiolo** grape. Of great body and richness, it is known as the "king of wine and the wine of kings." It has a long, noble history, especially since the 19th century when the House of Savoy adopted *Barolo* as its favorite wine. Originally *Barolo* was a sweet wine, but by the mid–19th century, it was being vinified dry and its tannin took a great deal of time to mature.

The principal zones of high quality are around the towns of Barolo, La Morra, Castiglione Falletto, Serralunga d'Alba, and the northern half of Monforte d'Alba, which produce nearly 90 percent of the region's *Barolo.* The wine maintains its reputation for big body and richness, though increasingly producers have aimed for a lighter, fruitier, easy–to–drink style. *Barolo Chinato* is an **amaro** made by steeping quinine in *Barolo* wine.

barrique (bah–REE–keh)   Small oak wine barrel used for aging wine. The term is from the French, but sometimes the Italian word *caratello* is used.

Basilicata (bah-see-lee-KAH-tah)   Southern Italian region located in the instep of the boot of Italy. The name is believed to derive from the basilica in the town of Acerenza, though the capital city is Potenza. In the eighth century B.C. the Greeks settled in the area, followed, five centuries later, by the Romans, who called the region Lucania. Later still, Basilicata was under the rule of the Byzantine Empire.

The rugged, mountainous character of Basilicata has made this one of the most impoverished regions of Italy. Poverty forced many to subsist principally on vegetables, which often served as the principal part of the meal, as in the stew called *ciambotta* or *ciammotta*. But the people of the area learned to make their food as delectable as possible by using every part of the animal, especially the pig, and by slowly cooking tough meat until succulent and tender. Mint figures in many dishes of Basilicata, including *scapece* with sardines preserved in vinegar flavored with mint, and *ciammaruchedde,* snails cooked with mint.

Pasta dishes are hearty and usually made from dried *maccheroni,* often served with a sauce containing meager bits of pork or mutton.

The cooks of Basilicata make generous use of the very hot chile pepper called *diavolicchio.*

Probably the best-known food product of Basilicata is *luganega* sausage, which takes its name from the old name of the region. Basilicata is known for the tastiness of its sausages; there is even one called *pezzente,* which means "very poor."

Cutturiedde is a lamb or mutton stew. *Pigneti* is a stew of mutton and other meats.

Burrata and *mozzarella* cheeses are found throughout Basilicata. Sweets include cookies and a local favorite called *torta di latticini,* literally "cake of cheeses," filled with eggs and various cheeses.

Basilicata's red wines are strong and robust, the best known being *Aglianico del Vulture.* Whites rarely rise above the quality of *vino da tavola.*

basilico (bah-SEE-lee-koh)   Basil. Basil originated in India but was well known in ancient Greece at least as early as 400 B.C. Today it is widely used as a seasoning and is the principal ingredient in *pesto.* From the Greek *basilíkon* (kingly) because St. Helena was said to find the True Cross where the air smelled like perfume.

bastarduna (bah-stahr-DOO-nah)   "Big bastard." Smyrna fig. Also prickly pear. A Sicilian term.

batsoà (baht-soh-AH)   "Silk stockings." Pig's feet dipped in an egg batter and fried in butter, served as an *antipasto,* from Piedmont. Though it would appear to be a heavy dish, it is considered quite delicate and therefore derives its name from a transliteration of the French *bas de soie.*

batticarne (bah-tee-KAHR-neh)   Heavy metal "meat pounder."

battuto (bah-TOO-toh)   "Beaten." A mixture of minced *pancetta* or fatback, onion, garlic, parsley, and other ingredients. It is sometimes added raw to soups and stews toward the end of the cooking process, but more often is lightly sautéed in olive oil, in which case it is called a *soffritto.* From the Latin *battuo* (beat).

Bauernbrot (BAU'RN-broht)   Dark rye bread of Alto Adige. The word is from the German *Bauernbrot* (farmers' or country bread).

bauletta (bau-LEH-tah)   "Little trunk." Bread roll from Mantua. The word also refers to *ravioli* filled with ham and cheese, from Friuli.

bava, alla (AH-lah BAH-vah)   "Dribble style." Any dish in which cheese is melted into thin strings that seem to dribble from the body of the cheese.

bavarese (ba-vah-REH-zeh)   Bavarian cream. A cold egg custard mixed with whipped cream and flavorings, particularly fruit puree, placed in a mold, and chilled. It is then unmolded.

The connection to Bavaria has never been satisfactorily explained, but Sandro Doglio in his *Gran dizionario della gastronomia del Piemonte* (1990) asserts that the original name came from a chocolate drink called *bevarèisa,* meaning "drinkable," which is similar to *bicerin.* He credits its invention to chef Giovanni Antonio Ari in 1678. Doglio further notes that in the next century the princes of Bavaria enjoyed such a beverage at the celebrated Paris café run by Sicilian confectioner and ice-cream maker Francesco Procopio de'Coltelli. Later on, the drink apparently evolved into a rich, thick custard that became known in French as *crème bavarois.*

bavette (bah-VEH-teh)   "Little dribbles." Ribbon-shaped pasta, often served with fava beans, from Tuscany. See also *linguine.*

bavosa (ba-VOH-sah)   Blenny. Any of several small fish in the family Blenniidae used in soups. The word means "slobbering," probably referring to the look of the fish's mouth and lips.

beccaccia (beh-KAH-ch'yah)   "Little beak." Woodcock. A migratory bird usually hunted only in October and November, then March and April. Until modern times, the giblets of the bird were favored for pâtés and mousses. The bird is usually barded and roasted.

beccaccino (beh-kah-CHEE-noh)   "Little beak." Snipe. A small migratory bird at its culinary best in autumn. Owing to its small size and lack of body fat, snipe is usually barded and roasted.

beccafico (beh-kah-FEE-koh)   "Fig pecker." Warbler. *Melanzane a beccafico* is a Sicilian dish of eggplant stuffed with bread crumbs, currants, pine nuts or **passoli e pinoli,** and **pecorino** so that they resemble fat little birds. The dish is then baked.

bellini (beh-LEE-nee) Cocktail made of equal parts fresh white peach juice and **prosecco.** The drink was concocted at Harry's Bar in Venice in the 1930s, but was not given its name until 1948, in honor of the Renaissance artist Giovanni Bellini, for whom an exposition was being held that year in the city. At Harry's Bar it is served in a slender but not very tall glass. Elsewhere it is commonly served in a champagne tulip glass.

According to Arrigo Cipriani, owner of Harry's Bar, the peach juice must be made by using a food mill to produce pulp, which is then pushed through a fine sieve. The cocktail is made by combining one-third fresh white peach juice (best if chilled before using) and two-thirds *prosecco,* poured into a chilled glass.

Bel Paese (bell pye-EH-zeh) "Beautiful country." A soft, mild cow's milk cheese from Lombardy. It was named by the man who created it in 1929, Egidio Galbani, after a children's photography book written by family friend Antonio Stoppani, whose picture is still on the wrapper.

ben cotta (ben KOH-tah) "Well cooked," as in cooking a piece of meat.

bensone (ben-SOH-neh) Lemon-flavored crumbly sponge cake of Modena. Baked in a spiral or the shape of the letter S, it is traditionally broken off into pieces and dipped into sweet wine, then eaten with a spoon. If jam is baked into the center of the cake, it is called *ciambella.*

bergamotta (behr-gah-MOH-tah) Bergamot. An orangelike, pear-shaped citrus fruit used in Calabria to make a marmalade. From the Turkish *bey armudu* (the bey's pear).

berlingozzo (behr-leen-GOH-t'zoh) Sweet ring cake flavored with anise, from Tuscany. Also *berlingaccio.* The dialect word derives from *berlingare,* which means to chatter on, as when one is stuffed with too much food and drink; it is also a slang term for food-loving Florentines.

bettelmat (BEH-tehl-maht) Unpasteurized cow's milk cheese similar to *fontina,* from Piedmont. Also *battelmat.* It is produced in Val d'Ossola as well as in the canton of Ticino. The name refers to *mattolina,* an aromatic herb of the Val Formazza that gives the cow's milk a characteristic flavor.

bettola (BEH-toh-lah) Tavern.

bev'r in vin (BEV'R een VEEN) Lombardian meat broth to which red wine has been added. The dialect term means "drunk in wine."

Biancale di Rimini   (bee-ahn-KAH-leh dee REE-mee-nee)   A white wine of San Marino based on *trebbiano* grapes grown around Rimini.

Bianchello del Metauro   (bee-ahn-KEH-loh dell meh-TAU-roh) *DOC* white wine of the Marches, made from *bianchame* grapes grown along the Metauro River.

bianchetti   (bee-ahn-KEH-tee)   "Little white (fish)." Anchovy or sardine spawn. Also *gianchetti*. They are usually boiled or fried and served with olive oil and lemon juice. In Calabria, made into a hot sauce called *mustica*.

bianchi di spagna   (bee-AHN-kee dee SPAH-n'yah)   "White Spanish [beans]." Large white kidney beans. Cooked and served warm or at room temperature with olive oil and lemon as an *antipasto*, as a side dish with meat, or in various stewed dishes. Also *spagnoni*.

bianco   (bee-AHN-koh)   White. Refers to wine.
   In bianco refers to a dish that is boiled and served plain or with little seasoning, or to a dish prepared without tomato sauce, such as *pasta con il tonno in bianco* (without tomato sauce), as opposed to *pasta con il tonno rosso* (with tomato sauce).

Bianco Capena   (bee-AHN-koh kah-PAY-nah)   *DOC* white wine of Latium, made from *malvasia* and *trebbiano* grapes grown around Capena.

Bianco dei Colli Maceratesi   (bee-AHN-koh DAY-ee KOH-lee mah-cheh-rah-TEH-zee)   *DOC* white wine of the Marches, made from *trebbiano* and *maceratino* grapes.

Bianco della Valdinievole   (bee-AHN-koh DEH-la vahl-dee-nee-EH-voh-leh)   *DOC* white wine of Tuscany, made from *trebbiano toscano* grapes.

Bianco dell'Empolese   (bee-AHN-koh dell-ehm-poh-LAY-seh)   *DOC* white wine of Tuscany, made from *trebbiano* grapes grown in the Empoli region.

Bianco di Custoza   (bee-AHN-koh dee kuh-STOH-zah)   *DOC* light white wine of the Veneto. It is made from several varietals, including *trebbiano toscano*, *garganega*, and *tocai friulano*, grown around Lake Garda. It is also made into a sparkling wine.

Bianco di Pitigliano   (bee-AHN-koh dee pee-tee-LY'AHN-oh) *DOC* white wine of Tuscany, made from *trebbiano, greco,* and *malvasia* grapes grown around Pitigliano.

Bianco di Scandiano   (bee-AHN-koh dee skahn-dee-AH-noh) *DOC* white wine of Emilia-Romagna, made from *sauvignon* grapes grown around the town of Scandiano. Sparkling and still versions are made.

bianco d'uovo   (bee-AHN-koh D'WOH-voh)   Egg white.

biancolello   (bee-ahn-koh-LEH-loh)   White wine grape of Campania, grown mainly on Ischia.

biancomangiare   (bee-AHN-coh-mahn-JAH-reh)   "White food." Jellied white custard flavored with almonds or (especially in Sicily) pistachios. This very old dessert (called *blancmange* in French), whose name derives from the whiteness of the custard, is said to have originated in France's Languedoc during the Middle Ages, and it was a very popular dish at aristocrats' banquets throughout the Renaissance. It is said that *biancomangiare* was served in the shape of a French poodle at the marriage feast of Caterina de' Medici of Florence and Henri II of France in 1533.

Bianco Pisano di San Torpè   (bee-AHN-koh pee-SAH-noh dee sahn tor-PEH)   *DOC* white wine of Tuscany made from *trebbiano* grapes grown around Pisa.

Bianco Vergine Valdichiana   (bee-ANH-koh VEHR-jee-neh vahl-dee-K'YAH-nah)   *DOC* white wine of Tuscany, made from *trebbiano* and *malvasia* grapes grown in the Valle di Chiana.

bicchiere   (bee-K'YEH-reh)   A glass.

bicerin   (bee-cheh-REEN)   Hot beverage made of chocolate, coffee, and milk, from Piedmont. It is a specialty of Turin, said to be created in the early 1700s at a café named Florio. The drink took the name *bicerin* from the little glass cup with a metal handle in which it was served.

bietola   (bee-EH-toh-lah)   Swiss chard. Believed to be native to Italy with no particular connection to Switzerland. The word *bietola* is from the Latin *beta*. It is used much like spinach and for the filling of Parma's *tortelli con erbette*. The ribs of Swiss chard are called *gambi*.

Biferno   (bee-FEHR-noh)   *DOC* white, red, and rosé wine of Molise.

biga   (BEE-gah)   Bread starter made from flour, yeast, and water. If the *biga* is left over from the previous day's baking, it is sometimes called *pasta vecchia* (old dough).

bigio   (BEE-j'yoh)   Whole wheat and white flour bread loaf.

bignè   (bee-N'YEH)   Cream- or chocolate-filled fried puff, from Rome. Called *beignets* (bumps) in French.

bigoli   (BEE-goh-lee)   Whole wheat pasta, slightly thicker than *spaghetti*—about one-tenth of an inch in diameter. It is very common in Venice, where it is made on a pasta press called a *bigolo* and served with a sauce of salted anchovies or sardines, *bigoli scuri in salsa*. In Lombardy and

Sicily, fresh sardines are more commonly used. Other traditional Venetian dishes include *bigoli all'anitra,* with a sauce of duck giblets and liver with the meat served in a duck broth, and *b. con sugo di oca conservato,* with preserved goose *confit. B. coi rovinazzi* is a Padua specialty made with a sauce of giblets, cockscombs, and sage. In Trentino-Alto Adige the pasta is called *bigoi.* In other regions a similar pasta is called *vermicelloni.*

binario di frolla   (bee-NAH-ree-oh dee FROH-lah)   "Pastry railroad track." Ricotta-filled cheesecake whose flat pastry strips resemble the track.

biova   (bee-OH-vah)   Lard bread from Piedmont. It has a fat round center and tapering ends and weighs up to 12 ounces. *Biovetta* is a smaller version of the same bread, weighing about 2 ounces.

biraldo   (bee-RAHL-doh)   Fresh blood sausage from Tuscany. Also called *biroldo* and *mallegato.*

birra   (BEE-rah)   Beer. That the word derives from the English or German word for beer, rather than from Latin *(cervisia),* indicates that beer drinking was not particularly popular until well into the 19th century, and Italian beers were brewed along the model of German lagers. By 1865, however, there were 114 *birrerie,* or beer taverns, serving their own brewery's beer, in Turin alone.

Since the 1980s young Italians have begun to drink more beer and less wine than previous generations. The best-known labels are Rome's Peroni, Udine's Birra Moretti, and Milan's Birra Dreher. *Birra alla spina* is draft beer.

bisato   (bee-SAH-toh)   Venetian dialect for eel, **anguilla.** Often sautéed in olive oil with bay leaf.

biscottato   (bee-skoh-TAH-toh)   Bread rebaked to give it a crisp, crunchy crust and texture.

biscotto   (bee-SKOH-toh)   "Twice baked." Dry cookie. Often containing nuts, *biscotti* are usually slices from a twice-baked flattened cookie loaf. In Tuscany, *biscottini* or **cantucci** are almond cookies. In Sicily, *biscotti a rombo* are diamond-shaped cookies and *b. regina* (queen's biscuits) are sesame seed biscuits. *B. tipo pavesini* are almond biscuits of Pavia. *B. de la bricia* are flavored with fennel seeds, a specialty of La Spezia. *B. aviglianesi* (Avigliano style) are made with unleavened bread flour.

biscuit Tortoni   (BEE-skweet tohr-TOH-nee)   French ice cream confection. Made of frozen vanilla mousse containing macaroons, almonds, and rum, it was created by the Italian confectioner Tortoni, who ran the fashionable Pavillon de Hanovre in Paris. *Biscuit Tortoni* became a very popular confection in Italian-American restaurants.

bistecca   (bee-STEH-kah)   Beef steak. In Florence, the classic *bistecca alla fiorentina* is a massive T-bone (***lombata***), at least 1¹/₂ inches thick, usually (though not always) marinated in olive oil, then grilled over charcoal. It is often served with olive oil and lemon, with white beans on the side. The best steak comes from young beef raised in the Valle di Chiana in eastern Tuscany. These *Chianina* cattle, which are not grown to full maturity, are known as *vitellone* (big veal). The meat may be aged for up to a month.

A *bistecchina* is a thin boneless slice of beef or veal, which is usually grilled.

BISTECCA ALLA FIORENTINA

T-bone beef steak, 1¹/₂ inches thick   *Olive oil infused with rosemary*
¹/₂ cup olive oil   *(optional)*
Salt and pepper   *Lemon wedges*

Marinate the steak in the olive oil for about 1 hour. Prepare a charcoal fire. Season steak with salt and pepper to taste. Grill for 6 to 8 minutes on each side, or until rare to medium-rare. If desired, brush with rosemary-flavored olive oil. Serve with lemon wedges. Serves 2.

bitter   (BEE-tehr)   Any of a variety of bitter beverages. See ***amaro***.

bitto   (BEE-toh)   Soft cow's milk cheese, from Valtellina in Lombardy. Aged about 40 days, longer if intended for grating.

blau Forelle   (blau foh-REH-leh)   "Blue trout." Trentino-Alto Adige version of France's *truite au bleu,* in which trout is cooked in white wine and vinegar to give it a blue color. From the German.

bobici   (boh-BEE-chee)   "Little pieces." Bean, potato, corn, and ham soup from Friuli.

Boca   (BOH-kah)   ***DOC*** red wine of Piedmont, made from ***nebbiolo,*** ***vespolina,*** and ***bonarda*** grapes grown around the villages of Boca and Maggiora.

bocca di dama   (BOH-kah dee DAH-mah)   "Lady's mouth." Sponge cake.

bocca d'oro   (BOH-kah DOH-roh)   "Gold mouth." Croaker, *Argyrosomus regius.* The name refers to the fish's gold-colored throat.

bocca nera   (BOH-kah NEH-rah)   "Black mouth." Dogfish, *Galeus melastomus.* The name refers to the fish's black mouth. Other regional names are used, including *moiella* in Genoa and *pesce 'impiso* in Naples. In Taranto, the fish is called *vooche de 'mfierne;* in Palermo, *pisci 'd'infernu.*

boccolotti   (boh-koh-LOH-tee)   "Big sockets." Short, squat *maccheroni* tubes.

bocconato   (boh-koh-NAH-toh)   "Big mouthful." Pastry stuffed with chicken livers, sweetbreads, and truffles. Served as an *antipasto.*

bocconcini   (boh-kohn-CHEE-nee)   "Small mouthfuls." Morsels of veal made into a stew.

Bocconcini modenesi, sandwiches from Modena, are made with crustless white bread filled with *prosciutto,* cheese, and white truffle. They are dipped in batter and fried. The term also refers to small *mozzarella* balls about 1 inch in diameter.

bocconotti   (boh-koh-NOH-tee)   "Big mouthfuls." Filled puff-pastry shells. Chicken livers, sweetbreads, and, in season, truffles are used. In Apulia, *bocconotti* are made in a half-moon shape.

In Abruzzo, they are muffin-shape pastries filled with a mixture of chocolate and almonds. The term also refers to *Marsala-*flavored sweet pastries filled with cream and jam.

boero   (boh-EH-roh)   "Boer." Liqueur-filled chocolate candy containing a cherry. The reason for the name is not clear.

boga   (BOH-gah)   Bogue, *Boops boops.* A Mediterranean silver fish, similar to sea bream, with large eyes. It is grilled or served with a sauce of tomato and Mediterranean seasonings.

boldro   (BOHL-droh)   See *rana pescatrice.*

Bolgheri   (bohl-GEH-ree)   *DOC* white and rosé wines of Tuscany, made from grapes grown around the Bolgheri-Castagneto Carducci area. The white is made from *trebbiano* and *vermentino* grapes, the rosé from *sangiovese* and *canaiolo nero.*

bollire   (boh-LEE-reh)   To boil. *Bollito* means boiled. From the Latin *bullire.*

bollito misto   (boh-LEE-toh MEE-stoh)   "Mixed boil." A dish based on boiled meats and vegetables, commonly containing beef, chicken, veal, tongue, calf's head, and *cotechino* sausages. One old Piedmontese tradition with cabalistic associations insists there must be seven cuts of beef; seven kinds of *ornamenti,* i.e., cuts like tongue, oxtail, and capon; seven vegetables; and three different sauces, one green made with parsley, one red made with tomato, and one yellow made with mustard. In Piedmont, where a wider variety of meats and vegetables is served, the dish is called *gran bui* or *grande bol-*

lito misto piemontese. In restaurants a *gran bollito misto* is usually served from a compartmentalized cart, sometimes with the broth ladled onto the pieces of chosen meat.

bolognese, alla   (AH-lah boh-loh-N'YEH-zeh)   "Bologna style." Usually refers to a hearty, long-simmered vegetable and meat sauce called *ragù,* which is served with pasta. A traditional *bolognese* sauce contains ground pork, beef, *pancetta,* garlic, tomatoes, vegetables, and, often, mushrooms and/or chicken livers.

RAGÙ ALLA BOLOGNESE

2 tablespoons butter	*¹/₂ cup dry red wine*
3 tablespoons olive oil	*1 cup beef or chicken broth*
1 celery stalk, chopped	*1 pound tomatoes, peeled, seeded, and*
1 carrot, chopped	* chopped*
1 onion, chopped	*Pinch of grated nutmeg*
6 ounces pancetta, diced	*Grated peel of 1 lemon*
6 ounces ground pork or veal	*Salt and pepper*
6 ounces ground beef	*2 tablespoons cream*

Melt the butter and olive oil in a deep saucepan. Add the celery, carrot, and onion and sauté for 1 minute. Add the *pancetta* and lightly brown for 1 to 2 minutes. Add the ground meats and cook until they lose their color. Add the wine and ¹/₂ cup of the broth and cook until the liquid has been absorbed. Add the remaining broth and reduce again. Add the tomatoes, nutmeg, lemon peel, and salt and pepper to taste. Cook over medium-low heat, covered, for about 2 hours. Add the cream, blend well, and serve. Serves 6 to 8.

bolzanese   (bohl-t'zah-NEH-zeh)   Fruit and nut buns from Bolzano.

bomba   (BOHM-bah)   "Bomb." Sweet or savory dish in a round, bomb-like shape. Usually refers to ice cream molded from two flavors.

In Emilia-Romagna, *bomba di riso* is a traditional molded rice dish filled with poultry, a specialty of Piacenza and Parma.

Bomba is also the name of a rare **robiola** cheese made around Alba and Langhe in Piedmont.

bombino bianco   (bohm-BEE-noh bee-AHN-koh)   A white wine grape of Apulia and Abruzzo, possibly originating in Spain. It is believed to be the actual identity of the grape called *trebbiano d'Abruzzo.*

bombino nero   (bohm–BEE-noh NEH-roh)   A red wine grape of Apulia, used in making rosé wines.

bombixeddas   (bohm–bee-SEH-das)   Meatballs, from Sardinia.

bomboloni   (bohm–boh-LOH-nee)   "Big bombs." Yeast and egg dough doughnuts usually without holes, from Tuscany. Usually sprinkled with sugar.

bomboniera   (bohm–bon-YEH-rah)   A small box of chocolates or other small candies. A *bomboniera* filled with *confetti* is usually given to the guests by the bride at the end of the wedding feast.

bonarda   (boh–NAHR-dah)   A red wine grape of Lombardy. The true *bonarda,* called *b. piemontese,* is little planted, but strains like *croatina,* propagated in **Colli Piacentini** and **Oltrepò Pavese** with a **DOC** designation, and *uva rara,* called *b. novarese,* are more widely propagated.

bonasai   (boh–nah-SAI)   "Very good." Modern cheese made from ewe's milk at the Sardinian Livestock and Cheese Institute. It is soft and square with a taste similar to yogurt.

bondiola   (bohn–dee-OH-lah)   A pork-and-beef cooked sausage. Flavored with red wine, it is a specialty of Polesine, an area in southern Veneto; it is usually eaten with mashed potatoes. It may be smoked.

bonèt   (boh–NEHT)   Chocolate custard pudding from Piedmont. It is flavored with rum and *amaretti.* The name is dialect for a little cap, referring to the shape of the copper or aluminum mold in which it is cooked. *Bonett de latimel* is a chilled vanilla pudding from Milan.

bongo   (BOHN-goh)   A fanciful Florentine name for *profiteroles* (cream-puff-pastry balls filled with whipped cream, pastry cream, or ice cream) piled in a mound and served with chocolate sauce. Also *bongo-bongo.*

bon hom   (bohn OHM)   "Good man." Sweet Easter bread in the shape of a man with an Easter egg under each arm.

bonissima, la   (lah boh–NEE-see-mah)   "The very best." A lavish cake, from Modena. Made with crushed walnuts, vanilla, grated lemon peel, honey, and rum with a chocolate or sugar icing, often with a double pastry crust.

bonito   (boh–NEE-toh)   Bonito, *Sarda sarda.* A large saltwater fish, related to tuna and mackerel. Bonito is usually sold in steaks and is best grilled. It is sometimes preserved in salt or canned.

boraggine   (boh–RAH-jee-neh)   Borage, whose flowers are used in salads and in tisanes. Also *borrana.* From the Old French *bourage.*

bordatino (bohr-dah-TEE-noh)   Soup made with vegetables, tomatoes, *pancetta,* and *polenta,* from Livorno.

boreto   alla   graisana (boh-REH-toh   AH-lah   grye-SAH-nah) Seafood soup, from Friuli. Usually containing turbot, the dish is a specialty of the town of Grado.

borlanda (bohr-LAHN-dah)   Soup made of cabbage and other vegetables in Piedmont. Once poor people's food in the town of Alto Verbano.

borlengo (bohr-LEHN-goh)   Huge crepes from Emilia-Romagna. Also *burleng* and *burteina.* Dressed with *pancetta* or lard, rosemary, and garlic, the crepes are folded into quarters and dusted with *parmigiano.*

The name derives from *burla* (joke), with various stories as to its origins. The simplest explanation is that this joke of a bread was served at a time of frivolity at open-air festivals. Others believe it dates to a time of crisis when the castle of Guiglia was besieged and the castle's lord, Ugolino, watered down the bread flour until it became a batter in order to feed his troops.

borlotti (bohr-LOH-tee)   Red-and-white beans. Similar to cranberry beans. If dried, they must be soaked overnight. *Borlotti* may be simply boiled and dressed with olive oil and garlic, or cooked with other ingredients. They are commonly stewed with a piece of pork rind called *cotica. Borlotti* may also be cooked with *polenta* and cabbage, cooled, cut into strips, and fried. In Venice, *borlotti* are called *lamoni.*

boscaiolo, alla (AH-lah boss-kye-OH-loh)   "Woodsman's style." A pasta sauce made with wild mushrooms and tomatoes, and sometimes fried eggplant.

bosco (BOSS-koh)   A white wine grape of Liguria. *Bosco Eliceo* is a **DOC** wine from Emilia-Romagna, made near the Comacchio lagoon. Versions include *bianco,* a white made from *trebbiano; fortana,* a red made from *fortana; merlot;* and *sauvignon. Bosco Romagno* is a **DOC** wine from Udine.

bosega (boh-SAY-gah)   Venetian term for a thick-lipped gray mullet, *Crenimugi labrosus.*

bottagio (boh-TAH-j'yoh)   Goose braised with savoy cabbage. A specialty of Piacenza, where it is traditionally made on the feast of *Santa Lucia* (December 13).

bottarga (boh-TAHR-gah)   The dried roe sac of gray mullet or tuna. The roe is removed from the fish and salted in its sac. It is then weighted, usually under two pieces of wood to remove the liquid and to compress it. It is then hung and dried. The mullet *bottarga* is preferred to tuna and is usually quite a bit more expensive.

Bottarga is sliced thin and served with oil and lemon or shaved or grated over pasta. It is particularly relished in Sicily, where it is called *uovo di tonno* (egg of tuna), in Sardinia, where it is called *butarega,* and in Calabria, where it is called *ovotarica.*

botte   (BOH-teh)   Large aging cask for wine, traditionally made with Slovenian oak. A *tino* is a cask that stands in a vertical position rather than the more common horizontal.

bottega   (boh-TEH-gah)   A shop of any kind, including a grocery. From the Latin *apotheca* (storehouse).

Botticino   (boh-tee-CHEE-noh)   *DOC* red wine of Lombardy, made from **barbera, marzemino, schiava,** and **sangiovese** grapes grown around the village of Botticino.

bottiglia   (boh-TEE-l'yah)   Bottle. From the Late Latin *buttis* (cask).

bovolo   (BOH-voh-loh)   Snail. *Bovoloni* are large snails, commonly consumed on Christmas Eve in Veneto. *Bovoletti* are small snails. They are sautéed in garlic with parsley. See also **lumaca.**

Bovolo is also a Veneto term for a bread loaf in the shape of a snail.

bra   (brah)   Strong, firm cheese from Piedmont. Named after the village of Bra, it is made from partly skimmed raw cow's milk, sometimes with ewe's or goat's milk added, and is aged for six months to a year.

brace, alla   (AH-la BRAH-cheh)   Grilled over coals.

brachetto   (brah-KEH-toh)   A grape of Piedmont, used in making a *DOC* sweet, bubbly, pale red dessert wine.

braciola   (brah-J'YOH-lah)   A slice or chop of meat, sometimes rolled around a stuffing. *Braciola alla brugia* is a Calabrian version cooked in lard and served with tomato sauce. The name *brugia* refers to an ancient people who lived in what is now Cozenza.

Braciolette are chops; *bracioline* are cutlets. *Braciolette a scottadito* are small lamb chops cooked, as in Rome, on a skillet and turned with and eaten with the fingers. From the Latin *brachium* (arm).

bramata   (brah-MAH-tah)   Cornmeal, finer than that used for *polenta.*

Bramaterra   (brah-mah-TEH-rah)   *DOC* red wine of Piedmont, made from **nebbiolo, croatina, vespolina,** and **bonarda** grapes grown in and around the village of Bramaterra.

branda   (BRAHN-dah)   *Grappa,* in Piedmontese dialect. From the Dutch, *bran-dewijn,* "burnt wine."

brandacujon (brahn-dah-koo-YAHN) Dish made of *stoccafisso* cooked with potatoes and olive oil, from Liguria. The dish is shaken vigorously for several minutes to incorporate all the ingredients and flavors. The name is from San Remo dialect meaning "shaken until tired."

branzi (BRAHN-zee) Cheese from Bergamo, made from cow's and goat's milk and ripened for a month, longer for grating.

branzino (brahn-ZEE-noh) Sea bass, *Dicentrarchus labrax* and *D. punctatus.* A white-fleshed fish with a clean, sweet flavor, ideal as a cold buffet dish. It is also grilled and prepared many other ways. Larger fish are usually poached or baked; smaller ones are often cooked *al cartoccio,* in parchment. Although a saltwater fish, the sea bass often swims upriver in the spring and lives in freshwater until fall. *Spigola* is the Neapolitan term.

brasato (brah-SAH-toh) Braised. Also *braciato.* From the French *braiser.*

brazedela (brah-t'zeh-DEH-lah) "Bracelet." Puff-pastry ring, from Ferrara. Served as a breakfast bun with eggs on Easter morning.

Breganze (breh-GAHN-t'zeh) *DOC* wines of the Veneto made north of Vicenza, including a **bianco,** from *tocai friulano* grapes; a **cabernet,** from **cabernet franc** or **cabernet sauvignon; pinot bianco; pinot grigio; pinot nero; rosso,** from **merlot;** and **vespaiolo.** Probably named after the commune of Bregenz in Austria.

bresaola (breh-SAU-lah) Dried salted beef. Usually made from the filet and aged for at least a month. It is sliced very thin and served with lemon and olive oil. A specialty of Valtellina in Lombardy.
  Violin di carne secca is a similar treatment for goat's meat.

brigidini (bree-jee-DEE-nee) Anise wafers from Tuscany. Named after *Santa Brigida* of Pistoia, they were originally made by nuns of the saint's order in the town of Lamporecchio.

Brindisi (BREEN-dee-see) *DOC* red and rosé wines of Apulia, made from **negroamaro** grapes grown near Brindisi.

brioche (bree-OHSH) Roll or bread made from a rich butter and egg dough. Sometimes served as a breakfast roll. From the French, derived from an Old Norman dialect word *brier* (to pound).
  Brioche rustica or *brioscia* is a bread served with meats and cheeses as an **antipasto,** sometimes with **ragù** or cheese in the center, or as a snack with ice cream. *Brioche* dates back at least to the 19th century, when French cooking in Naples was considered fashionable.

brocca (BROH-kah) Earthenware jug used in Rome as a wine carafe.

broccolo (BROH-koh-loh)   Broccoli, which may have been developed by the Etruscans or ancient Romans from cabbage; the plant seems to be native to Italy, and Caterina de'Medici is said to have introduced it to France in the 16th century. Also *broccoletto*.

There are three principal Italian varieties: *broccoli precocissima de Napoli* ("very precocious Neapolitan broccoli"), a very early spring variety; *b. precoce calabrese* ("precocious Calabrese broccoli"), an early Calabrese variety; and *b. tardiva d'inverno* ("winter broccoli"). *Broccoli nera* is a dark purple Calabrian variety. In Sicily, broccoli is called *spacarelli,* while *broccolò* or *broccoli* may refer to cauliflower, which most Italians call **cavolfiore.**

Broccoletti are the florets of broccoli.

The word *broccolo* derives from *bracco* (sprout).

brodettato (broh-deh-TAH-toh)   A dish made with veal or lamb cooked in white wine. A mixture of egg yolk and lemon juice is added at the end.

brodetto (broh-DEH-toh)   Fish stew, especially from the Adriatic. The broth is made from smaller fish and the larger fish are cooked in it. Often the broth is made from fish heads. The larger fish are cooked with tomato and oil and served separately. In the city of Ancona in the Marches, a traditional *brodetto* is made with 13 types of regional fish cooked in a tomato-garlic broth. *Brodetto alla romana* is a Roman meat soup. The cooked meat is removed from the broth and a mixture of egg yolks, lemon, marjoram, and **pecorino** is added and cooked until the eggs curdle. The soup is then poured over toast, with the meat served afterward as a second course.

In Florence, *brodetto* refers to an egg and lemon juice soup made at Easter.

brodo (BROH-doh)   Broth. Made from chicken, beef, and/or vegetables. *In brodo* refers to pasta served in such a broth. From either Middle English or, earlier, from Old High German *brod.*

bros (brohss)   Strong cheese from Piedmont. Also *bross, bruss,* and *bruz.* Mashed-up pieces of cheese are marinated in **grappa.** The word *bros* is an old dialect word for a cheese that has been fermented.

brovada (broh-VAH-dah)   Turnips marinated with **vinaccia,** or grape pomace, from Friulia. The turnips are tightly packed in wooden barrels and allowed to ferment. The cured turnips are usually shredded and then cooked with pork sausage or added to soup. The word *sbrovada* is dialect, means "to be scalded."

bruglione (broo-L'YOH-neh)   "Big mess." Sauté of wild and domestic mushrooms with potatoes and garlic, from Tuscany.

Brunello di Montalcino   (broo-NEH-loh dee mohn-tahl-CHEE-noh) *DOCG* red wine of Tuscany, made from grapes grown around the town of Montalcino. It is known for its power, complexity, and finesse. Made from a clone of the *sangiovese* called *sangiovese grosso,* the wine was first made in 1888 by Ferrucio Biondi-Santi (although the name *brunello* dates back at least to the 14th century) and has always been made in a long-lived, long-to-mature style. Only four vintages—1888, 1891, 1925, and 1945—were declared in the first six decades of production; and the fame of *brunello* as a unique wine grew steadily into the 1970s. Since then, nearly 90 vintners have begun producing *brunello* and acreage has increased rapidly. Many of these new producers have made *brunellos* in a lighter, early-maturing style, though *DOC* regulations of 1960 required the wine to be aged 42 months in casks. That was later dropped to 36 months in 1990, but most producers still age their wines a minimum of 48 months.

bruscandoli   (broo-skahn-DOH-lee)   "Brushes." Wild greens, similar to asparagus, from Friuli. The sprouts are gathered in spring and used in salads, pastas, and *frittata* or served with hard-boiled eggs, or blanched and jarred for later use.

bruschetta   (broo-SKEH-tah)   Toasted bread, often rubbed with garlic and drizzled with olive oil. Also *schiena d'asino, soma d'aj* in the south, and *fettunta* in Tuscany. *Bruschetta* has always been a way to salvage bread that was going stale by adding oil and seasonings. Sometimes the bread is entirely immersed in oil, but usually the oil is poured on the top after the bread is rubbed with a garlic clove. In recent years adding toppings, particularly chopped onions and tomatoes, has become popular in restaurants.

brüscitt   (BROO-sheet)   Cubed beef cooked with *pancetta,* red wine, and fennel seeds or dill, from Milan. Served with *polenta.* From *bruciacchiare* (to scorch).

brut   (broot)   French term meaning dry, used to designate a sparkling wine with little or no sweetness at all.

brutti ma buoni   (BROO-tee mah B'WOH-nee)   "Ugly but good." Dry, lumpy hazelnut or almond and egg white cookies. Also *brutti e buoni* and *belli e brutti.*

bucatini   (boo-kah-TEE-nee)   "Pierced [pasta]." A tubular dried pasta, slightly thicker than *spaghetti. Bucatoni* are even thicker. Also called *perciatelli.*

buccellato   (boo-cheh-LAH-toh)   Raisin-anise cake from Tuscany. Associated with the town of Lucca. The word dates to the Latin *buccellatum,* the bread eaten by the military, but this dessert bread is far more celebratory. It is traditionally presented by a grandfather to a grandchild on Confirmation day. In Sicily, the term refers to a short pastry dough filled with dried and candied fruits and nuts, shaped into a wreath. It is traditional at Christmastime.

buco (BOO-koh) "Small room." Term for a cellar *trattoria,* from Tuscany.

buddaci (boo-DAH-chee) Comber fish, *Serranus cabrilla.* Also *perchia.* Usually used for soups.

budella (boo-DEH-lah) Intestines. Also *budellame.*

budino (boo-DEE-noh) Sweet or savory puddings. From the French word *boudin* (sausage). *Budino belgo* is a chocolate and coffee pudding made in Mantua, though the name inexplicably associates the dessert with Belgium.

bue (BOO-eh) Cattle or beef. Once a rarity for Italians, beef is now readily available, with the best said to come from *Chianina* cattle in Tuscany. Beef is cooked many ways—grilled, roasted, or braised, and as *scaloppine, involtini,* and *rollatine.* All the parts are utilized. From the Latin *bubula.*

bufala (BOO-fah-lah) Buffalo, especially the water buffalo (not the American bison). The buffalo served for centuries as a work animal and for food, and its milk was the basis for *mozzarella di bufala.* During World War II, the herds were slaughtered by the retreating German army and not replaced (with animals from India) until well into the 1950s. From the Latin *bufalus.* Small balls of the cheese are called *bufaline.*

bugië (BOO-jee) "Little fibs." Fried, puffy fritters, from Liguria. They are a pre-Lenten treat, often served with *zabaione.* In Genoa they are called *boxie.*

buglione (boo-L'YOH-neh) "Mess." Peasant stew of leftover meat and poultry with vegetables like zucchini and tomatoes, from Florence. Traditionally, the meat is removed from the broth, sautéed with chopped celery, carrots, garlic, and olive oil, covered with water, and cooked down to a rich consistency. It is then served on top of *fettunta.*

buon appetito (bw'ohn ah-peh-TEE-toh) "Good appetite." A phrase used by the host of a dinner to begin a meal.

buongustaio (bw'ohn-goo-STEYE-oh) "Good taste (person)." Gourmet.

buranelli (buh-rah-NEH-lee) Butter cookies, from the island of Burano, near Venice.

buridda (buh-REE-dah) Several fish soups go by this name in Italy, all similar to the French Provençal *bourride,* from the Provençal *bourrido* (to boil).

In Genoa, *burrida* is usually made with cuttlefish, angler, **stoccafisso,** and anchovies.

In Sardinia, the term refers to a fish steak, commonly dogfish, topped with bread crumbs, walnuts, garlic, and nutmeg.

burlenghi   (boor-LEHN-ghee)   "Little tricks." Unleavened bread covered with a spread of fatback, rosemary, and garlic and pan-fried, from Emilia-Romagna.

burrata   (boo-RAH-tah)   "Dairy [cheese]." Rich cow's milk cheese from Apulia and Basilicata. Made by inserting long strings of cheese, called *lucini,* with cream into a puffed-up single strand that is then tied up. Of recent origin, it is generally served before the meal.

burrino   (boo-REE-noh)   "Little butter." Small cow's milk cheese of the south, pear-shaped and often filled with butter or salami. Also **butirro,** *burriello,* and *provole.*

burro   (BOO-roh)   Butter, which is more widely used in the north than in the south, where olive oil is preferred. Anything cooked in butter is called *al burro. Burro fuso* is melted butter. From the Latin *butyrum.*

burtleina   (boort-LAY-nah)   Crisp savory fritter of Piacenza.

büsecca   (boo-SEH-kah)   Tripe. *Büsecca* is also the name for a thick soup made with beef tripe, white beans, and vegetables, traditionally made from what the Milanese call *la ciappa e la francese* (the cap and the Frenchwoman), referring to the caul that covers the brain and to the curly tripe of the stomach lining, said to resemble a French coiffure. Also *büsecchia sanguinaccio.*

busecchina   (boo-seh-KEE-nah)   Chestnut dessert from Lombardy. The chestnuts are boiled and pureed, cream is added, and the confection is baked. The word may derive from **busecca** (tripe) because of the dessert's resemblance to tripe.

busiati   (boo-see-AH-tee)   "Bruised." Fresh pasta from Sicily made in a long strand that is cut into small pieces, then wrapped around a long skewer or stalk of grass to give them a hole in the middle. A knitting needle used to be used. Also called *maccheroni inferrettati.* Commonly served with a tomato-and-oregano sauce.

bussolai   (BOO-soh-leye)   "Compass." Ring-shape butter cookies from Friuli. Made with **rosolio** and about 3 to 4 inches wide, these cookies are traditionally given to children on their Confirmation day. The name perhaps refers to the cookie being symbolic of the compass that guides a young person through life.

bussolano (boo-soh-LAH-noh)   "Alm's box." Potato and lemon cake from Lombardy.

butirro (boo-TEE-roh)   Calabrian mild cheese or a round of *caciocavallo* containing a center of butter. From the Latin *butyrum*.

buttafuoco (boo-tah-FOO-koh)   *DOC* red wine of Lombardy, whose name means "sparks of fire," made from *barbera, bonarda,* *uva rara,* and *ughetta* grapes grown in the *DOC* zone of *Oltrepò Pavese.*

C

cabernet (kah-behr-NEH) Two French grape varietals, *cabernet franc* and *cabernet sauvignon*. Both are now increasingly being planted in northeastern Italy. In the past, the lighter *cabernet franc* (sometimes called *c. frank* or *bordo* in Italy) was preferred, and it is often bottled under the name *Cabernet*. But the popularity and renown of *cabernet sauvignon,* which goes into the finest red wines of Bordeaux and California, has caused renewed interest in this big-bodied, highly tannic varietal, first planted in Italy in the 19th century.

In Tuscany, *cabernet* is usually blended with **sangiovese** to give a wine backbone, as in the so-called Super Tuscan proprietal wines like *Solaia* and **Sassicaia.**

cacao (kah-KAU) Cocoa. From the Spanish.

One of the beans Cortés brought back from the New World in 1528, *cacao* was initially regarded as a dangerous stimulant by the Catholic Church. Trade in *cacao* was monopolized by Spain until 1728, after English and Dutch smugglers successfully spread its popularity throughout northern Europe. Cocoa beans were introduced to Piedmont in 1557 after Emanuele Filiberto, Duke of Savoy, sided with the Spanish against France and won the battle of St. Quentin. Soon afterwards chocolate processing became a major industry in Turin.

Cocoa became the most fashionable drink in Europe in the 18th century, but it was only after the Dutch found a way to alkalize chocolate to release the cocoa butter that the substance became useful in making candies and flavorings. By the middle of the 19th century, Turin pioneered the refinements of making chocolate candies called *diablotins* (little devils) and *givu* (cigar tip). Chocolate combined with hazelnuts in the confection known as **gianduja** became famous.

Cacc'e Mmitte di Lucera (KAH-cheh MEE-teh dee loo-CHE-rah) **DOC** red wine of Apulia, made from **uva di troia** and other grapes grown around the town of Lucera. The dialect name (which translates as something like "take out and put in") refers to the local custom of adding fresh grapes to wine that is already fermenting and then drawing off the surplus to produce a light, fresh-tasting, fruity wine.

cacciagione   (kah-t'chah-J'YOH-neh)   General term for game meats. See also *selvaggio.*

cacciatora, alla   (AH-lah kah-chah-TOH-rah)   "Hunter's style." Refers to dishes with sautéed and braised meats, particularly game, often with a wild mushroom and tomato sauce.

POLLO ALLA CACCIATORA

1 ounce dried porcini
1 chicken, (3–3¹/₂ pounds), washed,
    dried, and cut into 10 pieces
¹/₂ cup flour
3 tablespoons butter
3 tablespoons olive oil
1 red onion, diced
1 small carrot, diced

1 garlic clove, minced
1 bay leaf
¹/₂ cup white wine
¹/₂ cup chicken broth
Salt and pepper
¹/₂ cup chopped tomato
2 tablespoons chopped parsley

Soak the *porcini* in ¹/₂ cup warm water and set aside. Dredge the chicken pieces in the flour, shaking off any excess. Heat the butter and oil in a large sauté pan, add the chicken, and brown on all sides. Push the chicken to the side of the pan, add the onion and carrot, and sauté for 3 minutes. Add the garlic and the bay leaf and sauté for another minute. Add the wine, bring to a boil for 1 minute, add the chicken broth, salt and pepper, tomato, and the *porcini* (which have been coarsely chopped) as well the liquid from the mushrooms (strained through cheesecloth). Bring to a boil and let simmer for 30 minutes. Add parsley 5 minutes before serving. Makes 4 servings.

cacciatori   (kah-chah-TOH-ree)   "Hunters' [sausage]." Salami from Lombardy. About 5 inches long, it is usually cut into chunks, rather than slices.

cacciottu   (kah-CH'YOH-too)   A soft roll slit open on one side, filled with strips of salami and cheese, sealed with more cheese, dipped in melted lard, and heated in the oven, from Sicily. The word may mean "little hunters," perhaps because hunters took them to eat when they went to hunt, or may refer to a low felt cone-shaped hat that resembles the bun.

cacciucco (kah-CHOO-koh) "Mixture." Fish stew from Leghorn. Traditionally made with tomato and five kinds of seafood like squid, red mullet, cod, shrimp, and scallops to correspond to the five *c*'s in the word. It is seasoned with garlic, sage, and rosemary.

CACCIUCCO

3 pounds fish and shellfish, including
*   5 different kinds*
3 garlic cloves, chopped
¹/₂ slice peperoncino
¹/₂ cup olive oil
¹/₂ cup dry white wine

Salt and pepper
1 pound tomatoes, peeled, seeded, and
*   chopped*
¹/₂ cup cold fish stock
Garlic-rubbed toasts

Cut the fish into 2-inch pieces. Mash together the garlic and *peperoncino* in a mortar with a pestle. Heat the olive oil in a saucepan, add the shellfish, the lighter-textured fish, and the garlic mixture and cook for about 1 minute. Add the wine, season with salt and pepper to taste, cover, reduce the heat, and simmer for 10 minutes. Add the firmer-textured fish and tomatoes and bring to a boil. Lower the heat and simmer, covered, for 8 minutes. Remove from the heat and add the fish stock to stop the cooking. Correct the seasoning and serve over the toasts. Serves 6.

cacimperio (kah-cheem-PEH-ree-yoh) "Imperial cheese." Fondue made with *fontina,* egg yolks, milk, and butter, a specialty of Turin.

cacio (KAH-ch'yoh) Term for cheese in the south. From the Latin *caseus.* Less commonly used than *formaggio.*
   Cacio all'argentiera (Argento-style cheese) is a Sicilian dish of fried *provolone* with garlic, oregano, and vinegar. *C. ricotta* is an Abruzzese dessert of coffee-flavored custard made from sheep's milk.

caciocavallo (kah-ch'yoh-kah-VAH-loh) "Horse cheese." A firm, sharp buffalo's or cow's milk cheese, aged three months, longer if intended for grating. Originally from Campania, this ancient cheese is now produced throughout southern Italy. The cheese's name may derive from its being dried in tandem on either side of a pole, as if on horseback. Others believe the name dates back to when the cheese was made from mare's milk.
   Caciocavallo siciliano is shaped into oblong molds, salted, and waxed. *Butirro* is a Calabrian *caciocavallo* (*casucàvaddu* in dialect) containing butter in the center. Called *casizolu* in Sardinia.

cacio e pepe (KAH-ch'yoh eh PEH-peh) "Cheese and pepper." Spaghetti dressed with *pecorino* and ground black pepper, from Rome.

caciofiore (KAH-ch'yoh-fee-OH-reh) "Flower cheese." A soft, creamy cheese from Sardinia, sometimes called *fiore sardo,* made from ewe's milk in the countryside and cow's milk in commercial production. See *caciotta.*

caciotta (kah-CH'YOH-tah) A soft fresh cheese made from the whey of ewe's milk cheese. It is most closely associated with Campania (where it is called *caciofiore),* although the term applies to many small, similar cheeses. Also *casciotta.* From the Italian *cacio* (cheese).

caffè (kah-FEH) Coffee. From the Arabic *qahwa.*
    Coffee may have come to Italy from the Middle East as early as 1580 (Constantinople already had its first coffeehouse as of 1154). There may have been a shop selling coffee in Venice as of 1640, but it was not until the drink became fashionable in England, where the first coffeehouse opened at Oxford in 1650, and Paris, whose first coffeehouse opened in 1672, that Europeans began to drink coffee in earnest. It was, in fact, a Sicilian named Francesco Procopio dei Coltelli, whose Café Procope opened in Paris in 1675 and soon became famous for its coffee and ice cream. Similar coffeehouses opened throughout Italy; they were called *bottege del caffè.* The first is said to have opened in Turin around 1705 and was called Bottega di Pompeo.
    Italy, which grows no coffee beans itself, imports them from tropical regions, principally Brazil, Colombia, and Costa Rica. The two principal kinds are the *robusta* and the preferred, more complex *arabica.* These are roasted at factories called *torrefazioni* and sealed in airtight packages for sale. Italians prefer to grind their own beans, though some producers now make little packets for individually measured cups.
    In Italy the term *caffè* usually refers to a small **espresso,** not to a large cup of coffee. **Cappuccino** is *espresso* topped with steamed milk. Italians usually begin the day with a *cappuccino,* then drink *espresso* throughout the day. *Caffè lungo* (long) means a weak cup of coffee; *ristretto* (tight) means a very strong cup. *Doppio* is a double *espresso. C. corretto* is coffee with a shot of liquor like **grappa** or brandy. *C. latte* is coffee with milk added. *Latte macchiato* (stained coffee) is predominantly milk flavored with coffee. *C. freddo* is iced coffee. Decaffeinated coffee, *c. decaffeinato,* is commonly called *Hag,* the principal commercial producer of such coffee. *C. d'orzo* is an ersatz coffee made from barley. Regional variations include *c. valdostano,* a mixture of coffee, citrus peel, sugar, and **grappa** drunk from the spouts of a **grolla,** a wooden pot with four spouts, which is passed around the table. A similar pot is called *coppa dell'amicizia.*

cagghiubbi (kah-G'YOO-bee) Pasta rolled around a spit to form a hole in the center, from Brindisi.

caglio (KAH-l'yoh)   Rennet. In Abruzzo, a junket dessert made with rennet is called *quagliata.*

Cagnina di Romagna (kah-N'YEE-nah dee roh-MAH-n'yah) *DOC* purple-red wine of Romagna, made from *cagnina* grapes. In Friuli, the *cagnina* grape is called *terrano* or *refosco nostrano.*

cajettes (kah-ZH'ETTS)   Pasta pellets made from flour, potatoes, vegetables, and *toma* cheese, from Piedmont. *Cajettes* are usually cooked in a broth.

Calabria (kah-LAH-bree-yah)   The southernmost region of Italy, aside from the island of Sicily. Located in the toe of Italy, Calabria has a long history of good food, and its remoteness has allowed the people to maintain their culinary traditions, which are generally robust and homey, such as *ciambotta,* a stew made with eggplant, potatoes, and peppers; *scarafuoghi,* made with pork and chile peppers; and the hearty veal or pork innards called *morseddu.*

Licurdia is both a savory onion sauce and an onion soup laced with hot pepper and *parmigiano,* while *millecosedde* translates as a "thousand things" because of the number of ingredients cooks put into it.

Pasta dishes are simple in Calabria, many using tomato sauces and chile peppers, as in *penne all'arrabiata.*

The Calabrese are superb sausage makers and world famous for their *soppressata* and *capocollo;* their pork is some of the finest in Italy.

The best-known cheeses include *caciocavallo, provolone, mozzarella,* and *scamorza.*

For dessert, Calabrian *gelati* are superb.

Calabria, with eight *DOC* wine regions, produces mainly reds, the best known being *Cirò,* which is also made in a white variety.

calamari (kah-lah-MAH-ree)   Squid, *Loligo vulgaris.* This cephalopod has a long body with swimming fins at the rear, two tentacles, and eight arms. Calamari take their name from the Latin *calamus,* which refers to the inky liquid excreted by the squid and used in pastas and sauces. Calamari are eaten throughout Italy, often dredged in flour and deep-fried, especially the small ones called *calamaretti.* Medium squid may be stuffed with bread crumbs, garlic, and herbs and sautéed in olive oil or cooked in white wine and olive oil; large squid is usually stewed. *Totani* (*Todarodes sagitatus*), or flying squid, are similar in taste but with a slightly tougher texture. See also *seppie.*

calcioni (kahl-CH'YOH-nee)   "Butts." Sweet pastry, stuffed with *ricotta, pecorino,* and lemon zest, from Ascoli.

caldaia (kahl-DYE-ah)   Cauldron. From the Latin *caldarius,* "used for hot water."

In Apulia, *caldariello* is lamb cut into pieces and cooked in a cauldron with fennel and ewe's or goat's milk, a specialty of the town of Gravina.

caldana   (kahl-DAH-nah)   A warming oven where bread dough is placed to rise. From *caldo* (warm).

Caldaro   (kahl-DAH-roh)   **DOC** wine of Alto Adige, made in great quantity from **schiava** *grossa, gentile,* and *grigia* grapes around Lake Caldaro. Also *Lago di Caldaro* and *Kalterersee.*

caldarroste   (kahl-dah-ROH-steh)   "Hot roasted." Chestnuts roasted in a pan over coals.

caldo   (KAHL-doh)   Hot. From the Latin *calidus.*

calza   (KAHL-t'zah)   "Stocking." Cheesecloth used for straining.

calzagatti   (kahl-zah-GAH-tee)   "Cat's stockings." **Polenta** dish from Emilia-Romagna, cooked with a **soffritto** of onions, tomatoes, and beans.

calzone   (kahl-T'ZOH-neh)   "Trouser leg." Half-moon filled pastry, from Naples. Made from **pizza** dough and stuffed with various fillings, from **ricotta** and **mozzarella** to spinach and sausage. In Apulia, these are called *scialcione* or *cappello di gendarme* (gendarme's hat) because of the shape.

calzonicchi   (kahl-t'zoh-NEE-kee)   "Little trouser legs." Half-moon **ravioli** with a stuffing of brains. A specialty of Rome's former Jewish ghetto.

cameriere   (kah-meh-R'YEH-reh)   Waiter in a restaurant. Refers to a person who takes care of a *camera* (room).

camomilla   (kah-moh-MEE-lah)   Chamomile. Also chamomile tea. From the Latin *chamaemelon.*

camoscio   (kah-MOH-shoh)   Chamois, preferably less than two-and-a-half years old. From the Late Latin *camox. Camoscio alla piemontese* is a chamois stew. *C. alla tirolese* is a chamois stew from Alto Adige, cooked with vinegar and spices, and served with sour cream. See also **cervo** and **daino.**

Campania   (kahm-PAH-n'yah)   A region of Italy south of Rome and north of Calabria on the Tyrrhenian Sea. Its principal city, Naples, has long guided the gastronomy of the region, and the cooking of Naples has had the most influence on the way non-Italians regard Italian cooking. Rich in tomato sauces, with a prolific use of garlic, olive oil, and black olives, Neapolitan cookery was exported to the United States and other countries in the memories of emigrants from Campania, most of them very poor.

The cooking of Naples and Campania is rich in vegetables and pasta, often in layered casserole dishes. Meat was rarely affordable and seafood was expensive, except for those who were fishermen themselves. Naples was the first to accept the tomato from the New World as a basic food, when other Europeans believed it poisonous. And it was in Naples that a poor people's dish—*pizza*—was created.

Yet Naples, dominated by so many foreign powers in its history, also developed a court cuisine as rich as any in Italy. Dishes like *braciola,* a stuffed beef roll; the intricately layered *timballo* of pasta, eggplant, cheese, and tomato; and lavish desserts like *babà* and *sfogliatelle* have their origins in that baronial tradition.

Antipasto tables are grand displays of marinated vegetables and cold seafood, the fried mozzarella sandwich called *mozzarella* in carrozza, and excellent *salame.*

The wines of Campania, with its 14 **DOC** regions, are predominantly robust reds like *Taurasi* and *Lacrima Christi del Vesuvio;* the whites like *Fiano di Avellino* and *Greco di Tufo* are pleasant and light in body and fruit.

campagnola, alla   (AH-lah kahm-pah-N'YOH-lah)   "Country style." Refers to a dish made in a hearty, robust style, usually with onions and tomato.

Campari   (kahm-PAH-ree)   Trademark name for a bittersweet alcoholic beverage. It is served as an *aperitivo* and used in many other aperitifs, such as the *Americano,* the *Negroni,* and the *Milano-Torino.* It was created in Milan in the 1860s by Gaspare Campari, who owned a café in Milan's Galleria Vittorio Emanuele. *Campari* is a brilliant rose-red color and is made from herbs, quinine bark, and orange peel, with an alcohol content of 25 percent. On its own it is usually served with a twist of lemon. *Campari soda* is a bottled mixture of *Campari* and carbonated water, with about 10 percent alcohol.

Campidano di Terralba   (kahm-pee-DAH-noh dee teh-RAHL-bah) **DOC** red wine of Sardinia, made from *bovale* grapes grown in the region of Campidano around the town of Terralba.

canaiolo nero   (kah-nye-OH-loh NEH-roh)   A red wine grape of Tuscany, used in making *Chianti.* In central Italy, it is usually a white wine grape.

canarino   (kah-nah-REE-noh)   "Canary." Lemon tisane. The word possibly refers to the yellow color of the bird and the lemon. Italians drink this after a big meal to settle the stomach.

candelaus   (KAHN-deh-lauss)   "Candle holder." Almond-paste cookies from Sardinia. Small cup shapes are glazed and filled with almond paste.

Candia dei Colli Apuani   (KAHN-dee-yah DAY-ee KOH-lee ah-poo-AH-nee)   **DOC** white wine of Tuscany, made from *vermentino* grapes grown in the Apuan Alps region.

candito   (kahn-DEE-toh)   Candied. From the Old Italian *quand.*

canederli (kah-NEH-dehr-lee)   Dumplings from Trentino-Alto Adige. Also *Kenerderli* and *Knödl*. Made with eggs, stale bread, flour, milk, **speck,** onion, and herbs. The dough is shaped into large balls, then cooked in chicken or meat stock. They may be served in a soup or alone, usually just one or two per person, with melted butter and **parmigiano.** From the Austrian word for dumpling, *knöedel*.

canestrato (kah-neh-STRAH-toh)   "Big basket." Originally a ewe's milk cheese pressed into a *canestro* (wicker basket), from Sicily. Now any cheese so made. Also *incanestrato.* See also **pecorino.**

canestrelli (kah-neh-STREH-lee)   "Little baskets." Ring-shape sweet biscuits, from Liguria.

canestrello (kah-neh-STREH-loh)   "Pretty basket." Pilgrim scallop, *Pecten jacobaeus.* Usually fried. Also *canestrello di mare.*

canestrini (kah-neh-STREE-nee)   "Little baskets." Small pasta shape pinched at the middle and having ridged edges. Even smaller versions are called *panierini*.

cannariculi (kah-nah-REE-koo-lee)   Christmas honey-coated fritters from Calabria. Made with sweet wine and shaped into sticks.

cannateddi (kah-nah-TEH-dee)   "Little flat [pastries]." Easter pastries from Sicily. Shaped like a lyre and containing a whole, often colored, egg. Also *cannatunni.*

cannella (kah-NEH-lah)   "Little stalk." Cinnamon. The Saracens brought this spice to Sicily in the 9th century. The Crusaders brought cinnamon to the rest of Europe. For centuries, it was very expensive and used only by the wealthy until the Renaissance, when it was used liberally in the royal kitchens. In the 18th century the Dutch began cultivation of cinnamon in Southeast Asia, making it far more widely and cheaply available. As elsewhere, cinnamon is used in Italy as a spice, particularly in sweet foods and desserts. It is often sprinkled on **cappuccino.**

cannellini (kah-neh-LEE-nee)   "Tiny rods." White kidney beans.

cannelloni (kah-neh-LOH-nee)   "Large tubes." Large pasta tubes about 4 inches long, stuffed with many different ingredients, including meat and cheese. In Campania, they are called *cannaruozzoli* or, when stuffed with meat, hard-boiled eggs, salami, sausage, and vegetables, *schiaffettoni. Cannelloni alla napoletana* are stuffed with **ricotta** and sauced with tomato, cream, or other sauces, and, usually, baked. *C. alla piemontese* are stuffed with veal, **parmigiano,** and **prosciutto** and baked with a **balsamella** sauce. In Sicily, *cannelloni* are called *crusetti* or *rosette* and are filled with meat, tomato, and zucchini; they have closed ends and are baked with a **balsamella** with a little tomato.

cannoli   (kah-NOH-lee)   "Pipes." Crisp fried pastry tubes. The dough is shaped around a cylinder, fried, and filled with sweetened **ricotta** and other ingredients. In Naples, *cannoli* are usually flavored with rosewater or orange flower water and cinnamon, with candied fruit, pistachios, and chocolate added to the filling. Sometimes *cannoli* are stuffed with pastry cream. In Sicily, the crust is flavored with wine or **Marsala.**

cannolicchi   (kah-noh-LEE-kee)   "Short pipes." Very short dried pasta tubes.
   Cannoliccho also refers to the razor clam, *Solen vagina,* which is commonly eaten raw with a little lemon juice, grilled, or made into a stew or soup.

cannonau   (kah-noh-NAU)   Red wine grape of Sardinia. It produces a hard, deep red wine as well as some sweeter versions. The grape originated in Spain, where it is called *granacha (grenache* in French). Also *cannonao.*

cannoncini   (kah-nohn-CHEE-nee)   "Little cannons." Spirals of puff pastry shaped like little cannons.

canocchia   (kah-NOH-k'yah)   "Pipe eye." Mantis shrimp, *Squilla mantis.* The best are found in the Adriatic waters from the Marches north to the Veneto. Also *panocchia.*

cansonsei   (kahn-sohn-SAY)   "Little britches." **Ravioli** stuffed with sausage, bread, and **parmigiano,** a specialty of Bergamo and Brescia. In the Veneto, they are called *casunziei* and made with **ricotta** and beets, spinach, or winter squash. They are usually served with melted butter and **parmigiano.**

cantalupo   (kahn-tah-LOO-poh)   Canteloupe. The melon came from Armenia in the 15th century and was first planted in a papal garden near Rome called Cantalupo. See also **melone.**

cantina   (kahn-TEE-nah)   A winery or wine cellar.

cantina sociale   (kahn-TEE-nah soh-SH'YAH-leh)   Winery society. A cooperative of several growers or producers. Also *cantina coopertiva.*

cantucci   (kahn-TOO-chee)   Almond cookies from Tuscany. Commonly served with a glass of **vin santo.** Also *biscotti di Prato.*

capelli d'angelo   (kah-PEH-lee D'AHN-jeh-loh)   "Angel's hair." Very thin strands of pasta, often made with eggs. Especially popular in Genoa, Rome, and Naples, *capelli* are either sauced, usually with a light sauce of cream, vegetables, or seafood, or cooked in a broth. *Capellini,* also called *fidelini,* are also very thin, though sometimes slightly thicker than *capelli d'angelo,* and curled into small nests before cooking. *Spaghettini,* a specialty of Naples, are slightly thicker than both.

In Sicily, the term refers to such pasta fried and sweetened with honey.

capieddi 'e preddi (kah-pee-EH-dee eh PREH-dee) "Priest's hairs." Pasta with a very thin, slightly curled shape, from Calabria.

capitone (kah-pee-TOH-neh) A very large saltwater eel, *Anguilla anguilla.* The eels, which grow to 5 feet long, are commonly preserved in oil. They are a traditional dish at Christmastime all over Italy but particularly in central and southern Italy. The best eels are said to come from the mouth of the Po River. See *anguilla.*

caponata (kah-poh-NAH-tah) A Sicilian vegetable dish made of various ingredients but usually including cooked eggplant, celery, capers, anchovies, chile peppers, olives, tomato, vinegar, and onions. In Palermo they use a diminutive, *caponatina.* A similar dish in Piedmont is called *caponèt.*

The word may derive from the Latin *caupo* (tavern), suggesting the kind of robust food served at a tavern or inn. Sailors' taverns in Sicily were called *caupone,* where the dish was usually made with sea biscuit with sugar and vinegar to soften it, which is mimicked in the *friselle* bread rings used in Capri's *caponata del marinaio.* The Genoese *cappon magro* still contains sea biscuit in its preparation. But more modern versions of *caponata* are usually free of the biscuit and contain many more ingredients than the original.

CAPONATA

2 medium eggplants (approximately 2 to 2¹/² pounds), cut into 1-inch pieces	1 pound tomatoes, peeled, seeded, and diced
Olive oil for frying	2 tablespoons capers, rinsed
¹/⁴ cup extra virgin olive oil	1 tablespoon sugar
1 large onion, coarsely chopped	¹/² cup red wine vinegar
¹/² cup chopped celery	¹/² cup green olives
	Salt and pepper

Put the cubed eggplant into a colander and sprinkle with salt, tossing to make sure salt is evenly dispersed. Let drain for an hour, then pat dry with paper towels. Heat 1 inch of olive oil in a frying pan to 360°F and fry the eggplant until brown and crisp. Drain and set aside. Drain the leftover oil. In the same frying pan heat ¹/⁴ cup of the eggplant oil and the extra virgin olive oil. Add the onion and celery and sauté until golden brown. Add the tomatoes, bring to a boil, and simmer for 10 minutes. Stir in the capers, sugar, vinegar, and olives. Sprinkle with salt and pepper to taste and cook for 10 minutes. Remove from the heat and let cool to room temperature. Serves 6.

---

caponèt   (kah-poh-NET)   Small, finger-size stuffed cabbages or zucchini flowers, from Piedmont. From a dialect term for "castrated" because the zucchini flowers are not fertile.

cappa santa   (KAH-pah SAHN-tah)   "Holy cloak." Scallop. A large mollusk in the family Pectinidae. Also *pettine maggiore* and *ventaglio*. The best-known species in the Mediterranean are *Chlamys opercularis, Pecten jacobaeus,* and, principally, *C. varia.* The meat is known as the **noce,** and the roe or coral, the *corallo.*

Scallops have long been associated with holiness, owing to a legend of Galicia in which a pagan nobleman's horse leapt suddenly into the sea only to emerge carrying the body of Saint James the Greater covered with scallop shells—a miracle that caused the pagan to convert to Christianity. Pilgrims wearing or begging with scallop shells still make their way to the shrine of Santiago de Compostela in Spain.

Scallops are sometimes eaten raw, but they are usually cooked. Italians generally do not use heavy sauces with scallops, preferring them simply grilled, sautéed, or marinated as in a seviche.

Canestrell is a small scallop.

cappellacci   (kah-peh-LAH-chee)   "Big hats." Large, rather flat **ravioli** stuffed with squash or pumpkin, a specialty of Ferrara and Cremona. In Cremona, the squash is mixed with **mostarda.** Similar to what are called **tortellini** in Bologna and Modena, *cappellacci* are usually sauced with butter and **parmigiano.** At Christmastime, crushed **amaretti** are often added to the filling. The name *cappellacci* dates back at least to the late 16th century.

cappelletti   (kah-peh-LEH-tee)   "Little hats." Small stuffed pasta shaped like three-cornered hats. The shape is said to be styled after the hats of Spanish soldiers who invaded Italy in the 17th century. Usually filled with pork, veal, beef, or brains, *cappelletti* are often served in broth. They are a specialty of Reggio. In Ferrara, *cappelletti in brodo alla ferrarese* contain the neck gland of the pig. *C. faentini,* a specialty of the town of Faenza, are meatless, stuffed instead with fresh cheese and grated lemon peel.

cappello da prete   (kah-PEH-loh dah PREH-teh)   "Priest's hat." A pork sausage shaped to resemble a priest's three-cornered hat. Like **zampone** but stuffed into hog casings, it is commonly boiled and served with lentils or beans.

The term also refers to a triangular cut of beef and to a Tuscan stuffed pasta also shaped like a priest's hat, called *nicchi*.

cappello da gendarme (kah-PEH-loh dah jehn-DAHR-meh)   "Policeman's hat." Lavish *pasticcio* from Bari. Made of layers of *maccheroni*, pork, turkey, *prosciutto*, *mozzarella*, and seasonings, which, when assembled, supposedly resemble a policeman's hat.

capperi (KAH-peh-ree)   Capers. The best are said to come from the islands of Pantelleria and Salina. Capers are mixed with sea salt, which creates a brine, then aged for two months. From the Latin *capparis*.

cappone (kah-POH-neh)   Capon. *Cappone natalizio* is a Christmas dish of Reggio in which the capon is flavored with *prosciutto* and *Marsala* and roasted on a spit.

Cappone is also the word for a gurnard. Of the family Triglidae, most common are the gray gurnard, *Eutrigla gurnardus;* the red gurnard, *Aspitrigla cuculus;* and the tub gurnard, *Trigla lucerna*. They are often used in fish stews; a Piedmontese version takes the same name, *cappone*.

cappon magro (KAH-pohn MAH-groh)   "Lean capon." Seafood dish from Liguria. Layers of cooked vegetables, garlic-scented crackers, hard-boiled eggs, pickles, olive oil, garlic, capers, and at least a dozen kinds of fish, usually including tuna, crayfish, bass, and shrimp, are molded, then topped with lobsters and oysters. Despite its name, there is no capon in the dish at all.

cappuccino (kah-poo-CHEE-noh)   *Espresso* topped with steamed milk. The steam is built up by pressure in a machine devised for the process. Also *cappuccio*. The color resembles that of a Capuchin monk's habit.

cappuci guarniti (kah-POO-chee gwahr-NEE-tee)   "Garnished sauerkraut." Sauerkraut dish made with pork from Istria.

capra (KAH-prah)   Goat. From the Latin. *Capretto* is roast kid. *Capro* is a male goat. In Milan, the term may refer to roast lamb.

caprese (kah-PREH-seh)   In the style of Capri. Such a sauce is usually made from lightly cooked tomatoes, basil, olive oil, and mozzarella, to use on pastas, meats, fish, or salads. *Insalata alla caprese* is a salad of tomatoes, basil, and *mozzarella* dressed with olive oil and vinegar.

capretto (kah-PREH-toh)   Kid. Slaughtered between one-and-a-half to four months old, kid is usually roasted. From the Latin *capra*.

Capri (KAH-pree)   *DOC* zone of Campania that produces a white wine from *falanghina*, *greco*, and *biancolello* grapes, and a red from *Piedirosso* grown in Capri.

Capriano del Colle   (kah-pree-AH-noh dell KOH-leh)   *DOC* zone of Lombardy that produces wines made from *sangiovese* and *trebbiano* grapes grown around the town of Capriano del Colle.

capricciosa, alla   (AH-lah kah-pree-CH'YOH-sah)   "In a capricious style." Any dish done according to the whim of the cook, usually implying some degree of fancy.

caprignetti   (kah-pree-NYEH-tee)   "Little goat's [cheeses]." Small balls of goat's milk cheese, usually containing herbs, a specialty of Sorrento. From the Latin *capra* (goat).

caprini   (kah-PREE-nee)   "Little goat." Small cheeses from Piedmont. Cylinder shape. Originally made from goat's milk, now also made from cow's milk. The goat's milk version has a green wrapper; the cow's milk, blue. *Caprini* are produced mainly in Cùneo and Ossola. From the Latin *capra*.

caprino   (kah-PREE-noh)   "Little goat's [cheese]." Fresh goat's or cow's cheese molded into a cylinder shape. *Capra* means "goat."

capriolo   (kah-pree-OH-loh)   Roebuck.

carabacia   (kah-rah-BAH-ch'yah)   Tuscan onion soup.

caraffa   (kah-RAH-fah)   Carafe. From the Arabic *gharrafah*.

carbonade   (kahr-boh-NAH-deh)   Beef stew cooked with red wine, from Valle d'Aosta. The name supposedly refers to the "charcoal" black coloration of the dish. Also *carbonada* and *carbonata*.

carbonara, alla   (AH-lah kahr-boh-NAH-rah)   "Charcoal style." A Roman pasta preparation usually made with *spaghetti* sauced with cream, *pancetta* (or *guanciale*), *pecorino,* and *parmigiano* onto which a raw egg is dropped and cooked by the heat of the pasta itself. It is then tossed and served with plenty of black pepper.

The origin of the name has never been established. Some believe it refers to black *spaghetti* made with squid ink by Roman cooks in the seafood market, others to a 19th-century radical group called *I Carbonari*. Still others believe it was a dish created by the coal miners of the mountains between Abruzzo and Lazio. Or the name may simply describe the look of the cooked bits of *pancetta* in the preparation.

SPAGHETTI ALLA CARBONARA

2 tablespoons olive oil
4 ounces pancetta or guanciale,
   chopped into small pieces
3 egg yolks

4 ounces parmigiano, grated
Salt and pepper
1 pound spaghetti

Heat the olive oil in a sauté pan, add the **pancetta,** and cook over low heat until golden brown. Remove the *pancetta* from the pan and drain on paper towels.

Whisk the egg yolks, **parmigiano,** and salt and pepper to taste in a small mixing bowl and set aside.

Boil the **spaghetti** in salted water until **al dente,** drain, then place in a large bowl. Add the *pancetta* and the egg mixture. Toss thoroughly just until the egg yolks are cooked by the heat of the *spaghetti* and serve. Makes 4 servings.

carciofo (kahr-CH'YOH-foh)   Artichoke. Also *cacuocciulu* and *iscarzofa.* From an Italian dialect word *articiocco,* which itself derives from the Arabic *al-khurshuf.*

In Italy, the size of artichokes is distinguished by the names *la mamma* for the largest (usually boiled), *figli* (children), and the tiny *nipoti* (nephews) which are usually pickled and served as an **antipasto** dish. The principal variety is the *romanesco.*

Artichokes are usually served boiled or steamed with a dipping sauce of oil and lemon or stuffed with seasoned bread crumbs and often anchovies.

The artichoke may well be native to Sicily, where its propagation was principally confined (although the vegetable was well known among the ancient Romans) until the 15th century, when the kingdom of Naples, of which Sicily was a part, dispersed the artichoke throughout Italy. A century later Tuscan Caterina de' Medici introduced the vegetable to France.

Cuori di carciofi are the hearts of artichokes. *Carciofi alla giudea* (Jewish style) is a Roman specialty associated with the former Jewish ghetto there. Small local artichokes called *c. alla romano* are stuffed and roasted.

CARCIOFI ALLA GIUDEA

6 artichokes, trimmed	**1 tablespoon pepper**
1 lemon	**2 cups olive oil**
2 tablespoons salt	**Lemon slices, for garnish**

Clean the artichokes by removing the outer leaves and fibrous choke from the centers, leaving the tender leaves intact. Slice off about one-third of the top of each artichoke. Rub the artichokes with lemon or place in lemon water to prevent discoloration.

In a small mixing bowl, combine the salt and pepper, then sprinkle the mixture on the artichokes, making sure the mixture goes between the leaves. Heat the olive oil in a deep saucepan and cook the artichokes, standing up, for about 20 minutes. Sprinkle with a few drops of cold water so that steam will cook the insides. (It is traditional to do this step by placing one's fist in cold water, then releasing the moisture over the artichokes.)

Remove the artichokes from the pan and set on a plate. Using tongs, carefully pick up the artichokes by their bottoms and place them, top down, into the hot oil until golden brown. Serve with slices of lemon. Serves 6.

---

cardo   (KAHR-doh)   Cardoon, whose stem is eaten raw or baked with *parmigiano*. It is one of the traditional ingredients in **bagna caôda**.

carema   (kah-REH-mah)   **DOC** red wine of Piedmont, made with the *nebbiolo* grape, which in this region is called *picutener* or *pugnet*.

Carignano del Sulcis   (kah-ree-N'YAH-noh dell SOOL-chees) **DOC** zone of southwestern Sardinia that produces red wine from the Spanish/French grape *carignan* in the area of Sulcis.

Carmignano   (kahr-mee-N'YAH-noh)   **DOCG** red wine of Tuscany. A wine of great power, made from **sangiovese** and, increasingly, **cabernet** *sauvignon* grapes. Rosé and **vin santo** wines are also made. The wines have had legal status since 1716.

carne   (KAHR-neh)   Meat. From the Latin *carno*. *Carne cruda* is raw meat. *C. secca* is dried beef. Salted raw beef, a specialty of Trentino, is *c. salata* or *c. sala*. *C. macinata* is ground meat. *C. suina* is the meat of swine.

carota   (kah-ROH-tah)   Carrot. From the Late Latin, via the Greek *karoton*. Carrots have long been part of the Mediterranean diet, mentioned in Greek writings as of 500 B.C., though not one of the major vegetables of the

Italian diet. They are usually served marinated in oil as part of an **antipasto** selection.

carpa (KAHR-pah)   Carp, *Cyprinus carpio.* From the Late Latin, probably of Germanic origin. A freshwater fish, originally from eastern Asia, now widely farmed. The carp was unknown to the ancient Greeks and Romans; it was probably not brought to the Mediterranean and Europe until the late Middle Ages.

Carp are most relished in winter, when the fattened fish are stewed or grilled. Smaller carp are usually fried. Also *carpione.*

carpaccio (kahr-PAH-ch'yoh)   Paper-thin slices of chilled raw meat or fish lightly dressed with various condiments or **parmigiano.** It was a dish created in 1950 at Harry's Bar in Venice by owner Giuseppe Cipriani after a frequent customer, Contessa Amalia Nani Mocenigo, told him her doctor had placed her on a diet forbidding cooked meat. Cipriani prepared for her a dish of sliced raw beef dressed with a sauce of mayonnaise, lemon juice, horseradish, and milk. It became very popular at the restaurant. Cipriani named the dish after the 16th-century Renaissance painter Vittore Carpaccio (known for his use of reds and whites mirrored in the dish), whose works were on exhibition in Venice at the time. Since then *carpaccio* has been made in many forms, including seafood *carpaccio,* which was popularized in 1986 by chef Gilbert Le Coze at his restaurant, Le Bernardin, in New York.

CARPACCIO ALLA HARRY'S BAR

1¹/₂ pounds trimmed shell of beef	*1 teaspoon lemon juice*
³/₄ cup mayonnaise	*2 ¹/₂ tablespoons milk*
2 teaspoons Worcestershire sauce	*Salt and white pepper*

Place the beef in the freezer until it is fairly firm and easy to cut. Slice paper-thin. Combine the mayonnaise, Worcestershire, and lemon juice in a bowl. Add enough milk to make a thin sauce. Add salt and pepper to taste. Drizzle the sauce over the slices of beef. Serves 6.

carpeselle alla Vastese (kahr-peh-SEH-leh AH-lah vah-STEH-seh) Seafood dish from Vasto in Abruzzo. The seafood is marinated in vinegar and then fried and garnished with marinated vegetables and fruits.

carpione, in (een kahr-pee-OH-neh)   A way of preserving fish or meat, such as *tacchino in carpione.* See also **saor** and **scapece, a.**

carrello   (kah-REH-loh)   Food trolley. *Al carrello* is a menu term meaning something chosen from the cart at a restaurant.

carrettiera, alla   (AH-lah kah-reh-tee-EH-rah)   "Truckers' style." *Spaghetti* with a sauce of browned parsley, onions, garlic, anchovies, capers, and bread crumbs. The name would seem to associate the quick, simple directness of the dish with the image of the trucker. In Basilicata, ginger is added, and the sauce is called *alla trainiera,* which also means "truckers' style."

carricante   (kah-ree-KAHN-teh)   A white wine grape of Sicily, used in making **Etna bianco.**

Carso   (KAHR-soh)   **DOC** zone of Friuli-Venezia Giulia extending into Trieste and Yugoslavia that produces red wines from *terrano,* a strain of **refosco,** grapes.

carta da musica   (KAHR-tah dah MOO-zee-kah)   "Music paper." Unleavened sheets of bread from Sardinia. The sheets are so thin and fragile that they are said resemble old sheet music. They are crumbled into soup, eaten with olive oil as a snack, or ground into meal. Because it keeps so well, shepherds take it with them to the pastures. It is the basis for the main course called **pane frattau.**

carteddate   (kahr-teh-DAH-teh)   "Big sheets." Fried ribbons of sweetened dough traditional to Apulia at Christmas. The dough is often flavored with Marsala and after frying topped with cinnamon and honey. Also called *cartellate.*

cartoccio, al   (ahl kahr-TOH-ch'yoh)   "In a bag." Food that is steamed inside of a parchment, paper, or aluminum foil bag.

carulà   (kah-roo-LAH)   Cheese from Piedmont, from Ossola.

casa, della   (DEH-lah KAH-sah)   "Of the house." A dish that is a specialty of the kitchen or restaurant. *Vino della casa* is the house wine at a **trattoria.**

casadello   (kah-sah-DEH-loh)   "Big house (bread)." Vanilla-flavored cake from Ravenna.

casalinga, alla   (AH-lah kah-sah-LEEN-'gah)   "Housewife style." Done in a homey style, or homemade. Also *casareccia.* Has come to mean country or peasant cooking.

casatiello   (kah-sah-T'YEH-lo)   "Homestyle [bread]." Spicy Easter cheese bread, from Naples. Eggs in the shell are set in the dough and strips of dough are folded over.

casa vinicola   (KAH-sah vee-NEE-koh-lah)   "Wine house." A wine producer that uses grapes purchased from others' vineyards.

casiddi   (kah-SEE-dee)   Small, firm cheese from Basilicata.

casigliolo   (kah-see-L'YOH-loh)   Cheese similar to *caciocavallo,* from Sicily. Also *panedda* and *pera di vacca.*

cassa   (KAH-sah)   Cashier at a restaurant or food store. From the Latin *capsa* (chest).

cassata   (kah-SAH-tah)   Lavish Holy Week sponge cake from Sicily, often brick-shaped, filled with *ricotta,* candied fruits or *zucca candita,* and chocolate; flavored with *Marsala,* rum, or *strega;* and coated on all sides with marzipan. It was once made exclusively by nuns. Sometimes it is made with layers of chocolate, vanilla, pistachio, and strawberry ice cream. *Cassatine* are small *cassate.*

The word *cassata* may come from the Latin *caseus* (cheese), while others believe it derives from an Arabic word *qas'at,* for a deep, sloping dish in which such cakes were made.

cassatedde   (kah-sah-TEH-deh)   "Little cases." Fried turnovers from Sicily. Sweet ricotta-filled turnovers, glazed with honey, traditionally served on the feast of *San Giuseppe* (March 19).

cassoeula   (kah-soh-OO-lah)   "Casserole." Pork and savoy cabbage stew from Lombardy. Served with *polenta* on the feast of *Saint Antonio* (January 17). Also *cazzoeula* and *bottaggio.* From the French *casserole* (saucepan), ultimately from Greek *kyathos* (ladle).

CASSOEULA

1 pig's foot, cut in two lengthwise	*1 medium onion, diced*
2 tablespoons butter	*2 carrots, diced*
2 tablespoons olive oil	*1 cup diced celery*
1 pound pork sausage, cut into 4 to 6 pieces	*2 cups diced tomatoes*
1 pound pork ribs, cut into 4 pieces	*3 pounds savoy cabbage, cut into strips*
¹/₂ pound pork skin, cut into 6 pieces	*Salt and pepper*

Put the pig's foot in a large saucepan and cover with water. Bring to a boil, skim, and boil for about 45 minutes. In a large pot, melt the butter and the oil and brown all the meats including the boiled pig's foot. Halfway through the browning, add the onion and sauté until golden. When the meat is browned, add the carrots, celery, and tomatoes. Stir and cook over medium heat for about

30 minutes. Then add the cabbage and salt and pepper to taste and cook for another 45 minutes, stirring every 10 to 15 minutes so that the bottom does not burn. Serve with *polenta.* Serves 4.

cassola (kah-SOH-lah)   Seafood stew, from Sardinia. Made with John Dory, eel, octopus, chile peppers, tomatoes, and garlic and served over a slice of bread.

cassono (kah-SOH-noh)   Fritter stuffed with spinach and raisins, a specialty of Emilia-Romagna.

castagna (kah-STAH-n'yah)   Chestnut. Used widely in Italian cookery, the chestnut has a long history in Italy, and it is believed the Romans spread the chestnut to the rest of Europe. From the Latin *castanea.*

Chestnuts are shelled and boiled or cooked over an open fire in their shells and eaten fresh or made into a soup called **busecchina.** They are used as a stuffing for birds, pureed as a side dish, made into a flour for bread and pasta, and dried. Dried chestnuts are boiled in milk with bay leaf. In Modena, chestnuts are boiled in wine must, then roasted. Candied chestnuts in Piedmont have been made at least since the 15th century.

Castagnaccio is a cake made from chestnut flour, with pine nuts, almonds, raisins, and candied fruits, from Tuscany, Piedmont, and Liguria. *Monte bianco,* taking its name from the Alpine peak, is pureed chestnuts topped with whipped cream.

castagneto (kah-stah-NYEH-toh)   Goat's milk cheese from Piedmont. Made in discs and wrapped in chestnut leaves, now usually paper leaves.

castagnole (kah-stah-N'YOH-leh)   Small balls of fried sweet dough rolled in sugar. A specialty of Carnival time.

In Friuli, *castagnole* are chestnut cookies.

Casteller (kah-STEH-ler)   *DOC* light red wine of Alto Adige, made from **schiava, merlot,** and **lambrusco** grapes. Often made in an *amabile* style.

Castelli Romani (kah-STEH-lee roh-MAH-nee)   Red, white, and rosé wines of Latium based on grapes grown around the Castelli Romani southeast of Rome.

castelmagno (kah-stehl-MAH-n'yoh)   A sharp, blue-veined cow's milk cheese from Piedmont. Named after the town of Castelmagno in the region, although it has many local dialect names, including *ravajun* in Cùneo, *gariga* in Valle Susa, and *castaneul* in Monferrato and Langhe. It is made in 12-pound cylinders.

Castel del Monte (KAH-stehl dell MOHN-teh)   **DOC** zone of Apulia that produces white wine from the *pampanuto* grape, rosé from **bombino nero,** and red from **uva di troia** and other grapes. The name comes from an eight-sided mountain castle built by the Roman Emperor Friedrich II von Hohenstaufen of Swabia.

castrato (kah-STRAH-toh)   Any castrated male animal. Usually refers to lamb. From the Latin *castro* (to castrate).

castrino (kah-STREE-noh)   Small knife with a curved blade used to score chestnuts. From the Latin *castro* (to castrate).

casu marzu (KAH-soo MAHR-t'zoo)   Pungent, crumbly cheese from Sardinia. The dialect name means "rotten cheese" because small black worms are allowed to grow in the cheese. Also *casu becciu* and *casu Iscaldidu.*

casuzzolu (kah-soo-T'ZOH-loo)   "Little cheese." From Sardinia, similar to **provolone dolce**. It is commonly toasted before a fire.

catarratto (kah-tah-RAH-toh)   Widely planted wine grape of Sicily, used in making **Marsala** and *Bianco* **Alcamo**. Its surplus production is usually made into grape concentrate or distilled by the European Economic Union.

cavaleggera, alla (AH-lah kah-vah-leh-JEH-rah)   "Cavalryman style." A pasta sauce. Made with cream, **parmigiano,** walnuts, and eggs.

cavallo (kah-VAH-loh)   Horse meat. Also *carne equina.* Still a popular meat sold almost exclusively by designated horse butchers, who make it into sausages or prepare it for cooking like beef. **Pastissada di cavallo** is a Venetian dish of horse meat stewed in wine.

cavallucci (kah-vah-LOO-chee)   "Ponies." Spice cookies from Tuscany. Traditionally baked at Christmastime. The name comes from the cookie's horse-like shape.

cavatappi (kah-vah-TAH-pee)   Corkscrew. Also, a corkscrew-shaped pasta of southern Italy.

cavatelli (kah-vah-TEH-lee)   "Little plugs." Homemade pasta from Apulia. The flour is usually a mixture of white and semolina flours and **ricotta** is commonly added to the pasta dough itself. Resembling flattened almonds, sometimes ridged, *cavatelli* are often served with arugula. Also *cavateddi* and *rascatelli. Cavateglie e patate* is a Molise dish of *cavatelli* and potatoes with a **ragù** of rabbit and pork.

caviale (kah-vee-AH-lay)   Caviar. The Po delta of Emilia-Romagna produces a small quantity of sturgeon caviar, but most caviar used in Italy is imported. From the Turkish *havyar.*

caviciunetti (kah-vee-choo-NEH-tee) Savory deep-fried pastries from the Marches and Abruzzo.

cavolata (kah-voh-LAH-tah) Pig's feet and cauliflower soup from Sardinia.

cavolfiore (kah-vohl-F'YOH-reh) Cauliflower. From the Late Latin *caulis* (stem) and *fiore* (flower). In Sicily, several other terms for cauliflower are used, including *broccolò* and *vruoccolo pieno*.
    In Sardinia, a cauliflower soup is *la cauledda*.

cavolini di Bruxelles (kah-voh-LEE-nee dee brook-ZEHLS) Brussels sprouts. Also *cavoletti*. The word *cavolini* is from the Late Latin *caulis* (stem).

cavolo (KAH-voh-loh) Cabbage. Italian cabbages are divided into common cabbage, *cavolo cappuccio,* and savoy cabbage, *c. verza* or *c. di Milano. C. nero* (black cabbage) is similar to kale.

cavolo con le fette (KAH-voh-loh kohn leh FEH-teh) "Cabbage with slices." A dish of toasted bread slices topped with *cavolo nero* and its cooking water and drizzled with olive oil, from Florence.

cavolo rape (KAH-voh-loh RAH-peh) Kohlrabi.

cazmarr (kahz-MAHR) Stew of lamb innards with **prosciutto,** wine, and cheese, from Basilicata.

cazzilli (kah-T'ZEE-lee) "Little penises." Sicilian fried potato croquettes, so called because of their shape.

ceca (CHEH-kah) Young eel. See also **anguilla.**

cecamariti (CHEH-kah-mah-REE-tee) "Blind husbands." Dish of leftover bread, garlic, chile pepper, **fava** or **cannellini** beans, and greens like broccoletti, from Apulia. The name supposedly implies that a husband will greedily eat so much of the dish that he will go blind.

ceceniello (cheh-cheh-N'YEH-loh) Smelt, *Osmerus mordax*. Also *eperlano*. They are usually floured and fried.

ceci (CHEH-chee) Chickpeas. One of the oldest cultivated foods in the world, chickpeas were grown in Neolithic Sicily; during the time of the Roman Empire they were shipped in jars from Sicily to the rest of Italy. The chickpea is said to have resulted in the massacre of Charles I's French soldiers in 1282, when Sicilian rebels identified the foreigners by asking them to pronounce the word *cece* correctly. Those who did not were killed.
    Ceci are used in many preparations in Italy, as part of an **antipasto** table, cooked in soups and stews, or served with pasta or as a side vegetable. In Genoa *ceci in zimino* is a stew of chickpeas, celery, onions, and, sometimes pork.

It is traditional to serve **panelle** made with chickpea flour *(farina di ceci)* on the feast of *Santa Lucia* in Sicily. **Ciceri e tria** is a dish from Apulia made with chickpeas and homemade pasta. The rarely seen *cicherie* are similar to chickpeas but have a slightly smokier flavor.

cecina (cheh-CHEE-nah) Pizza made from chickpea flour, from Livorno.

cedro (CHEH-droh) Citron, *Citrus medica.* Closely related to the lemon but much larger. Italians candy citron by placing the skin in brine, cooking it, and then treating it with sugar syrup. Candied citron is used in many cakes and pies.

cefaletto (cheh-fah-LEH-toh) Small squidlike sea creature. In Campania, it is cooked *alla zi' Teresa* (Aunt Teresa's way)—marinated in lemon and oil, then grilled and served with a sauce of vinegar, garlic, chile pepper, oregano, and parsley.

cefalo (CHEH-fah-loh) Gray mullet, *Mugil cephalus.* A good fatty fish with white meat and an edible liver. Its egg sac is made into **bottarga**. Gray mullet can be cooked many different ways. Also *muggine* and *volpina.* From the Greek *kephalo-* (head). See also **triglia.**

celestina (cheh-leh-STEE-nah) "Sweet heaven." A clear consommé containing star-shaped pasta. From the Latin *caelestiis* (celestial).

Cellatica (cheh-LAH-tee-kah) **DOC** wines of Lombardy, made from **schiava gentile, barbera,** and **marzemino** grapes produced around the town of Cellatica.

cena (CHEH-nah) Dinner. Usually lighter than the midday meal in Italy. Often begins with soup and follows with a simple main course, then cheese and fruit, with wine and mineral water. *Cena,* which comes from the same Latin word, has an upper-class connotation as a meal taken late in the evening, while the same class refers to an earlier dinner as *pranzo.*

cenci (CHEN-chee) "Rags." Egg noodles flavored with anise, vanilla, orange peel, and **vin santo,** fried in lard, and sprinkled with sugar, from Tuscany. Also *frappe alla romana.*

ceppetello (cheh-peh-TEH-loh) "Little stump." Oyster mushroom, *Pleurotus ostreatus.* Light gray mushroom, both wild and commercially grown. See also **orecchiette.**

cerasuolo (cheh-rah-S'WOH-loh) "Cherrylike." A light wine, a bit darker in color than a **rosato.**

Cerasuolo di Vittoria   (cheh-rah-S'WOH-loh dee vee-TOH-ree-yah) *DOC* red wine of Sicily, made from *calabrese* and *frappato* grapes, grown around Vittoria. It is light red with a cherrylike flavor and color from which it takes its name.

cereali   (cheh-reh-AH-lee)   Grains. Wheat *(frumento)* is the most widely propagated grain in Italy. Rice (**riso**), corn (**granoturco**) for **polenta,** and barley (**orzo**) are also grown. From the Latin *cerealis* (of grain).

Italians do not, as a rule, eat the kind of hot or cold cereal flakes popular as American breakfasts.

cerfoglio   (chehr-FOH-l'yoh)   Chervil. From the Latin *caerefolium.*

cernia   (CHEHR-nee-yah)   Grouper. There are many groupers, all under the genus *Epinephelus,* with five species in the Mediterranean that grow to 40 inches or more. The most common in Italian waters is *E. guaza.* Grouper is a firm-fleshed, heavy fish that takes well to grilling, boiling, and baking and may be cut into steaks.

Cernia di fondale is a rarely marketed fish called the stone bass, *Polyprion americanus.*

certosino   (chehr-toh-SEE-noh)   Christmas cake, from Bologna. Said to have been created by the monks of the *certosa* (charterhouse) of the city for Cardinal Lambertini, later Pope Benedetto XIV. It is a spice cake with raisins, sherry, cinnamon, lemon peel, pine nuts, and apricot jam.

Cervellata   (chehr-veh-LAH-tah)   A sausage from Milan. Made with pork, often pig's brains, spices, and saffron.

cervello   (chehr-VEH-loh)   Brain. Calf's brains are often prepared *al burro nero* (with brown butter) or **alla fiorentina,** breaded and fried and served with anchovies and spinach. *Cervello in carrozza* ("brains in a carriage") is a dish of brain fritters, so called because the brains are enclosed in a batter; it is a specialty of Trentino, where they are also called by the German name *Hirn-Profesen,* which means "brains that take the veil."

Cerveteri   (cher-veh-TEH-ree)   *DOC* zone of Latium that produces red wines from *montepulciano* grapes and white wines from **trebbiano** and **malvasia** grapes.

cervo   (CHER-voh)   Stag. *Carne di cervo* is venison. It may be roasted over an open fire or grilled, but is more commonly marinated and braised.

cervone   (cher-VOH-neh)   Spice cake, from Abruzzo. Shaped like a snake for the feast of *San Domenico* (the first Thursday in May).

Cesanese del Piglio   (cheh-sah-NEH-seh dell PEE-l'yoh)   *DOC* wine of Latium, made from *cesanese* grapes grown around the villages of Piglio, Anagni, and Paliano in a wide range of styles, from dry to sweet.

cestino di frutta   (cheh-STEE-noh dee FROO-tah)   Basket of fruit.

cetriolo   (cheh-tree-YOH-loh)   Cucumber. Gherkins are called *cetriolini*. In Tuscany, *cetrioli marinati* are cucumbers marinated in sugar and lemon and eaten as a sweet.

chardonnay   (shahr-doh-NAY)   A white grape famously known for producing the great white wines of France's Burgundy region. Long cultivated in northern Italy, where it was once called by the German names *Gelber* (golden) and *Weissburgunder* (white burgundy) in the Tyrol, it was only in the 1980s that Italian vintners latched onto the international popularity of the grape, especially after its success in California; Alto Adige chardonnay received *DOC* status in 1984. *Chardonnay* grapes are used to make *spumante* and are blended with *garganega* grapes in the Veneto.

cheppia   (KEH-pee-yah)   Twaite shad, *Alosa fallax*. A bony fish, usually grilled.

chiacchiere della nonna   (kee-AH-kee-EH-reh deh-lah NOH-nah) "Grandmother's chatter." Crunchy sweet fried pastries. In Milan, they are called *ciacer di monegh* and are flavored with Marsala and sprinkled with confectioners' sugar. In Abruzzo and Veneto, they are called *zacarette* (shavings). They are traditionally served during carnival week.

chiama vinu   (kee-AH-mah vee-NOO)   "Wine call." Dish of short pasta, like penne, with a sauce of salted anchovies, bread crumbs, and black pepper, from Catania. It is said to make one so thirsty one will call out for wine. In Naples, the dish is usually made with *vermicelli.*

Chianti   (kee-AHN-tee)   *DOCG* Tuscan red wines. Made traditionally from *sangiovese* and other grapes in seven delineated zones: *Chianti Classico, Chianti Colli Aretini, Chianti Colli Fiorentini, Chianti Colline Pisane, Chianti Colli Senesi, Chianti Montalbano,* and *Chianti Rufina.* The *Chianti Classico* zone was first identified in the 13th century, and by 1398 the name *Chianti* had been attached to a white wine of the region. The superiority of the *Chianti Classico* zone was recognized when delimited in 1716 by the Grand Duke Cosimo III.

In the 19th and early 20th centuries, *Chianti* was produced by sharecroppers who often combined their grape yields from varietals common in Tuscany. Traditionally they used what was called the *governo* process, by which the juice of dried grapes was added to induce a second fermentation, raise the level of alcohol, and soften the wines for early drinking and sale. With the fading of the sharecropper system after World War II, *Chianti* became known as a cheap, usually undistinguished red wine packaged in a distinctive green bottle wrapped in a straw basket known as a *fiasco.*

But in 1967, Italy's **DOC** law defined what *Chianti* should be: It required the use of between 10 and 30 percent white grapes (traditionally *trebbiano*) blended with the usual *sangiovese* and *canaiolo nero* red grapes. By the 1970s, *Chianti* plantings, especially in the prestigious *Chianti Classico* region, were plentiful enough to meet worldwide demand. Stronger *DOCG* regulations that took effect in 1984 allowed the white grape quantity to be reduced to 2 percent, while the amount of other red grape varieties, like **cabernet sauvignon,** was raised from 5 to 10 percent. Meanwhile, vineyard yields were reduced in order to raise quality, causing a 40 percent drop in production over a five-year period.

In response to *Chianti Classico* producers who insisted they could make better wines if the white grape requirement was dropped, the *DOCG* rules were changed in 1996 to allow producers to make their wines entirely from red grapes or, if they chose, to add up to 6 percent white. In addition, 15 percent of other red varieties, such as *cabernet, mammolo,* and *malvasia nera,* may be used.

chiara   (kee-AH-rah)   Egg white.

chiaretto   (kee-ah-REH-toh)   "Claret." A dark *rosato* wine.

chiavara   (kee-ah-VAH-rah)   *Caciotta*-style cheese from the region of Genoa.

chifel   (KEE-fehl)   Crescent-shape roll made with cumin seeds, from the Tyrol. Commonly eaten with frankfurters and beer. The name commemorates an Austrian pastry chef named Chiffering, who worked at the court of the Duke of Parma and who is said to have introduced the croissant to Italy. The *chifel,* however, is made without sugar. Its shape commemorates the crescent moon symbol of the Turks at the Battle of Vienna. *Chifeleti* are cresentshape biscuits.

chifferi   (KEE-feh-ree)   *Maccheroni* in a half-moon shape, about 1 inch long, a specialty of northern and central Italy. Usually served with tomato sauce. Also *chifferotti* and *gomiti.* See also *chifel.*

chinotto   (kee-NOH-toh)   An orange used in Liguria to make jams. *Chinotto* is also a trademark name for a bitter soft drink.

chinulille   (kee-noo-LEE-leh)   "Little stuffed ones." *Ricotta*-filled *ravioli* that are fried and sprinkled with sugar icing, from Basilicata. In Calabria, they are filled with chocolate, candied fruit, chestnuts, and nougat.

chiocciolo (kee-yoh-chee-OH-loh)   Black top-shell snail, *Monodonta turbinata*. In Sardinia, the snail is called *monzitta,* meaning "little nun," because the snails look like nuns covered up in their black habits. In Murano, they are called *bodoletti.*

Chioccioli also applies to a snail-shaped **maccheroni.**

chiodi di garofano (kee-OH-dee dee gah-ROH-fah-noh)   "Nails of Garofano." Cloves.

chiodini (kee-oh-DEE-nee)   "Little nails." Either of two wild fungi, *Armillariella mellea* (honey fungus) or *Clitocybe tabescens* (an edible agaric mushroom), commonly gathered in the woods.

chiscioo (kee-SHOO)   Unsweetened buckwheat tart filled with cheese, a specialty of Tirano in Lombardy. Also *cicc.*

chitarra, alla (AH-lah kee-TAH-rah)   "Guitar style." Fresh egg pasta from Abruzzo. Cut on a stringed instrument called a *chitarra* that shapes the pasta into four-sided, fairly thin strands. Also *quadrati.*

chizze (KEE-t'zeh)   "Exciters." Fried dough stuffed with **prosciutto** and cheese, from Reggio Emilia.

ciabatta (ch'yah-BAH-tah)   "Slipper." A bread loaf about 8 inches long with a light, thin crust; the shape resembles a common slipper.

ciacci montanari (CH'YAH-chee mohn-tah-NAH-ree)   Fried cakes eaten with **prosciutto** or sausage, from the mountains of Emilia-Romagna. The word *ciacci* may be a form of *chiacchiere* (chatter), but it also refers to gluttony. *Montanari* are mountaineers.

cialda (chee-AHL-dah)   **Antipasto** of boiled vegetables with tomato, from Apulia. Also *cialledda.*

Cialda is also the name of a paper-thin waffle cookie with an embossed top, from Umbria.

cialzone (ch'yahl-ZOH-neh)   "Pants legs." Pasta stuffed with various ingredients, such as **ricotta** and herbs, potatoes and cinnamon, or spinach and candied citron, from Friuli. Also *cjalsons, cjarsons,* and other names.

ciambella (ch'yahm-BEH-lah)   "Ring cake." Ring-shaped bun, sometimes filled. *Ciambellone* is a large bread ring made with fruit and nuts. See also **bensone.**

ciambotta (ch'yahm-BOH-tah)   "Big mixture." Name given to many regional vegetable stews. In Calabria, it is a stew of eggplant, potatoes, tomatoes, and onions. In Apulia, it is often made with seafood. Also *cianfotta* and *giambotta.*

ciapole (ch'yah-POH-leh)   Term for both dried tomatoes and dried peaches or apricots, from Piedmont.

ciaramicola (chee-ah-rah-MEE-koh-la)   Cake flavored with lemon peel and *alchermes,* from Umbria. The cake is topped with meringue.

ciaudedda (chow-DEH-dah)   Artichokes stuffed with potatoes, fava beans, salt pork, and onions and braised, from Basilicata.

ciauscolo (ch'yau-SKOH-loh)   Very soft, spreadable pork sausage, from Macerata in the Marches.

cibreo (chee-BRAY-oh)   Stew of unlaid chicken eggs, chicken livers, wattles, and cockscombs, from Florence.

cicala (chee-KAH-lah)   "Cicada." Either of two species of shrimp: *cicala* or *cicala gigaute. Cicala* (also called *cannocchia* and *pannochia)* is mantis shrimp (*Squilla mantis*) about 4 inches long, which is fried, poached, or made into soup. *Cicala gigante* (also called *magnosa)* is flat or slipper lobster (*Scyllarides latus);* it can weigh up to 4¹/₂ pounds and more resembles a lobster. The name refers to the cicada-like noises the creatures make underwater.

ciccioli (CHEE-choh-lee)   Cracklings.

ciccionedda (chee-choh-NEH-dah)   "Little chubbies." Pastry filled with cherry preserves, from Sardinia.

cicerchiata (chee-chehr-kee-AH-tah)   "Turn-arounds." Also *cicerata.* Honeyed fried dumplings, similar to *struffoli,* a specialty of Abruzzo. *Cicerchiata* is made during Carnival.

ciceri e tria (CHEE-cheh-ree eh TREE-ah)   "Chickpeas and tria." Chickpeas cooked with onion, garlic, and bay, with homemade *tagliatelle* called *tria,* from Apulia. Some of the *tria* is reserved and fried in olive oil until crisp, then mixed into the dish.

cicoria (chee-KOH-ree-ah)   Chicory. Also *catalogna.* See also *radicchio* and *scarola.*

cieche (chee-EH-keh)   Elvers. Gathered in the Arno River in spring, they are fried. Also *cie* and *cee.* See *anguilla.*

Cilento (chee-LEHN-toh)   *DOC* white, rosé, and red wines of Campania made from grapes grown in the Cilento region.

ciliegia (chee-L'YEH-j'yah)   Cherry. *Marosticana* is a red and white cherry with a crisp texture. Also *cirasa* in dialect. See also *amarena* and *marasca.*

cima   (CHEE-mah)   Breast, usually referring to a boned breast of veal. *Cima ripiena* is a stuffed breast.

cime di rapa   (CHEE-meh dee RAH-pah)   Turnip greens. Also *broccoletti di rapa.*

cinese   (chee-NEH-seh)   Sieve. Also *passino fino.*

cinghiale   (cheen-G'YAH-leh)   Male wild boar, *Sus scrofa,* which was in fact domesticated and bred as swine as long ago as 1500 B.C. in northern Europe. The preferred age for a wild boar is less than six months old, and it should be hung for four to five days. Older boars are marinated *in agrodolce* and roasted. Boar hams may be cured like **prosciutto.**

Cinqueterre   (cheen-kweh-TEH-rah)   "Five Lands." **DOC** wine of Liguria, made from **bosco,** *albarola,* and **vermentino** grapes grown around the villages of Monterosso, Vernazza, Corniglia, Manarola, and Riomaggiore.

cioccolata   (ch'yoh-koh-LAH-tah)   Chocolate. See also **cacao.**

cioccolata calda   (ch'yoh-koh-LAH-tah KAHL-dah)   Hot chocolate beverage.

cioccolatini   (ch'yoh-koh-lah-TEE-nee)   Small chocolate candies. *Cioccolatini ripieni* are stuffed chocolate candies.

ciociara, alla   (AH-lah ch'yoh-CH'YAH-rah)   "Ciociara style." Either of two pasta sauces: one of **mozzarella, pecorino,** tomatoes, olive oil, and oregano or one to which cream is added, from Ciociara, south of Rome.

ciopa   (CH'YOH-pah)   Thick, compact bread loaf. The Veneto version is rather large; the Trentino version, called *ciopetta,* much smaller.

cipolla   (chee-POH-lah)   Onion. From the Latin *caepa.* In ancient Rome the onion was held in low culinary esteem as a food for the poor, but it became a staple of cookery by the Middle Ages.

White onions are called *maggenghe* (May) or *giugnaiole* (June). Red onions are called *vernine* (winter). *Cipolline* are small white onions.

ciriola   (chee-ree-OH-lah)   Small, crusty bread roll, about three to four ounces, from Rome.

Cirole is an Umbrian term for thick **spaghetti,** which is also called *umbrici,* made with semolina and white flours. In Latium, it is a term for small eels.

Cirò   (chee-ROH)   **DOC** wines of Calabria named after the village of Cirò on the Ionian coast. The reds and rosés are made from *gaglioppo,* the whites from *greco bianco.*

cisrà   (chee-S'RAH)   Soup of chickpeas, carrots, celery, onions, and pork rind, from Piedmont. Traditionally served in country towns on Pentecost Sunday. The three points of the chickpea are symbolic of the Trinity.

The word is a dialect form of *ceciata,* derived from **cece** (chickpea).

ciuppin   (ch'yoo-PEEN)   "Little bowl of soup." A fish soup, from Genoa. Made with various fish like flounder, John Dory, whiting, and others with white wine, tomato, and herbs. The contents are pureed rather than left whole. The word *ciuppin* is from Genovese dialect.

Ciuppin is the basis for cioppino, a seafood stew made by Italian immigrants in San Francisco, California.

civet   (chee-VEHT)   Cut-up pieces of chamois or hare marinated in red wine, carrots, onions, garlic, cloves, sage, and juniper berries. It is cooked for a long time, and the liver of the animal is added toward the end. Also *sivet.*

The word and dish are derived from the French *civet,* which is itself from the French *civette,* meaning "cat," supposedly because some cooks, trying to save money, would use cat, rather than rabbit, in the dish.

civraxiu   (chee-V'RAH-see-oo)   Semolina bread, from Sardinia. Made into enormous round loaves weighing up to ten pounds. The word is Cagliari dialect meaning different types of flours.

classico   (KLAH-see-koh)   "Classic." A term to describe wines made according to long-established traditions maintained within a **DOC** zone.

Clastidium   (klah-STEE-dee-oom)   Small-production white wine from Lombardy made from **pinot nero** and **pinot grigio** grapes around the town of Casteggio, known in Roman times as Clastidium.

coccioca   (koh-CH'YOH-kah)   Red gurnard, *Aspitrigla cuculus.* Prepared many ways: baked, grilled, or fried. Also *capone coccio.*

Coccio is also the word for a Tuscan terra-cotta pot.

cocciola   (koh-CH'YOH-lah)   Cockle, *Cerastoderma glaucum.* Also *cuore edule.* The spicy cockle, *Acanthocardia aculeata,* is known as *cuore rosso* (red heart) and, in Naples, as *fasolara.*

cocco   (KOH-koh)   See **noce di cocco.**

coccoedu   (koh-KWEH-doo)   "Little toy." Braided hard-crusted bread, from Sardinia. Also *coccoi.*

cocomero   (koh-KOH-meh-roh)   Southern Italian term for watermelon.

coda   (KOH-dah)   Tail. *Coda alla vaccinara* (butcher's style) is a stew of oxtail braised with tomato, onion, celery, and white wine, from Rome.

coda di rospo (KOH–dah dee ROHS–poh)   See *rana pescatrice.*

colla di pesce (KOH–lah dee PEH–sheh)   "Fish glue." Isinglass (gelatin) made from the dried bladder of sturgeon and other fish.

colapasta (koh–lah–PAH–stah)   Colander. Also *colatoio.* From the Latin *colum* (sieve).

colazione (koh–lah–t'zee–YOH–neh)   The midday meal, still the major meal of the day for most Italians. *Piccola colazione* and *prima colazione* are terms for breakfast. From the Latin *collatio.* See also **pranzo.**

Colli Albani (KOH–lee ahl–BAH–nee)   *DOC* white wine of Latium, made from **trebbiano** and **malvasia** grapes in the Alban hills.

Colli Altotiberini (KOH–lee AHL–toh–tee–beh–REE–nee)   *DOC* zone in Umbria that produces red and rosé wines from **sangiovese** and **merlot,** and whites from **trebbiano.**

Colli Berici (KOH–lee beh–REE–chee)   *DOC* zone of the Veneto that produces seven varietals, including **cabernet, pinot bianco,** and *tocai rosso.*

Colli Bolognesi (KOH–lee boh–loh–N'YEH–see)   *DOC* zone of Emilia-Romana that produces eight varietals, including some notable sparkling wines like *pignoletto,* from grapes grown in the hills south of Bologna.

Colli del Trasimeno (KOH–lee dell trah–SEE–meh–noh)   *DOC* zone in Umbria that produces white wines from **trebbiano, verdicchio,** and **malvasia** grapes and reds from **sangiovese,** *ciliegiolo,* and **gamay.**

Colli di Bolzano (KOH–lee dee bohl–ZAH–noh)   *DOC* wine of Alto Adige, made from **schiava** grapes grown around the city of Bolzano.

Colli di Parma (KOH–lee dee PAHR–mah)   *DOC* zone of Emilia-Romagna known for its **malvasia** sparkling wines, as well as a red from **barbera** and other grapes and a white from **sauvignon,** grown in the hills around Parma.

Colli Euganei (KOH–lee yoo–gah–NAY'EE)   *DOC* zone of the Veneto that produces seven types of wines, from **merlot** to *tocai italico,* from grapes grown in the Euganean hills south of Padua.

Colli Lanuvini (KOH–lee lah–noo–VEE–nee)   *DOC* white wine of Latium, made from **malvasia** and **trebbiano** grapes.

Colli Martani (KOH–lee mahr–TAH–nee)   *DOC* zone of Umbria that produces wines from **grechetto, sangiovese,** and **trebbiano** grapes grown in the hills around the town of Martana.

Colli Morenici Mantovani del Garda   (KOH-lee moh-reh-NEE-chee mahn-toh-VAH-nee dell GAHR-dah)   *DOC* zone of Lombardy that produces red, white, and rosé wines from *rondinella,* **merlot, trebbiano, garganega,** and *rosanella* grapes grown around Mantua and Lake Garda.

Colline Lucchesi   (koh-LEE-neh loo-KEH-zee)   *DOC* zone of Tuscany that produces red wines from the **sangiovese** and **canaiolo nero** grapes and white wines from the **trebbiano, greco,** and **vermentino** grapes grown around the city of Lucca.

Colli Orientali del Friuli   (KOH-lee oh-ree-ehn-TAH-lee dell free-YOO-lee)   *DOC* zone of Friuli that produces 20 different kinds of wine, including **cabernet, picolit, refosco, ribolla** *gialla,* **riesling renano, schioppettino,** and **Ramandolo.** The term refers to the "eastern hills of Friuli."

Colli Perugini   (KOH-lee peh-roo-JEE-nee)   *DOC* zone of Umbria that produces white, red, and rosé wines from grapes grown around the city of Perugia.

Colli Piacentini   (KOH-lee pee-ah-chehn-TEE-nee)   *DOC* zone of Emilia-Romagna that produces 12 kinds of wine, including **Gutturnio** (a red made from **barbera** and **bonarda** grapes), *Otruga* (white), and *Trebbiano Val Trebbia* (a *frizzante*), from grapes grown around the city of Piacenza.

Colli Tortonesi   (KOH-lee tohr-toh-NEH-zee)   *DOC* zone of Piedmont that produces **Barbera** and *Cortese* from grapes grown around the city of Tortona.

colomba pasquale   (koh-LOHM-bah pas-KWAH-leh)   "Easter dove." Dove-shaped Easter cake, said to have been created in Milan to honor the legend of two white doves who settled on a Milanese war chariot until the city won the battle of Legnano in 1176. Pavia also claims the cake was created in the shape of a dove by a young girl who brought it to the Lombard conquerer of Pavia, Alboin, in 572, who was so impressed that he allowed her to go free.

colombo   (koh-LOHM-boh)   Dove. Wild doves are best taken young, when they can be roasted or grilled; older ones are marinated and cooked in a casserole. From the Latin *columba.* See also **piccione.**

coltello   (kohl-TEH-loh)   Knife. From the Latin *culter.*

coltivatore   (kohl-tee-vah-TOH-reh)   A grape grower. From the Latin *colere* (to cultivate).

comino   (koo-MEE-noh)   Cumin. Though a favorite spice of the eastern Mediterranean since antiquity, cumin is not often used in Italian cookery. From the Latin *cuminum.*

companatico (kohm-pah-NAH-tee-coh) "(Food) with bread." Any food eaten with bread, which would not include pasta and rice dishes.

composta di frutta (kohm-POH-stah dee FROO-tah) "Fruit mixture." Stewed fruit, often made with wine.

concia (KOHN-ch'yah) "Preparation." Marinade. Most closely associated with the cooking of Rome's former Jewish ghetto, where zucchini were fried and then marinated in vinegar, garlic, salt, and pepper.

The term also refers to a dish of *polenta* cooked with *fontina* and *toma* cheeses.

conchiglie (kohn-CHEE-l'yeh) "Shells." Shell-shaped pasta, usually ridged; they come in several sizes, a specialty of Campania, commonly served with tomato sauce. From the Latin *concha* (shell). Also *arselle.*

conchiglie delle monache (kohn-CHEE-l'yeh DEH-leh moh-NAH-keh) "Nuns' shells." Sicilian sweet made of pastry shells filled with sweetened squash and chopped nuts.

condiggion (kohn-dee-J'YOHN) "Dressed (salad)." Salad made with tomatoes, cucumbers, lettuce, cardoons, celery, and olive oil, from Liguria. Often made with sea biscuits, *bottarga,* or canned tuna. Also *condion* and *condijun.*

condimento (kohn-dee-MEHN-toh) Condiment or garnish. From the Latin *condimentum.*

confetteria (kohn-feh-teh-REE-ah) Sweet confection. A *confetteria* is a shop selling sweets.

confetti (kohn-FEH-tee) Sugar candies, often encasing almonds, given by the bride and groom or at a christening. From the Latin *conficere* (to put together).

The tradition of throwing *confetti* at a bride is related to the outdated Sicilian practice of having the bride "kidnapped" and brought to the chapel for the wedding. The *confetti* was thrown in imitation of ammunition used to repel the enemy.

coniglio (koh-NEE-l'yoh) Rabbit, wild or domestic. From the Latin. For roasting, a rabbit five to six months old is preferred; usually larded. In Ragusa, *coniglio alla portoghese* (Portuguese style) is a stew with mixed vegetables.

cono (KOH-noh) Ice cream cone. From the Latin *conus.*

conserve (kohn-SEHR-veh) Preserves. From the Latin *conserve.* The ancient Romans were well acquainted with preserving fruits, flowers, seeds, and plants with honey; these preserves were always part of the most lavish banquets. Throughout the Middle Ages and into the Renaissance, Italian confectioners were considered the masters of the practice of preserving, especially once sugar became affordable.

consorzio   (kohn-SOHR-t'zee-oh)   A consortium of grape growers or wine, cheese, and *prosciutto* producers who oversee standards, production, and promotion of their products within a region. From the Latin *consortium* (fellowship).

conto   (KOHN-toh)   Restaurant or hotel bill. From the Latin *compter* (count). It is not the same as a receipt, which is called a *ricevuto* or *fattura.*

contorno   (kohn-TOHR-noh)   Vegetable served with the main course of a meal. From the Latin *contortio* (twisting), meaning that the vegetables are served around the meat or seafood of the dish.

controfiletto   (kohn-troh-fee-LEH-toh)   "Against the filet." Sirloin or porterhouse steak.

Copertino   (koh-pehr-TEE-noh)   *DOC* red and rosé wines of Apulia, made from *negroamaro* grapes grown around the town of Copertino.

coperto   (koh-PEHR-toh)   Cover charge, usually for bread, glassware, and linen, at a restaurant. The word probably derives from the Latin *cooperire* (to cover).

coppa   (KOH-pah)   Cooked and pressed cured boneless pork neck, which is brined, then stuffed into a casing and air-dried for six months or more. *Coppa di testa* (also *coppa d'inverno*) is cooked, pressed, seasoned meat made from the pig's head. The word *coppa* derives from the Latin *cupa* (tub), in which the ham was pressed.

   Piacenza's *c. di piacentina* is made from the neck roll, which in southern Italy is called *capocollo* and in Lombardy, *bondiana.*

coppa gelato   (KOH-pah jeh-LAH-toh)   Cup of ice cream. From the Late Latin *cuppa.*

coppia   (KOH-pee-yah)   "Couple." Bread in which two long crescent rolls are joined to make a couple, from Emilia-Romagna. From the Latin *copula* (bond).

corada   (koh-RAH-dah)   Calf's lung, which is stewed or made into soup.

coraline   (koh-rah-LEE-neh)   "Little corals." Tiny ring-shape pasta used for soup. From the Latin *corallium.*

corallo   (koh-RAH-loh)   Coral. Shellfish roe, usually used to color and flavor sauces. From the Latin *corallium.*

corata   (koh-RAH-tah)   Mixed innards, including the intestines, heart, and lung of lamb, braised with artichokes in white wine, a specialty of Rome. Also *coratella.*

Cordula or *sa corda* is a stew of innards, from Sardinia.

coregono   (koh-REH-goh-noh)   Salmon trout, *Argentina sphyraena.* A small, slender, silver fish with a pale-green back. It is rare in the Mediterranean; when caught, it is commonly fried. Also *argentina.*

Cori   (KOH-ree)   *DOC* zone of Latium around the town of Cori that produces red wines from *montepulciano, cesanese,* and *nero buono di Cori* grapes and whites from **malvasia** and **trebbiano.**

coriandolo   (koh-ree-AHN-doh-loh)   Coriander. While very widespread in eastern Mediterranean cooking and used freely in ancient Roman kitchens, coriander is not used much in modern Italian cookery; it is used sparingly in the south. From the Greek *koriandron.*

cornetti   (kohr-NEH-tee)   "Cornets." Italian croissants. From the Latin *cornu* (horn).

Also **gnocchi** made with chestnut flour and served with a simple sauce of crushed pine nuts and olive oil, from Liguria.

Fagiolini are also called *cornetti.*

corollo   (koh-ROH-loh)   "Corollas." Anise-scented sweet bread from Tuscany. From a diminutive of the Latin *corona.*

Cortese dell'Alto Monferrato   (kohr-TEH-seh dell-AHL-toh mohn-feh-RAH-toh)   *DOC* white wine of Piedmont, made from *cortese* grapes grown in the Alto Monferrato hills.

corvina veronese   (kohr-VEE-nah veh-roh-NEH-say)   "Veronese crow." A red wine grape of Veneto, used in making **valpolicella, Bardolino,** and **amarone** wines. Also *cruina.*

corvo   "Raven." Either of two Mediterranean fish: corvina, *Corvina nigra;* or drum or croaker, *Sciaena umbria.* Both fish are best fried.

The word *corvo* seems also to apply to the now-rare grayling, a freshwater fish in the family Thymallus, found in only a few European lakes and rivers.

Corvo   (KOHR-voh)   Proprietary name for Sicilian wines made by Duca di Salaparuta, a cooperative that produces whites under the names *Bianca di Valguarnera* (from **inzolia**) and *Corvo Bianco* (*prima goccia* and *colomba platino* from *inzolia,* **grechetto,** and **catarrato**) and reds under the names *Corvo Rosso* (**Nero d'Avola, perricone,** and **nerello mascalese**), *Duca Enrico (Nero d'Avola)* and *Terre d'Agala (Nero d'Avola* and *frappato).*

corzetti (kohr–ZEH–tee)   Pasta made with white, whole wheat, or chestnut flour, shaped into rounds, and embossed with a pattern (commonly a star) with a wooden stamp, from Liguria. *Corzetti* are named after old Genovese stamped money pieces, and old stamps, many now family heirlooms, commemorate heraldry or Genoa's history. Olive oil, marjoram, and pine nuts make a simple dressing for *corzetti*.

Corzetti alla polceverasca (in the style of the Val di Polceverera) is a pasta shaped into a figure 8 and served with a mushroom sauce, from Liguria.

coscia (KOH–sh'yah)   Thigh, usually referring to a chicken.

cosciotto (koh–SH'YOH–toh)   Leg of meat. In Abruzzo, *cosciotto d'agnello all'abruzzese* is made by inserting garlic and rosemary into slits in a leg of lamb, covering it with fatback strips, and cooking it with wine and tomatoes.

costa (KOH–stah)   Chop. From the Latin. A *costata* is an entrecôte or rib steak. See also **costoletta**.

costardello (koh–stahr–DELL–oh)   "Pretty [fish] of the shore." Skipper, *Scomberesox saurus*. A garfish, usually fried, sometimes salted.

costoletta (koh–stoh–LEH–tah)   Veal chop or cutlet. Also *cotolette*. From the Latin *costa* (rib). *Costoletta alla milanese,* one of the most famous dishes of Milan, is a breaded flattened veal rib chop with the bone, fried in butter and served with lemon, which actually antedated the Austrian *Wiener Schnitzel* it is sometimes said to be copied from. *C. all'emiliana* is a similar dish from Emilia-Romagna, with the addition of **parmigiano** on top.

Costeletta alla valdostana is a veal chop stuffed with **fontina** cheese and white truffles and fried, from the Valle d'Aosta. *C. alla bolognese* is a chop baked with **prosciutto** and **parmigiano,** from Bologna. *C. di vitello alla Guido Reni* is a chop that is flattened and stuffed with green beans, tomato, basil, and cheese, then rolled up and tied and grilled. It is a specialty of Bologna, named after a native son, the Renaissance artist Guido Reni.

Costoletta di montone alla Byron is a mutton chop marinated in oil and spices, then sautéed in butter. It is named after the English Romantic poet Lord Byron and is a specialty of Ravenna.

COSTOLETTA ALLA MILANESE

4 veal rib chops	**1 ¹/₂ cups bread crumbs**
2 cups milk	**2 tablespoons butter**
2 eggs, beaten	**Salt and pepper**

Pound the chops to about 3/8 inch thick. Let stand in milk for about 30 minutes. Dip into beaten egg, then dredge in bread crumbs, patting the chops to make sure the crumbs adhere evenly.

Melt the butter in a large sauté pan over medium heat until foamy. Sauté the chops for 3 minutes on each side, or until golden brown. Season with salt and pepper to taste. Serve immediately. Makes 4 servings.

---

cotechino (koh-teh-KEE-noh)   A fresh pork sausage, from Modena. It often contains pork rind. From *cotica* or *cotenna* (pig's skin), which was once used as a wrapping. It is usually boiled and served *con lenticchie,* with cooked lentils. *Cotechino in galera (cotechino* in prison) is a lavish dish from Modena of half-cooked *cotechino* wrapped in slices of **prosciutto** and beef, then cooked in an earthenware dish with onions, consommé, and white **Lambrusco** wine.

Cotechinata is pork rind rolled around peppers, garlic, and salt pork, from Basilicata.

cotica (KOH-tee-kah)   Pork skin or rind.

cotogna (koh-TOH-n'yah)   See **mela cotogna.**

cotta a puntino (KOH-tah ah poon-TEE-noh)   "Cooked to the point." Meat cooked to medium.

cotto (KOH-toh)   Cooked. Also *cotta.* From the Latin *coquere.*

covaccine (koh-vah-CHEE-neh)   "Little beds." Very thin **pizzas** topped only with olive oil and salt, from Tuscany.

coviglie (koh-VEE-yeh)   Coffee or chocolate mousse topped with whipped cream, from Campania.

cozze (KOH-t'zeh)   Mussels, *Mytilus galloprovincialis, M. edulis,* et al. A bivalve, usually with a black shell. Also *mitilli. Cozze pelose* (hairy mussels) have particularly hairy shells. *Cozze* are widely cultivated for the market; they may be eaten raw but are more often steamed or stewed. They are often cooked **alla marinara** or served in a **risotto** or cold rice dish. See also **datteri di mare, muscoli,** and **peoci.**

cozzolo   (koh-T'ZOH-loh)   Stargazer fish, *Uranoscopus scaber*. With its eyes seemingly fixed on the stars, this weever fish has spiny, sharp dorsal fins that must be removed before cooking. The fillets are usually fried, but they are also cooked in stews and soups.

cozzuledda   (koh-t'zoo-LEH-dah)   "Little mussels." Doughnut-shape pastry, from Sardinia. It is filled with a mixture of honey, almonds, walnuts, orange zest, and bran. Also *cozzula*.

cranu pestatu   (KRAH-noo peh-STAH-too)   "Pounded grain." Dish of pounded wheat berries and wild greens, from Apulia. The berries are soaked, drained, and pounded with a pestle called a *stompatura* to husk the grain. They are then steamed and often mixed with greens and tomato. Also *grano pestato*.

crauti   (KRAU-tee)   Sauerkraut, from Alto Adige.

crejoli   (kreh-J'YOH-lee)   Pasta from Molise, similar to **maccheroni alla chitarra** from Abruzzo.

crema   (CREH-mah)   Cream. For a soup, *crema* refers to a puree of vegetables. *Alla crema* refers to a dish with a cream sauce. From the Late Latin *cramum,* itself derived from a Celtic word for crust.

Crema also refers to custard, like *c. caramella* (caramel custard). *C. cotta* (also *panna cotta*) is cooked custard with gelatin and flavorings. *C. fritta* is **crema pasticceria** coated with egg and bread crumbs and fried.

Crema is also the creamlike foam on top of a well-made **espresso.**

Whipping cream is **panna.**

crema di peperoni   (CREH-mah dee peh-peh-ROH-nee)   Red or yellow pepper soup, from Tuscany.

crema inglese   (KREH-mah een-GLEH-seh)   "English cream." Egg custard made without flour and used as a sauce for desserts. From the original French name for this kind of sauce, *crème anglaise.*

crema pasticceria   (KREH-mah   pah-stee-cheh-REE-ah)   Pastry cream. See also **millefoglie** and **zuppa inglese.**

cremolata   (kreh-moh-LAH-tah)   **Granita** with a sherbetlike consistency.

cren   (krehn)   Horseradish. From an Austrian dialect word *Kren*. Horseradish is not much used in Italian cooking.

crescente   (kreh-SHEHN-teh)   Yeast starter. From the Latin *crescere* (to grow).

crescentina (kreh-shehn-TEE-nah)   A pizzalike bread, often made with lard or *prosciutto,* usually cut into slices and fried or baked in ashes. Also *cresentina* and *crescenta.*

crescenza (kreh-SHEHN-zah)   Soft, mild, creamy uncooked cow's milk cheese, from Lombardy. It has the consistency of butter. Aged for 15 days, it is then shaped into large or small slabs. Also **stracchino** or *stracchino di crescenza.*

crescione (kreh-SH'YOH-neh)   Watercress, an aquatic cress widely eaten since ancient times. The word *crescione* is of relatively recent origins, however, deriving not from the Latin but from Old High German *kressa* in the Middle Ages. It is used in salads and as a garnish.

crespelle (kreh-SPEH-leh)   Crepes. Also *screpelle.* Light batter pancakes usually rolled with a sweet or a savory filling, like French crêpes, though the word derives from the Latin *crispus* (curled). Also fried dough strips dusted with sugar, from Emilia-Romagna. Also called *sfrappole* or *sfrapel.*

   Crespolini are smaller and thinner, often stuffed and baked with a cream and **parmigiano** sauce. In Abruzzo, they are the basis for a carnival dish called *scrippelle 'mbusse* (bathed crepes) stuffed with **parmigiano** and rolled, then eaten in broth. See also **fazzoletti.**

creste di gallo (KRES-teh dee GAH-loh)   Cockscombs. Also a curved pasta shape with curly ridges, resembling a cockscomb.

creta, alla (AH-lah KREH-tah)   "Clay pot style." Method of cooking birds in a clay pot without using any fat, salt, or pepper. It is commonly used to cook guinea hen. Sometimes clay is packed onto the bird, the bird is cooked, then the clay is broken with a hammer.

crispeddi (kriss-PEH-dee)   "Curly [fritters]." Fritters, sometimes in a savory version made from anchovy- and fennel-flavored dough, from Sicily. Also *fritteddi.*

croatina (kroh-ah-TEE-nah)   "Little Croatian." Red wine grape of Lombardy. Called **bonarda** in Emilia's Colli Piacentini, though it is actually a strain of the true *bonarda.* The varietal is used to make the **DOC** wine of **Oltrepò Pavese.**

croccante (kroh-CAHN-teh)   "Crunchies." Pralines. In Umbria, *croccante quaresimale* (Lenten punches) are made with hazelnuts and chocolate.

crocchetta (kroh-KEH-tah)   Croquette. From the French.

crostacei (kroh-STAH-chay'ee)   General term for shellfish. From the New Latin *crustacea.*

crostata   (kroh–STAH–tah)   Tart, open face or with a lattice top. From the Latin *crusta* (crust). *Crostata di pere alla milanese* is a pear tart with apricot jelly and rum, from Milan. *C. di ricotta,* from Rome, has a filling made with **ricotta,** sugar, and eggs, flavored with lemon peel and **Marsala.** *C. alla siciliana* has a crust made of cream, potato starch, citrus, and pistachios, from Sicily.

crostini   (kroh–STEE–nee)   Thin slices of toast covered with various ingredients, such as chicken livers. From the Latin *crusta* (crust). They are a Tuscan specialty. In Rome, *crostini* are spread with bone marrow. A *crostino* differs slightly from a **bruschetta** in that the former is thinner and brushed with olive oil before being toasted.

crostoli   (kroh–STOH–lee)   Fried pastries, commonly shaped into bows.

crotonese   (kroh–toh–NAY–seh)   Ewe's milk cheese from Calabria, around the town of Crotone.

crudo   (KROO–doh)   Uncooked, referring to any kind of food in its raw state, especially when consumed that way. *Carne cruda* would be raw meat. From the Latin.

crumiri   (kroo–MEE–ree)   Cornmeal butter cookies shaped like a horseshoe or a boomerang, from Piedmont. The word means "strikebreaker," and probably refers to horseshoes thrown by or at strikebreakers in a labor dispute. In Piedmont, similar biscuits are called *ciapini,* which means horseshoes.

cu a siccia   (koo ah SEE–chee–ah)   A pasta dish of southern Italy containing cuttlefish, celery, tomato, and wine. The term translates as "cooked with cuttlefish."

cubbaita di giuggiulena   (koo-bah-EE-tah dee joo-joo-LEH-nah) Sicilian sesame seed and honey brittle.

cucchiaio   (koo-K'EYE-oh)   Spoon. From the Latin *cochlear.* See also *dolce al cucchiaiao.*

cuccìa   (koo-CHEE-yah)   Sicilian pudding made with wheat berries and mixed with **biancomangiare** or sweetened **ricotta** and candied fruit. The dish, of Arab origins, is traditionally served on the feast of *Santa Lucia* (December 13) because legend has it that on that day the people of Palermo were saved from starvation when a ship laden with wheat arrived in the harbor. In commemoration, no milled wheat is eaten on that day.

   Also in Palermo, they make a pastry called *cuccidata* with dried figs, candied squash, raisins, hazelnuts, chocolate, and almond cream.

cucina   (koo-CHEE-nah)   Cooking. Also kitchen. From the Latin *coquere* (to cook).

La cucina povera, which means cooking of the poor, is regarded as simple, hearty, and filling.

cuculli (koo-KOO-lee) "Little chubby ones." Chickpea fritters from Liguria, sometimes made with potatoes.

cucuzza (koo-KOO-t'zah) Sicilian term for squash.

Cucuzzara is a squash bread commonly made with tomato, onions, and sweet peppers, from Puglia.

cuddurini (koo-doo-REE-nee) "Round [breads]." Fried bread dough with honey, from Sicily. In Agrigento, the term refers to a *pizza* made with tomato.

cugghiuni dell'ortolano (koo-G'YOO-nee dehl-ohr-toh-LAH-noh) "Farmhand's testicles." Dish of small eggplants stuffed with bread crumbs, mint, garlic, and capers and sautéed, from Sicily, so called because of their shape.

culatello (koo-lah-TEH-loh) "Little rump." Cured pork rump cut from the bone and eaten as ham, a specialty of the Po Valley villages of Soragna, Zibello, Colorno, and Busseto in Emilia-Romagna. It is aged for a year to 18 months, then placed in a white wine bath.

culurzones (koo-loor-T'ZOH-nehs) Large *ravioli,* from Sardinia, stuffed either with cheese, egg, spinach, mint, and saffron and served with a *ragù* or with eggplant. Also *culurgiones, cu'irgionis,* and *culingiones.* The word may come from the Arabic.

cuore (KW'OH-reh) Heart. *Cuore di bue* is beef heart. *C. rosso* is a cockle (*cocciola*). From the Latin *cor.*

cupeta (koo-PEH-tah) Sweet bun with walnuts, traditionally served at Christmastime, from Lombardy.

cuscus (KOOS-coos) Couscous. Made from coarsely ground semolina flour rubbed with water, then steamed, usually with other ingredients, and eaten as a main or side dish. The origins are North African and the word is from the Arabic *kuskus.* Couscous probably entered Italy first through Sicily as a result of the Arab invasions.

In Sicily, where the term *cuscusu* is used, the dish is often made with seafood. In Trapani, seafood and chicken are combined in a large earthenware or china dish called a **mafaradda,** and the couscous is cooked in a *cuscusiera.* In Pantelleria, the couscous is closer to Arab versions, meatless but with both seafood and vegetables. *C. di Carloforte,* named after an island off Sardinia, is made with pork, lamb, chicken, and vegetables and served as a first course. Chicken flavored with saffron is the basis of *cascà,* from Sardinia, where they also make a casserole using *fregola*, a coarse couscous, combined with seafood. Italian Jews make *cuscussù all'Ebraica*, with cabbage, cauliflower, artichokes, Swiss chard, tomatoes, and other vegetables together with chicken. It is served with a hot sauce called *thursi* that is made from yellow squash and chile peppers. In Livorno, *cuscus* is combined with chickpeas and little meatballs wrapped in lettuce leaves.

cutturìedde   (koo-too-REE-yeh-deh)   "Innards stew." Lamb stew, usually flavored with wild dandelions and chile peppers, from Apulia and Basilicata.

cvapcici   (CH'VAHP-chee-chee)   Oval meatballs of ground veal, pork, and beef, from Trieste. Usually grilled and served with chopped onion and *ajvar*, a puree of roasted sweet and hot peppers, onions, vinegar, and oil.

Cynar   (chee-NAHR)   Trademark name for an alcoholic **digestivo** made from artichokes.

D

dado (DAH-doh)   Bouillon cube.

daino (dye-EE-noh)   Fallow deer. Probably from the Latin *dama*.

datteri di mare (DAH-teh-ree dee MAH-reh)   "Sea dates." Mussels, *Lithophaga lithophaga* and *Lithodomus lithophagus*. Most common off the coast of La Spezia, where they are called **muscoli**.

dattero (DAH-teh-roh)   Date, the edible fruit of the date palm, *Phoenix dactylifera*. From the Latin *dactylus,* which referred to both "finger" and the fruit. Dates have a long history in the Mediterranean basin. The ancient Romans imported them from Egypt. Today they are mainly produced in the Middle East. In modern Italy, dates are eaten fresh or dried, by themselves or as part of desserts.

delfino (dell-FEE-noh)   Dolphin, *Delphinus delphis*. Rarely eaten, except in Liguria. There, strips of the meat dried in the sun, which are called *musciamme,* are served as an **antipasto.**

della casa (DEH-lah KAH-sah)   "Of the house." A special dish of a restaurant.

dente, al (ahl DEHN-teh)   See **al dente.**

dentice (DEHN-tee-cheh)   Dentex, *Dentex dentex*. A good fish for baking and grilling. The name refers to its sharp teeth. *Dentice corassiere (D. gibbosus)* is found principally in the western Mediterranean.

denti di cavallo (DEHN-tee dee kah-VAH-loh)   "Horse's teeth." Small, stubby tube **maccheroni** of Tuscany.

denti d'elefante (DEHN-tee deh-leh-FAHN-teh)   "Elephant's teeth." Tube **maccheroni** about 1^1/$_2$ inches long.

diavola, alla   (AH-lah dee-AH-voh-lah)   "Devil's style." A dish heavily seasoned with black pepper or chile peppers. From the Late Latin *diabolicus.* See also *pollo alla diavola.*

diavolicchio   (dee-ah-voh-LEE-k'yee-oh)   "Devil [pepper]." Hot chile pepper, particularly those grown in Abruzzo, where they are widely used in the local cookery. From the Late Latin *diabolicus.*

digestivo   (dee-jeh-STEE-voh)   A drink taken at the end of the meal to aid digestion, such as *amaro, grappa,* or other spirit. From the Latin *digestus.*

dischi volonti   (DEES-kee voh-LOHN-tee)   "Flying saucers." Small round pasta shape with a hole in the center, which looks like a flying saucer.

ditalini   (dee-tah-LEE-nee)   "Little toes." Short tube-shape *maccheroni,* usually used for soup.

DOC   Abbreviation for *Denominazione di Origine Controllata* (dee-noh-mee-nah-t'zee-OH-neh dee oh-REE-jee-neh kohn-troh-LAH-tah), denomination of controlled origin. A phrase used by various agricultural government bodies that set and oversee the standards of some Italian foods, most significantly cheese and wine.

In 1955 *DOC* laws were drawn up to govern Italian cheese making, designating the various delimited regions in which specific cheeses could be made, describing the type of milk to be used, the composition, the process of production, and the special attributes of the cheeses. Not all cheeses are covered by the *DOC* laws; currently only 26 cheeses have such distinction.

In compliance with the European Economic Community, Italian wine regulations, both national and regional, were established in 1966 (and put into effect in 1967) under the *DOC* designation that applied to wines made from specific grape varieties grown within delimited zones. Standards were based on traditions within the regions, but to win *DOC* status, a wine had to meet prescribed norms of aroma, flavor, color, alcohol content, acidity, and other factors. There are currently about 250 zones covering more than 650 distinct types of wine. *DOC* regulations do not guarantee excellence, but only that certain standards of production were met. The **DOCG** designation demands a higher standard of quality, currently designating only 18 wines at this level. Nevertheless, both the *DOC* and *DOCG* regulations are regarded by many vintners as politicized and not closely monitored. Together the *DOC* and *DOCG* wines constitute about 10 to 15 percent of Italian production.

DOCG   Abbreviation for *Denominazione di Origine Controllata Garantita* (dee-noh-mee-nah-t'zee-OH-neh dee oh-REE-jee-neh kohn-troh-LAH-tah gah-rahn-TEE-tah), denomination of guaranteed controlled origin. Like the **DOC** regulations for delimited wine zones in Italy, the *DOCG* regulations require wines to be made from specific grapes and to meet prescribed norms of aroma, flavor, color, alcohol content, acidity, and other factors. The *DOCG* regulations, however, go much further in assigning the designation only to wines of "particular esteem" that meet higher-quality criteria that try to guarantee excellence. There are currently 18 *DOCG* wines—**Barbaresco, Barolo, Brunello di Montalcino, Vino Nobile di Montepulciano, Chianti, Chianti Classico, Albana** di Romagna, **Gattinara, Carmignano, Torgiano** Rosso Riserva, **Taurasi, Asti, Bracchetto d'Aqui, Ghemme, Franciacorta, Vernaccia di San Gimignano, Vermentino** di Gallura, and **Sagrantino** di Montefalco. If wines within these zones do not meet *DOCG* standards, they must be labeled **vino da tavola** (table wine).

dolce (DOHL-cheh) "Sweet." A sweet of any kind. In viniculture, the word *dolce* indicates a wine with 5 to 10 percent residual sugar. In cheese making, *dolce* refers to a fairly young, mild cheese. From the Latin *dulcis.*

Dolci di lunga conservazione are sweets that can be stored, like preserves, jams, candies, and hard cookies.

dolce al cucchiaio (DOHL-cheh AHL koo-K'YAI-oh) "Sweet for a spoon." A dessert that is eaten with a spoon, such as pudding, **tirami sù,** and **semifreddo.**

dolce del principe (DOHL-cheh dell PREEN-chee-peh) "Prince's sweet." Anise-flavored plum cake doused with **alchermes,** rum, and cognac, then filled with an egg and **mascarpone** mixture. *Dolce della principessa* (princess's sweet) is similar, made with ladyfingers.

dolce per i morti (DOHL-cheh pehr ee MOHR-tee) "Cookies for the dead." Spice cookies made with cinnamon, cloves, orange peel, lemon peel, and chocolate or **espresso** flavoring, from Molise. Traditionally made on All Souls' Day.

dolce torinese (DOHL-cheh toh-ree-NAY-seh) A rum-soaked chocolate cake with biscuits and almonds, served chilled, from Turin.

dolcetto (dohl-CHEH-toh) A red wine grape and seven **DOC** zones of Piedmont that produce several wines of soft tannins and good fruit. Although the name would seem to suggest the wine is sweet, *dolcetto* is, in fact, a very dry wine. The seven zones are *Dolcetto d'Acqui, Dolcetto d'Alba, Dolcetto d'Asti, Dolcetto delle Langhe Monregalesi, Dolcetto di Diano d'Alba* (sometimes called Diano), *Dolcetto di Dogliani,* and *Dolcetto di Ovada.*

donnici (DOH-nee-chee) **DOC** red wine of Calabria, made from **gaglioppo** and **greco** nero grapes grown near Cosenza.

donzella (dohn-ZEH-lah) "Young lady." Rainbow wrasse, *Coris julis,* an orange-banded fish best fried or used in soup.

dorato (doh–RAH–toh) "Golden." Refers to an ingredient that is dipped in egg and fried to a golden brown. From the Latin *aurum* (gold).

dragoncello (drah–gohn–CHEH–loh) Tarragon. From the Arabic *tarhun*. Tarragon is sometimes erroneously called **serpentaria** in Italy, which is actually snakeroot.

durella (doo–REH–lah) "Hard (grape)." A white wine grape of the Veneto, used mainly in making sparkling wines.

E

Elba (ELL-bah) **DOC** zone of Tuscany that produces red and white wines from grapes grown on the island of Elba.

elice (EH-lee-cheh) "Screws." Screw-shaped *maccheroni.*

elicoidali (eh-lee-koy-DAH-lee) "Spirals." Fat, tube-shaped *maccheroni* with a slight twist.

Emilia-Romagna (eh-MEE-l'yah roh-MAH-n'ya) Region of northern Italy stretching from the Adriatic Sea to the border of Piedmont. Emilia-Romagna has long prided itself on its gargantuan appetite for rich foods, and its capital city, Bologna, is still referred to as *La Grassa,* the Fat One.

Two of Emilia-Romagna's greatest contributions to world gastronomy are *prosciutto* ham and *Parmigiano-Reggiano* cheese; both are fundamental to Italian cookery and widely exported. The region is also known for its wide range of pastas, like the green spinach *lasagne* verdi, the layered *pasticcio* of *tortellini,* and *tagliatelle* alla duchessa, with a rich sauce of chicken livers, beaten egg yolks, and *parmigiano.*

Emilia-Romagna has its own version of *bollito misto,* and the region's sausages and salami, like *zampone,* are highly regarded. Its seafood stew, called *brodetto,* is made with fish and shellfish from the Adriatic.

Breads like *burlenghi* are heavily larded and spread with rosemary and garlic. Even vegetables get complex treatments in dishes like *erbazzone,* a tart filled with Swiss chard or spinach.

Zuppa inglese, a dessert of liqueur-soaked sponge cake with layers of *crema pasticcera,* is said to have been invented in the region.

Despite Emilia-Romagna's reputation for grand cuisine, its wines are generally of modest quality, many of them sparkling, and the region possesses only four **DOC**s and a single **DOCG,** for the white wine *Albana di Romagna.* The best-known red of the region is the *lambrusco,* usually *frizzante.*

emiliano   (eh-meel'-YAH-noh)   Pale yellow *grana* cheese, from Emilia, ripened for one to two years.

Enfer d'Arvier   (ahn-FEHR d'ah-vee-EHR)   *DOC* red wine of the Valle d'Aosta, made from *petit rouge* grapes grown around Arvier. *Enfer* is a reference to the inferno-like heat of the region.

enologia   (eh-noh-LOH-jee-ah)   Enology. From the Greek *oinos* (wine).

enoteca   (eh-noh-TEH-kah)   "Wine library." A collection of wines, a wine shop, or public and commercial displays.

eporediesi al cacao   (eh-poh-reh-dee-EH-see AHL kah-KAU) "Chocolate Ivreans." Hazelnut and chocolate macaroons, from the town of Ivrea.

erba cipollina   (EHR-bah chee-poh-LEE-nah)   "Onion herb." Chives.

Erbaluce di Caluso   (ehr-bah-LOO-cheh dee kah-LOO-soh)   *DOC* white wine of Piedmont, made from the *erbaluce* grape. Best known for its *passito* dessert style. Also *Caluso.*

erbazzone   (ehr-bah-t'ZOH-neh)   Savory pie with a filling of Swiss chard or spinach, *pancetta, parmigiano,* and eggs, from Emilia. When baked without a crust, it is called *scarpazzone.* When made in a sweet version, the *pancetta* is omitted and almonds are added.

erbe fini   (EHR-beh FEE-nee)   "Fine herbs." A finely chopped mixture of herbs.
   Erbe odorose are aromatic herbs. *Erbe selvatiche* are wild herbs. Fresh herbs are sold in an *erborista.*

erbette   (ehr-BEH-teh)   Swiss chard. See also *bietola.*

ermelline   (ehr-meh-LEE-neh)   "Little ermine." Bitter almonds.

escabecio   (ess-kah-BEH-ch'yoh)   Preservation and cooking method by which vinegar and other ingredients are used to marinate fish or are poured over cooked fish. From the Spanish *escabeche.* Also *scapece* and *scabecio. Scapece di vasto* is a version from Vasto in Abruzzo that contains chile peppers and saffron. See also *saor.*

espresso   (eh-SPREH-soh)   Coffee, in Italy. Made by forcing steam through ground coffee to make a strong brew. Italians drink more than 9 billion cups of espresso annually. There are several stories as to the origin of *espresso.* Some say that it was first sold at the Milan train station as people boarded the express trains. But the word *espresso* connotes a squeezed-out, stretched stream of coffee, which is what the *macchina a vapore* coffeemaker, invented in Naples in 1901, provided.

A well-made espresso has a creamy foam floating on top, called *crema* or *schiuma,* though there is no cream or milk involved, as there is in *cappuccino.* The coffee should be poured into a small cup called a *tazzina.* See also *caffè.*

esse di Raveo   (EH-say dee rah-VEH-yoh)   S-shaped cookies, a specialty of the town of Raveo in Friuli.

Est! Est!! Est!!! di Montefiascone   (EST EST EST dee mohn-teh-fee-ah-SKOH-neh)   *DOC* white wine of Latium, made from *trebbiano* and *malvasia* grapes. The odd name supposedly commemorates the legend of a German bishop named Johann Fugger who, on his way to Rome for the coronation of Emperor Henry V in 1111, sent his servant, Martin, ahead to inns in order to find good wines. He instructed him to write the Latin word *Est* (It is) on the door of the inn. When the bishop reached Montefiascone, he found the enthusiastic servant had scrawled the word three times, with extra exclamation points, to emphasize the high quality of wines in that town.

estratto   (eh-STRAH-toh)   Extract or a concentrated flavoring. In Sicily, *estratto di pomodoro* is a very concentrated tomato sauce.

etichetta   (eh-tee-KEH-tah)   Label, as in a wine label. From the Middle French *etiquet* (attached notice).

Etna   (ETT-nah)   *DOC* zone of Sicily that produces white, red, and rosé wines from grapes grown around Etna.

ettaro   (EH-tah-roh)   One hectoliter (100 liters). Europe's standard measure of wine volume.

etto   (EH-toh)   Standard Italian unit of measure, equaling 100 grams ($3^1/_3$ ounces).

F

fagiano (fah-J'YAH-noh) Pheasant, preferably one 12 to 14 months old. It is often hung for two days or more. *Fagiano alla norcese* (Norcia style) is stuffed with truffles and served with a sauce that includes **grappa.**

fagioli (fah-J'YOH-lee) Beans. Two kinds of beans are eaten in Italy: the Old World beans (**ceci, fave,** and **lenticchie**) and the New World beans, *Phaseolus vulgaris,* which came to Europe in the 16th century. There are two basic types: those eaten with their shells (called **fagiolini** or *cornetti)* and those that are first shelled, with only the bean itself eaten.

Probably the most widespread use of beans in Italy is in the dish **pasta e fagioli,** in which beans are cooked with seasonings, then combined with short pasta shapes like **ditalini** or broken **spaghetti.** Tuscans, who are called *mangia fagioli* (bean eaters) by other Italians, have a wide repertoire of bean recipes. *Fagioli toscani con tonno* is a Tuscan salad of white beans tossed with chunks of tuna and dressed with lemon juice, olive oil, and black pepper. *F. all'uccelletto,* so called because the beans are cooked the same way Tuscans cook small birds, is beans cooked with garlic, sage, and tomato sauce. Tuscans also cook beans *in fiasco*—that is, in a thick wine flask set in hot coals to simmer.

F. con le cotiche is a dish of white beans cooked with onions, **cotica prosciutto,** rosemary, and garlic, from Rome. In Campania, *f. alla maruzzara* is beans cooked with tomatoes, celery, basil, and parsley. *Faseula* is a dish of beans, tomato sauce, **pancetta,** and **salame,** usually served with **polenta,** from Piedmont.

fagiolini (fah-j'yoh-LEE-nee) "Little beans." Green beans, also called *cornetti;* they range in size from 2 inches up to 20 and in color from bright green to white. They are either boiled in salted water until tender, or blanched and then sautéed in butter or tossed with vinegar.

fagottini (fah-goh-TEE-nee) "Little bundles." Filled pancakes, savory or sweet. The term also refers to small bundles of goat's milk curd. From the Middle French *fagot.*

falanghina (fah-lahn-GHEE-nah) An ancient white wine grape of Campania and Sardinia. In Campania, a **DOC** white wine is made from *falanghina* grapes, a red from **primitivo,** and another red from **aglianico,** *Piedirosso,* and *primitivo.*

Falerio dei Colli Ascolani (fah-LEH-ree-oh Day-ee COH-lee ah-skoh-LAH-nee) **DOC** white wine of the Marches, principally made from **trebbiano** grapes grown around the hills of Ascoli Piceno. From the Latin wine *falernian.*

falernum (fah-LEHR-noom) Table wine of Latium whose name derives from the ancient Roman wine *falernian.*

Fara (FAH-rah) **DOC** red wine of Piedmont, made from **nebbiolo,** **vespolina,** and **bonarda** grapes grown in the hills around Novarra.

faraona (fah-rah-OH-nah) Guinea hen. The best are considered to be six to eight months old and weigh a maximum of two pounds. The full name in Italian is *gallina faroana,* which means "Pharoah's hen," because they were originally imported from Egypt.

farcia (fahr-SEE-yah) Forcemeat. From the Latin *farcio. Farcito* means stuffed.

farfalle (fahr-FAH-leh) "Butterflies." Pasta shaped like butterflies or bow ties. In Calabria, they are called *nocchetedde.* Smaller versions, called *farfalline, nastrini,* or *cravattine,* are commonly used in soups.

farina (fah-REE-nah) Flour. From the Latin *farina* (flour).
    Two types of wheat flour are used in Italy, one of which is made from *grano tenero* or soft wheat (*Triticum aestivum)* used principally for bread and cake, and the other from *grano durum* or hard durum wheat (*T. durum)* used for pasta. *Grano tenero* is classified in five categories according to the amount of fiber in the flour: from 00 *(zero zero),* the finest and whitest, to *Integrale,* or whole wheat flour.
    Farina gialla (yellow flour) is cornmeal, sometimes called *f. di granoturco* because of the erroneous belief that corn came from Turkey, although it was more likely to be shipped to Italy from there. *F. rimacinata* is twice-milled **semolina** flour. *F. setacciata* is sifted flour.

farinacei (fah-ree-NAH-cheh'ee) Foods rich in starch, such as chestnuts, potatoes, and rice. From the Latin *farina* (flour).

farinata (fah-ree-NAH-tah)   Ligurian version of Niçoise *socca,* a very thin pancake made with chickpea flour. From the Latin *farina* (flour). Tuscans call it *calda calda* (hot, hot). If made with onions and fried, it is called **panìssa.** *Farinata* is also the term for a creamy Tuscan **polenta,** usually served with vegetables.

Faro (FAH-roh)   *DOC* red wine of Sicily, made from **nerello mascalese** and other grapes grown around Messina.

farro (FAH-roh)   Spelt, *Triticum spelta.* Widely cultivated by the ancient Romans (who called it *far*), for whose legions it was a major food. Though once used to make bread, porridge, and soup, *farro's* use faded somewhat in Italy after wheat became more plentiful. There has been a renewed interest in the grain in recent years. It is sometimes erroneously translated as emmer.

Gran faro is a thick soup made with *farro* and **borlotti** beans in Tuscany.

far sudare (FAHR soo-DAH-reh)   "Cause to sweat." To braise. From the Latin *sudor* (perspiration).

farsumagru (fahr-soo-MAH-groo)   "False lean." A braised beef or veal roll filled with hard-boiled eggs, salami, and cheese, from Sicily. It originated in Palermo, and its name refers to the lean meat that covers a rich interior. Also *falso magro.*

fasui cul muset (fah-SOO-ee KOOL MOO-seh)   "Beans with snout." Red beans with pork sausage, from Friuli. The dialect expression derives from the Italian words *fagioli* (beans) and *muso* (snout).

fatto in casa (FAH-toh een KAH-sah)   Food "made at home" or in a restaurant.

fattoria (fah-toh-REE-ah)   Farm or wine estate, most commonly used in central Italy. From the Latin *facere* (to make).

fave (FAH-veh)   Fava beans. From the Latin *faba,* named after an aristocratic Roman family, the Fabii. Fava beans have been cultivated for at least seven thousand years and spread early on from the Middle East to Europe.

Young fresh fava beans are often eaten raw. They are called *bacelli* (old women) in colloquial Italian. Because they are considered poor people's food, favas are sometimes referred to as *la carne dei poveri* (the meat of the poor).

La favata is a hearty soup of dried fava beans, various cuts of pork, tomato, cardoons, and wild fennel, from Sardinia. See also **macca.**

fave dei morti (FAH-veh DAY-ee MOHR-tee)   "Dead man's beans." Cookies in the shape of fava beans, made with pine nuts, almonds, and egg whites, from Umbria and Lombardy. Traditionally eaten on All Souls' Day.

favette (fah-VEH-teh) "Bean [cookies]". Fried cookies that resemble little beans, usually flavored with a liqueur, from the Veneto.

favorita (fah-voh-REE-tah) A white, rather citric grape of Piedmont that gives its name to wines grown in the Roeri hills. The name means "favorite" but may also refer to a king's mistress. From the Latin *favor* (favor).

fazzoletti (fah-t'zoh-LEH-tee) "Handkerchiefs." Folded stuffed crepes. The name *fazzoletti della nonna* (grandmother's handkerchiefs) probably refers to the triangular kerchiefs old Italian women wore. Especially delicate versions may be called **mandilli de saêa** (silk handkerchiefs), a specialty of Liguria.

fecola (FEH-koh-lah) Starch. *Fecola di patate* is potato starch.

fedelini (feh-deh-LEE-nee) Long pasta strands usually served in broth.

fegatelli di maiale alla toscana (feh-gah-TEH-lee dee mye-AH-lee AH-la toh-SKAH-nah) "Pork liver in the Tuscan style." Chunks of pork liver with sage, garlic, bread crumbs, and fennel seeds, wrapped in caul fat and grilled on skewers with alternating pieces of fried bread and bay leaves, from Tuscany.

fegato (FEH-gah-toh) Liver.

Fegato alla veneziana, very thinly sliced calf's liver with an abundance of slowly cooked onions and commonly served with **polenta** made from white cornmeal, is probably the most famous Italian liver dish, a specialty of Venice. *F. di vitello alla milanese* is a dish from Milan of veal liver marinated in oil, dredged in egg and bread crumbs, then fried. *F. alla salvia* is veal liver fried with fresh sage. *F. alla lodigiana* (Lodi style) is made with slices of liver marinated with fennel seeds, wrapped in caul fat, and sautéed in butter.

Fegato grasso is foie gras, the fattened liver of goose or duck. *Fegatini* are chicken livers.

FEGATO ALLA VENEZIANA

1 pound calf's liver, very thinly sliced	*Salt and pepper*
6 tablespoons olive oil	*2 tablespoons butter*
2 onions, finely sliced	*Chopped parsley*

Cut the liver into small pieces about 1¹/₂ inches square. Pat dry and set aside.

Heat 3 tablespoons of the olive oil in a sauté pan, add the onions, and sauté until soft and transparent but not browned. In a separate sauté pan cook the liver in the remaining 3 tablespoons olive oil at medium-high heat until seared and cooked through, about 1 minute on each side. Season with salt and pepper to taste. Place the liver in the sauté pan with the onions. Add the butter and parsley, mix well, and serve. Serves 2.

---

fegato ai Sette Cannoli   (FEH-gah-toh aye SEH-teh kah-NOH-lee) "Liver of the Seven Cannons." Squash baked with a sweet-and-sour sauce. The name refers to a district in Palermo where a street vendor who could no longer afford liver to put in his squash preparation dropped it from the dish and sold it without liver.

Felino   (feh-LEE-noh)   Salami named after the village of the same name in Parma.

fermentazione   (fehr-mehn-tah-T'Z'YOH-neh)   Fermentation. From the Latin *fermentum.*

ferrarese   (feh-rah-REH-zeh)   Bread of Emilia-Romagna's city of Ferrara, made with a firm dough. *Manini ferrarese* are shaped like a hand with fingerlike strips of dough.

ferretti   (feh-REH-tee)   "Little iron [rods]." Thin metal rods used to form macaroni. From the Latin *ferrum* (iron).

ferri, ai   (aye FEH-ree)   Grilled over an open fire. From the Latin *ferrum* (iron), referring to the iron grill grating.

ferro di cavallo   (FEH-roh dee kah-VAH-loh)   "Horseshoe." Bread shaped like a horseshoe, made with a firm dough, from Sicily.

fesa   (FEH-sah)   Cut of meat from the thigh or rump.

fetta   (FEH-tah) Slice, strip. *Fettine* are thinly cut slices of meat.

fette, le   (leh FEH-teh)   Black cabbage (**cavolo nero**) soup, served over slices of bread, from Tuscany.

fettuccine   (feh-too-CHEE-neh)   Long flat pasta ribbons, about $3/8$ inch wide, usually made with eggs. The term itself is used mostly in Rome and southern Italy. Elsewhere a similar, though sometimes slightly thinner, pasta is called *tagliatelle.*

Fettuccine all'Alfredo is made with butter and **parmigiano,** a dish more commonly called *f. al burro* (*fettuccine* with butter), but *f. all'Alfredo* is a specialty of Alfredo's restaurant in Rome. The original owner, Alfredo Di Lelio, created the dish in 1914 to restore the appetite of his wife after she gave birth to their son. Di Lelio distinguished his version by using triple-rich butter and only the core of the **parmigiano** wheel. It became famous after Hollywood movie stars Mary Pickford and Douglas Fairbanks came to Rome on their honeymoon in 1927 and dined at Alfredo's every night they were there. At the end of their stay, they presented Di Lelio with a golden fork and spoon and pronounced him "King of the Noodles." The fame of the dish spread when the couple returned to America, though it was not well known by this name in Italy until after World War II.

F. alla papalina (Pope's style) is another Roman dish of *fettuccine* with a sauce of butter, onion, **prosciutto,** and a beaten egg that is cooked by the heat of the pasta. It was created at the restaurant La Cisterna di Trastevere for Cardinal Eugenio Pacelli, who became Pope Pius XII in 1939.

FETTUCCINE ALL'ALFREDO

7 tablespoons butter
7 tablespoons grated parmigiano
1 pound fresh fettuccine, cooked al
    dente

Melt the butter in a sauté pan until just foaming. Add the **parmigiano** and mix well. Add the **fettuccine** and mix with butter and cheese over low heat until well coated. Serve immediately. Serves 4.

---

fettunta   (feh–TOON-tah)   Toasted or grilled bread rubbed with garlic and olive oil. Also **bruschetta.**

fiadone   (fee-ah–DOH–neh)   A **pizza rustica** made with cheese and eggs for Easter, from Abruzzo.

Fiano di Avellino   (fee-AH-noh dee ah-veh-LEE-noh)   **DOC** white wine of Campania, made from *fiano* grapes grown around the town of Avellino. The name supposedly derives from the Latin name *Apianum* (bees) because the grape was said to attract bees.

fiasco   (fee-AH-skoh)   Flask. Notably the old-fashioned **Chianti** bottles half-covered with a straw basket. From Late Latin *flasco* (bottle).

fico   (FEE-koh)   Fig. Originally imported from the Middle East, particularly Chios and Carthage, figs were, in turn, spread to southern Gaul by the ancient Romans. They are commonly eaten raw, especially accompanying slices of **prosciutto.** From the Latin *ficus.*

fico d'India   (FEE-koh D'EEN-d'yah)   "Indian fig." Prickly pear.

fidej   (fee-DEHJ)   Handmade *vermicelli* or *fettuccine* usually cooked in milk, a specialty of Cùneo in Piedmont.

fidelanza   (fee-deh-LAHN-zah)   *Spaghetti* cooked in a tomato sauce, from Liguria. The name may derive from *fido,* meaning trustworthy, as in an always dependable dish.

fieto   (fee-EH-toh)   Pomfret, *Stromateus fiatola,* a gray flatfish rarely seen in the market. It is best grilled.

filatelli   (fee-lah-TEH-lee)   "Little strands of yarn." Very thin *spaghetti* from Calabria.

fileia del Calabrese   (fee-LAY'ee-ah dell kah-lah-BREH-seh)   "Calabrian rows." Pasta shaped like two strips joined together in a row, from Calabria.

filetto   (fee-LEH-toh)   Fillet of meat. From the Latin *filum* (string).

filini   (fee-LEE-nee)   "Little cat's whiskers." Extremely fine, very short pasta shape used in soups. A slightly thicker version is called *fili d'oro* (gold cat's whiskers).

filu 'e ferru   (FEE-loo eh FEH-roo)   "Iron wire." Sardinian *grappa.* From the Latin *filum* (thread) and *ferrum* (iron).

finanziera   (fee-nahn-Z'YEH-rah)   In Turin, a lavish stew made of chicken giblets, sweetbreads, mushrooms, and truffles, though in other parts of Piedmont the dish might contain calf's brains and cockscombs. The word refers to a coat worn by dignitaries of Turin during the 18th century, and there are references to the dish as early as 1500 at the court of Carlo Emanuele I. It may well have started out as a peasant dish that was embellished for the wealthy court tables and grew in size and traditions as the centuries worn on.

finferli   (FEEN-fehr-lee)   See *gallinaccio.*

finocchio   (fee-NOH-k'yoh)   Fennel, *Foeniculum vulgare dulce.* Also Florence fennel. The bulb is eaten as a vegetable. *Finocchietto* is a wild form of fennel with tall, featherlike foliage, used more as an herb. *Carosella* is the variety *F. v. piperatum,* which is eaten raw as an **antipasto** item. *Semi di finocchio* are fennel seeds. *Finocchiona* is a a sausage from Tuscany studded with fennel seeds, in Chianti called *sbriciolona,* whose name is derived from *sbricolare* (minced). From the Latin *feniculum.*

fiocchetti   (f'yoh-KEH-tee)   "Tassels." Pasta cut into fairly thick diamond shapes, then pinched to resemble little bows, from Umbria.

fiore di latte   (F'YOH-reh dee LAH-teh)   "Flower of milk." Soft fresh cow's milk cheese.

The term also describes ice cream made without any flavorings but sugar.

fiorentina, alla   (AH-lah F'YOH-rehn-TEE-nah)   "Florentine style." Dishes made the way they are in Florence. Term commonly refers to a dish made with or placed on a bed of spinach.

fiore sardo   (f'YOH-reh SAHR-doh)   "Sardinian flower." A **DOC** *pecorino* cheese, from Sardinia. Aged for three months, longer as a grating cheese. When young it is eaten as a table cheese.

fiori di zucca   (f'YOH-ree dee ZOO-kah)   "Squash flowers." Usually battered and fried, sometimes stuffed. *Fiori di zucchini* are zucchini flowers.

fitascetta   (fee-tah-SHEH-tah)   A wreath-shaped *focaccia* containing sautéed red onions, from Lombardy.

Five Roses   Light cherry-red wine made around Salento in Apulia by Leone De Castris. The English name comes from a time in World War II when liberating U.S. troops in Salento found the wine to their liking and translated the name of the vineyard region, Cinque Rose. Another story goes that an American officer pronounced the wine better than the well-known blended whiskey called Four Roses, adding another rose to the name.

flics   (fleeks)   Pasta flakes, from Friuli. From the German *flecks* (shreds).

focaccia   (foh-KAH-ch'yah)   A dimpled yeast bread, similar to pizza but thicker. It is often served with savory toppings. From the Latin *focus* (hearth). Though most closely associated with Genoa, *focaccia* is known throughout Italy in various forms. *Focaccia del cavatore* (marble workers' *focaccia),* made with chopped walnuts in the dough, is named after the marble workers of Carrara. In Viareggio, *focaccia* is made with malt in the dough. In Maremma, anchovies and red onions are incorporated into the dough. In Naples, *focaccia* is shaped into a ring and called *tortano;* when eggs are inserted into the dough ring, it is called **casatiello.** *Fugassa,* from Venice, is sweetened. In Basilicata, *focaccia* is made with pork cracklings, lard, and oregano and called *f. a brazzaud.* In Emilia-Romagna, thick *focaccia* sprinkled with tomato is called *torta salata* or **spianata.** In the town of Recco in Liguria, *focaccia* is stuffed with the local *stracchinella* cheese. In Apulia, tomatoes, garlic, and oil are placed in the indentations in the dough before baking; this is called *puddica.* In Tuscany, *focaccine* are small versions of *focaccia,* sometimes made with lard and butter instead of oil. In Lombardy, the bread is called *filascetta* or *fitascetta* and contains a bit of sugar in the dough. In Puglia a soft *focaccia* topped with tomato, garlic and oregano is called *puddhica.*

focolare   (foh–koh–LAH–reh)   Open hearth or fireplace. From the Latin *focus.*

foggiano   (foh–J'YAH–noh)   *Pecorino* cheese made around the city of Foggia. Also *canestrato.*

foiolo   (foh–YOH–loh)   See *trippa.*

folaga   (FOH–lah–gah)   Coot, a small game bird usually marinated and grilled.

folpo   (FOHL–poh)   Venetian dialect word for octopus, elsewhere called *polpo.*

fondo   (FOHN–doh)   Term referring either to a cooked–down mixture of onion, vegetables, and fat at the bottom of a pan prior to adding the principal ingredients, or to the residue remaining at the bottom of the pan, like juices and drippings.

fonduta   (fohn–DOO–tah)   Northern Italian cheese fondue. From the French *fondre* (to melt). Made with melted *fontina* cheese. The dish dates in Italian cookery at least to the mid–18th century. *Fonduta* is often served on toast; it is also used as a sauce on vegetables.

FONDUTA

8 ounces fontina cheese	*8 ounces butter, cut into pieces*
2 cups milk	*Salt*
4 egg yolks	*White truffles (optional)*

Cut the cheese into small cubes and place in double boiler over low heat. Add 1 cup of the milk and allow the mixture to slowly melt.

Meanwhile, warm the remaining 1 cup milk in another saucepan and add the egg yolks, one at a time, beating constantly. Stir in the butter until smooth, then add to the cheese and milk mixture. Stir until creamy and smooth. Add salt to taste. If desired, shave white truffles over the *fonduta.* Serves 4 to 6.

fongadina   (fohn–gah–DEE–nah)   Stew made from the innards of a calf, kid, or lamb. It is seasoned with bay leaves, rosemary, marjoram, garlic, and lemon peel. From the Veneto. From *affogare* (to smother).

fontana   (fohn–TAH–nah)   "Well." Mound of flour with a well in the middle. Eggs and other ingredients are placed in the well and mixed into the flour. From the Latin *fons.*

fontina   (fohn–TEE–nah)   Ancient cheese from the Valle d'Aosta. A mild, semisoft cheese, it is made from whole unpasteurized cow's milk and aged for about four months. It melts easily, and it is the basis of *fonduta*. *Fontal* is a commercially produced semisoft cooking cheese from Trentino, similar to *fontina*.

forastera   (foh–rah–STEH–rah)   A white grape of Campania and Sardinia, used in making *Ischia bianco*.

forchetta   (fohr–KEH–tah)   Fork. From the Latin *furca,* which refers to a two-pronged agricultural fork. The ancient Romans had no forks to eat with, and it was not until the 11th century that we hear of anyone so using a handheld, two-tined fork in a blistering attack by the hermit and cardinal bishop of Ostia, St. Piero Damiano, on the unnatural use of such a device by the wife of Venice's Doge, Domenico Selvo. Three centuries passed before forks were again mentioned in print, in a 1361 list of the dinnerware of the Florentine Commune, and it was another two hundred years before forks became common at European tables, the knife remaining the principal utensil for the carriage of food to the mouth. The first picture of a fork appeared in an Italian cookbook, *Cuoco Secreto di Papa Pio Quinto,* by Bartolomeo Scappi in 1570. By the 17th century, when hard plates began to replace the traditional slice of bread called a trencher, forks were still being used mainly to transfer meat from a serving platter to one's plate, and the fork was often passed on to the next person. By the 19th century the fork, which had become shorter and now had three or four tines, had been adopted by most Europeans, at least those of a class that could afford to buy a set of them.

forma   (FOHR–mah)   "Shape." As in a wheel of cheese or loaf of bread. Also a mold. From the Latin.

formagella   (fohr–mah–JEH–lah)   Fresh soft cheese, from Liguria. Made from cow's, ewe's, or goat's milk, lightly ripened. Also *formagetta*. From the Latin *forma* (form).

formagelle   (fohr–mah–JEH–leh)   Saffron-flavored **ricotta** pastries, traditional at Easter, from Sardinia. Sometimes called *pardulas*. From the Latin *forma* (form).

formaggetta   (fohr–mah–GHEH–tah)   Soft round cheese made from cow's and ewe's milk, from Piedmont. From the Latin *forma* (form).

formaggio   (fohr–MAH–j'yoh)   General term for cheese. From the Latin *forma* (form).

formaggio all'argentiera   (fohr–MAH–j'yoh ahl-ahr-jen-T'YEH-rah) "Silversmith's cheese." Sliced **caciocavallo** cheese fried in olive oil with red wine and oregano and served on bread, from Sicily. Legend has it that a poor silversmith wanted to fool his neighbors into thinking him a rich man by cooking a dish with such a wonderful aroma and flavor.

formaggio di fossa   (fohr-MAH-j'yoh dee FOH-sah)   Ewe's or cow's milk cheese ripened for three months in caves, from Emilia-Romagna.

formaggio di Malga   (fohr-MAH-j'yoh dee MAHL-gah)   Cow's milk cheese made around the village of Malga in the Alps.

formaggio elettrico   (fohr-MAH-j'yoh eh-LEH-tree-koh)   "Electric cheese." *Robiola* cheese mixed with tomato, chile peppers, vinegar, and bread, from northern Italy. The spiciness gives it an "electric" tanginess.

fornaio   (fohr-NYE-oh)   Baker. Also *panettiere.* From the Latin *furnus* (oven).

forno   (FOHR-noh)   Oven. *Forno a legno,* literally wood oven, is a bread bakery. *Al forno* refers to a dish baked or roasted in the oven. *Fornello* is a range or stovetop. From the Latin *furnus.*

forti   (FOHR-tee)   "Strong [cookies.]" Almond spice cookies from Venice.

fracosta di bue   (frah-KOH-stah dee BOO-eh)   Rib of beef.

fra diavolo   (frah dee-AH-voh-loh)   "Brother devil." Dishes made with hot chile peppers, such as **diavolicchio.**

fragola   (FRAH-goh-lah)   Strawberry. From the Latin *fragum.*
    Wild strawberries were known to the ancient Romans, but the fruit was not cultivated to any extent until the 16th century, and even then only in royal gardens. It was the wild American strawberry, *Fragaria virginiana,* that impressed first the English, then the rest of Europe, and eventually the world, enough to grow strawberries. Even more successful has been the large Chilean strawberry, *F. chiloensis,* thought to be hybridized with the American variety.
    In Italy, *fragoline di bosco* are wild forest strawberries. *Fragoloni* are large strawberries. The fruit is now used in a many ways, particularly in desserts such as **gelato** and **sorbetto.** They may also be served simply dressed with vinegar or **balsamico.**

fragoline di mare   (frah-goh-LEE-neh dee MAH-reh)   "Strawberries of the sea." A form of octopus.

fragolino   (frah-goh-LEE-noh)   "Strawberry [fish]." Pandora, *Pagellus erythrinus.* A reddish sea bream, good baked or grilled.

franceschino   (frahn-cheh-SKEE-noh)   "French (melon)." Small, sweet melon, similar to a canteloupe.

francesina (frahn-cheh-SEE-nah) "French (breadstick)." Breadstick, from Lombardy.

Franciacorta (frahn-ch'yah-KOHR-tah) *DOC* zone in Lombardy that produces a red wine from *cabernet franc, barbera, nebbiolo,* and *merlot;* a white from *pinot bianco* and *chardonnay;* and a *spumante* from *chardonnay* and *pinot bianco, pinot grigio,* and *pinot nero.*

franconia (frahn-KOH-n'yah) A *DOC* red wine of Friuli made around Isonzo. The name refers to the German wine-producing region of Franken. Locally called *Blaufränkisch, bleufrancs,* and *Limberger.*

frantoio (frahn-TOY'oh) Olive press. *Zuppa alla frantoiana* is a *borlotti* bean soup made with extra-virgin olive oil, from Tuscany.

Frappato di Vittoria (frah-PAH-toh dee vee-TOH-ree-ah) Red wine of Sicily, made from the *frappato* grape grown around Vittoria.

frappe (FRAH-peh) "Fringes." Strips of fried sweet dough, popular at carnival time.

frasca (FRAH-skah) In Friuli, casual restaurant set near a winery.

frascadei (frah-skah-DEH-ee) *Polenta* dish with vegetables, pork, and *mortadella,* from Liguria.

Frascati (frah-SKAH-tee) *DOC* white wine of Latium, made principally from *malvasia di Candia, malvasia del Lazio, Greco,* and *trebbiano* grapes. An *amabile* version is sometimes made, as is a sweet version called *cannellino* and a *spumante. Frascati* is produced in enormous quantities, with up to 7.9 million gallons in a good vintage year. The wine takes its name from the town of Frascati near Rome.

frattaglie (frah-TAH-l'yeh) Organ meats or giblets.

freddo (FREH-doh) Cold. From the Latin *frigidus.*

fregamai (FREH-gah-mye) Pasta dumplings from Liguria. Perhaps from the word *fregare* (to rub), as one would rub the pasta dough when making the dumplings.

fregola (FREH-goh-lah) A larger form of *cuscus,* from Sardinia, though it is not made with flour but with coarsely ground semolina grains that have been sprinkled with lukewarm water in a terra-cotta pot (called a *sa scivedda),* then dried and grated. The word probably derives from *fregare* (to rub to make grated cheese), a very old method that denotes its Sardinian origins rather than an analogy to Arabian couscous. *Fregola* is used in soups and stews or sauced like pasta. *Fregola* dishes are often scented with saffron. Also *fregula* and *succù.*

fregolata (freh-goh-LAH-tah) "Crumbly (pastry)." Cornmeal short-bread covered with nuts. The word 'may derive from *fregare* (to rub to make the crumbly texture of the shortbread).

freisa (FRAY-sah) A cherry-colored *frizzante* or *spumante* wine of Piedmont, made around Alba. *Freisa d'Asti* is produced around Asti, *Freisa di Chieri* near Balbiano.

fresa (FREH-sah) Cheese in the *caciotta* style, from Sardinia.

fresco (FREH-skoh) Fresh. *Al fresco* refers to a meal taken out of doors in the fresh air. From the Old High German *frisc*.

fresse alla cunese (FREH-seh AH-lah koo-NEH-zeh) Hash of pork liver and beef flavored with juniper and fried in butter, a specialty of Cùneo.

friarelli (free-ah-REH-lee) Tips of *broccoletti*. In Naples, the term is used for green pickling peppers.

fricandò (free-kahn-DOH) Larded cut of veal seared, then braised with *Marsala*. From the French *fricandeau,* for the same preparation.

fricassea (free-kah-SEH-yah) Fricasee, a term that applies to stewed poultry or veal dishes usually cooked in wine or served with a white cream sauce. *Fracassare* means to break into small pieces, but the word may also derive from the Latin *frigere* (to fry).

fricco dei Friuli (FREE-koh DAY-ee free-OO-lee) A fairly sharp cheese. Friulian cheese is sometimes fried with salt pork and eggs in butter.

frico (FREE-koh) "Little trifles." Crispy melted cheese fritter from Friuli, made with *montasio.* Sometimes the center is left quite runny. Also *fricco.*

frienno e magnanno (free-EH-noh eh mah-N'YAH-noh) "Frying and eating." Festive dish of fried foods including fish, organ meats, *mozzarella,* hard-boiled eggs, a thick *balsamella,* potato and rice *crocchette,* cauliflower, artichokes, zucchini, and zucchini flowers, from Campania.

friggere (free-JEH-reh) To fry. From the Latin *frigere. A friggitoria* is a shop specializing in fried foods.

frisceu (free-SHOO) Fritters from Liguria. Usually made with vegetables and codfish, though in some regions of Liguria they made be sweet and made with raisins and apples.

frisedda (free-SEH-dah) Ring-shaped roll made with whole wheat or white flour, from Apulia. It is twice-baked to make it very crusty, then, just before eating, softened in water and dressed with oil and sometimes tomatoes and onion. It is served as a lunch meal. The word may derive from *frisare* (to cause to kiss).

frittata (free-TAH-tah) A preparation of eggs and other ingredients such as onion, mushrooms, and peppers, sautéed and lightly browned. It is served both hot and cold. From the Latin *frigere* (to fry).

frittedda (free-TEH-dah) Sicilian vegetable stew made from fava beans, artichokes, and peas. Also *frittella*.

frittelle (free-TEH-leh) Fritters. From the Latin past participle *frictus*. *Frittelle* are traditionally eaten on the feast of *San Giuseppe* (March 19) because they were sold from carts similar to carpenter's carts. In Venice, the term used is *frittole,* often served with **malvasia** wine. *Fritules* are pumpkin fritters from Friuli.

fritto misto (FREE-toh MEE-stoh) "Mixed fry." An assortment of fried foods, such as meat, seafood, hard-boiled eggs, and vegetables. The word is from the Latin *frigere. Fritto misto alla fiorentina,* from Florence, includes brains, sweetbreads, chicken breasts, and artichokes. *F. m. alla milanese,* from Milan, includes veal, liver, brains, cockscombs, and vegetables. **Sciabbacheddu** (from Arabic for a fish net) is a Sicilian word for an assortment of fried fish prepared this way. In Piedmont, such a dish is called *fricia.*

frittura di paranza (free-TOO-rah dee pah-RAHN-zah) A dish of fried fish, from Naples. The term *paranza,* meaning a sailed fishing boat, is also Neapolitan slang for criminals, referring to the less desirable species of fish commonly used for this dish.

Friuli–Venezia Giulia (free-OO-lee veh-NEH-t'zee-yah JOO-l'yah) Small region of Italy located in the extreme northeast and bordering on Austria and Slovenia, whose cultures have influenced the region and vice versa. The character of the region's food is as varied as a peasant soup of spinach and cornmeal called **paparot** and the delicate Austro-Hungarian **Strudel.**

The pastas of Friuli–Venezia Giulia can be quite sophisticated, such as **cialzone,** which may contain as many as three dozen ingredients, or as unusual as a sweet **lasagne** *ai semi di papavero* (with poppyseeds).

Soups are very popular, like the barley and bean soup called *fasuj e uardi,* and stews, like *gulyas,* obviously derived from the Hungarian *gulyas.*

Montasio is a **DOC** cow's milk cheese of the region, traditionally used to make **frico,** a crisp cheese fritter.

Sweets tend to follow the Austro-Hungarian model, as in **gubana,** a cake filled with nuts, raisins, and figs.

The region is known principally for its clean, fruity white wines made from **tocai friulano, chardonnay,** and **sauvignon** grapes, especially those from

Colli Orientali del Friuli and *Collio Goriziano.* **Picolit** is a unique sweet wine of the area. Modest reds include **refosco, merlot,** and **cabernet.**

frizzante   (free-ZAHN-teh)   A lightly bubbly wine, not as bubbly as a *spumante. Frizzantino* refers to a wine with only slight bubbles.

frollini   (froh-LEE-nee)   "Tender [cookies]." Soft butter cookies made with potato starch in the dough, from Turin.

fruata   (froo-AH-tah)   Hollow loaf resembling pita bread, from Sicily.

frullato   (froo-LAH-toh)   "Whipped [drink.]" An iced fruit or coffee drink whisked to a frothy consistency.

frusta   (FROO-stah)   Wire whisk.

frutta   (FROO-tah)   Fruit. *Frutta cotta* is stewed fruit. *F. fresca di stagione* is fresh fruit of the season. *F. candita* is candied fruit.

frutta di bosco   (FROO-tah dee BOH-skoh)   Fruit of the woods. Berries such as *fragoline di besco* (wild strawberries).

frutta di martorana   (FROO-tah dee mahr-toh-RAH-nah)   Molded marzipan fruit supposedly invented by the mother superior of the convent of Martorana in Palermo for the paschal visit of the archbishop, although it has been traditional to make them for All Souls' Day. Similar candies of that day are called *frutta dei morti.*

frutti di mare   (FROO-tee dee MAH-reh)   "Fruit of the sea." Seafood.

fugazza   (foo-GAH-t'zah)   *"Focaccia."* Easter sweet yeast bread containing eggs, sugar, vanilla, figs, orange peel, and, sometimes, iris root, from Venice. Also *fugassa.*

fumetto   (foo-MEH-toh)   Concentrated broth, usually made from fish. From the French *fumet.*

funghetto, al   (ahl foon-GHEH-toh)   Sautéed in very hot oil, usually with garlic and parsley. See also **trifolato.**

funghi   (FOON-ghee)   Mushrooms. From the Latin *fungus. Funghi affogati* are poached mushrooms. *F. al trifolato* are often sautéed in garlic and olive oil with chopped anchovies, parsley, lemon, and butter. *F. secchi* are dried mushrooms.

Italians use a wide variety of wild and cultivated mushrooms, but the most prized are *funghi porcini, Boletus edulis,* known elsewhere as cèpes, whose plump meaty size and texture give them their name "little pig mushrooms." There are several types of these mushrooms found in many regions of Italy, the best from Alto Adige, Emilia-Romagna, Piedmont, Tuscany, Umbria, and the Veneto, and the best season for them is late August through the end of October. Simply sautéed with garlic and oil and sprinkled with parsley, or added to any number of dishes and sauces, *funghi porcini* are inseparable from Italian cookery.

Other mushrooms used in Italian cookery include the *agarico delizioso (Lactarius deliciosus)*, saffron milkcup; *cantarello (Cantharellus cibarius)*, chanterelle, also known as *gallinaccio* and *finferlo; chiodino (Armillariella mellea)*, honey mushroom; *lingua di bue (Fistulina hepatica)*, beefsteak mushroom; *orecchietta (Auricularia auricula)*, wood ear; *ovolo (Amanita caesarea)*, Caesar's mushroom; *pleuroto (Pleurotus ostreatus)*, oyster mushroom, also known as *fungo ostrica; prataiolo (Agaricus campestris)*, meadow mushroom; *prugnolo (Tricholoma gambosum)*, St. George's mushroom; *spugnola (Morchella esculenta)*, morel; **tartufo,** both black, *nero (Tuber melanosporum)*, and white, *bianco (T. magnatum)*, truffle; and *trombetta dei morti (Craterellus cornucopioides)*, horn of plenty.

fuori tavola   (foo'WOH-ree TAH-voh-lah)   "Away from the table." Sicilian term for snacks consumed at bars, taverns, or street stalls.

fusilli   (foo-SEE-lee)   Pasta shaped like a corkscrew, sometimes called *eliche* (propellers). *Fusilli lunghi* are the long strands. In Calabria, *fusilli* are called *fischietti* (little whistles). In Piedmont, a similarly shaped pasta is called *macaron del frèt*.

fuso   (FOO-soh)   Melted, as with butter. From the Latin *fusus* (spread out).

fusto   (FOO-stoh)   Cask or barrel used to age wine.

fuzi   (FOO-t'zee)   Quill-shaped fresh egg pasta, from Istria.

G

Gabiano (gah-bee-AH-noh) *DOC* red wine of Piedmont, made from *barbera* grapes grown around the village of Gabiano.

gaglioppo (gah-L'YOH-poh) A red wine grape of Calabria, used in making *Cirò.*

galani (gah-LAH-nee) "Tasseled ribbons." Bow-shape fritters flavored with *grappa* or *Marsala,* consumed during Carnival, from Venice.

galantina (gah-lahn-TEE-nah) Galantine. An aspic-covered cold dish of meat or fish that has been deboned and stuffed. From the Old French *galentine* (fish sauce), but ultimately from the Latin *gelatus* (congealed).

Also, a cooked salami made with veal, *pancetta,* pistachios, and spices.

galestro (gah-LEH-stroh) White wine of Tuscany, made from *trebbiano, chardonnay, pinot bianco, sauvignon blanc, riesling,* and other grapes. The name refers to the sandy, marl-like soil of the region.

gallanini (gah-lah-NEE-nee) "Little floaters." Tiny, twisted bow-tie shaped *maccheroni* for soups. Also *tripolini.*

galletta (gah-LEH-tah) "Ship's biscuit." Dry, unsweetened biscuit shaped something like a flattened bagel. Traditionally part of *cappon magro* in Liguria.

gallina (gah-LEE-nah) Fowl. In Sardinia, *gallina al mirto* is fowl that is boiled, then marinated with myrtle berries and leaves. It is eaten cold. From the Latin.

gallinaccio (gah-lee-NAH-ch'yoh) "Turkey cock." Chanterelle mushroom, *Cantharellus cibarius.* Also *giallino, finferlo,* and *cantarello.* From the Latin *gallina* (hen).

gallinella (gah-lee-NEH-lah) "Pretty fowl." Gurnard, *Trigla lucerna.* Also *cappone gallinella.* Long fish with highly colored fins. From the Latin *gallina* (hen).

gamay (gah-MAY) A red wine grape of French origin, planted in Valle d'Aosta but in small production. Used in making a wine of the same name.

Gambellara (gahm-beh-LAH-rah) A *DOC* white wine of the Veneto, made from *garganega* and *trebbiano* grapes grown around Vicenza. A *recioto* and *vin santo* are also made. The name comes from the town of Gambellara.

gambero (GAHM-beh-roh) Shrimp. Any of an enormous number of crustaceans. In the Mediterranean, the common brown shrimp, *Cragon cragon,* which is actually gray, is most readily found at the market. From the Latin *cammarus* (crab or lobster).

    Gamberetti are very small shrimp; *gamberoni* are very large shrimp. *Mazzancolla* (*Penaeus kerathurus*) also called *gambero imperialo,* is especially large, growing up to nine inches long. *Gambero rosso* is a large red shrimp.

    Gamberi di fiume (river shrimp) or *gamberi d'acqua dolce* (shrimp of sweet water) are crayfish, *Astacus fluviatilis,* a kind of small freshwater lobster.

    Italians prepare shrimp in many ways, from boiled and served with a little lemon juice, to sautéed in olive oil, to baked in a casserole.

    See also *canocchia* and *scampo.*

garganega (gahr-GAH-neh-gah) White wine grape of the Veneto, from the region of Garganega, used in making *Soave.* It is Italy's fifth most planted white grape variety.

garganelli (gahr-gah-NEH-lee) Pasta tubes from Romagna. The dough, which has cheese in it, is pressed with a device called a *pettine* (comb) that creates grooves intended to hold the sauce better; in Modena, *garganelli* are actually called *maccheroni al pettine.* Originally the pasta was rolled on hemp loom combs in the town of Castel Bolognese, where they were first made. *Garganelli* are traditionally served with either a sauce of butter, cream, nutmeg, boiled ham, and *prosciutto,* or with *pancetta,* tomato, butter, and oil.

garibaldi (gah-ree-BAHL-dee) Butter cookie bars containing raisins. Named after Giuseppe Garibaldi, the 19th-century revolutionary who helped free Italy from feudal and foreign control.

garofano (gah-ROH-fah-noh) Clove. Brought to the emperor Constantine by Arab traders from Asia, cloves were known in ancient Rome, but they disappeared from European cookery until brought to Sicily by the Arabs and brought back to Europe by the Crusaders. Even so, it was not until the

18th century that cloves became widely available in Europe. Today in Italy cloves are used as a seasoning for meats, poultry, sauces, and desserts.

From the Linnaean Latin *Eugenia caryophyllata.*

gastronomia   (gah-stroh-noh-MEE-ah)   Food store, particularly for delicacies. Also, prepared food bought at such a store and taken home.

The word derives from a 4th-century B.C. Greek poem of the same name, ultimately from the Greek *gaster* (stomach), and *nomos* (sum of knowledge).

Gattinara   (gah-tee-NAH-rah)   *DOCG* big-bodied red wine of Piedmont's Vercelli hills, made from the **nebbiolo** grape (known in the area as **spanna**) and a small quantity of **bonarda.** References to the wine date back at least to 1270. The name refers to the town of Gattinara.

gattò   (gah-TOH)   Cake. Also *gatò.* A southern Italian word for a cake, savory as well as sweet, from the French *gâteau. Gattò alla napoletana,* also called *gattò di patate,* is a potato pie, from Naples.

gattopardo   (gah-toh-PAHR-doh)   "Leopard [fish]." Large-spotted dogfish, *Scyliorhinus stellaris.* From the Latin *leopardus* (leopard). Because of its coarseness, it is often cooked with a fairly strong sauce or seasoning.

gattuccio   (gah-TOO-ch'yoh)   Dogfish, *Scyliorhinus caniculus.* The Italian word means "small cat," but it is no relation to the American freshwater catfish in the family Ictaluridae. See also **boccanera, boccanegra** (black mouth), and **palombo.**

Gavi   (GAH-vee)   *DOC* white wine of Piedmont, made from *cortese* grapes grown around the town of Gavi. Also *Cortese di Gavi.*

gazzosa   (gah-ZOH-sah)   Sweetened lemon-flavored carbonated water. The word ultimately comes from the Latin *chaos* (chaos).

gelatina   (jeh-lah-TEE-nah)   Aspic gelatin made from a calf's foot and beef shank. From the Latin *gelare* (to freeze). See also **colla di pesce.**

gelato   (jeh-LAH-toh)   Ice cream, made with egg custard, sugar, and flavorings. From the Latin *gelare* (to freeze).

The Arabs were the first to develop the kind of fruit ice that the Italians called **sorbetto,** but the Chinese seem to have invented milk-based ice cream, which Marco Polo described on his return from the Orient. The idea for both frozen desserts were brought to France by a cook named Bernardo Buontalenti, either with Caterina de'Medici in 1533 or with Maria de'Medici in 1600.

It was, however, a Sicilian who made custard-based ice cream, a wildly popular and fashionable confection: Francesco Procopio dei Coltelli, an impoverished Palermo aristocrat, emigrated to Vienna in 1672, first to work for a coffee purveyor, then as owner of his own coffeehouse. Before long he ran a chain of such cafés throughout Central Europe, then took the idea to Paris in 1675, where he opened the Café Procope (which still exists on its third site on the Rue de l'Ancienne-Comédie), where he began selling Viennese-style ices and, before long, custard-rich ice creams. Coffee houses in Italy followed the Paris model, and *gelato* became hugely popular.

In Italy today, the best ice creams in Italy are made by local *gelaterie,* which may display a sign reading *Produzione Propria* (produced by the proprietor), indicating a fresher ice cream than a commercially made one, which may contain emulsifiers and additives. See also **sorbetto** and **biscuit Tortoni.**

gelo di melone   (JEH-loh dee meh-LOH-neh)   "Ice and melons." Chilled sweet pudding made with watermelon juice, jasmine water, and cornstarch and decorated with jasmine flowers, pistachios, candied citron, and chocolate shavings, from Sicily. Called *gelu di muluni* in dialect.

gelso   (JEHL-soh)   Mulberry. The black variety has been cultivated for at least four thousand years.

gelsomino   (jehl-soh-MEE-noh)   Jasmine. From the Arabic *yasamin.*

gemelli   (jeh-MEH-lee)   "Twins." Pasta shape in which one side is folded and turned to look like two joined strands. From the Latin *gemini.*

Gemsenfleisch   (GEHM-sen-fleyesh)   Chamois cooked in red wine, vinegar, herbs, and sour cream, a specialty of the Tyrol in Trentino–Alto Adige. From the German meaning chamois meat.

genovese, alla   (AH-lah jeh-noh-VEH-zeh)   "Genoa style." A dish containing olive oil, garlic, and herbs, particularly basil. In Naples, *alla genovese* refers to a dish of beef braised in wine white and onions, supposedly introduced to the city by Genoese merchants and cooks in the 17th century.

gerbi   (JEHR-bee)   Bundles of wild greens such as thistle, salsify, leek greens, wild fennel, escarole, and others, from Liguria. They are boiled and eaten with green beans and potatoes dressed with olive oil. From the Latin *herba* (herb).

germinus   (jehr-MEE-noos)   Almond meringues, from Sardinia. The name refers to a white-yellow spring flower.

Gerstensuppe   (GEHR-sten-SOO-peh)   Barley soup with **Speck,** onion, garlic, and vegetables, from Trentino. From the German for barley soup. Called *orzetto* in Alto Adige.

Ghemme   (GEH-meh)   **DOC** red wine of Piedmont, made from **nebbiolo, vespolina,** and **bonarda** grapes grown around the Novara-Vercelli hills.

ghiaccio (GH'YAH-ch'yoh) Ice or ice cubes. From the Latin *glacialis* (icy).

ghineffi di riso (ghee-NEH-fee dee REE-soh) Fried rice cakes flavored with saffron, from Sicily.

ghiotta, alla (AH-lah G'YOH-tah) "Glutton style." Cooking method by which a sauce is made from pan drippings. It is usually served with fish. *Ghiotta* is the name of such a sauce.

Ghiotta is also a dish of peppers, potatoes, tomatoes, and zucchini cut into strips and baked together, from Abruzzo.

gialetti (jee-ah-LEH-tee) "Yellow [biscuits]." Cornmeal biscuits, from Romagna.

gianchi e neigro (jee-AHN-kee eh NAY-groh) "White and black." Breaded slices of organ meats sautéed till crisp, from Liguria. Also *bianco e nero*.

gianduja (jahn-DOO-yah) Chocolate and hazelnut paste. It is widely used in candy making and other sweet confections. *Gianduja* is a specialty of Piedmont, created in the early 18th century. Also **gianduia**.

There are several stories as to how the confection got its name. Turin tradition has it that the name derives from *Giovanni della doja* (John with a pint of wine in his hand), a popular marionette created by Gioacchino Bellone di Raccongi, who first exhibited the puppet in Turin in 1808. Some say the puppet was named after di Oja, a hamlet near Bellone's hometown of Racconigi, and that *Giovanni di Oja* is the actual name. Asti tradition has it that the name derives from a reconstruction of an ancient peasant dwelling called *casa di Giandoja* in Asti.

gianfottere (jahn-FOH-teh-reh) "Trifles." Stew of eggplant, roast peppers, zucchini, squash, and other seasonal vegetables, from Calabria.

giardinetto (jahr-dee-NEH-toh) Plate of cooked vegetables presented to resemble a garden. The diminutive derives from Middle English *gardin* (garden).

giardiniera, alla (AH-la jahr-dee-N'YEHR-ah) "Garden style." Made or served with chopped fresh or cooked vegetables. From Middle English *gardin* (garden).

gigantoni (jee-gahn-TOH-nee) "Super giants." Very large **maccheroni,** about 2 inches long and 1¹/₂ inches wide. From the Latin *gigant* (giant).

ginepro (jee-NEH-proh) Juniper, used as a flavoring for food and spirits. From the Latin *juniperus*.

ginestrata (jee-neh-STRAH-tah)   Soup made with wild broom, in the genus *Genista,* and chicken broth with a liaison of egg yolks, **Marsala,** and cinnamon. Nutmeg is sprinkled on the top. From Tuscany.

Gioia del Colle (jee-OYE-ah dell KOH-leh)   "Jewel of the Hills." **DOC** zone of Apulia that produces five types of wine, including **Aleatico** and **Primitivo.** The word *gioia* ultimately derives from the Latin *jocus* (joke).

giorno, del (dell J'YOHR-noh)   "Of the day." Refers to a restaurant's special dishes of the day. From the Latin *diurnus.*

girarrosto (jee-rah-ROH-stoh)   "Turned roast." Roasted on the spit or the roasting spit itself.

girelle (jee-REH-leh)   "Rings." Breakfast pastries made with croissant-like dough with raisins.

girello (jee-REH-loh)   Butcher's term for the internal muscle of the thigh, cut from the upper part of the shank. It may also refer to a rump roast.

giro di Cagliari (JEE-roh dee kah-L'YAH-ree)   **DOC** zone of Sardinia that produces a portlike sweet wine from the Spanish *giro* grape.

giudea, alla (AH-lah joo-DEH-yah)   "Jewish style." Refers to dishes prepared in the style of the Roman Jews when they lived in the city's ghetto, such as **carciofi alla giudea,** a dish of small, tender artichokes fried in olive oil. Also *alla giudia.*

glassa (GLAH-sah)   Icing. *Glassato* means glazed. From Middle English *glasen* (glazed).

gniumerieddi (n'yoo-meh-ree-EH-dee)   "Little gnomes." Apulian dish of grilled skewered sausages made from lamb or kid and its offal with salt pork, **pecorino,** and bay leaves. Also *gnumeredd, turciniedde,* and *gnomirelli.* The diminutive is derived from New Latin *gnomus* (gnome).

gnocchi (N'YOH-kee)   Dumplings, usually cooked in water or broth but also baked. The two principal forms are made with either potato or semolina dough. The former is used mostly in the north, the latter in Rome and the south.

Although some authorities believe *gnocchi* may have originated in Piedmont, potato recipes were far more popular in Liguria by the early 19th century, and there is a recipe for an elaborate form of potato *gnocchi* containing veal fat and hard-boiled eggs in the fifth edition of Vincenzo Corrado's *Il Cuoco galante* (1801).

In Sicily, semolina *gnocchi* are called *gnocculli. Gnocchi alla valdostana* are made with **fontina** cheese. *G. verdi* are made with **ricotta** and spinach that give them a green color. *G. di zucca* are Lombardian *gnocchi* made with pureed pumpkin in the dough. In Friuli, *g. di pane* are made with stale bread and *g. di susina* with prunes. *G. alla parigina* (Parisian style) are made with a choux pastry and browned in the oven. The Piedmontese enjoy *g. alla bava,* potato gnocchi with butter, **parmigiano,** and melted **fontina.** In Florence, *gnocchi* are called *topini* (field mice) because of their shape. In Genoa, *gnocchi* sauced with **pesto** are called **troffieti.** In Sardinia, where a ridged **semolina** *gnocchi* are called **malloreddus,** potato *gnocchi* are served *alla sassarese,* with a sauce of tomato, onion, and **pancetta.**

Gnocchi is also the name of a small, rippled dried pasta shell. The name *gnocchi* may derive from the Latin *nucleus* (nucleus), though some authorities believe it may derive from the Middle High German *knöchel* (knuckle).

GNOCCHI DI PATATE

1 pound baking potatoes	**Salt**
1 egg	**Sauce of choice**
1 cup flour	

Wash the potatoes, but do not peel them. Place in a saucepan with cold water to cover and bring to a boil. Cook until tender but not mushy. Drain the potatoes and when cool enough to handle, peel them. Put the potatoes through a ricer and place on a pastry board. Add egg, a small amount of the flour, and a little salt and mix with a spoon or your fingers. Keep adding flour, little by little, just until blended into a soft dough. Roll the dough into long cylinders about $1/2$-inch thick and cut into pieces about 1-inch long.

Cook the *gnocchi* in boiling salted water until **al dente.** Serve with a desired sauce. Serves 4.

GNOCCHI DI SEMOLINO

3 cups milk
10 tablespoons butter
Salt

1 ¹/₄ cups semolina flour
¹/₂ cup grated parmigiano
2 egg yolks

Bring the milk to a low boil in a saucepan. Add 2 tablespoons of the butter and a pinch of salt. Add the **semolina** little by little, constantly stirring to blend. Cook, constantly stirring, for about 30 minutes. Remove from the heat, add the **parmigiano** and egg yolks, and stir until well blended. Pour the *semolina* onto a marble surface and spread out with a wet spatula to a thickness of about ¹/₂ inch. With a round cutter about 1¹/₂ inches in diameter, cut the dough into disks and arrange them in a baking dish, overlapping one over another. Dot with the rest of the butter and more *parmigiano* and bake in a 400°F oven until the top is crisp and golden, about 30 minutes. Serves 4.

gnocco (N'YOH-koh) "Dumpling." Deep-fried pieces of dough made with **strutto,** usually topped with ham or cheese, from Emilia-Romagna.

gnudi (N'YOO-dee) "Nudies." Spinach and **ricotta** dumplings that resemble **ravioli** without pasta, from Florence. They are also sometimes called *ravioli malfatti* (badly made ravioli). From the Latin *nudus* (nude).

gobbi (GOH-bee) Cardoons. *Gobbi alla perugina* are deep-fried cardoons baked with a meat and tomato sauce, from Perugia. See also **cardo.**

goccia (GOH-ch'yah) Drop, as in a recipe instruction for a drop of flavoring. From the Latin *gutta.*

goccie al rosolio (GOH-ch'yeh ahl roh-SOH-l'yoh) "Rosolio drops." Pastel sugar candies with a liquid center. See also **rosolio.**

gorgonzola (gohr-gohn-ZOH-lah) Rich, blue-veined cow's milk cheese from Lombardy. It is named after the town of Gorgonzola and two legends have grown up about its origin. The first concerns a local shepherd who mistakenly left his milk behind and returned to find it had turned into blue cheese. The second involves a Gorgonzola innkeeper who received shepherds' cheese in payment for lodgings. One batch aged into *gorgonzola* and became much appreciated by visitors to his inn.
Originally *gorgonzola* was made through natural contact with spores of *Penicillium glaucum gorgonzola* in the air that penetrate the cheese, causing blue striations of mold called *erborinati* (a Lombard dialect word for parsley), then aging

the cheese in caves. Today, *gorgonzola* is commercially produced by inserting steel or copper needles into the cheese, allowing oxygen in and the penetration of a commercially made bacterium called *Penicillium gorgonzola*. The cheese ripens in 45 to 50 days and is then aged in wheels of about 20 pounds for three to six months. The rind is frequently brined during this aging process.

G. *dolce* is a sweeter, milder version, aged for three months; stronger, longer-aged versions are called *naturale, piccante, di monte,* and *stagionata* (aged), with the most pungent called *g. piccante* (piquant). There is also a rarely seen unveined version called *gorgonzola bianco* or *pannerone*.

governo (goh-VEHR-noh)   A vinicultural custom in Tuscany. Dried grapes or their must are added to wine that is already fermenting in order to induce a secondary fermentation. *Governo* gives **Chianti** its traditional tingliness as well as a certain roundness in the wine. Since the 1970s the practice has lost favor among *Chianti* producers, although there has been a new interest in *governo* recently among the producers of the *Putto Consortium*. From the Latin *gubernare* (to steer).

Gra-Car (GRAH-CAHR)   Liqueur made at the Carthusian monastery in Certosa. The name is short for the Latin *Gratium Cartusia* (gift of the Carthusians).

Gragnano (grah-N'YAH-noh)   Red, often fizzy wine of Campania, from the town of Gragnano.

gramigna (grah-MEE-n'yah)   "Grass." Curly pasta with a hole through the middle, from Emilia-Romagna. Commonly served with wine-braised sausage.

gramugia (grah-MOO-j'yah)   Soup of fava bean, artichoke, asparagus, and peas, a specialty of Lucca in Tuscany. It often contains beef. Also *garmugia*. The word may derive from the Latin *gramen* (plant or herb).

grana (GRAH-nah)   Grain. *Grano saraceno* (Saracen grain) is buckwheat flour. Also *grano*. *G. al ragù* is a Basilicata dish of wheat grains served with a sausage-tomato, garlic-and-olive-oil *ragù*. From the Latin *granum* (grain).

grana (GRAH-nah)   Any cheese of a hard and grainy texture, of which **Parmigiano-Reggiano** is the finest example. *Grana padana* is made in both Piedmont and Lombardy; *piacentina* around Piacenza; *lodigana* around Lodi. From the Latin *granum* (grain).

granatina (grah-nah-TEE-nah)   Ground beef, egg, and bread, shaped into a cutlet, dredged in egg and bread crumbs, and fried.

gran bui (grahn BOO-ee)   "Grand boil." A version of **bollito misto** served with several sauces, from Piedmont. Also *gran bouilli*.

granchio   (GRAHN-k'yoh)   General term for crab. From the Latin *cancer.* The shore crab, *Carcinus mediterraneus,* is sometimes called *granchio commune.*

Granceola (also *grancevola, granseola,* and *granzeola)* is the spider crab, *Maja squinado.* Large and hairy, the spider crab is usually boiled and the meat extracted from the shell. *Granzevola alla triestina* is a dish of crab baked with bread crumbs, parsley, and garlic, from Trieste. The *favollo (Eriphia verrucosa)* is the furry crab. *Granica d'arena (Macropipus puber)* is somewhat smaller. The blue crab of American waters (*Cancer pagurus)* is called *granciporro.* She-crabs are sometimes called *le femminelle.* A soft-shelled crab is called **moleca.**

grandinine   (grahn-dee-NEE-neh)   "Hailstones." Small pasta from Tuscany. From the Latin *grando.*

granita   (grah-NEE-tah)   A dessert ice flavored with coffee, lemon, or other flavorings that has a near-soupy, granular texture. A more granular version is called **gremolata.** From the Latin *granum* (grain).

grano   (GRAH-noh)   General term for a seed, grain, or fruit pit. In the plural, *granelli* refers to animal testicles that are eaten. From the Latin *granum* (grain).

grano al vincotto   (GRAH-noh AHL veen-KOH-toh)   "Grain in cooked wine." Dish of wheat berries sweetened with **vino cotto,** traditionally served on the feast of *Santa Lucia* (December 13), from Calabria.

grano dolce   (GRAH-noh DOHL-cheh)   "Sweet grain." Pudding of wheat, walnuts, pomegranate seeds, chocolate, and sweet wine, from Basilicata. From the Latin *granum* (grain) and *dulcis* (sweet).

granoturco   (grah-noh-TOOR-coh)   "Turkish grain." Corn. See also **mais.** The word *grano* derives from the Latin *granum* (grain).

gran pistau   (grahn pee-STOW)   "Crushed grain." Dish made with wheat berries crushed in a mortar and separated from the chaff, then mixed with a **soffritto** of leeks and pork, from Liguria.

grappa   (GRAH-pah)   A distilled spirit made from fermented grape pomace, called **vinaccia.** The word probably derives from the phrase *grappolo d'uva* (bunch of grapes). *Grappa* is made primarily in northern Italy. In France it is called *marc.*

Grappa is made by combining a volume of pomace with an equal volume of water in a copper cauldron for distillation. In the past, *grappa* was a fiery drink with little or no finesse, sometimes used as a flavoring, as in the Friulian sweet yeast bread called **gubana,** or as a fermenting agent, as in the Piedmontese cheese called **bros.** But in the last twenty years, producers have been making better and more refined *grappa* by using better grapes. *Monovitigno grappa* is a one-grape *grappa* popularized by the producer Nonino in Friuli, which also produces *ue,* distilled from grape must, and *le frutte,* distilled from fruits and berries.

grasso   (GRAH-soh)   Fat, specifically meat fat. From the Latin *grassus* (thick).

graticola, alla   (AH-lah grah-TEE-koh-lah)   Grilled over charcoal. From the Latin *cratis* (wickerwork).

gratinata, alla   (AH-lah grah-tee-NAH-tah)   Gratinéed, cooked with cheese on top that has been melted under the broiler. From the French *gratinée.*

grattini   (grah-TEE-nee)   Tiny pasta that look like grated cheese, used in soups. From Old High German *krazzon* (to scratch).

grattugia   (grah-TOO-j'yah)   Grater. Different sizes are used for cheese, citrus peel, and nutmeg. From Old High German *krazzon* (to scratch).

Graukäse   (GRAU-kay-seh)   Grainy, sharp cheese of Trentino-Alto Adige. The word is from the German (gray cheese).

Grave del Friuli   (GRAH-veh dell free-OO-lee)   Large **DOC** zone of Friuli that produces 15 types of wines, ranging from **cabernet** to **Refosco** *dal Peduncolo Rosso,* and **verduzzo.** *Grave* may be related to the Old French *gravele,* for "pebbly ground" of a kind the grapes grew in.

Gravina   (grah-VEE-nah)   **DOC** zone of Apulia that produces white wines, sometimes sparkling, from **malvasia, greco di tufo,** and *Bianco d'Alessano* grapes grown around Gravina.

Grecanico di Sicilia   (greh-KAH-nee-koh dee see-CHEE-l'yah)   A white wine of Sicily, made from *grecanico* grapes grown in the **Marsala** zone. The name suggests the Greek origins of the grapes.

grechetto   (greh-KEH-toh)   A white wine grape that falls under the **Colli Martani DOC,** from Umbria. The name suggests Greek origins of the grapes.

greco   (GREH-koh)   Term applied to vines originally brought by the Greeks to southern Italy. *Greco di Tufo* is a **DOC** zone of Campania that produces white wines from a clone of *greco* in Tufo and other villages. *Greco di Bianco* is a *DOC* white wine from around the town of Bianco in Calabria, made from *greco bianco* grapes. A *greco* is also made in Piedmont, with records of its existence dating back at least to 1381.

gremolata   (greh-moh-LAH-tah)   A mixture of chopped garlic, lemon peel, and parsley, commonly sprinkled over **ossobuco.**
  Gremolata is also a term for a granular water ice similar to **granita.**

griglia   (GREE-l'yah)   Grill. *Alla griglia* or *grigliata* refers to food cooked on the grill. *Grigliare* is to grill. From the Latin *craticulum*.

grignolino   (gree-n'yoh-LEE-noh)   A red wine grape of Piedmont that produces a pale red wine. *Grignolino d'Asti,* made around Asti, is a **DOC** red containing up to 10 percent *freisa*. *Grignolino del Monferrato Casalese* is another *DOC* red, made in the Casale Monferrato hills. The name comes from the Asti dialect word *grignòle* (grape pits), because the grape contains many seeds.

grillo   (GREE-loh)   A white wine grape of Sicily, used in making *Marsala*. It has been in decline since the 1980s. The word *grillo* in Italian means "cricket," though its relevance to the wine is not clear.

grissini   (gree-SEE-nee)   Breadsticks. The common legend of Piedmont has it that *grissini* were created by Turinese baker Antonio Brunero (who called them, in local dialect, *gherssin)* for the royal family of Savoy as a healthy form of bread to be eaten during the plague years 1679–1698. Nevertheless, there have been other claims as to the creator of *grissini,* some pre-dating Brunero. In any case, the best *grissini* are made in Turin.

griva   (GREE-vah)   Dish of fried pork liver, calf's brains, and eggs, flavored with juniper and other seasonings, from Piedmont. The taste of the dish is said to be similar to that of thrush *(griva* in dialect), which at one time fed on juniper. Also *flisse, frisse,* and *grisele.*
   Grive is also synonymous with **mortadella,** in Piedmont.

grolla   (GROH-lah)   Multi-spouted coffee pot for *caffè valdostana* (from Valle d'Aosta). It is passed around to guests to drink from. A similar pot is called a *coppa dell'amicizia* (cup of friendship).
   The word *grolla* is believed to derive from the German dialect word *Gral,* referring to the grail cup Christ sipped at the Last Supper, from which came the legend of the Holy Grail brought to England by Joseph of Arimathea.

grongo   (GROHN-goh)   Conger eel, *Conger conger.* A saltwater fish that grows to 8 feet in length, although the smaller ones are considered tastier. In Italy, *grongo* is both grilled and used in a soup or stew. From the Latin *conger.* See also **anguilla.**

groppello   (groh-PEH-loh)   A **DOC** red wine of Latium made around Riviera del Garda Bresciano.

Grumello   (groo-MEH-loh)   A red wine of Lombardy produced at a vineyard of the same name in Valtellina. It falls under the **Valtellina Superiore DOC** zone.

guanciale (gwahn-ch'YAH-leh)   Pig's jowl and cheek. Usually salted and cured for a month and hung to dry for another month. *Guanciale* is used like *pancetta.*

guarnaccia (gwahr-nah-CHEE-ah)   A red grape of Campania, used in making *Ischia rosso.* It is believed to be related to Sardinia's **cannonau,** France's *grenache,* and the *granacha* of Spain, where it probably originated.

guarnito (gwahr-NEE-toh)   Garnished. From the Middle French *garnir.*

guastedde (gwah-steh-DEH)   Sesame-seed roll filled with **caciocavallo** cheese and spleen, a specialty of Palermo. Also *pani cu'la meuza.*

guazzetto, in (een gwah-T'ZEH-toh)   Seafood cooked in a light sauce of white wine, garlic, parsley, and a little tomato. In Sardinia, capers are commonly added to such dishes. Also *sguazeto.*

gubana (goo-BAH-nah)   Sweet bread that is filled with cocoa, candied fruit, nuts, and **grappa.** Traditionally served at Easter in Friuli. In the Natisone valley, it is usually made with a yeast dough; in Cividale del Friuli it is made with a puff pastry. The name may derive either from *bubane,* Friulian dialect for abundance, or *guba,* Slavic for snail.

gulasch di manzo (GOO-lahsh dee MAHN-zoh)   Beef stew of Alto Adige, similar to Hungarian *gulyas* and called *gulyas* in Friuli.

gutturnio (goo-TUHR-n'yoh)   A red wine of Emilia-Romagna, made from **bonarda** and **barbera** grapes in the **DOC** zone of **Colli Piacentini.**

guvat (goo-VAHT)   Goby fish, *Gobius paganellus.* The small ones are inedible, but larger ones can be baked.

Legend has it that the *guvat* was the only fish that refused to raise its head from the water to listen to San' Antonio di Padua preach at Rimini circa 1221–1223. Also *guatto* and *ghiozzo.*

H

hammin   (HAH-meen)   A slow-cooked meat stew of Jewish origin, similar to *cholent*. From the Hebrew word *ham* (warm), referring to dishes that were kept warm for hours. Meats vary from region to region, with wealthier families using better cuts of beef or lamb or chicken. Beans and spinach are commonly included, and often matzoh meal is added toward the end to thicken the dish. Sometimes, though not always, *hammin* was tied to a religious feast such as Passover or Shabbat.

Hamin is also a pasta dish of ***tagliolini*** baked with raisins, pine nuts, and goose fat. It is a specialty of Ferrara, of Jewish origin.

Hauswurst   (HAUSS-vurst)   Sausage, served with noodles and sauerkraut, from Trentino. From the German (house sausage).

I

imbottigliato da (eem-boh-tee-L'YAH-toh dah) "Bottled by." Phrase used on wine bottles to name the producer, though not necessarily the grower or wine maker. The word derives from late Latin *buttis* (cask).

imbottito (eem-boh-TEE-toh) Stuffed or filled.

impanare (eem-pah-NAH-reh) To coat with bread crumbs.

impanata (eem-pah-NAH-tah) Turnover pastry, savory or sweet. *Impanata di Caltanisetta* is a form of pizza topped with cooked eel, tomato, and anchovies, a specialty of the town of Caltanisetta in Sicily. Also *impanada*.

impastare (eem-pah-STAH-reh) To knead.

indivia (een-DEE-vee-yah) Chicory, *Cicoria indivia*. Called curly chicory or curly escarole in the United States. *Indivia del Belgio* (also *indivia belga*) is witloof or Belgian endive *(C. intybus)*, the crown of which is blanched. Escarole *(scarola)* is also a form of *indivia*. All are used as salad greens. *Scarola* is added to soups and braised; Belgian endive is also sometimes braised. From the Latin *intubus*.

infarinata (een-fah-ree-NAH-tah) "Floured [soup]." Vegetable and cornmeal soup, from Tuscany.

inglese, all' (AHL een-GLEH-seh) "English style." Pasta or rice dressed with butter.

inglesine (een-gleh-SEE-neh) Butter cookies flavored with rum-soaked raisins, from Tuscany.

insaccato (een-sah-KAH-toh) General term for all salami and sausages. From the Latin *saccus* (wine bag).

insalata   (een–sah–LAH–tah)   Salad. From the Latin *sal* (salt), with which salads were dressed. In Italy, salads are made with greens or vegetables, alone or in combination with grains. The salad course comes before the cheese in the Italian menu plan.

Insalata condita is a salad dressed, at its simplest, with lemon and oil. *I. non condita* is a salad without dressing. *I. verde* is a simple green salad. *I. mista* is a mixture of greens and vegetables like fennel, tomato, and cucumber. *I. alla caprese* (from Capri) is made with tomatoes, **mozzarella,** basil, and olive oil. *I. di rinforzo* (invigorating salad) is a Christmas salad from Naples made with cauliflower, anchovies, capers, olives, and vegetables in vinegar and olive oil. It is actually made to last until Epiphany (January 6). *I. pantesca* is a salad from the island of Pantelleria off Sicily, which combines potatoes and tomatoes with capers. *I. di finocchio e arance* is a fennel and orange salad of Sicilian origin. *Insalatone* is a large salad often consumed after **pasta** at a **trattoria.**

insaporire   (een–sah–poh–REE–reh)   Cooking term meaning to add flavor to food, as by dressing vegetables with oil, onion, or garlic or by starting a dish with a **soffritto.** From the Latin *sapidus* (tasty).

integrale   (een–teh–GRAH–leh)   Whole wheat, as in flour, bread, or **pasta.** From the Latin *integer* (whole).

intingolo   (een–TEEN–goh–loh)   A rich meat sauce in which **polenta,** bread, or vegetables may be dipped. In southern Italy, the term refers to fish cooked with pieces of bread.

invecchiato   (een–veh–CH'YAH–toh)   Aged, as in wine. From the Latin *vetrus* (old).

involtini   (een–vohl–TEE–nee)   Stuffed rolls of meat or fish. *Involtini alla romana* are veal rolls stuffed with **guanciale** and garlic, then braised with tomatoes. *I. di* **pesce spada** are swordfish rolls stuffed with bread crumbs and **passoli** *e pinoli,* from Sicily.

INVOLTINI DI PESCE SPADA

2 tablespoons olive oil
1 onion, chopped
1 garlic clove, chopped
¹/₄ cup chopped parsley
basil
bread crumbs
2 tablespoons dried currants
2 tablespoons pine nuts
1 tablespoon capers
4 ounces sharp provolone cheese
2 eggs
Salt

Freshly ground black pepper
2 pounds swordfish, cut into thin
  slices
3 tablespoons olive oil, for sautéing

SALMORIGLIO SAUCE:
2 tablespoons lemon juice
Salt
Freshly ground black pepper
¹/₂ cup olive oil
1 garlic clove, minced
1 teaspoon minced fresh oregano

Prepare the sauce first. In a bowl, combine the lemon juice, salt, and pepper, and slowly add the olive oil, whisking the mixture to emulsify the dressing. Add the garlic and oregano and set aside.

In a skillet, heat the olive oil. Add the onion and sauté over medium heat until soft and translucent. Add the garlic and sauté for 1 minute. Then add the parsley, basil, bread crumbs, currants, pine nuts, and capers and sauté for another 2 minutes. Remove from heat and let cool. Add the cheese, eggs, and salt and pepper to taste and mix well. Flatten the swordfish slices slightly with a mallet and divide the filling evenly among the slices. Roll the slices and secure with a toothpick. Sauté the involtini in olive oil, turning them to cook evenly. They may also be grilled. Serve with the sauce. Serves 4.

inzolia   (een-ZOH-l'yah)   A native white wine grape of Sicily (grown to a small extent in Tuscany). Also **ansonica** and *anzonica*.

Ischia   (EE-sk'yah)   **DOC** zone of Campania's island of Ischia that produces a *bianco, bianco superiore,* and *rosso.*

Isonzo   (ee-SOHN-zoh)   **DOC** zone of Friuli-Venezia Giulia that produces 17 different kinds of wine along the Isonzo River.

Italico   (ee-TAH-lee-koh)   Semisoft cheese similar to **Bel Paese.** It was created in 1929 and is sold under various brand names.

J

'j jabre   (y'YAH-breh)   Wedges of sun-dried apples, from Ravenna. Dialect word for *labbre* (lips), which they resemble.

jambon de bosses   (jahm-BOHN deh boss)   *Prosciutto* from Valle d'Aosta.

jota   (YOH-tah)   A soup made with *polenta,* beans, onions, sage, cabbage, and *brovada,* from Friuli. Also *jotha, iota,* and *yota.* From the Spanish *judías* (beans).

jumache fellate di Saint'Antuon   (yoo-MAH-keh feh-LAH-teh dee sahn-tahn-T'WUON)   *Polenta* dish made with *broccoletti di rape,* *scamorza* cheese, and sausages, from Abruzzo. Originally fava bean flour was used. From the word *ammaccare,* meaning to crush the fava beans into flour.

K

kaki   (KAH-kee)   Persimmon. Originated in China and did not appear in European markets until it was first shown in Paris in 1873. Persimmons are not among Italians' favorite fruits, but when ripe and somewhat sweet, they may be served with slices of *prosciutto* as an *antipasto.*

kamostrelle   (kah-moh-STREH-leh)   Waffles, commonly filled with whipped cream, from the Valle d'Aosta. From *canesterlli* (small baskets).

Knödeln   (K'NOH-dehln)   Bread dumplings, sometimes made with rye flour, usually containing *speck* or liver, from Trentino. From the German (dumpling).

krafi   (KRAH-fee)   Sweet *ravioli* filled with raisins, rum, *fontina,* and citrus peel, from Istria.

Krapfen   (KRAHP-fenn)   Fried or baked dough served with jam, from Alto Adige. From the German (doughnut).
    Also *ravioli* made with rye flour, a specialty of Trentino-Alto Adige.

Kren   (krehn)   Fresh grated horseradish in vinegar. From an Austrian dialect word for horseradish.

L

laan (lahn) A kind of *tagliatelle,* commonly served with a puree of chickpeas, peas, or lentils, from Apulia.

lacciada (lah-CH'YAH-dah) "Lace [crepe]." Crepe traditionally made from the first milk of a cow after calving, from Lombardy. Black grapes are usually served with the crepes, or they are sweetened with sugar or jam. From the Latin *laqueare* (to ensnare).

Lacrima di Castrovillari (LAH-kree-mah dee kah-stroh-vee-LAH-ree) A pale red wine of Calabria, made from *gaglioppo* grapes, locally called *lacrima* (tears), grown around the town of Castrovillari.

Lacrima di Morro d'Alba (LAH-kree-mah dee MOH-roh DAHL-bah) *DOC* zone of the Marches that produces a light, purple-red wine from *gaglioppo (lacrima)* grapes.

Lacrima Christi del Vesuvio (LAH-kree-mah KRIS-tee dell veh-SOO-vee-oh) A white, red, rosé, or *liquoroso* wine made in the *DOC* zone of Campania near Mount Vesuvius. Also *Vesuvio.*

lagane (LAH-gah-neh) Pasta strips, similar to *fettuccine,* commonly served with chickpeas on All Souls' Day, in Molise, Abruzzo, and Calabria. Also *laganelle.* See also *lasagne.*

lagrein (LAH-green) A red wine grape of Trentino-Alto Adige used in making red wines *(Lagrein Scuro* and *Lagrein Dunkel)* and rosé wines *(Lagrein Rosato* and *Lagrein Kretzer)* in the Trentino, Alto Adige, and Valdadige *DOC* zones. The name derives from the Lagarina valley in Trentino.

lagrumuse (lah-groo-MOOZE) "Lachrymose." Pork sausage from Calabria, so called because when cut into, a drop of fat flows like a tear.

lambrusco   (lahm-BROO-skoh)   Red grape with at least 60 subvarieties of Emilia-Romagna used in making *lambrusco* wine. There are four **DOC** appellations: *Lambrusco di Sorbara, Lambrusco Grasparossa di Castelvetro, Lambrusco Reggiano,* and *Lambrusco Salamino di Santa Croce. Lambrusco* is usually vinifed as an **amabile** or **frizzante** wine. From the Latin *Vitis labrusca* (fruit of the wild grape).

Lamezia   (lah-MEH-t'zee-ah)   **DOC** red wine of Calabria, made from **nerello, gaglioppo,** and **greco** *nero* grapes, grown around Lamezia Terme and Nicastro.

lampascioni   (lahm-pah-SH'YOH-nee)   Bulbs of the wild tassel hyacinth, *Muscari comosum.* They are bitter onions, a specialty of the south, especially Apulia. After soaking to remove their bitterness, *lampascioni* are boiled, baked, or stewed and used in salads or as a puree. Also *lampagioni.*

lampone   (lahm-POH-neh)   Raspberry. Originated in Asia but was never cultivated in ancient Rome. Raspberries have always grown wild, but it was not until recently that they were cultivated for market and used in desserts, such as **gelato** and **sorbetto.**

lampreda   (lahm-PREH-dah)   Lamprey eel, *Petromyzon marinus.* Parasitic eel-shaped fish. It is grilled or made into a **pasticcio,** and the blood is usually retained to add to the sauce. Also *lampreda marina.* From Middle Latin.

lampuga   (lahm-POO-gah)   Dolphin fish, *Coryphaena hipparus.* Not the dolphin also known as a porpoise. It is often baked.

Langhe   (LAHN-geh)   **DOC** zone of Piedmont that produces wines from **nebbiolo, freisa, grignolino,** and **chardonnay** grapes grown around the Langhe hills.

lanzado   (lahn-ZAH-doh)   Chub mackerel, *Scomber colias.* A spotted, large-eyed fish with a good deal of fat. It is best grilled.

lardo   (LAHR-doh)   Fatback. *Lardo* also refers to the white fat from the pig's rump that has been layered with salt, pepper, cloves, cinnamon, sage, rosemary, and other herbs and spices and preserved in a salt brine for up to a year. In Italy, this is often served in paper-thin slices on top of toasted bread.

Lardellare means to lard a piece of meat. *Lardelli* are strips of fat used to lard meat.

Strutto, or rendered pork fat, is closer to the American form of lard. **Sugna** is pork fat. From the Latin *lardum* (fat).

lasagne   (lah-ZAH-n'yeh)   Wide pasta noodles layered with various ingredients and baked. *Lasagnette* or *lasagne festonate* pasta has rippled edges.

Though some authorities believe the word derives from Vulgar Latin *lasania* (cooking pot), the ancient Romans made *laganum,* which referred to strips of dough baked on a flat surface. Since *lasagne* requires a baking oven, which for most of Italian history was to be found only in the kitchens of wealthy families, the dish was considered to be a lavish one and is not mentioned in Pellegrino Artusi's *La Scienza in cucina e l'arte mangiar bene* (1891), the most important collection of Italian recipes appearing after the Unification. By the 20th century, however, *lasagne* became widely popular and was one of the staples of Italian–American kitchens.

Today there are scores of variations on *lasagne,* though the two principal forms are those of Bologna and Naples. *Lasagne alla bolognese* is made with spinach noodles made from flour and water, baked with ground veal, beef, and pork and **balsamella;** in Naples the noodles are layered with **ricotta, mozzarella,** and tomato sauce. In Friuli, *lasagna ai semi papavero* is a sweet version made with poppy seeds. In the south tiny meatballs are added. In Catania, *l. di catanese* is made with a sauce of eggplant, yellow peppers, anchovies, olives, capers, tomato, and garlic. *L. da fornel* is made with apples, figs, raisins, walnuts, and poppyseeds, a Christmas specialty of the Valle de Cordevole. In Molise, the name *lasagne* is shortened to *sagne.* A form of Sardinian *lasagne* is called *pillas.*

In Sardinia, the word *lasagne* refers to a form of **tagliatelle.**

lasca (LAH-skah)   Freshwater fish *(Chondrostoma genei)* of Lake Trasimeno in Umbria. It is considered a rare and great delicacy.

Latisana (lah-tee-SAH-nah)   **DOC** zone of Friuli-Venezia Giulia that produces 13 kinds of wine. Also *Latisana del Friuli.*

lattaiolo (lah-tye-OH-loh)   Milk custard of central Italy.

latte (LAH-teh)   Milk. In Italy, milk has never been widely consumed except as cheese.

Latticini are dairy products. A *latteria* is a shop that sells products and often pastries as well. It is also the name for a mild cheese of Friuli. From the Latin *lac* (milk).

latte di mandorla (LAH-teh dee MAHN-dohr-lah)   Almond milk. Sweetened almond-flavored milk, a beverage of southern Italy.

lattemiele (LAH-teh-mee-EH-leh)   "Honey milk." Whipped cream with honey (or sugar) and cinnamon.

latterino (lah-teh-REE-noh)   Sand smelt or silverside, *Atherina presbyter.* The fish are fried or poached and dressed with olive oil and lemon juice. Also *latterino sardaro* and *latterino capoccione.*

latteruolo   (lah-teh-roo-OH-loh)   Simple peasant dessert pastry topped with cooked milk, eggs, and either vanilla or crushed coriander, traditionally served on the feast of Corpus Christi, from Romagna. From the Latin *lac* (milk).

lattonzolo   (lah-TOHN-zoh-loh)   Suckling pig or unweaned calf. From the Latin *lac* (milk).

lattuga   (lah-TOO-gah)   Lettuce, which humans have eaten for at least three millennia. By 500 B.C., white lettuce with no formed heads was a favorite vegetable of the ancient Romans. Various varieties of cultivated lettuce *(Lactuca sativa)* include the cabbage lettuce *(l.s.* var. *crispa)* and Romaine lettuce *(l. s.,* var. *longifolia),* which came much later, apparently from Rome, and was only brought into Europe in the 14th century. The Romans got their Romaine from its place of origin, the Greek island of Cos. Today Italians generally eat lettuce as part of a green salad.

Lattuga nostrano (our lettuce) is a Sicilian lettuce with narrow, jagged leaves and a large rib.

lattume   (lah-TOO-meh)   Fish semen, usually from the tuna, which is air-dried, sliced very thin, and dressed with lemon and olive oil.

lauro   (LAU-roh)   See *alloro.*

Lazio   (LAH-t'zee-oh)   Latium, a region of central Italy whose capital, Rome, draws every strain of culinary tradition from every region of Italy and, as a result, has a highly developed gastronomy that combines the best of the north and south.

The historic, religious, and political importance of Rome has also provided it with a sense of exuberant abundance, and Romans like to eat well and probably consume more meat than do most other Italians. Indeed, though there is excellent fish to be found in Roman restaurants, they are not particularly known for their seafood.

Seasonal vegetables are very important in Latium, especially asparagus and artichokes in spring. Fried baby artichokes **alla giudea** is a vestige of the cooking of Rome's former Jewish ghetto.

When a dish is prepared **alla romana,** it often has a tomato sauce. Unlike the potato **gnocchi** of northern Italy, Latium's *gnocchi alla romana* are made with **semolina** and baked with cheese and tomato sauce. What other Italians call **tagliatelle con burro**—flat spaghetti with butter—Romans call **fettuccine** *all'Alfredo,* after the chef who made the dish famous in the 1920s. **Cacio e pepe** indicates a simple dressing of pasta with grated **pecorino** and black pepper, and **spaghetti alla carbonara** is made with a raw egg cooked by the heat of **spaghetti,** together with **pancetta** and plenty of black pepper.

One of Latium's best-known soups is **stracciatella alla romana,** a chicken broth made with egg drops that cook in the soup.

Rome is particularly known for spring lamb, which they call **abbacchio,** flavored with garlic and rosemary and roasted. **Coda** *alla vaccinara* is a stew of oxtail and red wine, and **saltimbocca** is veal cutlets topped with *prosciutto* and fresh sage leaves.

Latium's **pecorino** *romano* cheese varies in quality but its **ricotta** is excellent, and is often made into desserts.

There are 18 **DOC** zones in Latium, the best producing fresh white wines like **Frascati** and **Est! Est!! Est!!!** Most of the region's red wines are undistinguished.

Leberknödelsuppe   (LEH-behr-K'NOH-dell-SOO-peh)   Soup with liver dumplings, from Trentino. From the German for liver-dumpling soup.

leccarda   (leh-KAHR-dah)   Dripping pan placed under a roast on a spit.

leccia   (LEH-ch'yah)   Large silver and gray fish, *Lichia amia,* common in the western Mediterranean. Also called *leccia fasciata.* It is best grilled or baked.

leccia stella   (LEH-ch'yah STEH-lah)   Pompano, *Trachinotus ovatus.* A firm-fleshed fish suitable for many different preparations, particularly baked. From the Latin words *lichia* and *stella.*

legumi   (leh-GOO-mee)   Legumes. Peas, beans, chickpeas, fava beans, and lentils. From the Latin *legere* (to collect). See also **ortaggi** and **verdure.**

lenticchie   (lehn-TEE-k'yeh)   Lentils. From Latin *lenticula.* For centuries lentils were regarded as food for the poor. During World War II, shortages of many foods caused a new interest in lentils, and subsequently they were more widely accepted. Traditionally, they are eaten on New Year's Day for good luck.

Lentils, always bought dried, are eaten hot and cold, in soups and salads, often as an accompaniment to sausage, especially **cotechino** or **zampone.** *Pasta e lenticchie* is a mixture of small **ditalini** with lentils. In Abruzzo, very small mountain lentils are combined with chestnuts to make a soup called *zuppa di lenticchie e castagne.*

lepre   (LEH-preh)   Hare. *Lepre in salmi,* marinated in wine and herbs, then stewed, is a popular recipe for hare. *L. a ciffe e ciaffe* is hare cooked in a heavily herbed vinegar and wine marinade, from Molise. Also *lievero.* From the Latin *lepus.* See also **civet.**

Lessini Durello   (leh-SEE-nee doo-REH-loh)   **DOC** zone of the Veneto that produces a very dry white wine, mostly **spumante,** from **durello** grapes grown in the Lessini hills.

lesso   (LEH-soh)   Boiled. Refers both to the method and the food that is boiled. *Lesso rifatto* is boiled meat that is cooled, then reheated and served with a tomato and onion sauce.

Lesso misto is a mix of several kinds of meats. See also **bollito misto.**

Lessona   (leh-SOH-nah)   *DOC* zone of Piedmont that produces a red wine from **nebbiolo, vespolina,** and **bonarda** grapes grown in the Vercelli hills.

Lettere   (LEH-teh-reh)   A red wine, usually fizzy, made from *gragnano, olivella,* **piedirosso,** and other grapes, from the town of Lettere in Campania.

Leverano   (leh-veh-RAH-noh)   *DOC* zone of Apulia that produces a red wine from **negroamaro** grapes around the town of Leverano.

licurdia   (lee-KOOR-dee-yah)   Onion and potato soup or sauce seasoned with chile peppers, a specialty of the town of Cosenza in Calabria.

lievito   (lee-EH-vee-toh)   Leavener. *Lievito naturale* is a sourdough starter. *L. di birra,* literally "yeast of beer," is baker's yeast. *L. in polvere* is baking powder. From the Latin *levare* (to raise).

Liguria   (lee-GOO-ree-yah)   Northwest region of Italy along the Ligurian Sea. Liguria has very little farmland, and the sea is not as rich in species as in other parts of the Mediterranean. But Liguria does have the same aromatic herbs that flavor the cooking of France's nearby Provence—rosemary, thyme, basil, and marjoram—and its cooking is rich in vegetables and greens. Liguria's most famous dish is **pesto,** a fragrant, pungent sauce of basil, olive oil, garlic, nuts, and **pecorino** cheese, which is served with the thin pasta called **trenette,** a specialty of Genoa.

Given their reputation as sailors (Christopher Columbus hailed from Genoa), the Ligurians have learned to make dried fish, particularly **baccalà,** into a feast. Their **burrida** and **ciuppin** seafood stews are rich and savory, and **cappon magro** is a celebratory dish made of layers of fish, cooked vegetables, crackers, and olive oil. **Condiggion** is made with raw vegetables and, often, **bottarga.** The puffy bread known as *foccaccia* is commonly eaten with Ligurian dishes like these.

Sbira is a tripe and potato dish.

Pastas of the region include a figure-8 shape macaroni called **corzetti,** and **pansôti.**

Cima *all genovese* is veal breast stuffed with innards, cheese, pine nuts, and vegetables.

Ligurian cheeses include **stracchino** and **prescinseha.**

Genoese sweets include many cakes like **pandolce.** The sponge cake named in French *genoise* derives from Genoa models.

The wines of Liguria are few and produced in small quantities, including the white **pigato** and **vermentino** and the red *Orescinseha*.

limoncello   (lee-mohn-CHEH-loh)   A liqueur of the Amalfi coast and Sicily. Made by steeping lemon peels in alcohol and adding a sugar syrup. Cheaper versions are made by mixing lemon extract with alcohol. Also *lemoncello.*

limone   (lee-MOH-neh)   Lemon. The first citrus trees were probably brought to Italy in the 1st century B.C., possibly from Alexandria, Egypt, after the Romans annexed the area. The most widely propagated variety of lemon in Italy is called *Femminello ovale,* accounting for 75 percent of production. Lake Garda is the northernmost citrus-growing region in the world, propagation dating back to at least 1500, although most lemons come from the south of Italy. From the Arabic *laymun.*

Lumia is a highly perfumed lemon of southern Italy. *Limonata* is lemon soda.

lingua   (LEEN-gwah)   Tongue. *Lingua di bue* is beef tongue. Tongue in aspic is called *l. in gelatina. L. salmistrata* is cold pickled tongue. From the Latin.

linguatolo   (leen-gwah-TOH-loh)   "Big tongue." Flat, grayish fish, *Citharus macrolepidotas.* Best fried.

lingue algerine   (LEEN-gweh ahl-jeh-REE-neh)   "Algerians' tongues." Fried zucchini slices sandwiched with a cream and **parmigiano** sauce and fried again.

lingue di gatto   (LEEN-gweh dee GAH-toh)   "Cat's tongues." Crisp, thin butter cookies said to resemble a cat's tongue.

linguine   (leen-GWEE-neh)   "Little tongues." Narrow, flat pasta ribbons. Often served with a white clam sauce, at its best made with the **vongola verace** clam, and sometimes served with a red tomato and clam sauce. *Linguine* is a specialty of southern Italy; in northern Italy a similar pasta is called **trenette.** *Lingue di battone* (whores' tongues) are thin *linguine,* prepared with a spicy tomato sauce similar to **puttanesca.** *Lingue di passero* (sparrows' tongues) are extremely thin linguine. Also called *bavette.*

LINGUINE CON VONGOLE

2 pounds small clams	*Salt and pepper*
¹/₄ cup olive oil	*1 pound linguine, cooked al dente*
4 garlic cloves, minced	*Crushed red pepper (optional)*
¹/₄ cup chopped parsley	

Steam the clams in a large pot with ¹/₂ cup water until just opened and immediately remove from the heat. Let cool. Chop into small pieces. (Or leave the clams whole and serve them in their shells with the linguine.) Pass the broth through a sieve to remove any particles. Place the clams in the broth and set aside.

Heat the olive oil in a large sauté pan, add the garlic, and cook over low heat until slightly golden. Add two thirds of the clam broth and cook until reduced by one third. Add the rest of the broth, the clams, parsley, and salt and pepper to taste. Heat through very briefly. Add the *linguine,* turn up the heat to high, and toss to coat and heat through, about 1 to 2 minutes. Serve with red pepper, if desired. Serves 3 to 4.

---

liquirizia (lee-kwee-REE-t'zee-ah)   Licorice. A root used for its aromatic extract as a flavoring for sweets. From the Late Latin *liquiritia,* which relates to the Greek *glykus* (sweet) + *rhiza* (root).

liquore (lee-KOH-reh)   Liquor. *Al liquore* refers to a food or dish soaked or marinated in a liquor like rum or brandy. A *liquoreria* is a bar or liquor shop and a *liquorista* is a wine or spirits merchant. From the Latin *liquor.*

liquoroso (lee-koh-ROH-soh)   A wine of high alcohol content, usually fortified.

lisce (LEE-sheh)   "Smooth." Refers to the exterior finish of various *maccheroni* that might otherwise be *rigate* (ridged).

Lison-Pramaggiore (LEE-sohn-prah-mah-JOH-reh)   *DOC* zone of the Veneto that produces many kinds of wine, mostly from *tocai* and *merlot* grapes.

lista delle vivande (LEE-stah DEH-leh vee-VAHN-deh)   "List of foods." Restaurant menu, though the word *menu* is far more common.

litro (LEE-troh)   Liter, a standard European liquid measurement equivalent to slightly more than a quart. From Middle Latin *litra* (measure).

Lizzano (lee-T'ZAH-noh)   *DOC* zone of Apulia that produces five kinds of wines from *trebbiano* and *negroamaro* grapes grown around the town of Lizzano.

Loazzolo (loh-ah-ZOH-loh)   *DOC* zone of Piedmont that produces *passito* from *moscato* grapes grown around Loazzolo.

locanda (loh-KAHN-dah)   A country restaurant, usually a bit more refined than an *osteria*. Probably from the Latin *locus* (place).

Locorotondo (loh-koh-roh-TOHN-doh)   *DOC* zone of Apulia that produces white wines from *verdeca* and *bianco d'Alessano* grapes grown around the town of Locorotondo.

lodigiano (loh-dee-JAH-noh)   Strong cheese in the *grana* style made around Lodi.

logudoro (loh-goh-DOO-roh)   Commercially   made   mild   creamy cheese of Lombardy.

Lombardia (lohm-bahr-DEE-ah)   Lombardy, a northern region of Italy on the Swiss border. The region is dominated by the city of Milan, which has always drawn the best chefs and ingredients from Italy, France, and Austria. The cooking is rich in butter rather than olive oil, and pork is the preferred meat.

Robust stews like *cassoeula* and *büsecca* abound. Though landlocked, Lombardy gets excellent fish from Lake Maggiore, Lake Garda, and Lake Como. *Bresaola,* air-dried beef, is made in the Valtellina. One of the signature dishes of Milan is *ossobuco,* braised veal shank in a richly reduced sauce served with *gremolata*. It is traditionally accompanied by *risotto alla milanese,* made with saffron. Another famous dish is *costoletta alla milanese,* a flattened veal chop that is breaded and fried. *Vitello tonnato* is cold sliced veal covered with a tuna-and-mayonnaise sauce. *Minestrone alla milanese* is a vegetable soup, while *zuppa alla pavese,* in the style of Pavia, is beef broth with grated cheese and eggs that are poached in the broth.

Polenta is prepared in many ways, from porridge to slices of dried *polenta* fried in butter, and it is often served as an accompaniment to meat dishes. *Tortelli* are stuffed with vegetables, meat, or cheese. A famous pasta dish is *pizzoccheri* from Valtellina.

Lombardy's cheeses include *mascarpone, taleggio, stracchino, crescenza, robiola, gorgonzola,* and *Bel Paese*.

Panettone cake is traditional at Christmastime, from Milan. *Torrone,* an egg-white-and-nut nougat from Cremona, is also famous. Cremona is also famous for its pickled fruit condiment called *mostarda*.

Lombardy has 13 *DOC* zones, with *Valtellina* producing red wines from the *nebbiolo* grape. Good sparkling wines are made in *Franciacorta,* while *Oltrepò Pavese* produces a number of red, white, and *spumante* wines.

lombata (lohm-BAH-tah)   Loin of meat. Also *lombo. Lombatina* is a grilled veal chop or pork chop from the loin. From the Latin *lombus.*

lonza (LOHN-zah)   Cured pork tenderloin. Also a cured salami from the Marches.

luccio (LOO-ch'yoh)   Pike. A freshwater fish in the family Esocidae, much favored in the lake country of Lombardy, Latium, and Umbria. It is usually poached and sometimes made into quenelles.

luccio marino (LOO-ch'yoh mah-REE-noh)   "Sea pike." Barracuda, *Sphyraena sphyraena.* It is often fried or poached in a court-bouillon, though in Bologna it is cooked with cream and butter.

Lugana (loo-GAH-nah)   ***DOC*** zone of Lombardy that produces white wine, including a ***spumante.***

luganega (loo-GAH-neh-gah)   Long, thin pork sausage, with the best said to be made in Lombardy. It is often added to ***risotto.*** In Treviso, it is called *iuganega* or *xuganega.* Also *lucanica.* The origin of the name dates to the ancient Romans who named these sausages *lucani,* after a tribe of people of the same name who lived in southern Italy.

lumaca (loo-MAH-kah)   Snail. A gastropod mollusk within a spiral shell. *Lumache alla meranese* is a dish made of chopped snails sautéed with white wine and cooked with a puree of peas. In Rome, the feast of *San Giovanni* (June 24) is traditionally celebrated by cooking the very small snails called *grigette di vigna* with onion, garlic, olive oil, and chile peppers. In Bologna, *l. alla bobbiese* are shelled snails cooked with carrots, celery, leeks, and white wine. *Attuppatelli* is a Sicilian term for a very small brown snail. See also ***babbaluci, bovolo,*** and ***chiocciolo.***
  Lumache is also the term for snail-shape pasta.

luppoli (LOO-poh-lee)   Hops. From the taxonomic Latin *Humulus lupulus.* Also *bruscandoli.*

M

macca (MAH-kah) Soup made with fava beans, chile peppers, onion, tomato, and *spaghetti*. The word *macca* means abundance.

Macco or *maccù (u'maccù* in dialect) is a puree of dried fava beans flavored with borage and wild fennel, from Sicily. It dates back to antiquity and is served on the feast of *San Giuseppe* (March 19). From *macinare* (to smash or grind food).

maccheroni (mah-keh-ROH-nee) Also *macaroni*. Pasta, shaped into a multitude of forms, usually dried. Most commonly *maccheroni* refers to a dried, tubular pasta shape, often ridged, but it may also refer to long, thin strands of pasta like *spaghetti*. The first mention of the word *maccheroni* as a form of pasta was in a Genoa will in 1279 (suggesting the food had considerable value in a bequest), and the word may derive from *maccare,* meaning to flatten. Every region of Italy has its own favorite versions, from very small *maccheroncini,* such as *pastina* and *ditalini,* to the large *rigatoni.* See also individual shapes and *pasta.*

maccheroni alla campofilone (mah-keh-ROH-nee AH-lah kahm-poh-fee-LOH-neh) Thin egg pasta served with a pork and veal sauce, from the Marches.

maccheroni inferrettati (mah-keh-ROH-nee EEN-feh-reh-TAH-tee) See *busiati.*

maccù See *macca.*

macedonia di frutta (mah-seh-DOH-n'yah dee FROO-tah) Fruit salad. Some etymologists believe the term may refer to the number of ethnically mixed people in the region of Macedonia in ancient Greece.

macelleria (mah-cheh-leh-REE-ah) Butcher shop, from the Latin *macellarius.*

macerazione   carbonica (mah-cheh-rah-zee-OH-neh   kahr-BOH-nee-kah)   Carbonic maceration, a process in which whole grapes are placed in sealed containers under pressure in order to ferment partially and generate carbon dioxide gas. It is used principally in making *vino novello.*

macinare (mah-chee-NAH-reh)   To grind or crush food. From the Latin *maceratus* (to soften).

macis (MAH-chees)   Mace. The fibrous inner covering of nutmeg. It is native to the Moluccas. From the Greek *makir.*

madia (MAH-dee-ah)   Wooden trough used for making bread. Formerly used for making *pasta.*

mafalda (mah-FAHL-dah)   Braided semolina flour bread, from Sicily. The word is a Sicilian girl's name.

mafaradda (mah-fah-RAH-dah)   Earthenware dish used for making *cuscus* in Sicily.

maggiorana (mah-j'yoh-RAH-nah)   Sweet marjoram, *Origanum majorana.* Used as a seasoning in soups, stuffings, and many other foods. From Middle Latin *majorana.*
   Wild marjoram *(Origanum vulgare)* is known as **origano.**

magro (MAH-groh)   Lean, as applied to meat. Also, meatless. From the Latin *macer.*

maiale (MYE-ah-leh)   Pork. A principal meat of the Italian diet. It is eaten fresh, usually roasted, also cured and as sausages. The hams are cured as **prosciutto** and salami. The head *(testa)* is made into **soppressata.** The cheeks and jowls are cured as **guanciale;** the belly is cured as **pancetta. Lardo** and **strutto** are made from the fat.
   Whole suckling pig may be roasted or turned over an open fire, a preparation called **porchetta. Arista** is boneless roast pork. In the Marches, fresh ham is cooked in milk, a dish called *maiale al latte.* In Milan, the long-cooked **cassoeula** is made with the ribs and other parts and pork sausage.

maionese (mye-oh-NEH-zeh)   Mayonnaise. In Italy, it is made with egg yolks, oil, and lemon juice, without mustard. The origins of the name, which comes from French, are debated. French chef Marie-Antoine Carême wrote that the name comes from the French verb *manier* (to stir), while others believe the word is a corruption of the town of Bayonne, where it is said to have been created. The editor of France's *Larousse Gastronomique* contended that the word is from *moyeunaise,* derived from Old French *moyeu* (egg yolk). Still others insist it was created at and named after the town of Port Mahon, after its capture in June 1756 by the Duc de Richelieu.

maiorchino   (mah-yohr-KEE-noh)   Ewe's milk cheese made with black peppercorns and pressed into basket molds, from Sicily.

mais   (MYE-ees)   Corn, which arrived from the New World in the 16th century via the eastern trade routes to the Veneto, where it was called *grano-turco* in the mistaken belief that it was of Turkish origin. It was soon extensively grown. The flour became the basis for *polenta* and many breads and desserts, especially in northern Italy. From the Spanish *maiz,* derived from a Taino Indian word *mahiz.*

malaga   (MAH-lah-gah)   Rum raisin flavor, as in ice cream.

malfatti   (mahl-FAH-tee)   "Badly made." Cheese-and-spinach *gnocchi* of a lumpish shape that gives them their name. In Lombardy, they are made with spinach in the dough; in Emilia-Romagna, with Swiss chard.

malloreddus   (mah-loh-REH-duss)   "Small bulls." Also *maccarones, cravaos, gnocchetti sardi,* and *ciciones.* Tiny *gnocchi* made from *semolina,* saffron, and salt and shaped into small ridged dumplings with a slit down the center, from Sardinia. They are commonly dressed with a tomato, garlic, onion, and basil sauce or with a spicy sausage sauce flavored with saffron.

maltagliati   (mahl-tah-L'YAH-tee)   "Badly cut." Diamond-shape home-made pasta, often scraps of leftover pasta. They are added to soup.

malto   (MAHL-toh)   Malt extract. From Old English *mealt.*

malvasia   (mahl-vah-ZEE-ah)   The name of a great number of grape varieties grown in southern Europe and throughout Italy, to make such wines as *Malvasia, Istriana* in Friuli, *Malvasia di Casorzo d'Asti* and *Malvasia di Castelnuovo Don Bosco* in Piedmont, *Malvasia di Bosa (DOC)* and *Malvasia di Cagliari* in Sardinia. *Malvasia delle Lipari* is a Sicilian variety brought by the Greeks and made into a *passito.* The name comes from the Italian name for the Greek port of Monemvasia, which exported highly regarded dessert wines from the eastern Mediterranean. Also *malmsey.*

Mamertino   (mah-mehr-TEE-noh)   Sweet dessert wine from Sicily, said to be one of Julius Caesar's favorites.

mandarino   (mahn-dah-REE-noh)   Mandarin orange, also called tangerine. From the Malay *menteri* (counselor), referring to the officials of the Chinese Empire, whose robes were a bright red-orange color. The best Italian varieties are cultivated in Sicily.

Mandarinetto is a cordial made from the *mandarino.* The *mandarancio* is a cross between the mandarin orange and a regular sweet orange.

mandilli de saêa   (mahn-DEE-lee deh SAY'ah)   "Silk handkerchiefs." Very thin Ligurian *lasagne* pasta sheets, commonly served with a *pesto* sauce.

mandolino   (mahn-doh-LEE-noh)   Mandolin. A slicing utensil for vegetables, usually with several blades. It is named after the musical instrument.

mandorla   (MAHN-dohr-lah)   Almond. From the Late Latin *amandula*.
   Mandorlini are macaroons made in the town of Pontelagoscuro in Emilia-Romagna. *Mandorlato* is a nougat candy containing almonds, from the Veneto.

Mandrolisai   (mahn-droh-lee-ZAI)   *DOC* red wine of Sardinia, made from *bovale sardo* and *cannonau* grapes in the region of Mandrolisai.

mangiatutto   (mahn-jah-TOO-toh)   "Eat it all." Snow peas. Also refers to thin asparagus eaten whole, including the stems.

manicaretto   (mah-nee-kah-REH-toh)   Any kind of delicacy, from elaborate main dishes to pastries.

maniche   (MAH-nee-keh)   "Sleeves." A commercially made short dried *maccheroni,* sometimes ribbed. From the Latin *manica*.

manicotti   (mah-nee-KOH-tee)   Tube *maccheroni,* 4 to 5 inches long. Usually stuffed with *ricotta* cheese and ham and served with tomato sauce, sometimes baked. *Manicotti* derives from the Latin *manica* (sleeve).

manini   (mah-NEE-nee)   "Little hands." Bread shaped like crossed hands, a specialty of Ferrara. From the Latin *manus* (hand).

manteca   (mahn-TEH-kah)   Cheese with a center of butter, from Basilicata.

mantecato   (mahn-teh-KAH-toh)   "Pounded." A cooking term for ingredients pounded into a form of paste, as with *baccalà* when it is made into a creamy puree with olive oil and seasonings, or with *risotto* when butter and *parmigiano* are added at the end of the cooking process.
   Mantecato also refers to pasta quickly warmed in a skillet with some of its sauce and a little *parmigiano* just before serving it at the table.

manzo   (MAHN-zoh)   Beef. Refers also to a steer four years or older. *Bue* refers more specifically to one less than four years old. *Torello* is an uncastrated young bull, slaughtered at two years.
   Beef is widely used in Italian cooking and every part of the animal is used. Florence is famous for its thick T-bone steak, called *bistecca alla fiorentina,* and beef is usually one of the meats in a *bollito misto. Coda alla vaccinara* is oxtail stew, from Rome. Meat loaf is *polpettone.* Meatballs are *polpette.*

marasca   (mah-RAH-skah)   Morello cherry. A wild sour cherry used to make maraschino liqueur. From *marasca* (bitter), which comes from the Latin *amarus*. See also *amarena.*

Marasche are cookies containing such a cherry and covered with sliced almonds, from Bologna.

Marche   (MAHR-keh)   The Marches, a region of Italy bordered by the Apennines on the west and the Adriatic Sea on the east. The coastline provides a bounty of seafood—crustaceans, mollusks, and fish—much of it cooked with tomato sauce. The fish soup **brodetto** contains many kinds of fish and shellfish. Ancona is famous for its dried cod stew called **stoccafisso.** The mountains are a good source of game, especially hare and rabbit, which figure in dishes like *coniglio in* **porchetta,** rabbit stuffed with wild fennel and cooked like suckling pig.

A special pasta dish of the region, **vincigrassi,** is a very rich **lasagne.**

The best known cheese is **caciotta,** made from mixed cow's and ewe's milk, especially *caciotta d' Urbino,* and **pecorino,** such as *pecorino le marchigiano* and *pecorino sotto le foglie di noce,* wrapped in walnut leaves.

The Marches have 10 **DOC** zones that produce a number of crisp whites, including **verdicchio** and hearty reds like **Rosso Conero** and **Rosso Piceno.**

margarina   (mahr-gah-REE-nah)   Margarine, a butter substitute created in the late 1860s by French chemist Hippolyte Mège-Mouries in a contest sponsored by Napoleon III. Originally made with beef and pork fat, it is now made exclusively with vegetable oils. It is little used in Italy. From the French *margarine.*

mariconda, la   (lah mah-ree-KOHN-dah)   Soup with dumplings called *mariconde* made with bread crumbs, egg, butter, cheese, and nutmeg, from Lombardy.

LA MARICONDA

6 cups bread crumbs from 2- to 3-day-old Italian bread	**2 tablespoons minced Italian parsley**
1 cup milk	**Pinch of freshly grated nutmeg**
5 tablespoons butter	**2 eggs**
7 tablespoons grated parmigiano	**Freshly ground pepper**
	8 cups beef broth

In a bowl, moisten the bread crumbs in the milk and let stand for 20 minutes. Squeeze out the excess milk. In a sauté pan, heat the butter, add the bread crumbs, and stir constantly until the bread crumbs are dry. Put the bread crumbs into a bowl and let cool. Add 4 tablespoons of the *parmigiano,* the parsley, nutmeg, eggs, and pepper and mix. Bring the broth to a gentle simmer. In the meantime, with the help of a spoon, form little dumplings of the mixture about the size of marbles and place them on a floured board. Gently lower them into the broth and let cook for 5 minutes. Serve with the remaining *parmigiano.* Serves 6.

---

marille (mah-REE-leh)   Short, ridged *maccheroni.* Joined side by side, they form a double-barrel shape. Made by the Neapolitan company Voiello.

marinara, alla (AH-lah mah-ree-NAH-rah)   "Mariner's style." A freshly made sauce, commonly used on pasta. The ingredients may vary but usually include garlic, olive oil, and crushed tomatoes with oregano or other herbs.

Its name may be explained by the story of how fishermen's wives would make a fast, fresh sauce upon the arrival of their husbands with the day's catch, which would then be added to the sauce to cook. From the Latin *mare* (sea).

marinata (mah-ree-NAH-tah)   Marinade. In Italy, there are two basic types: *marinata corta,* which is quite mild and simple, like a concoction of oil, lemon, and salt; and *m. lunga,* which usually contains vegetables and wine. Also *conce.*

Marino (mah-REE-noh)   *DOC* white wine of Latium, made from *trebbiano* and *malvasia* grapes grown around the town of Marino.

maritozzo (mah-ree-TOH-t'zoh)   Lenten raisin buns, originally from Rome. In the Marches, they are flavored with lemon peel.

marmellata (mahr-mah-LAH-tah)   Jam. From the Portuguese *marmelo* (quince), the fruit from which the first marmalades were made.

marmitta torinese (mahr-MEE-tah toh-ree-NEH-seh)   Soup containing seasonal vegetables, potatoes, basil, onion, and garlic, served over a slice of bread, from Turin. *Marmitta* is a pot.

marmora (mahr-MOH-rah)   "Marble-smooth [fish]." Striped bream, *Lithognathus mormyrus.* Usually grilled. From the Latin *marmor* (marble).

marro (MAH-roh)   Dish of lamb intestines flavored with garlic, rosemary, and *pancetta,* a specialty of L'Aquila in Abruzzo.

marrone (mah-ROH-neh)   See *castagna.*

Marsala (mahr-SAH-lah)   *DOC* golden fortified wine of Sicily made from white *catarratto, grillo,* and *inzolia* grapes and red *perricone, calabrese,* and *nerello mascalese* grapes grown around Marsala. It was created by wine shipper John Woodhouse in 1773 for the English market after he discovered that fortifying the wine with grape spirit prevented it from spoilage on the journey to the English market. *Marsala* was popularized after Lord Nelson adopted the wine in 1798 as an onboard beverage. In 1832, the firm of Florio built enormous facilities for the production of the wine for export.

Today *Marsala* is fortified by adding *sifone,* made from sweet wine and alcohol and/or **vino cotto,** cooked-down must. *Marsala Fine* (17 percent alcohol) uses more of the latter than the former, while *Marsala Superiore* (18 percent alcohol) is well aged. *Marsala Vergine* or *Solera* (18 percent alcohol) is extremely dry and does not use either *vino cotto* or *sifone,* being instead a blend of aged wines from different barrels, as in the Spanish sherry system called *solera. Stravecchio* is a *Marsala Vergine* aged in wood for ten years.

In addition to sipping, *Marsala* is used extensively in the Italian kitchen, in such preparations as **mazariso** and **zabaione.**

Martina Franca   (mahr-TEE-nah FRAHN-kah)   **DOC** white wine, some sparkling of Apulia, made from grapes grown around the town of Martina Franca. Also *Martina.*

marubini   (mah-roo-BEE-nee)   "Little rubies." Stuffed scalloped pasta rounds, a specialty of Cremona. *Marubini* may be stuffed with roast pork, braised beef, beef marrow, or calf's brains, and **parmigiano.** In the past, *marubini* were meatless, made with **mollica, parmigiano,** and herbs.

marzapane   (mahr-t'zah-PAH-neh)   Marzipan. An almond and sugar paste that is shaped into forms such as **frutta di martorana** or rolled to coat the sides of **cassata.**

The word may derive from Latin for *marci pan* or *marco panis* (bread of Saint Mark); others believe it is from an old Italian word for a small candy box or a container of rare coins, which may itself derive from the Arabic *martaban* or *mawtaban,* which meant "king sitting still" and referred to the image of a sitting Christ imprinted on Venetian coins.

marzemino   (mar-t'zeh-MEE-noh)   Red wine grape widely grown in Lombardy and Trentino.

marzolino   (mar-t'zoh-LEE-noh)   Ewe's milk cheese, traditionally made in March *(marzo),* from Tuscany and Latium. See also **pecorino.**

masaro alla valesana   (mah-ZAH-roh AH-lah vah-leh-SAH-nah) Wild duck marinated in vinegar, thyme, and tarragon, barded with **pancetta,** baked, then cut into pieces and sautéed in butter with wine, anchovies, onions, and capers, from the Veneto.

mascarpone   (mah-skahr-POH-neh)   A fresh cow's milk cheese. It is soft, almost the consistency of butter but with slightly less butterfat. The best is made in Lombardy and Emilia-Romagna. *Mascarpone* originated in the area of Lodi, with references back to 1168, and its name probably derives from *mascherare,* meaning to dress up. Others believe the name refers to an Alpine *ricotta* called *macherpin*. A very small amount of *mascarpone* is made from goat's milk. Also *mascherpone*.

mastrich (mah-STREEK)   A mixture of **mascarpone,** egg yolks, sugar, rum, grated lemon peel, and olive oil served chilled with chocolate sauce, from Lombardy.

matagliati (mah-tah-L'YAH-tee)   "Badly cut." **Tagliatelle** cut into irregular pieces, from Modena.

mataloc (mah-tah-LOAK)   Large domed sponge cake similar to **panettone** in appearance. It contains nuts, raisins, grated citrus peel, fennel seed, and other spices. A specialty of the Lake Como region. From the Spanish *matalauga* (anise).

matasse (mah-TAH-seh)   "Tangles." Pasta ribbons similar to *fettuccine.*

Matino (mah-TEE-noh)   **DOC** red and rosé wines of Apulia, made from **negroamaro** grapes grown around Matino.

mattarello (mah-tah-REH-loh)   Rolling pin. Also *stenderello.*

mattone, al (ahl mah-TOH-neh)   "With a brick." Refers to a cooking technique of flattening an ingredient like chicken or artichokes with a heavy weight while grilling or roasting.

mazariso, il (eel mah-t'zah-REE-soh)   Cake made from ground pistachio flour, eggs, oranges, butter, and **Marsala,** from Sicily. After baking, it is iced with confectioners' sugar flavored with saffron and orange juice.

mazzafegati (MAH-t'zah-feh-GAH-tee)   "Liver bundle." Pork sausage with orange peel, pine nuts, and raisins, from Umbria.

mazzancolla (mah-t'zahn-KOH-lah)   Imperial prawn *(Penaeus caramote)*. It can grow up to 9 inches long. Also *mezzancolla, spannoccho, mazzacuogno,* and *gambero imperialo.*

mazzarelle d'agnello (mah-t'zah-REH-leh D'AHN-y'ehl-loh)   "Lamb bundle." Dish of lamb's innards wrapped in chard or beet greens, then braised in white wine, from Abruzzo.

mazzetto odoroso (mah-T'ZEH-toh oh-doh-ROH-soh)   "Fragrant bunch." Sprigs of parsley, rosemary, thyme, sage, and sometimes marjoram tied together with bay leaf and used as a flavoring in soups and stews.

medaglione (meh-dah-L'YOH-neh)   "Medallions." Thick slices of meat or fish.

megalolo (meh-GAH-loh-loh)   Fruit graft of lemon onto a bitter orange tree, from Calabria.

meino (meh-EE-noh)   Round sweet cornmeal bread served with heavy cream, a specialty of Lombardy.

mela (MEH-lah)   Apple. By the time of Pliny the Elder in the 1st century, there were at least 36 different kinds of apples known to the Romans. Today, apples are eaten as fresh fruit, as well as poached *(mele cotte)* and used as a flavoring, stuffing, and the base of many desserts. From the Latin *malum*.

mela cotogna (meh-lah koh-TOH-n'yah)   Quince. The ancient Romans imported quince from Cydonia on the island of Crete. Today, both wild and cultivated quince are used. The fruit is poached or baked or made into jam or into *cotognata,* a quince paste, from Sicily and Apulia. It is traditionally molded in special forms, though it can be molded in a pan and cut into squares. From the Latin *melilmelum* (sweet apple).

melagrana (meh-lah-GRAH-nah)   Pomegranate. The ancient Romans imported them from Carthage and called the fruit *malum punicum* (Punic apple), as well as *malum granatum* (seed apple), from which both the Italian name derives as well as the Middle French *pomme grenate*.

Italians use the juice of the pomegranate for fruit drinks, jellies, and desserts.

melanzana (meh-lahn-ZAH-nah)   Eggplant. The eggplant came to Italy from the Middle East, possibly during the Crusades. Today there are countless varieties of eggplant, in many sizes, shapes, and colors. Also *melanciana, mulignano, melo di giano,* and *petonciani.*

Many dishes made with eggplant are of southern Italian origin. *Melanzana alla **parmigiana** or parmigiana di melanzane,* a casserole made with sliced eggplant and tomato sauce topped with melted **mozzarella** and baked, is claimed by several regions as their own and would seem to refer to Parma style, but it is definitely of southern origins. One Sicilian culinary authority, Mary Taylor Simeti, believes the word *parmigiana* is actually a corruption of the Sicilian dialect word *palmigiana,* meaning shutters, referring to the layers of eggplant in the dish. *M. a quaglia* is deep-fried eggplant cut so that the slices curl to resemble a quail's tail from Sicily. *M. a beccafico* is slices of eggplant stuffed with **passoli e pinoli,** bread crumbs, and **pecorino,** plumped up to resemble the warbler known as **beccafico,** also from Sicily. **Pasta alla Norma** is pasta with eggplant in tomato sauce with **ricotta salata,** from Catania in Sicily. *M. al funghetto* or *fungetiello* is a dish of eggplant chopped up like mushrooms and sautéed in oil with garlic, pepper, and parsley, from Naples and Calabria. Eggplants may also be dried or preserved **sott'olio.** See also **caponata.**

melassa di miele (meh–LAH–sah dee mee–EH–leh) "Honey molasses." Bitter honey. From the Late Latin *mellaccum* (grape must) and *mel* (honey).

melica (MEH–lee–kah) Corn or cornmeal. *Meliga* is a cornmeal cookie from Piedmont. See also *mais.*

melone (meh–LOH–neh) Melon. Known to the ancient Romans, who called the fruit *melopepo,* but with the empire's downfall, the melon disappeared from Italy until the 14th century.

There are two principal groups of melons: muskmelons, including cantaloupes and winter melons; and watermelons, all of which are grown in Italy. Muskmelons are often eaten with *prosciutto* as an *antipasto.* See also *anguria* and *gelo di melone.*

melú (MEH–loo) Blue whiting, *Micromesistus poutassou.*

Menfi (MEHN–fee) Red and white wines of Sicily made on the coast near Menfi. Most are produced by the Settesoli Cooperative.

menola (meh–NOH–lah) Picarel, *Spicara maena,* a fish lowly regarded for culinary purposes.

mensa (MEHN–sah) A cafeteria-style eatery usually associated with a factory or university. The word is the equivalent of the English word for such a room, a *mess.* Both words derive from the Latin word for a table.

menta (MEHN–tah) Spearmint, *Mentha spicata.* The name derives from the Greek nymph named Minthe, who was trampled into the ground by Persephone after the goddess found her in the arms of Persephone's husband, Pluto. According to the myth, Minthe lives on as a fragrant plant.

Mentuccia is wild mint or peppermint, *Mentha peperita. Nepitella* is a form of catnip, *Nepeta cataria.*

menu (MEH–n'yoo) Restaurant menu. From the French. A *menu a prezzo fisso* is a fixed-price menu that usually includes the chef's specials of the day at a reasonable price. A *menu di degustazione* is a tasting menu of several small courses served at a restaurant. A *menu turistico,* which must be posted outside the restaurant by law, is a reasonably priced menu of standard items, which are usually not among the best the restaurant has to offer.

Meranese di Collina (meh–rah–NEH–zeh dee koh–LEE–nah) *DOC* zone in Trentino-Alto Adige that produces a red wine from *schiava* grapes grown around Merano. Also *meraner Hugel.*

merenda   (meh–REHN–dah)   A snack enjoyed at mid–morning, tea time, or the late afternoon. In Piedmont, an afternoon snack is called *l'dop disnè le marende*. *Merendare* means to go for a snack or a picnic.

merendine del granduca   (meh–rehn–DEE–neh dell grahn–DOO–kah) "Granduke's snacks." Crepes with a filling of strawberries, *ricotta,* and *malvasia* wine, from Tuscany. *Merendare* means to go for a snack or picnic.

meringa   (meh–REEN–gah)   Meringue. Meringue shells are called *gusci di meringa.*

merlano   (mehr–LAH–noh)   Whiting, *Merlangius merlangus.* Silver–sided, white–flesh fish, a member of the cod family.

merli   (mehr–LEE)   Blackbirds, rarely eaten unless nothing else is available. The word is from the Latin *merula.*

merlot   (mehr–LOH)   A Bordeaux grape variety widely propagated in northeastern Italy to meet the world market for a soft tannin red wine of the same name.

merluzzo   (mehr–LOO–t'zoh)   Hake, *Merluccius merluccius.* Atlantic cod, usually salted and dried as *baccalà.* The Mediterranean species is called *nasello. Merluzzo cappellano* is another species called the poor cod, *Trisopterus minutus.* See also **merlano.**

messciua   (meh–SHOO–ah)   "Mixture." Chickpea soup made with wheat or spelt berries, beans, and olive oil, from Liguria. A specialty of La Spezia. Said to derive from stevedores' habit of cooking up a dish made from the stray bits of vegetables and grains on the docks.

messicani   (meh–see–KAHN–nee)   "Mexicans." Dish of veal rolls filled with sausage and eggs, sautéed in butter and flavored with *Marsala,* from Milan. The name derives from their resemblance to Mexican stuffed tortillas.

Metapontum   (meh–tah–POHN–tum)   Wines of Basilicata, made on the Ionian coast around Metaponto. The red is from *negroamaro* and *malvasia nera* grapes, the white from *malvasia bianco* and *trebbiano.*

metodo classico   (MEH–toh–doh KLAH–see–koh)   "Classic method." A term used to signify sparkling wines made by the traditional French *méthode champenoise* of double fermentation for making Champagne.

mezzaluna   (meh–t'zeh–LOO–nah)   "Half moon." Curved chopping knife with two handles. It is rocked back and forth over the food to chop it as finely as desired. Also *lunetta.*

miascia   (mee–AH–sh'yah)   Bread pudding made with apples, pears, raisins, and rosemary, from Lombardy.

miccone (mee-KOH-neh)   "Big bread." Large loaf of bread with a soft center that keeps for several days, from Lombardy.

michetta (mee-KEH-tah)   Round, crusty roll, about 2 ounces in weight, with five sides coming to a button at the top, from Milan. Sometimes called *milanese*. See also *rosetta*.

midolla di pane (mee-DOH-lah dee PAH-neh)   "Bread pulp." The crumb or spongy interior part of a bread loaf.

midollo (mee-DOH-loh)   Beef marrow. From the Latin *medietas* (middle).

miele (mee-YEH-leh)   Honey, from the Latin, *mel*. Beekeeping and the production of honey were mastered by the ancient Romans. It was not until the 19th century, when sugar became cheap, that honey was surpassed as a sweetener. The best Italian honey generally comes from the south, particularly Sicily. Italians use honey in many ways, including eating it fresh with cheese.

migliaccio (mee-L'YAH-ch'yoh)   A baked cake or pudding made with blood pudding or chestnut flour. *Migliaccio napoletano* is a Neapolitan dish made by alternating slices of *polenta,* blood sausage, and *mozzarella.*

mignozzi (mee-N'YOH-t'zee)   Sweet fritters flavored with brandy, from Abruzzo. The word probably refers to the Italian word *mignolo* (little fingers), although *mignotta* means harlot.

mignuice (mee-N'YOO-cheh)   "Little (dumpling)." *Semolina* dumplings from Apulia.

milanese, alla (AH-lah mee-lah-NEH-seh)   "Milan style." Any dish associated with Milan, usually involving butter in the cooking process. *Costoletta alla milanese* and *risotto alla milanese* are two of the best-known dishes of the city.

millassata (mee-lah-SAH-tah)   Omelet made with artichokes, from Sicily.

millecosedde (MEE-leh-koh-SEH-deh)   "A thousand things." Soup of various dried beans, vegetables, and wild mushrooms served with *ditalini* or *spaghetti* broken into thirds, and olive oil, from Calabria.

millefoglie (mee-leh-FOH-l'yeh)   "Thousand leaves." A pastry made like the French *millefeuille*. Consists of layers of *pasta sfogliata* (puff pastry) and *crema pasticcera* (pastry cream) topped or dusted with chocolate.

millerighe (mee-leh-REE-geh)   "Thousand lines." A flattened, fat *maccheroni* with ridges, which give it its name.

milza (MEEL-zah)   Spleen, usually beef or calf. It is often pureed and spread on *crostini*. See also *guastedde*.

minestra (mee-NEHS-trah)   Soup. At one time this term referred to any first course, but today it refers to soup, specifically one with pieces of vegetable or grain in broth, as opposed to a *crema* (pureed soup) or a *zuppa*. From *minestrare* (to administer), probably because the food was portioned out as the only dish served at a meal. *Minestra* has a more liquid consistency than *zuppa,* which is often poured over roasted or fried stale bread. *Minestra di farro* is an ancient soup, still made in Tuscany and Abruzzo, using *farro*. M. *maritata* (married soup) is a vegetable soup made in the south in various local ways. In Naples, it is called *pignato grasso,* and meat is added to the vegetables. M. *paradiso* (paradise soup) is a light egg-based soup from Emilia. M. *mariconda,* made by cooking cheese, eggs, and bread in a broth, is from Brescia. In M. *del prete* (priest's soup), croutons made from a baked pudding of butter, eggs, and cheese are floated in a simple poultry or meat stock. It is a specialty of Emilia-Romagna. M. *di passatelli antica* is a thick soup made with beef marrow and eggs, in Emilia-Romagna. M. *di tennerumi* is a Palermo dish made with the tenderest leaves and shoots of zucchini, cooked with tomato, oil, onion, garlic, anchovies, and basil into a stewlike soup. Small pieces of pasta are added in at the end.

   Minestrina is a light broth containing *pastina* or *semolina*. In Modena *minestrina* is made with spinach. See also *crema, passatelli, minestrone,* and *zuppa.*

minestrone (mee-neh-STROH-neh)   "Big soup." Hearty vegetable soup. The ingredients vary from region to region. There are at least three or four vegetables in addition to onions, carrots, celery, potatoes, and tomatoes. From the Latin *ministro* (to serve).

   Minestrone alla fiorentina, from Florence, is made with a *soffritto* of pork, chile peppers, and chicken giblets. M. *fritto* (fried minestrone) is a peasant dish made from the leftovers of *minestrone* bound with a little flour, made into patties, and fried in olive oil, from Liguria. See also *minestra* and *zuppa.*

minni di Sant'Agata (MEE-nee dee sant-AH-gah-tah)   "Saint Agatha's nipples." Puffy, breast-shaped cookies or breads named after the Sicilian saint whose breasts were cut off as part of her martyrdom, from Catania. She was later healed by St. Peter, who appeared to her in a vision, but was thereafter roasted over hot coals. On the feast of *Sant'Agata* (February 5), parishioners bring loaves of bread to be blessed at the local church in some regions.

minni di virgini (MEE-nee dee veer-JEE-nee)   "Virgins' breasts." Semolina buns filled with pastry cream, so called because they are said to resemble virgins' breasts. They are a specialty of Sicily, traditionally made by nuns, but in deference to the nuns' propriety, they are sometimes called *panotti* (big breads). They are also called **minni di Sant'Agata.**

minuicci   (meen-WEE-chee)   "Little ones." Short *spaghetti* with a hole through it, usually served with tomato and boiled cauliflower in a dish called *cima di cola,* a specialty of Basilicata.

mirtillo   (meehr-TEE-loh)   Bilberry. From the Latin *myrtus* (myrtle).

mirto   (MEER-toh)   Myrtle, from the Latin *myrtus,* the basis for a liqueur called by the same name, from Sardinia.

missoltit   (mee-SOHL-teet)   Preserved fish made from Lake Como and Lake Maggiore. They are air-dried, then placed in barrels called *missolte.* They are skinned, reconstituted in red wine vinegar, and served with olive oil. Also *misortitt, misoltini,* and *missultitt.*

misticanza   (mee-stee-KAHN-zah)   Salad of greens, such as arugula, endive, sorrel, purslane, and watercress.

misto   (MEE-stoh)   "Mixed." A **bollito misto** is a mixture of boiled meats and vegetables. **Fritto misto** is a mixture of fried foods. **Insalata misto** is mixed greens and vegetables in a salad. From the Latin *mixtus.*

mocetta   (moh-CHEH-tah)   **Prosciutto** of chamois, or wild goat. A specialty of Valle d'Aosta, usually served as part of an **antipasto.** Now made from domesticated goat.

moleca   (moh-LEH-kah)   Soft-shell crab. Especially from the lagoon of Venice, where it is caught and eaten during April and May. See also **granchio.**

Molise   (moh-LEE-zeh)   Region of Italy north of Campania, east of Latium, and south of Abruzzo, on the Adriatic Sea. Its historic and political connection to Abruzzo ended when Molise became an independent region in 1963, but it still shares many of the same culinary traditions of Abruzzo, with more of a nod to the south. There is also a significant Albanian-speaking population, which increased after the fall of communism. The food of Molise is uncomplicated, rich in vegetables and pork, spiced with chile peppers, and sauced with tomatoes. There are, however, few dishes unique to Molise. *P'lenta d'iragn,* a white *"polenta"* made with potatoes and wheat and served with a tomato sauce, is one of the more unusual dishes. *Calcioni di ricotta rustici* are **ravioli** stuffed with **ricotta, provolone,** and **prosciutto,** then fried in oil.

The cheeses of Molise include **scamorza,** *mateca,* and **burrino.**

Molise has only two **DOC** zones, **Biferno** and *Pentro di Isernia,* and almost all the wine is consumed in the region itself.

mollica di pane (moh-LEE-kah dee PAH-neh)   The soft interior of bread, used as a binder or sauce thickener. The word *mollica* is sometimes used to refer to bread crumbs, which are more correctly called **pangrattato.** In southern Italy, bread crumbs are substituted in certain dishes for **parmigiano,** which was too expensive for poor people.

molva occhiona (MOHL-vah oh-K'YOH-nah)   "Big-eyed molva." Mediterranean ling, *Molva macrophthalma.* A long, wide-eyed fish similar to whiting. It is usually cut into steaks and fried.

monacone (moh-nah-KOH-neh)   "Fat monk." Casserole made with layers of eggplant, veal, **prosciutto, fontina,** and tomato, from Capri. The name refers to the hearty eating habits of monks.

mondeghili (mohn-deh-GHEE-lee)   Meat croquettes fried in butter, from Lombardy.

Monica di Cagliari (MOHN-nee-kah dee kah-L'YAH-ree)   **DOC** red wine of Sardinia, made from *monica* grapes that originated in Spain. It is usually vinified sweet.

Monica di Sardegna (MOHN-ee-kah dee sahr-DEH-n'yah)   **DOC** red wine of Sardinia, made from *monica* grapes that originated in Spain. Usually vinified sweet or as a **frizzante.**

montasio (mohn-TAH-zee-yoh)   Mild **DOC** cow's milk cheese of Friuli–Venezia Giulia. It was created at the monastery of Moggio in the 13th century. Commonly eaten as a table cheese, it sharpens with aging. It is also used to make **frico.** A more localized version is called *carnia.*

montasù (mon-tah-ZOO)   "Climbing up." Small northern bread made with oil and shaped in a spiral. It weighs between 7 and 10 ounces.

Monte Antico (MOHN-teh ahn-TEE-koh)   Red and white wines of Tuscany, made around Monte Antico (Ancient Mountain).

monte bianco (MOHN-teh bee-AHN-koh)   "White mountain." A dessert confection of chestnut puree topped with whipped cream to look like a snow-capped mountain. It gets its name from Mont Blanc, the highest peak in the Alps.

Montecarlo (mohn-tee-KAHR-loh)   **DOC** zone of Tuscany that produces red and white wines grown around the town of Lucca. The red is made from **Chianti** grapes, as well as *ciliegiolo,* **malvasia nero,** and *syrah.*

Montecompari-Colonna (mohn-teh-kohm-PAH-ree-koh-LOH-nah) **DOC** white wine of Latium, made from several grape varieties grown around Montecompari and Colonna.

Montefalco (mohn-teh-FAHL-koh) *DOC* zone of Umbria. Its best known reds are *Sagrantino di Montefalco*, whose name possibly refers to the sacramental wine of the Franciscan monks who grew the grape, and *Sagrantino di Montefalco passito*, a sweet red wine for dessert.

Montello e Colli Asolani   (mohn-TEH-loh eh KOH-lee ah-soh-LAH-nee)   *DOC* zone of the Veneto that produces *cabernet, merlot,* and *prosecco* wines from grapes grown around the hills of Asolo.

Montepulciano   d'Abruzzo (mohn-teh-pool-chee-AH-noh   dah-BROO-t'zoh) *DOC* red wine of Abruzzo, made from *montepulciano* and *sangiovese* grapes. A *cerasuolo* is also made within the zone. The *montepulciano* grape is used in wines made around Monte Conero in the Marches.

Montescudaio (mohn-teh-skoo-DYE-oh) *DOC* zone of Tuscany that produces white wines from *trebbiano, malvasia,* and *vermentino* grapes, reds from *sangiovese,* and a *vin santo* around the town of Montescudaio.

montone (mohn-TOH-neh)   Mutton, referring to a male sheep when it has reached a year-and-a-half old. It is consumed on occasion in the south of Italy but rarely served in the north. From the Old French *moton* (ram).

Montuni del Reno (mohn-TOO-nee dell REH-noh) *DOC* white wine of Emilia-Romagna from *montuni* grapes grown around the Reno river. Usually vinified as a *frizzante.*

monzette (mohn-ZEH-teh)   Also *cocoidu a pienu.* Stuffed snails, from Sardinia.

monzù (mohn-ZOO)   Cook, chef, usually with reference to the cook of a well-to-do house in southern Italy. The word dates from the 18th century, when the cuisine of France began to influence that of Sicily, and the word itself is a dialect corruption of the French *monsieur* (sir). The *monzù* was held in high esteem among the household staff and was extremely secretive about his work and recipes, which were passed down through an oral tradition to his successors.

morchella (mohr-KEH-lah)   Morel mushrooms, *Morchella esculenta* and *M. conica.* From the French *morille,* which probably derives from Vulgar Latin *maurus* (brown).

more (MOH-reh)   Blackberries. From the Latin *morum.*

Morellino di Scansano (moh-reh-LEE-noh dee skahn-SAH-noh) *DOC* red wine of Tuscany made from *sangiovese* grapes grown around the town of Scansano.

morena (moh-REH-nah)   Lamprey eel, *Muroena helena.*

morlacco (mohr-LAH-koh)   Mountain cheese from the Veneto. Made from partially skimmed cow's milk, it is formed into rounds about 3 inches high and 12 inches in diameter. It has a faintly bitter finish. The word refers to the Morlacchi, a tribe of people indigenous to Dalmatia.

morseddu (mohr-SAY-doo)   "Little morsel." Breakfast dish of Calabria. Pork tripe is stewed in red wine, tomatoes, chile peppers, and herbs. It is eaten in a round roll called a *pitta* or with *pane casareccio.* Also *u murzeddu* and *mursiellu.*

mortadella (mohr-tah-DEH-lah)   Pork sausage made of finely ground meat with spices and larded, from Bologna. It is usually flavored with peppercorns and coriander. The sausages are quite large, from 3 pounds up to 180 pounds. *Mortadella di Amatrice,* made in the town of Amatrice in the Apennines, is flavored with cinnamon and cloves and contains only a single larding of pork fat; it is smoked, then aged for two months.

M. di fegato, from Piedmont, is made with pork liver moistened with red wine.

The name probably derives from *mortaio* (mortar), because the ingredients are mashed down to make the sausage.

Moscadello di Montalcino (moh-skah-DEH-loh dee mohn-tahl-CHEE-noh)   *DOC* sweet, *amabile,* or *liquoroso* white wine of Tuscany made from *moscato* *bianco* grapes around the commune of Montalcino.

moscardino (moh-skahr-DEE-noh)   Small octopus, *Eledone cirrosa* and *Eledone moschata.* In Genoa, it is cooked in oil with garlic, rosemary, and tomatoes, in a dish called *moscardinetti all'inferno.* The term means dandy or fop.

moscato (moh-SKAH-toh)   A widely planted white grape variety. It has a very aromatic bouquet and is used primarily to make sweet or semisweet dessert wines and sparkling wines in Italy. From the Latin *muscus* (musk).

Many regions carry the *moscato* appellation, *Moscato di Trani* in Apulia (**DOC**); *Moscato della Lucania* in Basilicata; *Moscato di Scanzo* in Lombardy; *Moscato di Cagliari (DOC), Moscato di Sardegna (DOC)* and *Moscato di Sorso-Sennori (DOC)* of Sardinia; and *Moscato di Noto (DOC), Moscato di Pantelleria (DOC),* and *Moscato di Siracusa (DOC)* of Sicily. *Moscato d'Asti* is the best known of the *Moscato* wines, although most of the production is outside of the Asti zone.

moscatello (moh-skah-TEH-loh)   "Little Muscat." Muscatel grape or wine made from that grape. From the Latin *muscus* (musk).

mosciame (moh-SH'YAH-meh)   "Flabbies." Dried, salted strips of dolphin, swordfish, or tuna. It is an essential ingredient in *cappon magro.* Called *musseddu* in Sicily. Also *musciame.*

mostaccioli   (moh–stah–CH'YOH–lee)   Small cakes of southern Italy made of honey, flour, orange peel, almonds, and spices. They are cut into diamond shapes and baked, then covered with chocolate icing. Also *mustazzoli* and *mustazzuoli.*

In Piedmont, a cookie called *mostaceu* is made with cornmeal and sweet wine. Both names probably derive from Latin *mustaceum,* meaning a cake made with must.

Mostaccioli is also the name for a tubular pasta shape similar to *penne.*

mostarda   (moh–STAHR–dah)   Preserves. *Mostarda di Cremona* (mustard of Cremona), from Lombardy, is a sweet-and-sour condiment made of various fruits. It is the traditional accompaniment to boiled meats. *M. di Carpi,* from a town in Emilia, is similar but the fruits—pears, apples, and quinces— are cooked in must. In Sicily, *m. di mosto* is a sweet cooked-down must thickened with flour and flavored with orange peel. Nuts are added and it is poured into molds and dried. From the Latin *mustum* (must).

mosto del vino   (MOH–stoh dell VEE–noh)   Wine must, the fresh juice of pressed grapes. The term may also refer to grape pomace, the skins and pits left after the pressing and used to make *grappa,* more properly called *vinaccia.* From the Latin *mustum.*

motella   (moh–TEH–lah)   Three-bearded rockling, *Gadropsarus mediterraneo,* a fish similar to a whiting.

mozzarella   (moh–t'zah–REH–lah)   A soft fresh cheese made from cow's or buffalo's milk. One of the most important and ubiquitous cheeses in Italy, though southern ones are best. Since it is a *pasta filata* cheese, it melts well. The name comes from the verb *mozzare,* meaning the process by which handfuls of the cheese are torn off and twisted during the process. From the Latin *mutilis* (to mutilate).

Mozzarella was once made mostly from buffalo's milk *(mozzarella di bufala),* but when the Nazis retreated from Italy in World War II, they killed off most of the herds. The cheese was then made with cow's milk (today called *fior di latte),* although the buffalo herds have been restocked with animals from India. Today *mozzarella di bufala* is again common, though it often contains only a small percentage of buffalo milk.

Mozzarella is shaped into rounds, braids, basket shapes, or small balls called *bocconcini, ovolini di bufala* (buffalo eggs), or *ciliegine* (little cherries).

Mozzarella in carrozza (mozzarella in a carriage), a specialty of Campania, is slices of *mozzarella* and bread layered into sandwiches that are dredged in egg and bread crumbs, and fried. It is served with either a *marinara* or anchovy sauce. *Spiedini alla romana* is a Roman version of this dish for which the sandwiches are skewered on toothpicks before cooking. See also *provatura.*

'mpepata di cozze (m'peh-PAH-tah dee KOH-zeh) "Peppered mussels." Mussels cooked with lemon, black pepper, and parsley, from Campania.

muffa nobile (MOO-fah NOH-bee-leh) "Noble rot." A mold called *Botrytis cinerea* that attacks and shrivels grapes, concentrating their sugars to produce an intensely sweet wine. A dessert wine is made under this name in Umbria.

muffuliette (moo-foo-L'YEH-teh) Soft rolls flavored with saffron and anise, from Sicily. Often eaten *fuori tavola* or served at tea time.

muggine (MOO-jee-neh) See *cefalo.*

mugnaia, alla (AH-lah moo-N'YAI-yah) Cooked in the robust style of a miller or miller's wife.

Müller-Thurgau (MOO-lehr TOOR-gau) White grape variety that is a cross of *riesling* and *sylvaner,* now widely planted in northern Italy. The variety is named after Dr. Hermann Müller of the Swiss canton of Thurgau. In 1882 at a German viticultural station in Gaiesenheim, he hybridized *riesling* grapes, probably with *sylvaner.*

murianengo (moo-ree-ah-NEHN-goh) Blue-veined cow's or goat's milk cheese, made along the Italy-France border.

murice (MOO-ree-cheh) Murex or sea snail, *Murex brandaris.* Also *ginocchiello.* Also known for its purple dye.

muscoli (MOO-skoh-lee) Mussels, in Liguria (elsewhere in Italy called *cozze*), especially date mussels, *Lithodomus lithophagus,* elsewhere called *datteri di mare.* Called *muscioli* in the Marches, they are stuffed with ham and bread crumbs, then roasted with a tomato sauce. From the Latin *musculus.*

muset (MOO-sett) "Snout." Pork sausage from Friuli. Besides pork meat and rind, it contains chile peppers, cinnamon, and white wine; it is aged for one month. *Brovada* are often added. Also *musetto.*

mustella (moo-STEH-lah) Forkbeard, *Phycis phycis* and *P. blennoides.* Fish similar to whiting.

mustica (MOO-stee-kah) Anchovy or sardine spawn that is salted and dried, then preserved with chile peppers in olive oil, from Calabria.

N

napoletana, alla (AH-lah nah-poh-leh-TAH-nah) "Neapolitan style." Any dish associated with Naples. Usually connotes a dish made with tomatoes, garlic, oil, and eggplant. See also *Campania.*

nasco di Cagliari (NAH-skoh dee kah-L'YAH-ree) *DOC* grape of Sardinia, grown around the city of Cagliari, used in making semisweet amber wines and richer sweet fortified wines.

nasello (nah-SEH-loh) Hake. *Nasello alla palermitana* (Palermo style) is breaded with a mixture of anchovies and bread crumbs, then baked. See also *merluzzo.*

natalizia (nah-tah-LEE-t'zee-ah) Lemon-flavored Christmas bread (the word refers to the Nativity), a specialty of Verona. It is usually baked in a star-shape mold and sprinkled with nuts and *Marsala.*

navone (nah-VOH-neh) Parsnips, which comes in two varieties: one is long and carrot-like, the other more turnip-shape (introduced to European cultivation in the 17th century). Native to northeastern Europe, parsnips were very much a part of the ancient Romans' diet (the best were said to come from Germany) and became one of the principal root vegetables of the Middle Ages, but were superseded by the potato when it was brought back from the New World in the 16th century. Parsnips are usually boiled, added to soups and stews, or made into fritters.

'ncapriata (n'kah-pree-AH-tah) Soup or puree of fava beans and wild greens, particularly chicory, from Apulia.

'ncip 'nciap (n'cheep n'chahp) Neapolitan mixture of leftover chicken and eggs. The term seems to echo the chopping sound of the knife on the cutting board.

'ndocca 'ndocca (N'DOH-kah N'DOH-kah) A pork stew from around Teramo in Abruzzo, in which every part of the pig is cut into chunks and stewed with chile peppers, herbs, vinegar, and spices. The dialect term means a "light tap."

'ndugghia (N'DOO-j'yah) Very spicy pork sausage containing the lungs and liver, from Calabria. Also *'nnuglia.* The dialect word derives from the French name for a similar sausage, *andouille,* from a time when Calabria was occupied by the French.

nebbiolo (neh-bee-OH-loh) A generic name for Piedmont grapes not classified under the **DOC** or **DOCG** regulations. In print the name dates to 1303 and probably refers to *nebbia,* the fog that blankets the hills of the area during the October harvest.

 Nebbiolo is the principal grape in many of Piedmont's best wines, including **Barbaresco** and **Barolo.** A clone called *picutener* is the basis for **carema.** **Spanna** is the name for the grape used in eastern Piedmont, especially where **Gattinara** is made. *Nebbiolo d'Alba* is a **DOC** red wine of Piedmont that makes a wide range of wines that includes *Barolo* and *Barbaresco.* Outside of Piedmont, principally in the Valle d'Aosta and Lombardy, the grape is known as *chiavennasca.*

necci (NEH-chee) Chestnut flour crepes baked in terra-cotta forms and served with **pecorino** and **ricotta,** from Tuscany. *Neccio* is a chestnut cake.

negroamaro (neh-groh-ah-MAH-roh) A red grape of Apulia, whose name means "black bitter," used on its own or blended with **malvasia** *nera.* It is Italy's sixth most propagated varietal. Also *Negro Amaro.*

Negroni (neh-GROH-nee) Cocktail made with **Campari,** gin, and sweet vermouth. Said to be named after Count Camillo Negroni, who concocted the drink around 1935 at the Casoni Bar in Florence.

neonata (neh-oh-NAH-tah) "Newborn." Tiny fry fish. From New Latin *neonatus.*

nepitella (neh-pee-TEH-lah) Wild mint, *Nepeta cataria,* a variant of catnip. From the Latin *nepeta.*

nerello mascalese (neh-REH-loh mah-skah-LEH-seh) A red grape of Sicily, used to make *nerello siciliano* wine.

nero d'avola (NEH-roh D'AH-voh-lah) A red wine grape, considered among the best in Calabria and Sicily, used in a wide variety of wines. Also *Calabrese.*

nervetti in insalata (nehr–VEH–tee een een-sah-LAH-tah) Cold salad with calf's foot, from Lombardy. The name means "little nerves in a salad." From the Latin *nervi*.

nespola (NEH-spoh-lah) Medlar, *Mespilus germanica*. A tart fruit that must show signs of serious decay before it can be consumed. The term *nespola* also refers to a medlar-like fruit commonly called loquat in English. In the south, the Neapolitan medlar called *azarola (Crataegus azarolus)* is smaller and sweeter and may be eaten fresh or made into preserves or liqueurs. From the Latin *mespilus*.

nidi di carnevale (NEE-dee dee kahr-neh-VAH-leh) "Carnival nests." Dessert made of chocolate pasta ribbons coiled into nestlike shapes and allowed to dry. They are then deep-fried until crisp and served with a sauce of honey, brandy, and blanched almonds, from Tuscany.

nidi di schiuma (NEE-dee dee skee-YOO-mah) "Nests of white-caps." *Capellini* made into the shape of nests, then fried. They are then drizzled with honey, cinnamon, and candied orange peel, from Sicily.

nieddera (NEE-eh-deh-rah) Sardinian name meaning black, for the Spanish grape variety called *bovale,* used in making a strong red wine.

nocciola (noh-chee-OH-lah) Hazelnut. Both varieties, oblong and round, are cultivated in Italy, with the best grown in Sicily. Hazelnuts are eaten fresh, made into flour, put into sauces and stuffings, candied, covered with chocolate, baked in cakes, and are part of the recipe for *gianduja.* The word is a diminutive of *noce* (nut), which derives from the Latin *nux*.

noce (NOH-cheh) Nut, especially walnut. From the Latin *nux*. Called *cocoro* in Sardinia.

The term *noce* also refers to the eye of the round of beef or veal and to the meat of a scallop.

noce di cocco (NOH-cheh dee KOH-koh) Coconut, which appeared in Egypt in the 6th century, imported from the Indian Ocean. But it took several centuries for the coconut, which took the Latin taxonomic name *Cocos nucifera,* to come to Europe, and despite Marco Polo's mention of having eaten one in the Orient, the coconut was not known in Italy until the 18th century. Today in Italy, coconuts are eaten fresh, are a popular sidewalk concession, and may be added to desserts or made into ice creams and sorbets.

noce moscata (NOH-cheh moh-SKAH-tah) "Muscat nut." Nutmeg, which only came to Italy in the late Middle Ages through the trade routes of the Middle East after the Crusades, became one of the popular spices of Europe. It is used in a wide variety of sweets, stuffings, sauces, and condiments.

nocino (noh–CHEE-noh)   A liqueur made from green walnuts. Traditionally picked on the eve of the *Festa di San Giovanni* (June 24), the nuts are placed in alcohol with spices and lemon peel and left in the sun for 40 days. The liqueur is then filtered and drunk on All Souls' Day (November 2) to honor the dead.

nodino (noh-DEE-noh)   Noisette of veal, cut about 1½ inches thick, from Lombardy. From the Latin *nodus* (node).

nonna, della (DEH-lah NOH-nah)   "Grandma's style." A dish prepared with a homestyle traditional flavor. Also *alla nonna.*

norcina, alla (AH-lah nohr-CHEE-nah)   "Norcina style." Refers to a dish made as in Norcia in Umbria, usually denoting the use of pork in the dish. Also *alla norsina.* A norcineria is a pork butcher's shop. Norcia was famous for its butchers at least since the 17th century.

Norma, alla (AH-lah NOHR-mah)   Also *alla Bellini.* A pasta dish from Sicily. Usually made with **penne** or **spaghetti,** with a sauce containing tomato, fried eggplant, and **ricotta salata.** The dish, of which there are many versions—all containing eggplant—is widely believed to be named after the opera *Norma* (1821) by Vincenzo Bellini, who was born in Catania in eastern Sicily. Most authorities say the dish was created to commemorate the first performance of the opera. But Italian cooking authority Giuliano Bugialli insists the name merely means "pasta prepared in the normal way."

PASTA ALLA NORMA

1 eggplant	Salt and pepper
Salt	1 pound penne or spaghetti
½ cup olive oil	10 basil leaves, coarsely chopped
1 garlic clove, crushed	½ cup grated ricotta salata
10 ripe tomatoes, peeled, seeded, and chopped	

Slice the eggplant and place on a slanted board. Sprinkle with salt and place under a weight for 1 hour to force out the bitter water.

Heat ¼ cup of the olive oil in a saucepan, add the garlic, and cook until golden. Add the tomatoes and salt to taste. Bring to a simmer and cook over medium heat until the sauce has reduced by a third. Season with salt and pepper to taste, remove from the heat, and set aside.

Wash off the salt from the eggplant slices and pat dry. Heat the remaining ¼ cup olive oil in a sauté pan and fry the eggplant until golden brown on both sides. Remove from the pan, drain on paper towels, then coarsely chop.

Cook the *penne* or *spaghetti* in a large pot of boiling salted water until **al dente,** drain, and place in a large sauté pan on high heat. Add half the tomato sauce, the eggplant, half the basil leaves, and half the *ricotta.* Toss briefly and cook through. Serve in a large dish with the rest of the sauce, *ricotta,* and basil. Serves 4.

---

nosiola (noh-see-OH-lah)   A white grape variety of Trentino, used in making dry white wines and as the base for **vin santo.**

nostrale (noh-STRAH-leh)   Any food that is homegrown or locally grown. From the Latin *nostras* (native).

nostrano (noh-STRAH-noh)   "Our kind." In Trentino-Alto Adige it refers to locally made **grana** cheeses. In Sicily it refers to a local type of lettuce. See **lattuga.**

nucatuli (noo-kah-TOO-lee)   Sicilian Christmas almond and fig pastry whose name probably derives from Arabic *nuqulat,* meaning confectionary or dried sweet. When made into a single large version it is called *la luna di maometto* (the moon of Mohammed).

nuragus (noo-RAH-gus)   **DOC** white grape of Sardinia that once made a robust wine often cut with water but is now usually used to make a white light wine of little character. The name *nuragus* refers to ancient Sardinian cone-shaped stone houses in the area of Cagliari.

nzugna (N'ZOO-n'yah)   Dialect word for **sugna** (pork fat), from Naples. It may also refer to melted butter.

O

oca (OH-kah) Goose, which has been domesticated since Neolithic times. Also *papero*. The ancient Romans held the goose in high esteem and for centuries before Christ did not eat it all, reserving a place in the temple of Juno for the bird. Later the Romans found the geese of Gaul far more appetizing than their own, importing the birds through Naples, where they were fattened and then herded to markets in Rome and other cities of Italy. On the orders of Charlemagne, Europe became well stocked with domesticated flocks in the Middle Ages. The most popular geese for eating are the Embden and the Toulouse, preferably less than ten months old. They are usually roasted. The liver is often fattened to make *fegato grasso.*

occhialone (oh-k'yah-LOH-neh) "Big-eyed (fish)." Red bream, *Pagellus bogaraveo.* Grilled or used in soup. From the Latin *oculus.*

occhiata (oh-K'YAH-tah) "Fat-eyed (fish)." Saddled bream, *Oblada melanura.* Usually poached. From the Latin *oculus.*

occhi di pernice (OH-kee dee pehr-NEE-cheh) "Partridge eyes." Very tiny pasta rings used in soups. From the Latin *oculus.*

occhio di bue (OH-k'yoh dee BOO-eh) "Eye of the ox." A fried egg. From the Latin *oculus.*

odori (oh-DOH-ree) Aromatics, such as onion, carrot, and celery. From the Latin *odor* (smell).

ofelle (oh-FEH-leh) "Round (ravioli)." *Ravioli* made with a potato dough and stuffed with spinach, veal, and sausage, from Friuli.

offa (OH-fah) Small cake or cookie. *Offella* is more of a tart. In Lombardy, *offelle* are shaped into an oval and sometimes stuffed with apricot jam.

In Emilia, they are stuffed with marzipan. In Friuli, they are savory, made with spinach, pork, veal, and onion.

olio   (OH-l'yoh)   Oil. From the Latin *oleum.*

Italians principally use olive oil *(olio d'oliva)* and blends of olive and cottonseed oils for cooking. The best olive oil is never treated with chemicals. To be labeled *vergine,* the oil must be from the first pressing. It is very low in acidity and is best used as a dressing rather than as a cooking medium, especially since it is expensive. Newly developed **DOC** regulations will govern the quality of olive oil based on the means of extraction and on acidity. The grades are: *extra vergine,* from the first pressing of the olives by mechanical means only and with an acidity of less than 1 percent; *sopraffino vergine,* not more than 1.5 percent acidity; *fino vergine,* not more than 3 percent; *vergine,* not more than 4 percent. Olive oils above 4 percent are called simply *olio d'oliva,* and are usually blends of chemically rectified *(olio rettificato* or *olio miscelato)* or de-acidified oils. *Olio di sansa di oliva* is an oil made from the dregs *(sansa)* of the pressed olives.

Olii varii (various oils) is a general term for oils from sources other than olives.

Olio nuovo (new oil) is oil pressed from green, not fully ripe olives.

See also *oliva.*

olio santo   (OH-l'yoh SAHN-toh)   "Holy oil." Olive oil flavored by steeping chile peppers in the bottle.

oliva   (oh-LEE-vah)   Olive. From the Latin.

One of the most important foods and crops of Italy, the olive originated in the Middle East, or possibly Crete, and was first planted in Latium in the 6th century B.C. Olives are eaten by themselves as a snack, used in many dishes and breads, and pressed into olive oil. In Sicily, black olives are cured in brine, and when dried and shriveled are called *accirate* (in bloom). Purple *gaeta* olives come from Campania. Liguria produces many olives, including the salty *ardaino* and the small, black *ponentine.* In the Marches, stuffed olives are called *oliva all'ascolana.* See **olio.**

olivette   (oh-lee-VEH-teh)   "Little olives." Olive-size morsels of veal cooked in a white wine sauce, from the Marches.

Oltrepò Pavese   (ohl-treh-POH pah-VEH-seh)   **DOC** zone of Lombardy that produces several wine types, including **barbera, buttafuoco,** *sangue di Giuda,* and **spumante.** The name means "beyond the Po in the region of Pavia."

ombretta   (ohm-BREH-tah)   "Little shadow." Colloquialism for an aperitif taken in an outdoor café, mostly wine and mostly in the Veneto, although it is often sipped at breakfast in cold regions and winter as a stimulant. The word is said to refer to the shadow cast by the bell tower of St. Mark's Cathedral in Venice. In this shade was a wine bar where the term to "get a shadow" was a colloquialism for having a refreshing drink.

ombrina (ohm-BREE-nah) "Little dark (fish)." Grayling fish, croaker, *Thymallus vulgaris* or *Umbrina cirrosa*. A silvery fish of the Mediterranean coast, with black wavy lines. Cooked in a wide variety of ways. From the Latin *umbra* (shade).

onda, all' (ahl-OHN-dah) "Wavy." Term used to describe the creamy consistency of a well-made *risotto,* which should have a wavelike appearance. From the Latin *unda* (wave).

onde (OHN-deh) "Waves." Butter cookies with an almond or candied cherry at one end. From the Latin *unda.*

orata (oh-RAH-tah) Gilthead bream, *Sparus aurata*. Fine white fish with a golden band behind its eyes, thereby the reference to *orata* (gold) and gilthead. It is usually prepared rather simply, roasted or grilled.

orecchia marina (oh-REH-k'yah mah-REE-nah) "Sea ear." Abalone *(Haliotus tuberculata),* whose shape resembles a human ear. Abalone, which is brought up by divers and is becoming increasingly rare, must be pounded in order to make it tender enough to eat. It is usually eaten raw, briefly sautéed, or braised. From the Latin *auris* (ear) and *marinus* (of the sea).

orecchi di aman (oh-REH-kee dee AH-mahn) "Haman's ears." Ear-shape fried cookie containing eggs, sugar, and lemon peel and dipped in sugar syrup or confectioners' sugar. The cookie is named after the biblical character of Haman, a Persian who decreed death to all Jews, and is made during the feast of Purim celebrated by Italy's Jews. From the Latin *auris.*

orecchiette (oh-reh-K'YEH-teh) "Small ears." Pasta shape that resembles small human ears, from Apulia. From the Latin *auris. Orecchiette* are made from small, thin rounds of pasta that are pressed with the thumb to form a hollow in the center. They are traditionally served with cooked turnip tops and mashed chile peppers, garlic, anchovies, and oil or with *broccoli di rape,* chile peppers, and anchovies. In Apulia, small *orecchiette* are called *chiancarelle* and larger versions *pociacche*. In Molise, this shape is called *recchietelle. Orecchioni* are ear-shape pasta that is stuffed with *ricotta,* parsley, and nutmeg, parboiled, dressed with butter and cheese, and baked, from Modigliana in Emilia-Romagna.

Orecchiette is also a name for the *ceppetello* (oyster mushroom).

orecchio (oh-REH-k'yoh) Ear. Refers to an animal ear, most commonly from pigs, which is usually boiled first, then cut into strips and fried or eaten cold. From the Latin *auris* (ear).

origano (oh-REE-gah-noh) Oregano or wild marjoram, *Origanum vulgare. Origano* is used as a seasoning in soups, sauces, stuffings, and other preparations. It is always used dried. See also *maggiorana.*

Ormeasco (ohr-meh-AH-skoh) Red wine of Liguria made from *dolcetto* grapes grown around the town of Ormea in the upper Arroscio valley in the *DOC* zone of Riviera Ligure di Ponente. The name is also a local term for *dolcetto.*

orso bianco (OHR-soh bee-AHN-koh) "White bear." Colloquial term for a chef in Bologna. From the Latin *ursus.*

ortaggi (ohr-TAH-jee) Greens or pot herbs. From the Latin *hortus* (garden).

Orta Nova (OHR-tah NOH-vah) Red and rosé wines of Apulia, made from *sangiovese* and other grapes grown around the town of Orta Nova.

ortica (ohr-TEE-kah) Nettle. The tops are consumed either as a vegetable or in soups. From the Latin *urtica.*

ortrugo (ohr-TROO-goh) White wine grape of Emilia-Romagna made into wines of the same name in the *DOC* zone of *Colli Piacentini.*

Orvieto (ohr-vee-EH-toh) *DOC* white wine of Umbria, made from *procanico, verdello,* **grechetto,** and other grapes around the town of Orvieto. Though mostly vinified dry, there are **abboccato, amabile,** and *dolce* versions. Some of the *Orvieto* zone overlaps Latium.

orzo (OHR-zoh) Barley, one of the first grains cultivated by man, and eaten in its wild state in prehistoric times. From the Latin *hordeum.*

Barley probably originated in Ethiopia but was known throughout the Mediterranean and Europe by 3,000 B.C. The ancient Romans made bread from barley, as well as porridge, but when leavening gained dominance in bread making, barley, which does not interact well with yeasts, lost popularity to wheat.

Orzo perlato is pearl barley. *Orzata* is an almond-flavored drink. *Orzo* is also the name for a small rice-shape pasta.

ossi di morti (OH-see dee MOHR-tee) "Dead man's bones." Hard, crunchy cookies shaped to resemble a shank bone. In Sicily, they are sometimes formed to resemble skeletons. Also *muscardini.* From the Latin *os* and *mors.*

ossobuco   (OH–soh–BOO–koh)   "Pierced bone." Braised shank, usually veal, with a rich sauce of tomato and onion. It is a specialty of Lombardy, where it is usually served with *gremolata* and *risotto alla milanese*. The bone marrow is considered a delicacy, and a small, long spoon is commonly placed on the table with the dish so that the marrow may be drawn out. From the Latin *os*.

OSSOBUCO

4 veal shanks	*1 piece lemon peel, about 1 inch long*
1 cup flour	*Salt and pepper*
4 tablespoons butter	*¹/₂ cup dry white wine*
1 onion, chopped	*4 tomatoes, peeled, seeded, and*
1 stalk celery, chopped	*chopped*
1 carrot, chopped	*1 ¹/₂ cups veal stock*
2 sprigs fresh marjoram	*1 teaspoon grated orange peel*
2 garlic cloves	*1 teaspoon grated lemon peel*

Dredge the veal shanks in flour and shake off the excess. Heat the butter in a heavy pot until foamy, add the veal shanks, and brown evenly. Add the onion, celery, carrot, marjoram, one of the cloves of garlic, and the piece of lemon peel. Season with salt and pepper to taste and brown for about 2 minutes. Add the wine and cook until it is absorbed. Place the veal shanks in an upright position (so that the marrow does not fall to the bottom of the pot), add the tomatoes and veal stock, bring to a boil, cover, and reduce the heat to a simmer. Cook for about 45 minutes. Remove the cover and turn up the heat to reduce the sauce slightly. Continue to cook for 10 minutes more, add the remaining clove of garlic and the grated orange and lemon peels, stir, and cook for 3 minutes more. Serve with *risotto* or *polenta*. Serves 4.

ossocollo   (OH–soh–KOH–loh)   "Neckbone." Ham made from the neck of the pig, from Friuli. From the Latin *os* and *collum*.

osteria   (oh–steh–REE–ah)   Originally a Roman wine shop or tavern frequented by neighborhood people. The term *osteria* now denotes a simple inn or eating place.

ostie   (OH–stee'yeh)   Edible wafer paper.

ostrica   (oh–STREE–kah)   Oyster, *Ostrea edulis*. Also *ostrea*. Although once considered a food of the poor, oysters were enjoyed by all strata of ancient Roman society, as they are today by those who can afford them. They are usually eaten raw from the shell, but may be cooked, baked, or fried. The oysters taken from Adriatic waters, particularly around Venice, are especially prized. Oysters are farmed in the Gulf of Taranto, where they are breaded and baked with olive oil, *alla tarantina.*

Ostuni   (oh-STOO-nee)   *DOC* zone of Apulia that produces a white wine from *impigno* and *francavilla* grapes and a red called *ottavianello* from the grape of the same name around the town of Ostuni.

ottarda   (oh-TAHR-dah)   Bustard, a large game bird (Tetrax tetrax), usually roasted. From the Latin *avis tarda* (slow bird).

otto di Merano   (OH-toh dee meh-RAH-noh)   Rye bread loaf shaped with two balls of dough to resemble a figure 8 *(otto),* from Merano.

ovolo buono   (OH-voh-loh BWOH-noh)   "Good egg (mushroom)." Edible amanita mushroom, *Amanita caesarea.* Usually eaten raw and often sliced on top of **carpaccio.** From the Latin *ovum* and *bonus.*

ovotarica   (oh-voh-TAH-ree-kah)   Tuna **bottarga,** served on bread with tomatoes and olive oil, from Calabria. From the Latin *ovum* (egg).

P

paarl (pahrl) Coarse rye bread flavored with caraway and fennel, a specialty of Valvenosta in the Tyrol.

padedda (pah-DEH-dah) "Small pan." Dish of boiled chicken, beef, veal, and pigeon with tomatoes, cloves, onions, garlic, carrots, and celery, from Sardinia. Also *patedda* and *pingiada*. From the Latin *patella* (plate).

padella (pah-DEH-lah) Frying pan. A *padellina* is a small frying pan. From the Latin *patella* (plate).

paesana, alla (AH-lah pye-ZAH-nah) "Country style." Term suggests a robust, rustic style of cooking enjoyed by Italy's former peasant class. From the Late Latin *paginsis* (inhabitant).

paeta al malgaragno (pah-EH-tah ahl mahl-gah-RAH-n'yoh) Roast turkey barded with *pancetta* and basted with pomegranate juice. A sauce is made from the turkey giblets with more pomegranate juice. From Venice. Possibly from the Spanish *pato* (duck).

Pagadebit di Romagna (pah-gah-deh-BEET dee roh-MAHN'ya) *DOC* zone of Emilia-Romagna that produces a white wine from *bombino bianco* grapes, locally called *pagadebit* (debt-payer). Sometimes vinified as an *amabile*. Some experts believe this is the same grape as *bombino bianco*.

pagello (pah-GEH-loh) Sea bream, known in American waters as porgy, *Sparus pagrus*. A lean, firm-fleshed oval saltwater fish that is simply cooked by poaching, grilling, or broiling. *Pagro* is a large sea bream that grows to 30 inches and is not considered quite so delicate in taste as the *pagello*. *Pagro reale* is another species, *S. caeruleosticus*. See also *sarago*.

paglia (PAH-l'yah) Cow's milk cheeses from Piedmont and Lombardy. The name derives from the tradition of aging the cheese in *paglia* (straw).

paglia e fieno   (PAH-l'yah eh fee-EH-noh)   "Straw and hay." A mixture of fresh green spinach pasta and yellow egg *tagliatelle,* or *tagliolini,* commonly served with a light cream sauce with ham and peas.

pagliata   (pah-L'YAH-tah)   Roman dialect word meaning beef or veal intestine.

paglierina   (pah-l'yeh-REE-nah)   Small cow's milk cheese with a slightly acidic taste, from Piedmont. Similar to French Brie and Camembert, the cheese used to be sold on a little mat of straw, *paglia.*

pagnotta   (pah-N'YOH-tah)   Large round loaf of bread. *Pagnotta di Santa Chiara,* from Naples, is made with potato and wheat flours, lard, and pepper, shaped into two circles, stuffed with anchovies and tomato, rolled, and baked. From the Latin *panis* (bread).

paillard   (pye-ARD)   A very thinly pounded piece of meat. Usually sautéed or grilled. The word is from archaic French, after a dish made by a 19th-century Parisian restaurateur named Paillard.

paiolo   (pye-OH-loh)   Deep, round-bottomed copper pan, commonly used to make *polenta.*

pajata   (pah-Y'AH-tah)   Roman dish of newborn calf's or lamb's intestines filled with its mother's milk, cooked with a spicy tomato sauce, usually served with *rigatoni.*

pala   (PAH-lah)   Wooden or metal peel. Used to slide breads or pizza in and out of the oven. From the Latin (spade).

palamida   (pah-lah-MEE-dah)   Bonito, *Sarda sarda. Palamita bianca* is another species, *Orcynopsis unicolor.* See also *bonito.*

palombaccio   (pah-lohm-BAH-ch'yoh)   Squab. *Palombacci alla perugina* (Perugia style) is a roast squab in a red wine, juniper, olive, and sage sauce, sometimes served with the bird's intestines, from Umbria. Also *palombo.* From the Latin *palombes* (pigeon).

palombo   (pah-LOHM-boh)   Pigeon.   Also a small shark called smooth hound, *Musetlus mustelus.* The fish must be skinned before cooking. The Roman dish *Palombo coi piselli* is made with peas, tomato, and onion. In Sicily, the fish is marinated in vinegar before flouring and frying. Also *vitello di mare* (veal of the sea). See also *gattuccio.* From the Latin (pigeon).

pampepato   (pahm-peh-PAH-toh)   "Pepper bread." Sweet but peppery ring-shaped cake with nuts and chocolate icing, from Ferrara. A Christmas cake, it is offered to customers by bakers. It was created in the 15th century at the Corpus Domini monastery.

In Umbria and the Marches it is shaped into small rolls, which may contain nuts, raisins, and candied fruit.

panada (pah–NAH–dah)   Broth with beaten eggs, bread crumbs, and *parmigiano,* from the Veneto. Also a dish made of balls of dough filled with pork, eel, or lamb, from Sardinia.

pan al latte (PAHN ahl LAH–teh)   "Milk bread." Sponge cake–like bread. From the Latin *panis* (bread) and *lac* (milk).

panarda (pah–NAHR–dah)   Multi–course meal of the feast of *Sant'Antonio Abate* (January 17) in Abruzzo. Served in many stages and consisting of dozens of different dishes—from *antipasto* through sausages, pickles, pastas, soups, variety meats, cheeses, fruits, and desserts—the banquet sometimes numbers as many as 60 dishes.

panare (pah–NAH–reh)   To bread a food for sautéing. From the Latin *panis* (bread).

panata (pah–NAH–tah)   A pancake made of eggs, bread, cheese, and nutmeg served in broth. This Easter dish was called *tridura,* in Romagna. From the Latin *panis* (bread).

pan bigio (pahn BEE–j'yoh)   "Gray bread." Coarse gray-colored bread made of unrefined flour. From the Latin *panis* (bread).

pancetta (pahn CHEH–tah)   Cured pork from the belly of the pig. Also *carne secca.* It is made either as *pancetta stesa,* which is the whole piece of meat, or *p. arrotolata,* which is rolled and sometimes flavored with pepper and cloves. *P. affunicata* is much like American bacon. *Rigatino* is a lean *pancetta,* from Tuscany. From the Latin *pantic* (stomach).

pan con l'uva (pahn kohn LOO–vah)   Raisin bread. From the Latin *panis* and *uva.*

pan co'santi (pahn koh–SAHN–tee)   A walnut and raisin bread. Served on All Saints' Day in Siena.

pancotto (pahn–KOH–toh)   "Cooked bread." A rustic dish of stewed tomato, garlic, and oil with bread. In Lombardy, if an egg is added, it is called *pancot marida* (married *pancotto*). Also *pane cotto.* See also **pappa al pomodoro.** From the Latin *panis* and *coquus* (cook).

pan de frizze (pahn deh FREE–t'zeh)   Sweet cornmeal bun made with pork cracklings, from Friuli.

pan de mei (pahn deh MEH–yee)   Cornmeal yeast buns, from Lombardy. Also *man de mej.* From the Latin *panis.*

pan di miglio   (pahn dee MEE-l'yoh)   Brioche-like bread made with millet flour or cornmeal. From the Latin *panis* and *millium* (millet).

pan di ramerino   (pahn dee rah-meh-REE-noh)   Rosemary-flavored bread, from Tuscany. From the Latin *panis* and *ros marinus*.

pan di Spagna   (pahn dee SPAH-n'yah)   "Spanish bread." Sponge cake. Used as the basis for *tirami sù* and many other desserts. From the Latin *panis*.

pandolce   (pahn-DOHL-cheh)   "Sweet bread." Christmas cake shaped into a dome, flavored with nuts, fruits, and spices, and topped with a sprig of bay leaf, from Genoa. By tradition the first cut is made by the youngest member of the family. Also *pandoce*. From the Latin *panis* and *dulcis*.

pandorato   (pahn-doh-RAH-toh)   "Golden bread." Bread soaked in egg and milk, then deep-fried. It may be stuffed with cheese, anchovies, or ham. From the Latin *panis* and *aurum*.

pandoro   "Golden bread." (pahn-DOH-roh)   A tall Christmas cake like *panettone,* from Verona. Eggs and butter give it a golden color. It is usually baked into a star shape. From the Latin *panis* and *aurum*.

pane   (PAH-neh)   Bread. The ancient Romans, who called bread *panis,* were taught bread making by the Greeks in the 2nd century B.C., before that subsisting on a mush similar to *polenta* called *puls* made from *farro.* By the year 25 B.C. Rome had 329 public bakeries, and bakers were often freed slaves. By A.D. 100 Trajan had established a baker's school in Rome. Yet the cultivation of wheat was left largely to the imperial provinces of Africa and Egypt, lost to Rome when those territories were forfeited to the Byzantine Empire. During the barbarian invasions, wheat was all but unobtainable in Rome, and bread was made with beans, acorns, and other grains. The techniques of milling and bread making were, however, carried on in the monasteries and, in the Middle Ages, in newly formed bakers' guilds, which had strict quality controls for their members. Still, it was not until the late Middle Ages that bread was again widely available for the populace in Italy, and most breads were still made with flours other than wheat. The distinction between the rich and the poor for much of Italy's history, right into the 20th century, was the difference between those who ate white bread and those who ate dark.

Most bread in Italy today is made from wheat, usually with white flour (only about 2 percent is made with whole wheat). In the south, semolina flour is also used for bread, and in the north, especially the Tyrol, rye. Breads may take the form of flatbreads, like *pizza* and *focaccia,* or round loaves of all sizes, various shapes, and braided loaves often made for feast days. Most professional bakers in Italy work on a small scale making the traditional breads of their region, and most of the breads available in one region are not to be found in any other. Large commercial bakeries began to appear after World War II, but most Italians still prefer to buy their breads from local bakeries.

At a multi-course meal, bread is usually consumed at the beginning, with the *antipasto* and with the second course, but not with the pasta. Italians do not butter their bread nor dip it in oil, though slices of it may be spread with garlic and oil and toasted as *bruschetta, crostini,* or *fettunta.*

pane casareccio (PAH-neh kah-sah-REH-ch'yoh) "Rich house bread." Large, thick-crusted bread loaf. From the Latin *casa* (hut).

pane del marinaio (PAH-neh dell mah-ree-NYE-oh) "Mariner's bread." Sweet bread shaped like a dome and full of nuts, raisins, and spices, from Genoa. From the Latin *panis* and *marinus* (of the sea).

pane del sabato (PAH-neh dell SAH-bah-toh) "Sabbath bread." Bread loaf enriched with eggs, a specialty of the Italian Jews, similar to challah. From the Hebrew *Shabbath*.

pane di pollo (PAH-neh dee POH-loh) "Chicken bread." Chicken that has been boned, stuffed with a meat mixture, and formed into the shape of a bread loaf. It is then poached in broth and served with a green sauce. From Tuscany. From the Latin *panis* and the old French *poulet*.

pane di Terni (PAH-neh dee TEHR-nee) A saltless bread with a light crust and airy interior full of holes, from the town of Terni in Umbria. From the Latin *panis*.

pane francese (PAH-neh frahn-CHEH-zeh) "French bread." Originally called *pane di Como* because it came from the region around Lake Como. The more common name refers to a kind of crunchy-crusted French bread with an airy interior.

pane frattau (PAH-neh frah-TAU) "Broken bread." Dish made with *carta da musica* softened in hot water, arranged in a shallow dish, and eaten with a poached egg, tomato sauce, and *caciocavallo* or *pecorino sardo,* from Sardinia.

pane grattugiato (PAH-neh grah-too-J'YAH-toh) "Grated bread." Bread crumbs. Also *pangrattato*. From the Latin *panis* and the Middle French *grata*.

pane in cassetta (PAH-neh in kah-SEH-tah) "Bread in a box." Sandwich bread. Also *pain carré*. From the Latin *panis* and the Middle French (casket).

pane integrale (PAH-neh een-teh-GRAH-leh) Whole wheat bread, usually shaped into a sandwich loaf. From the Latin *integer* (whole).

panelle (pah-NEH-leh)   "Little breads." Sicilian fried crisps made with chickpea flour, especially popular as a *fuori tavola* snack in Palermo. Often stuffed into a soft roll. Also *panillaru*. From the Latin *panis*.

pane nero (PAH-neh NEH-roh)   "Black bread." Made with rye and whole wheat flour, which give it a dark color. From the Latin *niger*.

pane pugliese (PAH-neh poo-L'YEH-seh)   Large bread loaf with a rustic texture and a hard, crunchy crust, from Apulia.

pane tipo Altamura (PAH-neh TEE-poh ahl-tah-MOO-rah)   "Altamura-style bread." Bread made from a high-gluten durum wheat flour from the town of Altamura in Apulia. It has a thick crust and a very wheaty flavor. From the Latin *panis*.

panetteria (pah-neh-teh-REE-ah)   Bread bakery. Generally does not sell pastries. From the Latin *panis*.

panettone (PAH-neh-TOH-neh)   A tall, cylindrical, egg-rich cake with candied fruit, traditionally served at Christmas and Easter, from Milan. A 15th-century legend explains the cake's name as deriving from a Milan baker named Toni, whose beautiful daughter was courted by an aristocrat who offered to work as an apprentice in the bakery, where he created a very rich cake that became very popular in the city and was called *"pan di Toni."* The word may simply derive from a Milanese term for a big bread. From the Latin *panis*.

In Florence this type of cake is often called *panettone della passione,* "big bread of [Christ's] passion." *Panettoncino di mais* is a cornmeal sponge cake, commonly made with chocolate, from Molise.

panficio (pahn-FEE-ch'yoh)   Bread bakery. From the Latin *panis*.

panforte (pahn-FOHR-teh)   "Strong bread." A firm, sweet cake full of nuts, spices, white pepper, and candied fruit, traditionally served in winter, especially at Christmastime, a specialty of Siena. See also *pampepato*. From the Latin *fortis*.

pan giallo (pahn J'YAH-loh)   "Yellow bread." Fruit and nut cake flavored with rum, traditionally served at Christmastime, from Rome. From the Latin *helvus* (light bay).

pan graham (pahn GRAHM)   Graham-flour bread, named after American Reverend Sylvester Graham, a 19th-century advocate of temperance and nutrition. It includes unsifted whole wheat flour containing bran. From the Latin *panis*.

panino (pah-NEE-noh)   "Small bread." Small sandwich. The name was apparently coined at Milan's Paninoteca Bar Quadronno. *Panini cresciuti* (grown rolls) are fried Sicilian potato rolls containing ham and cheese. From the Latin *panis.*

panìssa   (pah–NEE–sah)   "Little bread." A *polenta*-like dish made with chickpea flour and water, dressed with olive oil, from Liguria. Also, a chickpea and onion tart, from Liguria.

In Piedmont, *panìssa* is a *risotto* flavored with **Barbera** wine and pork rind, **salame alla douja,** and **borlotti.** In Novarra, *paniscia* is a soup of beans, vegetables, and salami added to *risotto.*

panna   (PAH–nah)   Heavy cream. *Panna montata* is whipped cream. *P. cotta* is an eggless custard, usually served with berries. *P. acida* is sour cream. Called *rascu* in Sicily.

pan pepato   (pahn peh–PAH–toh)   "Spiced bread." Nougat candy containing raisins, candied fruit, and almonds, as made in the Marches. From the Latin *panis* and *piper* (pepper).

pan sciocco   (pahn SHOH–koh)   "Foolish bread." Unsalted Tuscan bread.

pansôti   (pahn–SOH–tee)   "Pot bellied." Egg-rich *ravioli* stuffed with herbs, egg, **prescinseha,** and **parmigiano,** from Liguria. Also *pansouti.* See also **preboggion.**

pan tranvai   (pahn tran–VYE)   "Tramway bread." Raisin bread from Milan. The name derives from its origins at a bakery in the tramway station *(tranvai)* on Monza.

panzanella   (pahn–zah–NEH–lah)   Summer salad of central Italy consisting of tomatoes, cucumber, onion, basil, vinegar, and olive oil. Also *pan molle* (soft bread) and *panbagnato* (soaked bread). From the Latin *panis* (bread).

panzanelle   (pahn–zah–NEH–leh)   "Little nonsense." Twisted bread sticks, from Tuscany. From the Latin *panis* (bread).

panzarotti   (pahn–zah–ROH–tee)   "Little bellies." Filled pastry or pasta half-moons, deep-fried or boiled. In Tuscany, *panzarotti* with a savory filling, such as tomatoes, anchovies, and **mozzarella,** are fried. In Apulia, they are also savory and fried, traditionally made on the feast of *Sant'Antonio Abate* (January 17). In Basilicata, they are made with sweetened chickpea flour paste and chocolate. From the Latin *pantic* (stomach).

papalina   (pah–pah–LEE–nah)   "Pope's hat." Sprat, *Sprattus sprattus.* Similar to the anchovy and usually fried.

paparot   (pah–pah–ROHT)   Soup made with spinach, garlic, and cornmeal, from Friuli-Venezia Giulia.

papassinos   (pah-pah-SEE-nohs)   "Raisin (pastries)." Pastries with a topping of raisin-walnut paste, from Sardinia. If cinnamon, cloves, and anise are added, they are called *pabassinus.*

papero   (PAH-peh-roh)   Duckling. Also *papera.* See also **anitra.**

pappa al pomodoro   (PAH-pah ahl poh-moh-DOH-roh)   "Tomato pap." Lightly cooked tomatoes, garlic, olive oil, and stale bread, from Tuscany. It is a homestyle dish, often served as baby food, though it has in recent years become popular in fashionable restaurants in Italy and the United States. In Lazio, it is called *pancotto col pomodoro.* Also *pappa col pomodoro.* From the Middle English *pap.*

PAPPA AL POMODORO

4 tablespoons butter	*Salt*
¹/₄ cup extra-virgin olive oil	*Freshly ground black pepper*
2 cups diced (small) yellow onion	*3 cups diced Italian bread or country*
3 tablespoons minced garlic	*bread, in ³/₄-inch pieces*
12 tomatoes, very ripe, peeled, seeded,	*Parmigiano for shaving*
and chopped	*3 tablespoons truffle oil (optional)*

In a stockpot, melt the butter and the olive oil, add the onions, and cook gently until translucent. Add the garlic and cook for another 2 minutes. Add the tomatoes, bring to a boil, and simmer until tomatoes fall apart a bit and are soupy, about 15 minutes. Season with salt and pepper, add the bread, and stir to mix. Serve in soup plates, shaving some ***parmigiano*** on top and drizzling some truffle oil on each dish. Serve immediately. Serves 4 to 6.

pappardelle   (pah-pahr-DEH-leh)   "Gulp down [pasta]." Homemade long, flat pasta shape, about ¹/₂ to 1 inch wide and 6 inches long, usually made with eggs. In Tuscany, it is traditionally served *con la* **lepre,** with a hare sauce. *Pappardelle di Prato* is served with a sauce made from a ewe, carrots, onion, celery, and tomatoes, as made in Prato. *P. alla Sienese* is a Sienese version made with squab, **Chianti,** and fresh sage. Also *larghissime* and *fettucce.*

paradell   (pah-rah-DELL)   Apple custard or bread pudding, a specialty of the Valtellina.

parmigiana, alla   (AH-lah pahr-mee-J'YAH-nah)   A dish made in the style of Parma, which suggests copious amounts of ***parmigiano*** and ***prosciutto.***

In America, it connotes something in bread crumbs, fried, topped with tomato sauce, *mozzarella,* and *parmigiano,* and baked. See also *parmigiano.*

parmigiano (pahr-mee-J'YAH-noh)   A cow's milk cheese made in huge wheels and aged. One of the most esteemed Italian *grana* cheeses. The cheese of the region has been noted for its quality at least since the days of Boccaccio, who noted it in *The Decameron* (14th century).

Parmigiano-Reggiano, which was made around Parma and Reggia at least as early as the 17th century, was established in 1955 under the *Consorzio del Formaggio Parmigiano-Reggiano* as a cheese of controlled origin, from a limited zone around Parma, Reggio nell' Emilia, Bologna, Modena, and Mantua. Each round is stamped by the producer.

The cheese may be made year-round but must be made in the morning and must contain no additives except rennet (*caglio*) and salt. The cheese must be aged for at least a year. Only 2.5 million wheels, weighing 50 to 90 pounds each, are produced each year, and the highest quality is stamped for export. *Parmigiano nuovo* (new *parmigiano*) is aged less than a year; *P. vecchio* (old) is aged up to two years; and *P. stravecchio* (very old) is aged for at least two years and usually more. See also *grana.*

Parrina (pah-REE-nah)   *DOC* zone of Tuscany that produces red, white, and rosé wines. From various grapes grown around the village of Parrina.

parrozzo (pah-ROH-t'zoh)   Almond cake with chocolate icing, from Abruzzo. The name derives from *pan rozzo* (rough cake).

passare (pah-SAH-reh)   To strain. From the Latin *passus* (step).

passatelli (pah-sah-TEH-lee)   Tiny dumplings made from eggs, cheese, nutmeg, lemon peel, and bread crumbs. The word derives from *passato,* meaning "passed through" the disk of a food mill into simmering chicken or beef broth. In the Marches, ground veal and spinach are added to the mixture; in Tuscany, spinach and lemon peel. In Pesaro, ground beef is added.

The word *passatelli* also refers to the elderly because this is a digestible soup commonly served to the old and infirm.

passato (pah-SAH-toh)   Pureed. The term, which derives from the Latin *passus* (step), also refers to a creamed soup, a soup of pureed vegetables, or a smooth tomato sauce. Also *purea.* See also *crema.*

passerino (pah-seh-REE-noh)   "Little sparrow." Plaice, *Pleuronectes platessa.* A flatfish of the western Mediterranean. They are bottom feeders, so the most prized come from sandy bottoms. Plaice are best simply sautéed, grilled, or broiled, as is the *passera (Platichthys flesus),* a flounder.

passero (PAH-seh-roh)   Sparrow. Usually cooked on a spit or braised and served with *polenta.* From the Latin *passer.*

passito   (pah-SEE-toh)   Sweet wine made from partially dried grapes. *Passito* is also a Lombardian dialect word meaning "past it," as applied to cheeses that are very old.

passoli   (pah-SOH-lee)   Dried currants, from the Latin *uvae passae.*

pasta   (PAH-stah)   "Paste." A general term for dough, but more specifically for any of an enormous range of boiled farinaceous dishes made with flour and water, sometimes with the addition of egg yolks. (When the word takes an article, e.g., *una pasta,* it refers to a pastry bought at a shop.) From the Late Latin.

While pasta has become an international food, it is, in its myriad forms and shapes, the food most identified with Italians, who consume more than 60 pounds per person annually. (By comparison, Americans eat about half as much.) The myth that Marco Polo brought pasta back from China somehow persists despite all historical evidence to the contrary. Records show that pasta was well established in Italy before Marco Polo's return in 1295.

The ancient Greeks called a flat cake cut into strips *laganon,* which in Latin became *laganum,* a dish composed of dough strips roasted on hot stones, not boiled in water. (Latin references to *pastillum* are to a bread roll, not noodles.) Nevertheless, the word *laganum* was a direct antecedent of **lasagne,** and in Naples the word *laganatura* is still used to describe a rolling pin for pasta. (Other etymologists trace *lasagne* to Greek *lasana,* a trivet or stand for a pot.)

Some scholars believe the ancient Persians ate a form of noodles they called *rishta,* while others have proposed the possibility that the first forms of pasta arrived via the Arab invasions between the 7th and 13th centuries. But culinary scholar Charles Perry says that boiled noodles called *itriyah* are actually mentioned in the Jerusalem Talmud of the 5th century. In the book *Kitab-Rugiar* (1154), an Arab geographer named Al-Idrisi describes pasta making on a large scale in the Sicilian town of Trabia (near Palermo), which exported its pasta throughout the Mediterranean. He used the Arab word *itriyah,* referring to long strands of dough, and this entered the Sicilian dialect as *tria,* still heard today as a synonym for **spaghetti.**

The first printed reference to **maccheroni** is by a citizen of Genoa named Ponzio Bastone, who left a *bariscella piena de macaronis* (a basket full of macaroni) in his will, suggesting that such a food was of considerable value.

By the 14th century references to various forms of pasta, generally referred to as **vermicelli** (little worms) are numerous, as well as to manufacturers of the food item, and preparations ranged from stuffed pastas to baked casseroles, some with savory sauces, others with sweet or sour sauces. Stuffed pasta like **ravioli** date at least to the 14th century, when they were usually deep fried or served in broth.

By 1800, the generally used term *vermicelli* had been superseded by *maccheroni,* and Naples, which had 280 shops selling pasta as of 1785, was the capital of pasta production. The drying of *maccheroni* had been perfected in Torre Annunziata, south of Naples, and from then on it became a staple of the Italian diet. In those days pasta was made in a large trough called a **madia,** and the work of kneading the dough was done by foot, but by the end of the 19th century the process had been nearly all mechanized. Die-cut pasta was created by Féreol Sandragné in 1917, and the entire process of commercial pasta making was perfected by the Braibanti family in 1933. Before commercial, boxed pasta was produced, many dried pastas like **spaghetti** were longer than the now-standard size.

Pasta takes two principal forms in Italy. *Pasta fresca* is freshly made (not dried) pasta, made from soft wheat *(Triticum vulgare aestivum)*. *Pasta secca* or *pastasciutta* is dried pasta, usually commercially made. Under Italian law, the latter may be made only with hard *semola di grano duro* wheat flour *(Triticum durum)*. If it contains eggs *(pasta all'uovo)*, spinach, tomatoes, beets, or other ingredients that gives it color, it is called *pasta speciali*. *Pasta tricolore* (three-color pasta) is a combination of regular pasta, spinach pasta, and tomato pasta, to represent the colors of the Italian flag, though this pasta is also called *Arlecchino,* after the Commedia dell'Arte's colorful Harlequin character. *P. di ceci* is made with chickpea flour. *P. glutinata* has gluten added to the dough and is cooked in broth. It is considered more nutritious for children and elderly people. *P. tirata* is a rolled northern Italian pasta, preferably done by hand. *P. in forma* or *uno* **timballo** refers to pasta shaped and baked in a form, usually layered with many other ingredients.

There are literally hundreds of pasta shapes, cut from large sheets called **sfoglie,** and sizes under the two main categories of **spaghetti** and **maccheroni.** There are also many regional names for the same shape or cut of pasta. The principal shapes are covered under their own names in this book.

pasta alla deficeira   (PAH-stah AH-lah deh-fee-CH'YEH-rah)   *Maccheroni* cooked in wine; from Liguria. The term refers either to a "dolt's pasta" or a "deficient pasta."

pasta asciutta alla marchigana   (PAH-stah ah-SH'OO-tah AH-lah mahr-kee-GAH-nah)   "Dry pasta Marches style." Yeast pasta cut into ribbons, then allowed to rise before being boiled.

pasta e ceci   (PAH-stah eh CHEH-chee)   Dish of pasta and chickpeas. See also *tuoni e lampo.*

pasta e fagioli   (PAH-stah eh fah-J'YOH-lee)   "Pasta and beans." Hearty pasta and bean soup or stew, also containing pork, olive oil, garlic, and aromatic vegetables. Although it is a specialty of the Veneto, where it is called *pasta e fasioi,* this dish is made all over Italy.

PASTA E FAGIOLI

3 tablespoons olive oil
2 garlic cloves, chopped
1 onion, chopped
1 celery stalk, chopped
2 tablespoons chopped parsley
1 cup dried borlotti, soaked overnight
   in water

1 ham bone (optional)
7 to 8 cups meat stock
Salt and pepper
4 ounces ditalini, cooked
Grated parmigiano
Olive oil (optional)

Heat the olive oil in a large pot and sauté the garlic, onion, celery, and parsley until the onion is transparent. Drain the beans, add them to the pot, and sauté for about 1 minute. Add the ham bone, if using, and the stock. Cook over low heat for about 4 hours, adding more stock if necessary to keep a liquid consistency. Remove the ham bone and about one-third of the beans and set aside. Pass the soup and remaining beans through a food mill, add any pieces of ham that remain on the bone, and return it to the pot with the reserved beans. Season with salt and pepper to taste. Add the *ditalini* and simmer for about 5 minutes. Turn off the heat and let stand for about 10 minutes. Serve with *parmigiano* and, if desired, olive oil. Serves 4.

pasta filata   (PAH-stah fee-LAH-tah)   "Pulled or spun dough." Cheese made by stretching the curds into strands, then molding them. See also *mozzarella* and *provolone*. From the Latin *filatim* (thread by thread).

pasta frolla   (PAH-stah FROH-lah)   "Soft pastry." Short pastry, with a high amount of fat.

pasta grattugiata   (PAH-stah grah-too-J'YAH-tah)   "Grated dough," literally meaning that dried dough is grated into very small grains, cooked as for *cuscus,* or served in broth. Commercially it may go under the name *grandinine* or *pastina.*

pasta 'ncasciata   (PAH-stah n'kah-sh'YAH-tah)   "Encased pasta." *Maccheroni* and meatball dish baked with eggplant, salami, peas, *caciocavallo,* and *mozzarella,* from Sicily.

pastarasa   (pah-stah-RAH-sah)   Soup dumplings made with bread crumbs, *parmigiano,* egg, and nutmeg, a specialty of Reggio Emilia. Similar to *panatelli* but without meat. From the Late Latin *pasta* (paste).

pasta reale (PAH-stah reh-AH-leh) "Royal dough." Name for Sicilian *marzapane*. From the Latin *regilis.*

pasta sfogliata (PAH-stah s'foh-L'YAH-tah) Also *pasta soffiate.* Flaky puff pastry, used for pastries. See also *millefoglie.* From the Latin *folium* (leaf).

pastatella (pah-stah-TEH-lah) "Pretty pastry." Dessert tart made with oranges, almonds, and chocolate.

paste (PAH-steh) Small pastries sold in pastry shops. From the Late Latin *pasta* (paste).

pastella (pah-STEH-lah) Batter for frying. Commonly a mixture of flour, lightly salted water, and sometimes eggs or egg yolks. From the Late Latin *pasta* (paste).

pasticcere (pah-stee-T'CHEH-reh) Pastry cook. From the Late Latin *pasta* (paste).

pasticceria (pah-stee-t'cheh-REE-ah) Pastry shop, which usually does not sell bread.

pasticcini (pah-stee-CHEE-nee) Cookies. From the Late Latin *pasta* (paste).

pasticcio (pah-STEE-ch'yoh) Also *pasticciata.* A layered baked dish, such as *pasticcio di **maccheroni**.* A *pasticcio* differs from a **timballo** in that the latter is made in a mold rather than simply layered in a baking dish. In Bologna, a *pasticcio* is made with **tortellini** and **ragù** baked in a pie crust, sometimes with white truffles. *P. di maccheroni alla padovana* is a macaroni pie filled with mushrooms, squab, truffles, and a **balsamella,** from Padua. In Pesaro *pasticciata alla pesarese* is a dish of sautéed beef cooked with tomato puree, cloves, and cinnamon. From the Vulgar Latin *pasticium* (pasty).

pastiera (pah-stee-EH-rah) A wheat-berry cake filled with **ricotta** cheese and candied fruit, prepared in several places in the south. *Pastiera napoletana* is a Neapolitan Easter version specialty using puff pastry, sometimes made with barley flour and buttermilk.

pastina (pah-STEE-nah) Very tiny specks of *pasta,* cooked in soup. From the Late Latin *pasta* (paste).

pastissada di cavallo (pah-stee-SAH-dah dee kah-VAH-loh) "Big messy mixture of horse." Stew made with horse meat and served with **polenta,** from Venice. In Verona, it may be called *pastissada de caval,* a traditional dish that supposedly dates back to 489, when King Theodoric the Great gave the horses killed in battle to the starving inhabitants of the beseiged city of

Verona. In Friuli-Venezia Giulia, it is made with beef and called *pastizzade*. From the Vulgar Latin *pasticium* (pasty).

pasto   (PAH-stoh)   A meal. From the Latin *pastus* (feeding). See also *cena, colazione,* and *pranzo.*

pastuccia   (pah-STOO-ch'yah)   A yeast bun incorporating egg and sausage, a specialty of Teramo. From the Late Latin *pasta* (paste).

pasutice   (pah-soo-TEE-cheh)   Lozenge-shape egg pasta, from Istrian. From the Late Latin *pasta* (paste).

patata   (pah-TAH-tah)   Potato. The name comes from the Taino Indian word *batata*. The Spanish brought potatoes back to Europe from the New World in 1536, and potato flowers adorned the garden of Pope Pius V by 1572. At that time the tuber was called a truffle *(tartufo),* and it was not until 1585, when a Carmelite monk named Nicolo Doria brought the potato from Spain to Genoa, that the tuber was regarded as having much culinary interest. Still, right into the 19th century, the potato was regarded more for its value as animal fodder than as desirable food for human beings. In 1801 a Celestinian monk published a *Treatise on Potatoes* that noted many different preparations, including creamed potatoes, potato fritters, roast potatoes, stuffed potatoes, and the first recipe for *gnocchi.*
   Patatine novelle are new potatoes. *Fecola di patate* is potato starch.

patella   (pah-TEH-lah)   Limpet, *Patella caerulea,* a shellfish best eaten in late winter but rarely in the market because of its leathery texture.

pavone   (pah-VOH-neh)   Peacock. The name comes from the Latin. Peacock would probably never be seen on a contemporary Italian table or anywhere else, but in ancient Rome the bird was considered an exotic contribution to a banquet table. Peacocks were raised and sold for such a purpose, though, as the poet Horace notes in his *Satires,* the service of such a bird was out of pretense rather than good taste.

peara   (peh-AH-rah)   Sauce of beef marrow, pepper, and grated bread served with *bollito misto,* from the Veneto.

peccato di gola   (peh-KAH-toh dee GOH-lah)   "Sin of gluttony." A compliment paid to a cook or restaurateur, indicating a meal or dish was so delicious that it was a temptation to gluttony.

pecora   (PEH-koh-rah)   Ewe. Used more for its milk to make cheese and its wool than for its meat.

pecorino   (peh-koh-REE-noh)   "Little sheep." A sharp hard cheese made from fresh ewe's milk.

There are four principal regional kinds. *Pecorino romano, p. saldo, p. siciliano,* and *p. toxano. P. romano,* also called simply *romano,* from around Rome, is always aged (about eight months). *P. sardo* and *p. siciliano* can be eaten as table cheeses or, when aged, used for grating. *Pecorino* is also called *crotonese. P. pepato, pecorno,* and **maiorchino** are Sicilian terms for *pecorino* with black peppercorns. *P. toscano* must by law be made from ewe's milk drawn between September and June and aged for at least six months. It is usually eaten as a table cheese.

P. senese has a rind rubbed with tomato paste. *P. toscanello* is a Sardinian version. See also **canestrato, crotonese, fiore sardo, marzolino, piacintinu,** and **ricotta salata.**

pegai (peh-GYE)   Chestnut-flour **ravioli,** from the Apennine mountain towns of Emilia-Romagna. Originally a Lenten pasta, it is traditionally meatless, stuffed with **ricotta,** walnuts, and **parmigiano.**

pelara (peh-LAH-rah)   "Skin." A red grape of the Veneto, known for its hardiness. It withstood the invasion of American phylloxera in the 19th century.

pelare (peh-LAH-reh)   To peel. From the Latin *pilare* (to remove hair).

Pellaro (peh-LAH-roh)   Red and rosé wines of Calabria made from *alicante* and other grapes grown around the town of Pellaro.

penne (PEH-neh)   "Quills." Short, quill-shaped macaroni, about $5/16$-inch wide, sometimes ribbed. They are a specialty of Campania, though widely used in Italy. From the Latin *penna* (feather), whose quill would be used as a pen. Also *ziti tagliati,* **mostaccioli,** and **maltagliati.**

Pennette are smaller *penne; penne ziti* and *penne di natale* (or *natalini)* are fatter; *pennoni* are fatter still. In Tuscany, *penne* are served **strascicare,** "dragged through" a meat sauce. *P. alla pizzaiola* refers to a Neapolitan dish of *penne* cooked **pizza** style, that is, with a herbaceous tomato sauce and baked with pieces of **mozzarella** on top, from Naples.

pentola (PEHN-toh-lah)   General term for a pot or pan.

peoci (peh-OH-chee)   Mussels in Venetian dialect. The word also means "lice," perhaps referring to the tiny size of the mussels. See also **cozze.**

pepato (peh-PAH-toh)   "Peppered [cheese]." **Pecorino** cheese, with black peppercorns throughout the cheese, from Sicily. *Pecorino ragusano* contains red chile pepper shreds, from Ragusa. From the Latin *piper* (pepper).

pepe (PEH-pe)   Black or white pepper. Black pepper was introduced to Europe around the 5th or 6th century B.C. from the East. First used as a medicine, it gradually became a major spice *(piper)* in the cookery of ancient

Rome. During the Middle Ages, Venice monopolized the pepper trade. *Peperata* is a sauce of beef marrow, ground black pepper, bread crumbs, and ***parmigiano,*** served with meat or poultry.

peperonata (peh-peh-roh-NAH-tah)   Stew of sweet peppers (***peperoni***) cooked with onions, garlic, and tomatoes in olive oil, usually served at room temperature. From the Latin *piper* (pepper).

peperoncino (peh-peh-rohn-CHEE-noh)   Chile pepper, *Capsicum annuum annuum* Linné. Similar to an Anaheim chile but probably developed from a sweet pepper in Italy. In Abruzzo, it is called ***diavolicchio;*** in Sardinia, *piberoneddu* or *arrabiosu;* in Sicily, *pipi* or *ardenti. Peperoncino in povere* is ground chile pepper. From the Latin *piper* (pepper).

peperoni (peh-peh-ROH-nee)   Sweet peppers. They came to Italy soon after their discovery in the New World, but for two more centuries, peppers, both sweet and hot, were considered poor people's food and not included in any of the Italian culinary encyclopedias until the 19th century.

Peppers in Italy are categorized by shape: *peperoni quadrati* (four-sided) has a square, box-like shape; *p. a cuore di bue* (bull's heart) is heart-shaped; *p. a corno* (horn-shaped) is elongated, either curved or straight; and *p. a pomodoro* (tomato-shaped) is small and compressed. From the Latin *piper* (pepper).

See also ***peperonata*** and ***peperoncino.***

pepolino (peh-poh-LEE-noh)   Wild thyme, *Thymus serpyllum.*

peposo (peh-POH-zoh)   Beef shank or pork shank stew braised with red wine, garlic, and black peppercorns, from Tuscany.

pera (PEH-rah)   Pear. This fruit came to Italy via Greece and Europe, and there were dozens of varieties available to the ancient Romans; by the 17th century there were more than two hundred. Nearly all the world's pears are now derived from either of two species, Europe's *Pyrus communis* or Asia's *P. sinensis.* From the Latin *pirum.*

Pears in Italy are eaten fresh, often with cheese, or poached. They are used in pastries and to make an eau-de-vie.

perchia (PEHR-ch'yah)   Comber, *Serranus cabrilla.* A yellow-striped fish mostly used in soup. From the Latin *porcus* (spiny fish).

perciatelli (pehr-ch'yah-TEH-lee)   Dried   fat   hollow   strands   of ***spaghetti,*** approximately $^1/_{10}$ inch in diameter. From southern dialect word *perciato* (pierced through). Also *foratini, fedelini bucatini,* and *fide bucate.*

per'e palummo (PEH-reh-eh pah-LOOM-moh)   "Pigeon's feet." A red grape of Campania, used in making a dark red wine in the **DOC** zones of Vesuvio and Capri. Also *piediosso.*

pernice (pehr-NEE-cheh)   Partridge, particularly the common gray partridge, *Perdix perdix*. They are roasted on a spit or in the oven.

perricone (peh-ree-KOH-neh)   Red wine grape of Sicily. Also *pignatello*.

persegi in guasso (per-SEH-jee een GWAH-soh)   Cooked peaches flavored with almonds and liqueurs, from the Veneto. From the Latin *persica* (peach).

persicata (pehr-see-KAH-tah)   Peach preserves. Also *marmellata di pesche*. From the Latin *persica* (peach).

persico (PEHR-see-koh)   Perch, *Perca fluviatilis*. A freshwater fish of the family Percidae, with green-gold back and vertical stripes. Small perch may be fried, while large perch are most often poached with vinegar.

pesca (PEH-skah)   Peach. The name derives from the Latin *persica,* because the ancient Romans originally brought the fruit from Persia, probably in the 1st century, when Pliny called it the "Persian apple," *Malum persicum*. The Romans thereafter developed several varieties of peach. In Sicily, peaches are still called *persiche*. Today, peaches are eaten fresh, or are stuffed with cream custard and macaroons and baked, or poached.

Little round, chocolate-stuffed cakes made in Latium to resemble peaches are called *pesche*.

pesca noce (PEH-skah NOH-cheh)   "Peach nut." Nectarine has been known for at least 2,000 years and in the 16th century was called the "nut of Persia." Also *nettarina*. From the Latin *persica* and *nux*.

pescati carbonaretti (peh-SKAH-tee kahr-boh-nah-REH-tee)   "Carbonized catch of fish," so called because the fish are grilled until charred, at which point the scales are removed and the insides seasoned and consumed, from Umbria.

pescatora, alla (AH-lah peh-skah-TOH-rah)   "Fisherman's style." A dish made with seafood. From the Latin *piscator*.

pesce (PEH-sheh)   General term for fish. *Pesce azzurro* (blue fish) refers to mackerel, anchovies, and sardines, though not to the bluefish of the North Atlantic, called **pesce serra** in Italy. From the Latin *piscus*.

pesce balestra (PEH-sheh bah-LEH-strah)   "Bow fish." Trigger-fish, *Balistes carolinensis*. The tough skin must be removed before cooking.

pesce castagna (PEH-sheh kah-STAH-n'yah)   "Chestnut fish." Ray's bream, *Brama brama*. The Italian name refers to the fish's brownish color.

pesce-cavallo (PEH-sheh-kah-VAH-loh) "Horse fish." Mackerel, *Scomber scombrus.* A plentiful pelagic fish that the ancient Romans often salted, as it still is today. Mackerel may also be canned or pickled. Fresh, it is best broiled. See also ***sgombro.***

pesce d'uovo (PEH-sheh D'WOH-voh) "Egg fish." Fish omelet with the elongated shape of a fish, from Tuscany.

pesce lucertola (PEH-sheh loo-CHER-toh-lah) Lizard fish, *Synodus saurus.* Not an important species for human consumption.

pesce martello (PEH-sheh mahr-TEH-loh) Hammerhead shark, *Sphyrna zygaena.* The best are young and small. Usually cut into steaks and grilled.

pesce persico (PEH-sheh PEHR-see-koh) Perch, *Perca fluviatilis.* Principally taken from the northern Italian lakes. Usually pan-fried.

pesce pilota (PEH-sheh pee-LOH-tah) Pilot fish, *Naucrates ductor.* So called because it follows ships or swims ahead of sharks. Best for grilling.

pesce prete (PEH-sheh PREH-teh) Priest fish, *Uranoscopus scaber.* So called because its eyes turn upward toward heaven. Also *boch-in-chev* and *lucerna.*

pesce sciabola (PEH-sheh shee-AH-boh-lah) "Sabre fish." Scabbard fish, *Lepidopus caudatus.* A long, silver fish. Usually cut into pieces and fried or grilled.

pesce serra (PEH-sheh SEH-rah) "Clenched fish." Bluefish, *Pomatomus saltator.* A voracious fish with a strong flavor, best grilled or baked. Its Italian name derives from the fish's strong jaws and teeth.

pesce spada (PEH-sheh SPAH-dah) "Sword fish." Swordfish, *Xiphias gladius.* Usually cut into steaks and grilled or baked.

According to legend, Sicilian fishermen, known for their prowess in catching swordfish, lured the fish to the boat with words of Greek. Otherwise, upon hearing Sicilian spoken, the fish would quickly retreat. To this day swordfish is a very popular fish among Sicilians. One Sicilian specialty is to dress the swordfish with ***salmoriglio,*** a mixture of oregano, parsley, garlic, salt, pepper, lemon juice, and olive oil, sometimes with a little seawater added. *Agghiotta di pesce spada* is another Sicilian dish made with tomato, herbs, currants, pine nuts, and olives. *Rustutu cu'sammurigghiu,* also Sicilian, is swordfish fried in oil and seasoned with marjoram or sometimes with a coating of grated cheese and/or bread crumbs. In Calabria, the fish is cooked *alla bagnarese,* roasted with capers, lemon, parsley, and olive oil. See also ***involtini.***

pescestocco (peh-sheh-STOH-koh) Sicilian term for **stoccafisso.** In one Sicilian recipe, the dried fish is soaked, then cooked with potatoes, onion, celery, and tomatoes. Capers and black olives are added at the end of the cooking time.

pesce violino (PEH-sheh vee-oh-LEE-noh) "Violin fish." Flat ray fish, *Rhinobatus rhinobatus.* Particularly abundant around Sicily. So called because of its shape, which resembles a violin. It is best sautéed or broiled.

pesce volante (PEH-sheh voh-LAHN-teh) "Flying fish." Flying fish, *Cypselurus rondeleti.* Not much favored as an edible species.

pescheria (peh-skeh-REE-ah) Fishmonger. Also *pescivendolo.* From the Latin *piscarius* (of fish).

pesciolini (peh-sh'yoh-LEE-nee) "Little fish." Small fry fish such as whitebait.

pesto (PEH-stoh) "Pounded." Any food mashed with mortar and pestle, but more specifically a verdant green sauce made with mashed fresh basil leaves, olive oil, pine nuts or walnuts, and **pecorino** cheese. Forms of *pesto* date back to the ancient Romans' *moretum,* which was made from crushed garlic, parsley, olive oil, vinegar, and ewe's milk. The first mention of the word *pesto* dates to a Florentine cookbook of 1848, but the condiment has become most closely associated with Liguria and, specifically, with Genoa, where **trenette al pesto,** with green beans and potatoes, is a classic dish. From the Late Latin *pestare.*

Purists insist that *pesto* be made only from sweet basil *(Ocinum basilicum),* not bush basil *(O. minimum),* and that metal containers or utensils be used.

TRENETTE COL PESTO

1 garlic clove, chopped	*¹/₂ cup grated parmigiano*
Salt	*¹/₂ cup olive oil*
3 tablespoons pine nuts	*¹/₂ pound potatoes*
2 cups fresh basil leaves	*¹/₂ pound thin green beans, trimmed*
¹/₂ cup grated pecorino	*1 pound trenette*

Crush the garlic, a pinch of salt, and the pine nuts in a large mortar to a smooth paste. Little by little, add the basil leaves and continue to crush to a coarse paste. Gradually add the **pecorino** and **parmigiano,** then begin to work in the olive oil, a little at a time, to produce a smooth pesto.

Peel the potatoes and cut them into thin slices, about ³/₈-inch thick. Place the green beans and potatoes in a large pot of boiling salted water and cook for about 3 minutes. Remove with a slotted spoon and set aside to drain. Plunge the *trenette* into the same boiling water and cook until *al dente,* about 8 minutes. Drain the *trenette,* reserving about 2 tablespoons of the cooking water. Stir the water into the *pesto,* pour over the *trenette,* and toss with the beans and potatoes. Serves 4.

petto   (PEH-toh)   Breast. From the Latin *pectus.*

pevera   (PEH-veh-rah)   Wooden funnel for filling wine casks.

pevera alla padovana   (PEH-veh-rah AH-la pah-doh-VAH-nah)   Seasoned beef marrow, served with salad, from Padua.

peverada   (peh-veh-RAH-dah)   "Pepper (sauce)," used as a condiment to roasted or boiled meats. In Venice, this sauce is a descendant of the medieval *peverata* that once included pomegranate juice. It is now made with chopped poultry liver, salami, lemon peel, bread crumbs, and black pepper.

pezzata   (peh-T'ZAH-tah)   "Big pieces." Stewed ewe with onion, tomatoes, chile peppers, and rosemary, from Molise.

pezzente   (peh-T'ZEHN-teh)   "Beggar." Once a poor man's sausage of Basilicata, made with inferior cuts of pork and a good deal of pepper, it is now popular throughout Italy.

pezzo   (PEH-t'zoh)   Piece, probably from the Vulgar Latin *pettia.*

pezzo duro   (PEH-t'zoh DOO-roh)   "Hard piece." Molded ice cream. See also *gelato.*

pezzo forte   (PEH-t'zoh FOHR-teh)   "Strong piece." Main course of a meal. Also *pièce forte.*

pezzogna   (peh-T'ZOH-n'yah)   Species of fish found off the coast of Capri.

piacere, a   (ah p'yah-CHEH-reh)   Prepared "to your liking," referring to a dish made according to the customer's wishes. From the Latin *placere* (to please).

piacintinu   (pee-ah-cheen-TEE-noo)   "Pleasing [cheese]." *Pecorino* cheese made with saffron, from Messina. From the Latin *placere* (to please).

piadina   (pee-ah-DEE-nah)   "Little plate." Thin round of bread grilled on an earthenware pan called a *testo.* It is topped with a slice of *prosciutto,* salami, or cheese and folded over. *Piada dei morti* is a sweet version with raisins and nuts, from Romagna. Also *piada.* From the Vulgar Latin *plattus.*

piatto (pee–AH–toh)   Plate, both as a piece of dinnerware or a dish served at a meal. *Primo piatto* is the first course of a meal. *Piatti del giorno* are special "dishes of the day" served at a restaurant. *Piatto di mezzo* is an in-between course, such as a vegetable. The word derives from the Vulgar Latin *plattus.*

Piave (pee–AH–veh)   **DOC** zone of the Veneto that produces eight wines, including **merlot, raboso, tocai,** and **verduzzo.**

piccage (pee–KAH–jeh)   Genoese term for "ribbons," referring to a pasta like **tagliatelle.** They are often made with Swiss chard and sausage kneaded into the dough. *Piccage* are often served with **pesto.** The word probably derives from *picché,* piqué cotton fabric, which itself comes from the French *piqué.*

piccante (pee–KAHN–teh)   Sharp, spicy, tangy. From the Middle French *piquer.*

piccata (pee–KAH–tah)   Thin escalope of veal. *Piccatina* is a small escalope.

picchiapo (pee–K'YAH–poh)   "Slap." Boiled beef with onions and tomato, from Rome.

picchiettare (pee–k'yeh–TAH–reh)   "To speckle." To insert spices into meat for flavoring while cooking.

picchi–pacchiu (PEE–kee–PAH–k'yoo)   Any of a variety of spicy tomato–based sauces containing chile peppers and served with a grating of **caciocavallo** cheese, from Sicily. Also *pic-pac.*

The dialect phrase is a combination of slang "slap" and "lazy," whose meaning suggests a well-seasoned life of ease.

piccione (pee–CH'YOH–neh)   Also *torresani.* Squab, farm-grown birds, preferably less than seven months old. The most available in Italy would be the wood pigeon (*Columba palumbus*). *Piccioni selvatici* are wild pigeons. They are best roasted or braised. From the Latin *pipere* (to chirp). See also **colomba** and **palombaccio.**

piccola colazione (PEE–koh–lah koh–lah–t'zee–OH–neh)   "Small collation." Breakfast, which in Italy usually consists of coffee and a roll. Also *prima colazione.* From the Latin *collatio* (light meal).

picellati (pee–cheh–LAH–tee)   "Short fat (pastries)." Pastries filled with nuts, grapes, and honey, from Molise.

pici (PEE–chee)   "Short (pasta)." Short, very thin, hand–rolled egg pasta, from Tuscany. Also *pinci.*

picioni (pee-CH'YOH-nee)   Pastries filled with *ricotta* and raisins and flavored with rum and cinnamon, a specialty of Macerata in the Marches.

picolit (PEE-koh-leet)   A highly regarded semisweet or sweet golden wine of Friuli's **Colli Orientali del Friuli DOC** zone. The name refers to the "small" amount of grapes produced. It has had a long popularity, noted for its quality in the papal courts of the 18th century, and it has been compared to Hungary's *Tokay*. *Picolit* has recently had renewed popularity, owing to new clones developed by Perusini family of the Rocca Bernarda of Ippilis. Also *Piccolit* and *Piccolito*.

piedini di maiala (pee-eh-DEE-nee dee mye-AH-lah)   Pig's feet. From the Latin *pes* (foot).

Piemonte (pee-eh-MOHN-teh)   Piedmont, a region in the northwest of Italy. The most significant factor in Piedmont's gastronomy—as well as its attractiveness to foreign powers ranging from the Romans to the French—is the vast, fertile Po River valley, which produces most of the rice grown in Italy, including the best rice for *risotto.* Piedmont's culinary traditions can be traced to the royal court of Savoy, which ruled from the 15th century until 1861, and to French fashion and style. Many of the best-known dishes of Piedmont are rich with truffles, egg pastas, wild game, and pork products.

There is an equally rich tradition of peasant dishes, some of which have become classics served only in the finest restaurants. **Bollito misto,** a mixture of meats and vegetables simmered for a long time and brought to the table to be ladled out, is familiar to most Italians but finds its most sumptuous realization on Piedmontese tables. **Bagna caôda** is a winter dish of raw vegetables dipped into a hot bath of olive oil. Here, **panissa** is a robust stew of rice, beans, and sausage.

The most famous Piedmontese pastas are the homemade *tajarin* and stuffed **agnolotti;** during the late fall and winter, pasta and *risotto* may be topped with shaved white truffle (**tartufo**) from around Alba. Breadsticks, called **grissini,** are a Piedmontese creation.

Cheeses of note include **bra, gorgonzola, toma,** and **Castlemagno.**

Piedmont is well known for its sweets, including **torrone,** desserts and candies made with **gianduja,** and the **Marsala**-rich egg fluff called **zabaione.**

The most famous wines of Piedmont, which has 37 **DOC** zones, are big, robust reds that also have, in their best examples, tremendous finesse. **Barolo** and **Barbaresco** are the most famous of them all (both have **DOCG** designations), made from the **nebbiolo** grape that also goes into lesser reds, such as **nebbiolo, Gattinara,** and **spanna. Dolcetto** is another well-known medium-bodied red; **barbera** may be found as a somewhat raw, common red or, as in *Barbera d'Asti,* a supple red wine. Of the whites produced, by far the most common and best known is the sparkling **Asti Spumante,** made from **moscato** grapes. *Arneis* is a white wine now gaining some recognition. Piedmont is also known for its *amaro* digestives and for the creation of *vermouth*.

pietanza (pee-eh-TAHN-zah)   Main course, or any kind of food accompanied by bread. See also *companatico*.

pietrafendola (pee-eh-trah-FEHN-doh-lah)   "Rock splitter." A very hard cylindrical cookie, traditionally made on the Feast of the Immaculate Conception (December 8th), from Sicily.

pigato (pee-GAH-toh)   A white wine of Liguria made in the **DOC** zone of Riviera Ligure di Ponente.

pignato grasso (pee-N'YAH-toh GRAH-soh)   Neapolitan dialect for "fat pot," referring to a cabbage, vegetable, and sausage soup, sometimes called *minestra maritata* (wedded soup). In Basilicata, *pignata di pecora* is a stew made with ewe, tomatoes, potatoes, and pork cooked in a large clay pot.

pigneti (pee-N'YEH-tee)   "Small stew." Mutton stew made with tomatoes, chile peppers, salami, and *pecorino,* from Basilicata. It is traditionally cooked in a clay jar that is sealed after the ingredients are placed in it.

pignola (pee-N'YOH-lah)   "Pine (grape)." White grape variety of Valtellina.

pignolata (pee-n'yoh-LAH-tah)   "Pine cone." Traditional Christmas dessert cake made of little balls of fried pastry built up into a cone shape, a specialty of Messina. Also *pignoccata*. From the Latin *pinus.*

Large *amaretti* cookies covered with pine nuts are also called by this named. *Pinolate* are similarly made cookies.

pignolo (pee-N'YOH-loh)   "Big pine nut." Native red grape of Friuli-Venezia Giulia, used in making a cherry-like wine. It was probably first planted in the hills of Rosazzo and was noted in print in the late 17th century. It is considered a promising varietal for quality wine.

pinna (PEE-nah)   Fan mussel, *Pinna nobilis.* Eaten like scallops, fresh, steamed, or sautéed.

pinoccate (pee-noh-KAH-teh)   Traditional Christmas pine nut cookies, from Umbria.

pinoli (pee-NOH-lee)   Pine nuts, especially those from the Italian stone pine tree, *Pinus pinea.* They are eaten raw or toasted and are used widely in Italian cookery, and are essential to a true Ligurian *pesto.* In Sicily, they are often used together with currants as in *passoli e pinoli.* Also *pignoli.*

pinot bianco (PEE-noh bee-AHN-koh)   "White pinot." Widely planted white grape of northern Italy, known in France as *pinot blanc.* The name pinot refers to the pine cone *(pin* in French) shape of the grape bunches.

pinot grigio   (PEE-noh GREE-j'yoh)   "Gray pinot." Widely planted white grape in northern Italy, known in France as *pinot gris* and as *Ruländer* in Alto Adige. See also *pinot bianco* and *pinot nero.*

pinot nero   (PEE-noh NEH-roh)   "Black pinot." The same red grape planted in northern Italy, known as *pinot noir* in France and as *Blauburgunder* (blue burgundy [grape]) in Alto Adige. See also *pinot bianco* and *pinot grigio.*

pinza   (PEEN-zah)   Sweet bread made with cornmeal, fennel seeds, dried figs, candied fruit, and *grappa,* from the Veneto. It is traditionally served on the feast of the Epiphany.

pinzimonio   (peen-zee-MOH-n'yoh)   "Combination." A dip of sea-soned virgin olive oil served after the main course with raw vegetables. In Rome it is sometimes called *cazzimperio.*

piovanello pancia nera   (pee-oh-vah-NEH-loh PAHN-ch'yah NEH-rah)   "Fat little black priest." Snipe, which are in season from August until March. The most common variety in Europe is *Gallinago gallinago.* Snipe is best roasted. See *beccaccino.*

pippiare   (pee-pee-AH-reh)   Cooking term meaning to simmer slowly for a long time, from Naples.

pirrichittus   (pee-ree-KEE-toos)   "Little pear." Pear-shaped pastry puff flavored with orange-blossom water, some with empty centers, some filled with pastry cream, from Sardinia.

pisarei e faso   (pee-SAH-ray eh FAH-zoh)   Small morsels of fresh pasta made with bread crumbs and formed with a crease in the middle, mixed with braised beans, and served in tomato sauce or broth, a specialty of Piacenza and Monferrato.

pisci d'ovu   (PEE-shee D'OH-voo)   Term meaning "fish [made] of eggs," referring to a mixture of eggs and bread crumbs fried in batches, as are small fish, from Sicily. A *fuori tavola* snack.

piselli   (pee-SEH-lee)   Peas. *Piselli novelli* are "new peas." Peas were known to the ancient Romans, who used them dried. The garden variety was developed in Italy during the 16th century, and was a favorite of Caterina de'Medici. Today, Roman peas still have a high reputation for flavor and sweetness; they are often cooked with *prosciutto.* From the Latin *pisum.* See also *taccola.*

pissaladeira   (pee-sah-lah-DEY-rah)   A soft *pizza* of the Italian Riviera, similar to the French *pissaladière.* Thicker than Neapolitan *pizza,* it is topped with tomatoes, anchovies, and olive oil. Sometimes called *pizza all'Andrea,* for the 16th-century naval hero Andrea Doria, whose favorite food it supposedly was.

pistacchio   (pee-STAH-ch'yoh)   Pistachio. Pistachios were introduced to Rome in the 1st century, but were probably grown in southern Italy long before that. Sicily leads in their production. From the Middle Persian *pistak.*

pistada   (pee-STAH-dah)   A condiment of **lardo,** garlic, and parsley crushed into a paste, from Emilia. See also **pesto.** From the Late Latin *pistare* (pounded).

pistum   (PEE-stuhm)   Dumplings made with raisins and sugar, boiled in pork broth.

pitta chicculiata   (PEE-tah kee-koo-L'YAH-tah)   Calabrian **pizza** topped with anchovies, tomato, capers, and black olives. The word *pitta* means flat in Calabrese dialect and *chicculiata* means little pits, referring to the chopped pieces of ingredients on top.

pittenguise   (pee-tehn-GWEE-seh)   Christmas cake shaped in a rosette and containing raisins, nuts, honey, cinnamon, and cloves, from Calabria. It is made two months before Christmas, wrapped carefully, stored, and given as a present. Also *dolce antico.*

pivieressa   (pee-v'yeh-REH-sah)   Plover, a small wading bird, with about 60 species. The eggs are considered a delicacy. The birds are usually roasted. From the Vulgar Latin *pluviarius.* Also *barosala.*

pizza   (PEE-t'zah)   Flat yeast bread topped with a wide variety of ingredients, but principally tomato, **mozzarella,** and basil. *Pizza* is one of the most identifiable of Italian foods, though it was not until after World War II that this Neapolitan item became well known even in the rest of Italy. Indeed, Americans in East Coast cities like New York, Boston, New Haven, and Baltimore, with large Neapolitan immigrant populations, were more familiar with *pizza* than most Italians until the 1950s. Today *pizza* is found throughout Italy, made in 40,000 *pizzerie* (with about 5,000 ovens in Naples alone), and Italians consume 2.5 billion *pizzas* each year.

The term *pizza* is clouded in some ambiguity, though it may derive from an Old Italian word meaning a point, which in turn led to the Italian word *pizzicare,* to pinch or pluck. The word shows up for the first time in print as a Neapolitan dialect word—*piza* or *picea*—about 1000 A.D., possibly referring to the manner in which something is plucked from a hot oven. In Calabria, the term used is *pitta* (flat), where tomatoes are rarely used.

While many Mediterranean cultures and regions of Italy have long had their versions of flatbreads, including the Middle Eastern *pita,* Sicily's **sfincione,** and Tuscany's **schiacciata,** the baked flatbread most people now think of as *pizza* originated in Naples and was a favorite snack of occupying Spanish soldiers at the Taverna Cerriglio in the 17th century. The soft, baked crispy dough that the Neapolitans called a *sfiziosa* would be folded over into a *libretto* (little book) and consumed in the hand. It was baked by men called **pizzaioli,** who worked in small shops called *laboratori.* By the middle of the 19th century the word *pizza* had become common parlance for the food item.

The tomato, with which *pizza* is so closely associated, did not come to Italy from South America until the 16th century and was long considered potentially poisonous, because the fruit is a member of the nightshade family. But the poor of Naples used it to make their daily bread more appetizing, and the tomato grew particularly sweet on the farms of nearby San Marzano.

Then, on June 11, 1889, an official of the Royal Palace asked a local *pizzaiolo* named Raffaele Esposito to create a special *pizza* for the visit of King Umberto I's consort, Queen Margherita, to Capodimonte. Esposito created three examples, but the one most favored by the Queen was made with ingredients in the three colors *(tricolore)* of the Italian flag—red (tomato), white (**mozzarella**) and green (basil) atop the *pizza* dough. Esposito quickly named the newly fashionable *pizza* after the queen, and thus was born the *pizza alla Margherita* that was to become the classic Neapolitan *pizza,* recognized as such by the *Associazione Vera Pizza Napoletana* (The True Neapolitan Pizza Association), which is currently trying to get **DOC** status for Esposito's contribution to world gastronomy. (There is also an *Associazione Pizzaioli Europei e Sostenitori* that represents 175,000 *pizza* workers throughout Europe.)

The *Associazione* also recognizes the excellence of three other types of *pizza: pizza* **alla marinara** (or *all'olio e pomodoro),* with a *marinara* tomato and oil sauce; *p. al formaggio e pomodoro* (grated cheese and tomato); and *p. ripieno* (stuffed pizza), better known as a **calzone,** in which the *pizza* dough is wrapped around a filling of **ricotta, mozzarella** and other condiments.

The following rules have been set by the *Associazzione* for the denomination of a true Neapolitan *pizza:*

1. The crust must be made only with flour, natural yeast or brewer's yeast, salt, and water. All types of fat are absolutely forbidden from inclusion in the *pizza* dough.

2. The diameter of the *pizza* should never exceed 30 centimeters (10 to 12 inches).

3. Dough must be kneaded by hand or by approved mixers that do not cause the dough to overheat.

4. The *pizza* dough must be punched down by hand and not by mechanical means or a rolling pin.

5. The cooking is done directly on the floor of the oven. The use of sheet pans or other containers is not allowed.

6. The oven must be lined with brick and refractory material similar to volcanic stone and must be fired with wood.

7. The oven temperature must be at least 400° C (750° to 800° F).

8. Variations on the classic *pizzas* above, which are inspired by tradition or fantasy, are accepted, provided they are not in conflict with the rules of good taste and culinary laws.

9. The *pizza* must have the following characteristics: not too crusty, well done, and fragrant, with the border *(cornicione)* high and soft.

The traditional *pizza alla margherita* dough is made by hand from a ball of dough called a *pagnotte;* it is stretched and flattened by hand, never with a rolling pin, and must have a puffy crust border called a *cornicione. Fior di latte mozzarella,* fresh tomatoes, and fresh basil are then added, and the *pizza* is baked in a wood-burning stone oven whose temperature reaches upwards of a thousand degrees and cooks the pizza in less than two minutes. The ideal pizza should emerge very hot and crispy, with a brown, semi-charred crust and bubbles, the other ingredients bubbling or melted together.

In Italy *pizzas* are served either as an individual pie for one person or as a square slice called a *taglio,* cut from a larger pie. By custom, inexpensive, simple red wines or cold beer are the beverages of choice with *pizza.*

P. bianca usually refers to a *pizza* with a topping of nothing more than garlic, rosemary, ground pepper, and olive oil, although sometimes the term refers to white cheeses used as a topping, as it does in the United States. *P. all'Andrea* (also, *pizzalandrea* and *pissadella*) is Ligurian *pizza* topped with onion, tomato, garlic, black olives, and anchovies. It is named after 16th-century Italian naval hero Andrea Doria. *P. e fuie* is a corn flour flatbread baked with wild greens, a specialty of Molise. *P. quattro stagioni* (four seasons *pizza*) refers to a *pizza* with four toppings representing the four seasons of the year. *P. alla Siciliana* is Sicilian *pizza* that is usually thicker than Neapolitan *pizza,* baked in a square pan and topped with tomato sauce and, often, anchovies. Sicilians also make a stuffed *pizza* called *carbuchu* (from an Arabic word for bread bakery), filled with anchovy fillets. They also fry plain *pizza* dough called *mitilugghia* (from the Arabic *mitilua,* meaning risen) and *tarongie,* from an Arabic word, *turung,* for orange, referring to the *pizza's* golden color; *mitilugghia* is topped with anchovies. In Apulia *p. del giovedi grasso,* served the last Thursday before Lent begins, is two circles of *pizza* dough enclosing a filling of ground pork, **pecorino, ricotta,** eggs, and lemon zest.

A *pizzetta* is a small, very thin-crusted *pizza,* sometimes eaten without a topping and dipped in sugar or honey.

pizza dolce   (PEE-t'zah DOHL-cheh)   "Sweet pizza." Sweet form of **pizza** topped with a variety of nuts, candied fruit, citrus, and sweet flavorings, usually served at celebrations and feast days. *Pizza di Pasqua ternana* is an Easter bread, from the town of Terni in Umbria. *P. sette occhi* is so called because pastry strips are latticed across the top to show holes resembling seven eyes, from Abruzzo.

pizzaiola, alla (AH-lah pee-t'zye-OH-lah)   Fresh tomato sauce seasoned with herbs and garlic and sometimes containing meat or fish, from Naples. It is so called because it resembles the seasoned tomato topping for *pizza.*

pizzaiolo (pee-t'zye-OH-lo)   *Pizza* maker. See also *pizza.*

pizza rustica (PEE-t'zah ROO-stee-kah)   "Rustic *pizza.*" Savory tart made with **ricotta, mozzarella, prosciutto, mortadella,** and seasonings baked in a pastry crust, from Abruzzo. From the Latin *rusticus.*

pizzicheria (pee-t'zee-keh-REE-ah)   Grocery and delicacies shop of southern Italy. The name refers to "plucking" *(pizzicare)* items from the shelf.

pizzoccheri (pee-T'ZOH-keh-ree)   Baked pasta dish made with buckwheat *tagliatelle* mixed with cooked savoy cabbage and potatoes and layered with cheese, from Valtellina. One Italian language authority contends the word was originally *pinzocchero,* which means provincial.

podere (poh-DEH-reh)   Small wine estate or farm.

polenta (poh-LEHN-tah)   Cooked cornmeal. In Roman times the people made a similar dish which they called *puls* or *pulmentum,* with *farro,* dressed with meat and cheese. When corn came to Italy in the 16th century, the ground meal was used in a wide variety of dishes, beginning with boiled cornmeal that might be served as a porridge, baked and cut into squares, grilled or fried, as a main course in Sicily, as a side dish elsewhere, or as a pasta course as the base for a *ragù,* mushrooms, and other ingredients. *Polenta* is usually cooked to a desired thickness, then poured onto a wooden board called a *taglier* and cut with a string. In Venice they say the texture of freshly made *polenta* should be like *la seta,* "silk," with a glossy finish to it.

Polenta bianca (white *polenta*) is made from white cornmeal of the Veneto and Friuli. *P. edosei (polenta* with birds) is a Lombardian dish of *polenta* covered with small roasted birds like thrushes and skylarks, though the term also refers to a flat-domed layer cake spread with apricot preserves and decorated with little chocolate birds. *P. maritata* is *polenta* layered with red beans and **peperoncino** fried in oil scented with garlic, a specialty of Isernia in Molise. *P. alla rascard* is a Valle d'Aosta version of sliced *polenta* baked with layers of *fontina* and a beef and sausage *ragù.* In Lombardy, *p. in fiur* is cooked with milk, while *p. taragna* is done with butter and *scimudin* cheese, and *gras pista* is a *polenta* dish topped with ground salt pork. In Liguria, *p. incatenata* (enchanted *polenta*) is made with white beans and kale or cabbage. *P. pastizzada* is a Veneto dish made with alternating layers of *polenta* and minced veal, mushrooms, cockscombs, and vegetables. In Abruzzo, there is a tradition of serving *p. sulla tavola* (*polenta* on the table) for which the *polenta* is placed on a table and spread with a hare sauce, at which point everyone at the table consumes it without benefit of plates. *P. sarda* is a Sardinian version made with sausages and a tomato sauce.

pollame   (poh-LAH-meh)   Poultry. From the Latin *pullus.*

Pollino   (poh-LEE-noh)   ***DOC*** light red wine of Calabria, made from *gaglioppo* and *greco nero* grapes grown around the Pollino range.

pollo   (POH-loh)   Chicken, usually referring to a broiler three to five months old and weighing two to three pounds. From the Latin *pullus.*

Pollo novello is a spring chicken, about three months old. *Pollastra* or *pollastrella* is a pullet, a female chicken five to seven months old but not yet laying eggs. *Gallina* is an egg-laying hen. *Galletto* is a young rooster. *Pollo ruspante* is a free-range chicken.

pollo alla diavola   (POH-loh AH-lah dee-AH-voh-lah)   "Devil's style chicken." In Tuscany, the chicken is flattened and heavily seasoned with black pepper. When cooked with a heavy brick on top, it is called *pollo al mattone.* In Florence, *p. alla diavola* is served with a ginger sauce. In Abruzzo, *pollo alla diavola* is cooked with the chile pepper called **diavolicchio.**

POLLO ALLA DIAVOLA

1 chicken (3 pounds)	*Salt*
3 tablespoons olive oil	*Lemon wedges*
Coarsely ground black pepper	

Cut the chicken down the backbone and split open. Place a clean, heavy weight on the chicken to flatten it for at least 1 hour. Brush the chicken on both sides with olive oil, then season heavily with coarsely ground black pepper and salt to taste. Set under the broiler and cook until browned and tender. Serve with lemon wedges on the side. Serves 4.

pollo alla franceschiello   (POH-loh AH-lah frahn-cheh-SK'YEH-loh) Chicken cooked in garlic and olive oil with green olives and **sottaceti** added just before serving, from Abruzzo. Named after Francesco II of the Kingdom of the Two Sicilies.

pollo alla Marengo (POH-loh AH-lah mah-REHN-goh) Chicken sautéed in butter, cooked with white wine, tomatoes, and mushrooms, garnished with parsley, and served with crayfish and fried bread. Named after the Battle of Marengo on June 14, 1800, in Piedmont, where Napoleon defeated the Austrian army, this dish was created by his chef to commemorate the day.

pollo alla melagrana (POH-loh AH-lah meh-lah-GRAH-nah) Chicken cooked with pomegranate seeds.

pollo alla potentina (POH-loh AH-lah poh-ten-TEE-nah) Chicken braised with basil, onion, tomato, peppers, and wine, from Polenza in Basilicata.

pollo alla scarpariello (POH-loh AH-lah skahr-pah-ree-EH-loh) "Chicken shoemaker's style." Spicy chicken dish made with chunks of chicken, usually on the bone, cooked with garlic, vinegar, and white wine, commonly with the addition of sausage slices and mushrooms. Probably of southern Italian origins, it is better known in Italian-American kitchens than in Italy.

POLLO ALLA SCARPARIELLO

3 tablespoons olive oil	4 garlic cloves, chopped
1 chicken (3 pounds), cut into small pieces	1/4 cup vinegar
	1/4 cup dry white wine
1/2 pound Italian sausage, cut into pieces	Salt and pepper

Heat the oil in a large sauté pan, add the chicken pieces, and brown evenly. Add the sausage pieces and brown evenly. Drain off the excess fat, add the garlic, and cook until chicken is golden brown and tender. Add the vinegar and reduce for 3 minutes. Add the white wine and salt and pepper to taste, cover the pan, and simmer until the chicken is cooked through and the sauce is reduced to a minimum. Serves 4.

pollo ripieno alla lunigianese (POH-loh ree-pee-EH-noh AH-lah loo-nee-j'yah-NEH-seh) Chicken stuffed with beets, greens, eggs, and *ricotta,* boiled, and served with *salsa d'agresto* made with **agresto,** walnuts, bread crumbs, sugar, and garlic, from Lunigiana, a valley between Liguria and Tuscany.

polmone (pohl-MOH-neh) Lung. From the Latin *pulmo.*

polpa (POHL-pah)   Boneless beef or veal. The term also means pulp, as of tomatoes. From the Latin *pulpa* (flesh).

polpette (pohl-PEH-teh)   Meatballs. Also *polpettine* and *purpetti*.

polpettone (pohl-peh-TOH-neh)   Meat loaf.

polpettone di tonno (pohl-peh-TOH-neh dee TOH-noh)   Tuna sausage bound with bread crumbs and eggs.

polpo (POHL-poh)   *Octopus vulgaris*. Also *polipo*. A cephalopod with eight arms with two rows of suckers. *Moscardino* is a small octopus *(Eledone cirrosa)*, while *polpetto, polpessa,* or *fragoline di mare* (sea strawberries, *Octopus macropus*) are the smallest.

Larger octopuses should be skinned and tenderized by being pounded. They are usually stewed or boiled, often served cold with a little lemon and olive oil. In *polpi in purgatorio* (octupuses in Purgatory) they are cooked with **diavolicchio,** from Abruzzo.

polsonetto (pohl-soh-NEH-toh)   Small, round-bottomed copper cooking pan used to make custards.

polverino (pohl-veh-REE-noh)   "Little powder." Flour mixture sprinkled on **panforte** before baking. From the Latin *pulver* (powder).

Pomino (poh-MEE-noh)   **DOC** zone of Tuscany restricted to land owned by Marchesi de'Frescolbaldi, who has made well-regarded white and red wines on the property, as well as a **vin santo.**

pomodoro (poh-moh-DOH-roh)   Tomato. Though closely associated with Italian cooking, the tomato actually only reached southern Italy from the New World in the 16th century. It was supposedly brought by two Jesuit priests from Mexico and flourished in the region around Naples. The Italian botanist Piero Andrea Mattoli first mentions the fruit (the tomato is not a vegetable) in 1544, calling them *pomi d'oro,* "golden apples," referring to their yellow color before fully ripened. Mention is made of tomatoes' cultivation in Italy in 1607, but the first known recipe for cooked tomatoes in Italy did not appear until 1705 in a Roman manuscript. The first tomato sauce recipe appeared in 1797 in a cookbook by Francesco Leonardi, former cook to Russia's Catherine the Great, but this was more in the style of a French *coulis.* The first mention of **spaghetti** (actually **vermicelli***)* with a sauce of tomato was in 1839, described by Ippolito Cavalcanti, Duke of Buonvicino, in *Cucina casareccia in dialetto napoletano (Home Cooking in Neapolitan Dialect).*

By the 19th century tomatoes were widespread throughout Italy, though not yet synonymous with Italian cooking, as it became among the emigrants to America at the end of the century. In 1875, however, Francesco Cirio began to process tomatoes, canning them commercially, and the fruit became widely used and a major industry in Italy.

Pomodori seccati al sole are sun-dried tomatoes. *Concentrato di pomodoro* is tomato paste. Canned tomatoes are called *pomodori in scatola. Pommarola* is a tomato sauce.

pomodoro a strica-sale (poh-moh-DOH-roh ah STREE-kah-SAH-leh) "Salt-rubbed tomato." Just-picked, ripe tomatoes rubbed with salt and eaten, from Sicily.

pompelmo (pohm-PEHL-moh) Grapefruit. Appeared in the New World only about 200 years ago as a new species, which probably arose from mutation. The name derives from the Dutch name for the fruit, *pompelmoes,* which means "big lemon," and refers more specifically to the *pummelo,* which itself may have been an ancestor of the grapefruit. Only after its commercial cultivation in Florida around 1890 did the grapefruit achieve a popularity that has made it second in importance to the lemon among citrus fruits.

porchetta (pohr-KEH-tah) Roast suckling pig. A spit-roasted suckling pig flavored with rosemary and garlic is called *porceddu* in Sardinia. It used to be cooked in a pit lined with stones. a dish called *carne a carrarglu* (meat in a hole). The term *in porchetta* refers to any dish prepared the way suckling pig is. From the Latin *porcus* (pork).

porcini (pohr-CHEE-nee) "Little pigs." Boletus mushrooms, *Boletus edulis.* Grown mainly in Alto Adige, Emilia-Romagna, Piedmont, Toscany of Umbria, and the Veneto. The best season for them is late August through the end of October. They are eaten fresh, often sautéed in oil with garlic and parsley, and added to everything from pasta sauces to stews. They are also available dried. From the Latin *porcus* (pig).

porrata (poh-RAH-tah) Either of two preparations: a sauce made of pounded leeks, olive oil, and crusted bread, or a leek tart made with egg and topped with ***pancetta,*** from Florence. From the Latin *porrum* (leek).

porro (POH-roh) Leek. *Porrina* is the white portion. The origins of the leek are obscure, but it was well known in ancient Egypt and earlier in Mesopotamia. Leeks have remained a favorite vegetable of Europeans since the Middle Ages. In Italy today, leeks are sautéed, braised, and added to soups or stews. From the Latin *porrum.*

portulaca (pohr-too-LAH-kah) Purslane. Grows wild around the Mediterranean. Used as a salad green and to flavor stews and soups. The plant may have originated in India but was spread early on to the Mediterranean and Europe. From the Latin.

Posillipo, alla   (AH-lah poh-SEE-lee-poh)   "Posillipo style." Dish using shellfish and tomato, as is done in the area of Naples called Posillipo.

potacchio, in   (een poh-TAH-ch'yoh)   Stew containing chile peppers, tomato, white wine, and herbs with meat, poultry, or seafood, from the Marches.

poveraccia   (poh-veh-RAH-ch'yah)   "Poor little (clam)." Term for a small clam.

pranzo   (PRAHN-zoh)   In some parts of Italy this term means lunch, elsewhere called *colazione.* In other regions *pranzo* may mean dinner. From the Latin *prandium.*

prataiolo   (prah-tye-OH-loh)   "Field [mushroom]." Horse mushroom, *Psalliota arvensis.* Large white mushroom prepared *trifolato* style.

preboggion   (preh-boh-J'YAHN)   Mixture of borage, beets, dandelions, chicory, and chervil used to stuff *pansôti,* from Liguria. From the Old French *bourage* (borage).

Predicato   (preh-dee-KAH-toh)   "Preached." Tuscan wines created in 1980 by a consortium of producers, led by Ambrogio Folonari of Ruffino, to bring order to those table wines that did not conform to traditional **DOC** and **DOCG** designations. *Predicato di Biturica* is a red made from **cabernet** and **sangiovese;** *P. di Cardisco,* a red from *Sangiovese* and 10 percent other grapes; *P. del Muschio,* a white from **chardonnay** or **pinot bianco, riesling, Müller-Thurgau,** or **pinot grigio;** and *P. del Selvante,* a white from **sauvignon** *blanc* and other varieties. In 1993 the name *Predicato* was changed to *Capitolare* so that it would not be confused with the German wine label term *Prädikat.*

prescinseha   (preh-sheen-SEH-ah)   Acid-curd fresh cheese, like clabbered cream, from Liguria. Also *prescinsena.*

presine   (PREH-see-neh)   One-inch square unsweetened wafers of the kind used in Holy Communion and formerly by pharmacists to be soaked with a dose of liquid medicine.

pressato   (preh-SAH-toh)   "Pressed [cheese]." A firm yellow cow's milk cheese similar to *asiago,* originally from Vicenza.

preznitz   (PREHZ-neetz)   Triestian sweet pastry rolls with raisins, nuts, and candied fruits.

prezzemolo   (preh-T'ZEH-moh-loh)   Parsley, which is said to have originated in Sardinia. Flat-leaf Italian parsley is somewhat more pungent than other European varieties of parsley. Owing to the liberal use of *prezze-*

molo in so many dishes, there is a saying in Italy that children are like parsley, because "they get in everything."

From the Latin *petroselinum,* in turn from the Greek *petroselinon* (stone celery).

prezzo fisso   (PREH-t'zoh FEE-soh)   "Fixed price." A meal at a set price in a restaurant, as opposed to à la carte. From the Latin *pretium* and *figere.*

primaticci   (pree-mah-TEE-chee)   "First little (vegetables)." The first vegetables or fruit of the season. Also *primizie.* From the Latin *primus* (first).

primavera, alla   (AH-lah pree-mah-VEH-rah)   "Springtime style." Any dish served with fresh vegetables. In Venice, **risotto** *primavera* is very popular.

primitivo   (pree-mah-TEE-voh)   "Primitive." Also *primitiva.* A red grape of Apulia that produces big-bodied red wines. *Primitivo* is believed to be related to the American grape called Zinfandel. The name *primitivo* refers to the grapes' early-ripening characteristics. From the Latin *primus* (first).

P. di Manduria is a **DOC** red of Apulia used widely for blending as well as for wines in the **secco, amabile,** and **dolce** *naturale* styles.

primo   (PREE-moh)   So-called first course of the meal, although it follows the **antipasto.** It is usually soup, pasta, or **risotto.** From the Latin *primus* (first).

procanico   (proh-KAH-nee-koh)   Grape of Umbria, used in making **Orvieto.**

produttore   (proh-doo-TOH-reh)   Producer. From the Latin *produco.*

profiterole   (proh-fee-teh-ROH-leh)   Cream-puff-pastry shells filled with whipped cream, pastry cream, or ice cream and served with chocolate sauce, like their French namesake. In Florence, they are sometimes called **bongo.**

profumo   (proh-FOO-moh)   Aroma. From the Latin *fumus* (smoke).

prosciutto   (proh-SHOO-toh)   Cured ham. *Prosciutto* has been made for more than two thousand years in the region around Langhirano, near Parma. *P. di Parma* must come from one of three regions to be entitled to a **DOC** label: Parma, San Daniele (in Friuli), or the Veneto. By law the ham must come from a cross of five different breeds of pig born and raised in those regions, and be fed on corn, barley, cereals, and the whey from **Parmigiano**-*Reggiano* cheese production; the pig must reach a minimum weight of 340 pounds and be a year old. It is said that the winds, both from the sea and the mountains, give *p. di Parma* its taste and delicacy.

At production houses called *prosciuttifici,* the hams are treated to an exacting process of curing and aging. A minimum of salt is used in the curing process, and the use of nitrites, sugar, smoke, water, or additives is forbidden.

The hams must be cured for at least 300 days, usually more for export. About 7 million *p. di Parma* are produced each year. Other, non-**DOC** *prosciutti* are produced in other parts of Italy. *Prosciutto* is usually served in paper-thin slices as an **antipasto,** though it is often cut into small pieces and added to many dishes, including **pastas** and savory pies.

Prosciutto crudo refers both to raw and to cured ham. *P. cotto* is cooked ham. *P. fresco* is fresh ham; it is sometimes braised in **Marsala** with vegetables. *P. di capriolo* is made from roebuck; *p. di cinghiale* is from boar.

prosecco   (proh-SEH-koh)   A white grape of Friuli, used in making *frizzante* wines, best known in the Veneto as the topper in the **bellini** cocktail. The sparkling quality is accomplished through the French *Charmat* process of inducing a second fermentation in a tank. *Prosecco di Conegliano-Valdobbiadene* is a **DOC** varietal made in a range of *frizzante* and **spumante** wines.

provatura   (proh-vah-TOO-rah)   Cow's milk **mozzarella,** from Latium, commonly breaded and fried. It is sometimes called **marzolina** because it is best made in the month of March (*Marzo* in Italian). The word translates roughly as "try it."

provola   (PROH-voh-lah)   A semisoft cow's milk cheese, **pasta filata,** from southern Italy. Once made from buffalo's milk, and sometimes smoked, it is similar to **mozzarella** but ripened longer. The word means globe-shaped.

provolone   (proh-voh-LOH-neh)   A sharp, spicy, very aromatic cow's milk cheese, usually with a hard wax rind, originally from southern Italy. The word derives from a Campanian dialect word *prova* (globe-shaped). *Provolette* is a small version, *provole* medium, and *provoloni* large, which may reach 5 or 6 feet in length. *Provolone piccante,* a strong-flavored version, is made with lamb or kid's rennet and aged; *p. dolce,* which is much milder, is made with calf's rennet.

prugna   (PROO-n'yah)   Plum. *Prugna secca* (dried plum) is a prune. From the Latin *prunus* (prune). Plums were first brought to ancient Rome from Damascus. See also **susina.**

puccia   (POO-ch'yah)   Olive bread or rolls of Apulia. In Piedmont, the name of a pork and cabbage stew served with **polenta.**

puddighinus   (poo-dee-GHEE-noos)   "Baby chicken." Roast chicken stuffed with giblets, bread crumbs, egg, and tomatoes, from Sardinia.

Puglia   (POO-l'yah)   Apulia, a region in the heel of Italy with a rather flat topography and a long seacoast. There is a significant wheat-growing zone around Foggia, and vegetables like artichokes, fava beans, and arugula that do well in bright, hot, sunny weather flourish throughout the province.

Though one of Italy's poorest regions for centuries, Apulia has come a long way in the past decade, and its tradition of eating large amounts of meat and cheese has never been more evident than now. Its *pasta* includes the ear-shape *orecchiette* and the almond-shape *cavatelli*. *Ciceri e tria* is composed of fried pasta strips with chickpea, and *'ncapriata* is a hearty dish of pureed fava beans, chicory, and olive oil. *Gniumerieddi* are lamb innards cooked with *pecorino* cheese.

As befits its prospect on the sea, Apulia offers abundant seafood, from the baby octopus of Bari to the mussels of Taranto.

Of its cheeses, *caciocavallo, provolone,* and *scamorza* are widely available. For dessert there is a quince concentrate called *cotognata.*

Despite its 26 **DOC** zones, the wines of Apulia are of modest quality, the best known being the reds from **Salice Salentino.** The best white is *Locorotondo.*

pummarola   (poo-mah-ROH-lah)   Plum tomatoes, from San Marzano in Campania. *A pummarola 'ncoppa* means topped with tomato, from Naples. From **pomodoro.**

punta   (POON-tah)   Shoulder of meat.

puntarelle   (poon-tah-REH-leh)   Wild chicory spears. Eaten raw, dressed with olive oil, lemon juice, vinegar, garlic, and anchovies, in a salad, from Rome. From **pomodoro.**

pupazze   (poo-PAH-t'zeh)   "Doll babies." Calabrian Easter bread whose dough is braided to swaddle an Easter egg, as if in a blanket. From the Latin *pupa.*

purea   (poo-REH-ah)   Puree. Also *pure.*

pusteria   (poo-steh-REE-ah)   Soft, mild cow's cheese of Trentino-Alto Adige.

putizza   (poo-TEE-t'zah)   Easter cake roll filled with nuts, chocolate, coffee beans, *grappa,* and vanilla wafers and formed into a snail shape, from Istria. The word may come from the Slovenian *potivica* (rolled one).

puttanesca, alla   (AH-lah poo-tah-NEH-skah)   "Harlot style." A robust southern Italian tomato sauce. Usually made with tomatoes, onions, garlic, chile peppers, capers, olives, anchovies, and oregano. The reference to prostitutes supposedly suggests this was a sauce quickly made by such women between clients. It is most often associated with Naples and Calabria, although versions are found throughout Italy.

SPAGHETTI ALLA PUTTANESCA

¹/₄ cup olive oil
2 garlic cloves, crushed
1 peperoncino, chopped
4 anchovies, chopped
1 ¹/₂ pounds ripe tomatoes, peeled,
*   seeded, and chopped*

4 ounces black olives
1 tablespoon capers
Salt and pepper
1 pound spaghetti, cooked until al
*   dente*

Heat the olive oil in a large saucepan and add the garlic and **peperoncino**. When the garlic is golden, remove from the pan. Add the anchovies, tomatoes, olives, and capers and cook for 7 to 8 minutes. Add salt and pepper to taste. Serve over **spaghetti**. Serves 4.

puzzone (poo-T'ZOH-neh) "Big, smelly (cheese)." Strong-smelling cow's milk cheese made around the city of Moena in Trentino.

Q

quadrucci (kwah-DROO-chee) "Little squares." Stuffed pasta squares added to soups. In Lombardy, *quadrucci* are stuffed with ham, eggs, sweetbreads, bread, and cheese. *Quadratini* are extremely small squares used in soups. From the Latin *quadratus*.

quagghiaride (kwah-gh'yah-REE-deh) "Innards." Sheep's stomach stuffed with **scamorza,** eggs, chicken giblets, and salami, baked, and served with boiled arugula, from Apulia.

quaglia (KWAH-l'yah) Quail. The bird is usually barded and then roasted on a spit or braised. *Quaglie alla stemperata* (diluted quail) is quail stewed in a mixture of vegetables and diluted vinegar and served with olives, from Sicily. *Melanzane a quaglia* is deep-fried eggplant cut so that the slices curl to resemble a quail's tail, from Sicily. From Middle Latin *quaccula*.

quagliette (kwah-L'YEH-teh) "Little quail." Tiny balls of leftover stuffing wrapped in cabbage leaves and fried.

quaresimali (kwah-reh-see-MAH-lee) "Lent." Lenten biscuits, usually made with ground almonds, sugar, vanilla, and egg whites. In Tuscany, they are made with cocoa powder and shaped like alphabet letters.

quartirolo (kwahr-tee-ROH-loh) Also *milan stracchino*. Smooth, uncooked, mild soft cow's milk cheese made around Bergamo, Pavia, and Lodi in Lombardy. It is shaped into a square. The name refers to the milk from cows that in the past had been fed the fourth *(quarto)* cutting of the sweetest grass in late September and early October; the cheese is now made year-round.

quattro formaggi, ai (eye KWAH-troh fohr-MAH-jee) "With four cheeses." A pasta sauce made by mixing four different cheeses, of which two are usually **fontina** and **parmigiano.**

quinquinelle (kween–kwee–NEH–leh)   Quenelles. Skinless forcemeat in the shape of a sausage, made with meat or seafood that is bound with eggs and fat, then poached. Gastronomic authority Giuliano Bugialli contends that the word dates at least to the 14th century in Italian print, but it derives from the German *Knödel* (dumpling).

quinto quarto (KWEEN-toh KWAHR-toh)   "Fifth fourth." Organ meats and variety items including sweetbreads, brains, hooves, and testicles, from Rome. Called *quinto quarto* because the meats make up an additional fifth part of the animal's carcass, which is traditionally butchered into four quarters.

R

rabarbaro (rah-BAHR-bah-roh) Rhubarb. The rhubarb root came to Europe in the Middle Ages and mainly was used medicinally. The edible plant itself did not arrive in France until 1724. Still, with the exception of the English, Europeans cared little for the taste of rhubarb, and it is not an important comestible in Italy. From the Latin *Rhabarbarum* (Rha of the barbarians), which referred to the river Rha (now the Volga) on whose banks the plant was cultivated by the barbarian tribes that came to be known as the Tatars.

raboso (rah-BOH-soh) A red wine grape of the Veneto, used in making a wine of the same name, which is said to derive from *rabbioso* (angry), because of the wine's roughness and high acidity.

radiatori (rah-dee-ah-TOH-ree) Radiators. A pasta shape so called because it resembles a radiator heater.

radicchio (rah-DEE-k'yoh) A red- or purple-leaf chicory. There are four principal varieties: *radicchio di Castelfranco, r. di Chioggia, r. di Verona,* and *r. di Treviso,* known locally as *spadone.* The round *r. di Chioggia,* developed after World War II, is the most widely exported red variety.

Radicchio is eaten as a salad or garnish, braised or grilled and served as a vegetable, and sometimes added to sauces. *Risotto al radicchio* is made with *r. di Treviso.* The word *radichio* probably derives from the Latin *radix* (root).

radice (rah-DEE-cheh) Roots, specifically the radish. The radish is not a favorite vegetable for Italians, though it appears in an *antipasto* or a salad. From the Latin *radix* (root). Also *rapanelli* and *ravanelli.*

rafano (RAH-fah-noh) Radish or horseradish, from Piedmont. See also **radice, ramolaccio,** and **Kren.**

ragù (rah-GOO) Meat sauce, usually referring to the long-simmered Bolognese classic, *ragù alla bolognese,* made with vegetables, tomatoes, heavy cream, and beef.

The word *ragù* is a corruption of the French word for stew, *ragoût,* which in turn derives from the Latin *gustus* (taste). During the Renaissance and afterward, French and Italian stews shared similarities in aristocrats' kitchens. Emilia-Romagna also had an affinity for French culinary style, and by the end of the 18th century the term *ragù* was used to refer to a **maccheroni** meat sauce seasoned with meat, cinnamon, and black pepper. By the next century *ragù* always referred to a meat sauce, not to a stew, and Bologna's was the best known. *Ragù alla napoletana,* however, is made with meat that is removed and eaten on its own as a second course after the pasta course which is sauced with the *ragù.* Colloquially, the Neapolitans refer to their *ragù* as *guadaporta,* which means doorman, because such a person could stand in a doorway all day and watch the *ragù* simmer. See also **salsa** and **sugo.**

ragù del macellaio   (rah-GOO dell mah-cheh-LYE-oh)   "Butcher's-style ragù." Mixed meat sauce with tomatoes and onion, from Bari. The sauce is traditionally served on **orecchiette** or **cavatelli,** then the meat is eaten on its own. See also **sugo.**

ragusano   (rah-goo-SAH-noh)   Cow's milk cheese, a kind of **provolone**, made around Ragusa, in Sicily. It is usually shaped into small cushions tied with string.

Ramandolo   (rah-MAHN-doh-loh)   *DOC* zone of Friuli that produces sweet **verduzzo** wines. Also a white wine in the *DOC* zone of **Colli Orientali del Friuli.**

rambasici   (rahm-bah-SEE-chee)   Meat-filled rolls of savoy cabbage, from Friuli.

ramerino   (rah-meh-REE-noh)   Rosemary. The term also refers to a Tuscan bread loaf containing rosemary. From the Latin *rosmarinus.* See also **rosmarino.**

ramolaccio   (rah-moh-LAH-ch'yoh)   Horseradish. *Ramolaz nero* (black horseradish) is a type found and used in cooking in Lombardy.

rana   (RAH-nah)   Frog. Frogs' legs are called *cosce di rane.* From the Latin.

rana pescatrice   (RAH-nah pess-kah-TREE-cheh)   "Frog fish." Also *boldro* and *coda di rospo.* Angler fish, *Lophius piscatorius.* Known by more than a dozen names in English (including monkfish, bellyfish, and goosefish) and as *lotte* in France, this large-mouthed saltwater fish has a broad, ugly head and pointy teeth. It is so ugly that the fish is often sold with the head cut off, though it may be used for fish stock or soup. The tail *(coda)* provides the principal edible part of the fish. It is caught in the eastern Atlantic and Mediterranean and is particularly flavorful in winter months.

rapa (RAH-pah)   Turnips. See also **brovada.** From the Latin.

raschera (rah-SKEH-rah)   A hearty cow's milk and ewe's milk cheese, made around Cùneo in Piedmont.

raveggiolo (rah-veh-J'YOH-loh)   Tangy fresh cheese made from goat's, sheep's, or cow's milk, principally from Campania but also in northern Italy. Also *ravaggiolo.*

Ravello (rah-VEH-loh)   A wine region centered in the town of Ravello in Campania. A red and a rosé are made from **per'e palummo, aglianico, merlot,** and other grapes. The white is made from *coda di volpe, San Nicola,* **greco,** and other grapes.

ravioli (rah-vee-OH-lee)   Square **pasta** shape (sometimes with ridged edges) enclosing any of a wide variety of ingredients, most commonly **ricotta** and spinach.

The word may derive from the Latin *rabiola,* for rape turnip, whose shape was imitated in the *ravioli,* or from *ravolgere* (to wrap). The city of Cremona claims to have created *ravioli.* But Genoa claims them, too, insisting the word actually dates to their dialect word for the *pasta, rabiole,* which means "something of little value" and supposedly came from the practice of thrifty sailors who stuffed any and all leftovers into pasta to be used as another meal. Today *ravioli alla genovese* uses a stuffing of liver and lamb's brains, cow's udder, capon, spinach, **prescinseha,** egg, ham, and egg yolks. Another Ligurian version called *zembi d'arzillo* is stuffed with fish, escarole, and watercress, then sauced with tomatoes, garlic, butter, and marjoram. *R. alla piemontese* is a Piedmont dish made with meat and vegetables served with a brown sauce and **parmigiano.** In the Marches, *r. ai filetti di sogliola* are filled with *ricotta* and dressed with a sauce made from tomatoes and fillet of sole. *R. alla pustterese* are filled with sauerkraut, from Trentino-Alto Adige. *R. alla caprese* is made with **caciotta** cheese and served with tomato sauce, as in Capri. *R. di Purim* are spinach-stuffed *ravioli* served by Italian Jews at the feast of Purim. There are, as well, many *ravioli*-like regional *pastas* with names such as **agnolotti, cansonei, cappellacci, pansôti, tortellini, turteln,** and others. *R. in camicia* (*ravioli* in their undershirts) or *ignudi* (nudies) are actually poached meat or vegetable dumplings that look like *ravioli* filling but are not actually wrapped in dough at all.

RAVIOLI IN CAMICIA

1 pound fresh spinach, after stemming
  and cleaning
2 tablespoons butter
1 teaspoon kosher salt
1 ²/₃ cups ricotta cheese
1 ¹/₂ cups freshly grated parmigiano
¹/₄ teaspoon freshly grated nutmeg
1 egg yolk

3 tablespoons flour, for the ravioli
¹/₄ cup flour, for rolling the ravioli
6 quarts water, salted

SAUCE:
5 tablespoons unsalted butter
10 fresh sage leaves
¹/₄ cup freshly grated parmigiano

In a large pot, place the washed, wet spinach over medium heat, cover, and cook for a few minutes until the spinach wilts. Immediately rinse under cold water, and drain in a colander. Take a wooden spoon and squeeze the spinach against the sides of the colander with the spoon until all liquid is gone. One can also take spinach in handfuls and squeeze excess water through the fingers. In a sauté pan, add the butter and sauté the spinach until there is almost no water left. On a cutting board, chop the spinach leaves finely and put into a bowl and let cool. Add the salt, **ricotta, parmigiano,** nutmeg, egg yolk, and the flour, and mix well. If the mixture is too soft, refrigerate for 1 to 2 hours.

Heat the water. In the meantime, shape the *ravioli* into walnut-size ovals and lightly roll in the flour. Set aside. Lower the *ravioli,* a few at a time, into the boiling water and poach for 2 to 3 minutes, long enough for them to rise to the top. Remove them, drain them, and repeat with the rest. Preheat the oven to 375° F. In a saucepan, melt the butter with the sage leaves. Place the poached *ravioli* in a baking dish, drizzle with the sage butter, and sprinkle with the cheese. Bake until lightly browned, about 10 minutes. Serve immediately. Serves 4.

---

razza   (RAH-t'zah)   Ray fish. Any of a large group of flat, cartilaginous fish in the genus *Raja,* including *razza chiodata (R. clavata)* and *r. quattrocchi (R. miraletus),* which means "four-eyed ray" because of two dark spots on the body that look like eyes. Rays have long tails and thick skin, and the wings are the only truly edible part. The fish's nimbleness gives it the alternative name *arzilla.*

reblec   (REH-blehk)   A fresh, cow's milk curd cheese of Valle d'Aosta.

recioto   (reh-chee-OH-toh)   Wine process of drying grapes to a raisin-like state on straw mats to concentrate their sugar, which make high-alcohol dry wines like **amarone**. *Recioto* is a dialect word of the Veneto meaning ears, referring to the tops of the dried grape bunches.

refosco   (reh-FOH-skoh)   **DOC** red wine of Friuli. From *fosco* (fog), which may refer to the climatic conditions of the vineyard area.

regina in porchetta   (reh-JEE-nah een pohr-KEH-tah)   "Queen in suckling pig." Carp taken from Lake Trasimeno and cooked in the manner of roast piglet called **porchetta,** from Umbria. From the Latin *regina*.

reginette   (reh-jee-NEH-teh)   "Little queens." Sweet dipping biscuits rolled in sesame seeds, a specialty of Sicily.
 Also a **lasagne**-width noodle with ruffled edges.

resta   (REH-stah)   "String." Plaited strings of garlic or onions hung outdoors to dry.

resti di cibo   (REH-stee dee CHEE-boh)   "The remainders of the meal." Leftovers.

rete di maiale   (REH-teh dee mye-AH-leh)   Caul fat. Taken from the membrane lining a pig's stomach. The word *rete* means network, because the caul has a lattice-like composition and texture; *maiale* means pig.

rhum   (rum)   Rum, first made in the Caribbean from sugar cane. The word, though of British origin, may ultimately derive from the Latin *saccharum* (sugar). None is made in Italy, but it is drunk as a spirit or used as a flavoring.

ribel   (REE-bel)   Buckwheat fritters, from Alto Adige.

ribes   (REE-bess)   Currant, both black *(nero)* and red *(rosso)*. The word is derived from the taxonomic genus *Ribes*. Dried currants (small grapes) are *passoli*.

ribolla   (ree-BOH-lah)   **DOC** white grape of Friuli whose history dates to the 13th century and was mentioned by Bocaccio in an essay on gluttony. Its quality declined in the 19th and 20th centuries, but there have been recent attempts to upgrade the wine. Also *ribolla gialla*. See also **schioppettino.**

ribollita   (ree-boh-LEE-tah)   "Re-boiled." Hearty Florentine soup made with beans, olive oil, vegetables (usually red cabbage), bread, and cheese, left to stand, and reheated. It is traditionally made with the leftover soup from the day before and should be thick enough to be eaten with a fork. Sometimes it is colloquially referred to as *zuppa del cane* (soup for the dog) because of its simplicity.

ricciarelli   (ree-chee-ah-REH-lee)   "Curly [biscuits]." Almond-shaped cookies, from Siena, whose shape is associated with the feast of the Annunciation (March 25) and with fertility.

ricci di donna   (REE-chee dee DOH-nah)   "Lady's curls." Pasta shape resembling curly hair, from Calabria.

riccio di mare   (REE-ch'yoh dee MAH-reh)   "Curl of the sea." Sea urchin, *Paracentrotus lividus.* When opened, these spiny round creatures reveal the only part that is eaten—the five orange or pink ovaries known as coral. They are commonly eaten raw with a squeeze of lemon juice, although they may be cooked with other ingredients.

ricciola   (REE-ch'yoh-lah)   Amberjack, *Seriola dumerili.* A bluish fish with a yellow streak. Best grilled or baked. Also *leccia.*

riccitelle   (ree-chee-TEH-leh)   "Little curls." Curly, crimped strands of pasta. Also *tripolini.*

riccoli   (REE-koh-lee)   "Curlies." Curly macaroni shape.

ricevuta   (ree-cheh-VOO-tah)   Receipt, as for a restaurant meal. Also *ricevuta fiscale* and *fattura.* Under recent Italian law, a restaurant customer must carry a receipt called a **scontrino** with him upon leaving the restaurant. Otherwise, a policeman may issue a *multa,* a ticket that requires paying a fine.

ricotta   (ree-KOH-tah)   "Re-cooked." Fresh soft cow's milk cheese made from the whey, although it was traditionally made with ewe's milk. Roman-style *ricotta* is quite moist, while Piedmontese-style *ricotta* is creamier.
    Ricotta salata or *canestrata* is firmer and salted. *R. secca* is dried and used for grating. *R. infornata* is a Sicilian version that is baked until brown. *R. marzotica* is a Puglian version ripened in herb leaves. *R. forte* is a double-fermented *ricotta,* from Apulia. In Venetian dialect, *ricotta* is called *puina.*

ridurre   (ree-DOO-reh)   To reduce, as a sauce or heated liquid. From the Latin *reducere.*

riesling italico   (REE-s'ling ee-TAH-lee-koh)   White wine grape planted in northern Italy. Not a true riesling, which is called **riesling renano.** In Alto Adige, it is called *Welschriesling* ("foreign riesling" in German). See also **riesling renano.**

riesling renano   (REE-z'ling reh-NAH-noh)   White wine grape planted throughout northern Italy. Known as *Rheinriesling* in Alto Adige because it is the true *Johannisberg* or *white riesling* used in Germany's Rhine Valley. From the German.

riffoli   (REE-foh-lee)   Sponge cake filled with **ricotta,** citron, chocolate, and **pistachios,** then glazed, from Campania.

rigaglie   (ree-GAH-l'yeh)   Giblets.

rigate   (ree-GAH-teh)   "Ridged." Ribbed **maccheroni,** as opposed to *lisce* (smooth). *Rigatoni* is a fat, ribbed macaroni, about 2 inches long.

rigatino   (ree-gah-TEE-noh)   **Pancetta** covered with black pepper and cured flat, from Tuscany.

ripasso   (ree-PAH-soh)   "Revision." A vinicultural practice in the Veneto of adding **amarone** pomace to a wine to provide bigger body and complexity through a second fermentation.

ripieno   (ree-P'YEH-noh)   "Filled." Stuffed or stuffing.

ris e corata   (REES eh koh-RAH-tah)   "Rice and offal." Rice in consommé with bacon, onion, sage, and calf's lungs, a specialty of Lombardy.

ris e lovertis   (REES eh loh-VEHR-tees)   "Rice and hops." Rice in consommé with buttered hops and grated cheese, a specialty of Lombardy.

riserva   (ree-ZEHR-vah)   "Reserve." **DOC** and **DOCG** wines that have undergone specific aging requirements may be called *riserva. Riserva speciale* requires even longer aging. From the Latin *reservare.*

ris e verz   (REES eh VEHR'tz)   Soup of rice and savoy cabbage, from Lombardy.

riso   (REE-soh)   Rice, of which 50 varieties are grown in Italy. From the Greek via Iranian *(oryzon).*

Rice is produced in four principal categories, according to the length of the grain. The shortest grain is called *comune,* next comes *semifino,* then *fino,* and *superfino.* The last two are ideal for making **risotto.** The most valued in the *superfino* category are *arborio* (a cross between *vialone* and an American strain called Lady Wright), *carnaroli* (a cross between *vialone* and *lencino), baldo, corallo, volano grita,* and a very rare variety called *razza* 77. Unpolished rice is called *vialone,* while unrefined rice that still contains the germ is *r. integrale* or *sbramato.*

Despite erroneous assertions that ancient Greece and Rome acquired rice for propagation from the Orient, the grain was first brought into Europe, to Spain, by the Moors in the 8th or 9th century. From Andalusia it was brought to Sicily, where it may have been grown on a small scale in Piedmont as early as the 10th century. It was documented as being grown in the Po Valley as of 1475, and after Vasco da Gama brought back spices and rice from India to Portugal in 1499, rice production increased rapidly. By 1522 farmers in the Po Valley had constructed complex watering systems for rice cultivation, and the grain became a major part of the northern Italian diet.

Riso in bianco is simple boiled white rice. *R. giallo* is saffron-scented rice served with **parmigiano** and butter. *R. al salto* is a crisply cooked rice pancake.

Risi e bisato is a Veneto dish of rice and eel cooked with bay leaves, lemon, and oil. Venetians also cook *r. in cavroman,* a dish of rice with spiced mutton. *R. e bisi* is a Veneto dish of rice and fresh peas. *Ris e fasui* is a Friulian soup of rice, bean, and potatoes. In Lombardy, **ris e corata** is made with veal lung; *ris e ran* with frog's legs; and *ris e spargitt* is a soup with asparagus. *Ris an cognon* is a Piedmontese soup with rice and **fontina** cheese, while in Lombardy the same dish is made with **parmigiano.** *R. alla pitocca* is a simple boiled rice and chicken dish of Lombardy. *Riso con i bruscandoli* is a Veneto rice dish cooked with springtime wild hops. *Bombo di riso* is a molded dish of rice and pigeon or squab, a specialty of Piacenza and Parma dating back to the 16th century.

RISI E BISI

6 cups beef broth	**¹/₃ cup chopped parsley**
5 tablespoons butter	**3 pounds fresh peas, shelled**
2 tablespoons olive oil	**12 ounces long-grain rice**
2 ounces pancetta, chopped	**Salt to taste**
1 small onion, chopped	**6 tablespoons grated parmigiano**

In a large pot, heat the beef broth. In another large pot, heat the butter and the olive oil. Add the **pancetta** and onion and sauté over moderate heat until onion is soft but not browned. Add the parsley, mix, and cook for another minute. Add the peas, toss with the onion mixture, and add 1 cup of the broth. Let simmer for 10 minutes. Add the rice and another cup of broth and stir. Let cook, stirring every few minutes and adding ¹/₂ cup of broth as it gets absorbed, until rice is **al dente,** about 20 minutes. The final dish should be thick but soupy. Add salt as needed, and the **parmigiano**. Serve immediately. Serves 4 to 6.

risone   (ree-SOH-neh)   "Rice [pasta]." Also *riso* and *orzo.* Rice-shaped macaroni, used for soups.

risotto   (ree-SOH-toh)   A dish of creamy cooked rice that has absorbed a good quantity of broth to make it flavorful and tender. The best varieties of rice are plump and stubby *superfino* varieties (see **riso**), and the best known are regional varieties like *canaroli, arborio,* and *baldo.* The correct consistency for *risotto* should have a creamness of liquid, called *all' onda,* or "wavy."

The most famous *risotto* is made *alla milanese,* from Milan. It is flavored with saffron and contains beef marrow. Legend has it that the dish dates to 1574, when a stained-glass worker on Milan's cathedral, who was known for the yellow color of his glass, which he achieved by adding saffron to his pigments, colored the rice at the wedding of his boss's daughter, whereupon the guests pronounced the dish *"Risus optimus"* (Latin for "excellent rice"). Thereafter such yellow–tinted rice was called *risotto alla milanese.*

The Milanese also make *risott rusti,* with pork and beans. *R. bianco* (white *risotto)* is the simplest, begun with sautéed onions and broth, served with butter and **parmigiano.** *R. nero* (black *risotto)* is made with cuttlefish or squid ink. *R. certosina* or *r. di frutti di mare* is made with seafood and fish stock, the latter usually with crayfish. *R. ai funghi* is made with mushrooms. *Sartu di riso alla napoletana* is a Neapolitan baked **timbale** made with molded rice filled with many ingredients from meatballs and chicken livers to hard-boiled eggs and eggplant, usually containing melted **mozzarella** and tomato. *R. alla montovana* (also *r. alla pilota)* is done with sausage and onion. *R. alla valtellinese* is done with cabbage and beans. *R. alla sbirraglia* is a Veneto *risotto* cooked with spring-time's wild hops, chicken, and veal. It is a dish that takes its name from the word *sbirraglia,* a Venetian slur for the Austrian police who occupied the city and refers either to their habit of stealing chickens from the people or to Venetians' desire to hack the police into pieces, like the chicken in the dish. Venetians also make a *risotto* with mutton called *r. in capro roman* and *r. alla gondoliera* (gondolier's style), made with mussels. *R. di secole (risotto* with scraps) is another Veneto variety utilizing the scraps of meat left on a beef or veal bone after the rest of the meat has been cut away. A third Venetian dish is *r. alla chioggiota* made with a paste made from local fish. *R. primavera* is made with spring vegetables. *R. "chi cacuoccioli" alla siciliana* is made with fava beans, peas, artichoke hearts, and onion. In Siena during the Palio horse races held July 2 and August 16, *r. fratacchione,* made with sausage, red onions, and pepper, is traditionally served. It takes its name from monks who liked to eat well. *R. al salto* (jumping risotto) is made with leftover *risotto* that is mixed with beaten egg and made into pancakes that are quickly cooked and flipped over on a pan.

RISOTTO ALLA MILANESE

1-inch piece of beef marrow	*¹/₂ cup dry white wine*
3 tablespoons butter	*6 cups chicken broth*
2 tablespoons olive oil	*Pinch of saffron*
1 onion, chopped	*1 cup grated parmigiano*
1 ¹/₂ cups Italian rice	*Salt and pepper*

Soften the beef marrow in boiling water for a few moments, then coarsely chop. Melt the butter and oil together in a large saucepan, add the marrow, and brown lightly. Add the onion and sauté until wilted. Add the rice and stir to coat completely. Sauté until slightly toasted. Pour in the wine and let it be absorbed by the rice. Add the broth, ladleful by ladleful, stirring after each addition until the liquid is absorbed.

After 10 minutes of cooking, dissolve the saffron in a small amount of broth, and add to the saucepan. Cook for about 10 minutes more, or until the rice is tender but *al dente*. Add the *parmigiano* and blend thoroughly to create creamy waves (*all'onda*) in the *risotto*. Serve immediately. Serves 4 to 6.

---

ristorante   (ree-stoh-RAHN-teh)   Restaurant. A higher class of eating establishment than a *trattoria* or *osteria*.

The word *restaurant* derives from the Latin *restaurer* (to restore), but there was no such establishment in ancient Rome or anywhere else where a person could come to have his own table, choose from a menu, and pay according to what he chose. Until the middle of the 18th century, travelers had to subsist on whatever was being prepared at a local inn, usually in the company of strangers at a long, communal table. In 1765 a Parisian cookshop owner named Boulanger served a soup of sheep's foot he called a *restaurant* as a restorative dish for his customers. The dish became popular, but the word *restaurant* did not come to mean an eating establishment until 1782, when a cookshop owner named Beauvilliers (former chef to the Comte de Provence) began serving guests at separate tables at La Grande Taverne de Londres, after which the word *restaurant* was applied to any such establishment.

The French Revolution spurred the growth of this new concept by abolishing the monopolistic cooks' guilds and by forcing aristocrats' former chefs to find new venues for their talents, so that by 1804, Paris had between 500 and 600 restaurants. The idea made headway in other countries, though in Italy, a formal restaurant was a rarity until the 20th century, while *trattorie* and *osterie* continued more in the traditional mode of offering a single, set meal at a set price. When restaurants did become fashionable in Italy after the turn of the century, they were usually in grand hotels and copied the French model set by Auguste Escoffier. Only after World War II did Italian restaurateurs focus more on their own regional dishes, as is now the case throughout the country, so that a restaurant in Venice will by and large feature Venetian cooking and one in Rome, Roman cooking.

ristretto   (ree-STREH-toh)   "Tight." The rich consistency of a reduced sauce or stock and the strong, syrupy consistency of a well-made *espresso.*

Riviera del Garda Bresciano   (ree-vee-EH-rah dell GAHR-dah breh-SH'YAH-noh)   *DOC* zone of Lombardy that produces a rosé wine called *chiaretto,* and a white and a red *groppello* from grapes grown around Lake Garda. Also *Garda Bresciano.*

robiola   (roh-bee-OH-lah)   Soft, creamy cow's milk cheese. It was originally made in the town of Robbio in Lombardy. *Robiola di Roccaverano,* from the village of the same name, is a well-known version made from goat's, ewe's, or cow's milk, or a mixture, from Piedmont. See also *stracchino.*

rocciata   (roh-chee-AH-tah)   "Rocky." Folded triangle of strudel-like pastry, filled with prunes, nuts, and cinnamon, a specialty of Assisi and Perugia.

Roero   (roh-EH-roh)   *DOC* red wine of Piedmont, made from *nebbiolo* and *arneis* grapes grown around Roero. A white called *Arneis di Roero* is also made.

rognone   (roh-N'YOH-neh)   Kidney, usually from a young calf. Kidneys are usually sautéed or grilled and served simply. From the Latin *renes.*

rognosa   (roh-N'YOH-sah)   "A mess." *Frittata* made with eggs, *parmigiano,* and salami, from Piedmont.

rollatine   (roh-lah-TEE-neh)   Rolls, as in beef rolls stuffed with a filling.

romana, alla   (AH-lah roh-MAH-nah)   "Roman style." This term covers dishes specific to Roman cookery, usually involving tomato sauce.

rombo   (ROHM-boh)   Name derived from the Latin *rhombus,* for a number of large oval flatfish of the Atlantic and Mediterranean savored for their white flesh. The best is *rombo chiodato (Psetta maxima)* or "nailed rombo," because of the hooked points on its back—in France known as *turbot.* So treasured was this fish that the emperor Domitian supposedly asked the Roman Senate to debate the correct way to cook it. *R. liscio,* is brill (*Scopththalmus rhombus),* called *suaso* in Emilia-Romagna. Also *rombo maggiore.*

ronco   (ROHN-koh)   Friulian term referring to a vineyard hill site, commonly added to wine labels to indicate a wine made from grapes grown on the best-exposed hillsides for maximum quality.

rosato   (roh-SAH-toh)   Rosé wine. From the Latin *rosa* (rose).

rosbif   (rohs-BEEF)   Roast beef. From English.

roscani   (roh-SKAH-nee)   Acidic-tasting greens, from the Marches. In Ancona, they are cooked and dressed with oil, vinegar, mint, and garlic, and garnished with hard-boiled eggs.

roschette   (roh-SKEH-teh)   Crisp baked dough rings, a specialty of the Sephardic Jews of Livorno.

rosetta   (roh-ZEH-tah)   "Rosettes." Hollow, very crisp roll resembling the shape of a rose, from Venice. From the Latin *rosa* (rose).

rosmarino   (rohs-mah-REE-noh)   Rosemary. The name comes from the Latin *rosmarinus* (dew of the sea), so called, according to Pliny, because it grows in regions around the Mediterranean where there is a good amount of dew (*ros* in Latin). Rosemary is commonly used as a seasoning for roasted and grilled meats, especially lamb.

rosolare   (roh-soh-LAH-reh)   To brown food in a skillet or to roast until browned in the oven. From the Old High German *rosten* (to roast).

rosolio   (roh-SOH-l'yoh)   Cordial. Originally made from rose petals, rose oil, and honey, dating back to the 15th century and said to be a favorite drink of Caterina de' Medici. By the 18th century, lemon was favored over rose as a flavoring. Today, *rosolio* is still made in Calabria and Sicily and is used more as a flavoring in desserts and pastries than as a cordial. *Rosolino* is a version made with less alcohol than the regular *rosolio*. From the Latin *rosa* (rose).

rospo   (ROH-spoh)   See *rana pescatrice*.

Rossese di Dolceaqua   (roh-SEH-seh dee dohl-cheh-AH-kwah) Red *DOC* wine of Liguria, made from *rossese* grapes near the town of Dolceaqua.

rossetti   (roh-ZEH-tee)   "Little red [fish]." Spawn of red and white mullet, floured and fried. From the Latin *rosa* (rose).

rosso   (ROH-soh)   Red. From the Latin *rosa* (rose).

Rosso Barletta   (ROH-soh bahr-LEH-tah)   *DOC* red wine of Apulia, made from *uva di troia* grapes grown around the port of Barletta.

Rosso Canosa   (ROH-soh kah-NOH-zah)   *DOC* red wine of Apulia, made from *uva di troia* and other grapes grown around Canosa.

Rosso Conero   (ROH-soh koh-NEH-roh)   *DOC* red wine of the Marches, made from *montepulciano* grapes grown around Monte Conero.

Rosso di Cercatoia   (ROH-soh dee chehr-kah-TOY-ah)   Big-bodied red wine from Tuscany's Cercatoia region.

Rosso di Cerignola   (ROH-soh dee cheh-REE-n'yoh-lah)   *DOC* red wine of Apulia, made from **uva di troia** and **negroamaro** grapes grown around Cerignola.

Rosso di Montalcino   (ROH-soh dee mohn-tahl-CHEE-noh)   *DOC* red wine of Tuscany, made, as is **Brunello di Montalcino,** from **sangiovese** grapes grown around the town of Montalcino. But because it requires only one year of aging compared with four for *brunello,* it is a less tannic, lighter wine that sells for much less.

Rosso di Montepulciano   (ROH-soh dee MOHN-teh-pool-chee-AH-noh)   *DOC* red wine of Tuscany, made from *prugnolo gentile* grapes grown around the town of Montepulciano.

Rosso Piceno   (ROH-soh pee-CHEH-noh)   *DOC* red wine of the Marches, made from **sangiovese** and *montepulciano* grapes grown around Ascoli Piceno.

rosticceria   (roh-stee-cheh-REE-ah)   Rotisserie grill. Also, a snack bar serving hot and cold food. From the Middle French *rotisserie.*

rosticiana   (roh-stee-ch'YAH-nah)   Onions cooked with the pieces of pork left over after the cuts for meat and sausage have been used, from Milan. Also *rosticiada.*

rostin negaa   (roh-STEEN neh-GAH)   Veal chops braised in white wine, from Lombardy.

rotella dentata   (roh-TEH-lah dehn-TAH-tah)   "Teethed roller." Kitchen instrument with a rolling, toothed blade used to cut sheets of pasta dough for **ravioli** and other stuffed pastas.

rotolo   (roh-TOH-loh)   Roll, as of meat or pasta, usually stuffed. From the Latin *rota* (wheel).

roventini alla toscana   (roh-vehn-TEE-nee AH-lah toh-S'KAH-nah)   "Tuscan scorchers." Blood pudding cooked with lard and sprinkled with **parmigiano,** from Tuscany.

rubino   (roo-BEE-noh)   Ruby-colored wine. From the Latin *ruber* (red).

Rubino di Cantavenna   (roo-BEE-noh dee kahn-tah-VEH-nah)   *DOC* red wine of Piedmont, made from **barbera, grignolino,** and *freisa* grapes grown around Cantavenna.

ruche di Castagnole Monferrato   (ROO-keh dee kah-stah-N'YOH-leh mohn-feh-RAH-toh)   *DOC* red grape of Piedmont used to make a violet-red wine. It is believed to have been brought from Burgundy in the 18th century. Also *rouchet and roche.*

rucola   (ROO-koh-lah)   Arugula, also called *rocket,* which originated in Asia. Arugula is used in salads, soups, sauces, and as a vegetable. The word derives ultimately from the Latin *eruca* (colewort). Also *rocola, arugula, rughetta,* and other names.

ruote di carro   (roo-OH-teh dee KAH-roh)   "Cartwheels." Pasta shape resembling a cart's wheel, usually served with tomato sauces. Also *rotelle* and *rotelline.*

rustica, alla   (AH-lah ROO-stee-kah)   "Rustic style." Any dish done in a rustic, robust style. See also **torta rustica.** From the Latin *rusticus.*

rustici   (ROO-stee-chee)   "Rustics." Snacks made of puff-pastry dough filled with **balsamella** and tomato, a specialty of Lecce; or any savory pastries. From the Latin *rusticus.*

rustisana   (roo-stee-SAH-nah)   Peppers and tomatoes quickly simmered with garlic, basil, and rosemary, often served with **polenta,** from Piacenza. The word probably derives from the Latin *rusticus* (rustic).

S

saba (SAH-bah)   Grape juice and grape pulp cooked to a thick consistency to be used in sweet-and-sour dishes and desserts. Also *sapa*.

sagnarelli (sah-n'yah-REH-lee)   Pasta ribbons about 1¹/₂ inches long, with ruffled edges.

sagne chine (SAH-n'yeh KEE-neh)   "Stuffed lasagne." *Lasagne* stuffed with meatballs, hard-boiled eggs, *mozzarella, scamorza,* and *pecorino* layered with tomato sauce, from Calabria. In Campania, the dish is called *sagna chiena*.

sagrantino (sah-grahn-TEE-noh)   Tannic red wine grape of Umbria. *Sagrantino di Montefalco* is a **DOC** wine. The word may refer either to the wine of the Sacrament or the Sacramentine religious order. Also *sacrantino*.

salame (sah-LAH-meh)   Salami. Since salt was one of the original preservatives for salami, the word derives from the Latin *sal* (salt).

There are three basic types of *salame*: fresh, dry aged, and precooked; and two kinds of casing: natural, made from animal parts like bladder and intestines, and artificial, which may come from animal skins, cellulose, or polyvinyl.

Every region has its salamis, whose flavors differ according to the local pig used, the cuts of meat, the seasonings and filler, the coarseness, and the casing. *Salame cotto nell'aceto* is a Friulian dish of fresh salami cooked in vinegar and served with **polenta.** *S. toscano* is a fat-rich pork sausage with pepper. *Salamella* (also called *salsicca napoletana)* is made with both pork and buffalo meat. *S. gentile* is an Emilian sausage that is quite lean and mildly seasoned. *S. da sugo* is another Emilian sausage, controlled by a consortium, made from the best parts of the pig and blended with cinnamon, cloves, nutmeg, and red wine. In Piedmont, *s. alla douja* is aged in an earthenware pot called a *douja*. *S. di Varsi,* from the Lombardian town of Varzi, is made with lean pork and fresh **pancetta**. *S. di Felino,* from the Parma village of Felino, is made with high-quality pork and knotted. *S. Fabriano,* from the town of Fabriano in the Marches, is made with pork and baby beef. An Emilia-Romagna garlic *salame* is called *s. al zantil,* a local dialect name for a part of the pig's intestine used for the casing. In the Abruzzi, *ventricina* is a pork, fennel, and **peperoncino** sausage studded with orange peel, a specialty of Chieti. *S. ungherese* is smoked in the style of Hungarian salamis.

salame inglese (sah-LAH-meh een-GLEH-zeh) "English salami." Jelly-roll sponge cake.

salamini (sah-lah-MEE-nee) Sausage links.

salamoia (sah-lah-MOI-yah) Brine. From the Latin *sal* (salt), which would be used in the brine.

salatini (sah-lah-TEE-nee) Square crackers, usually flavored and salted (in Latin, *sal* means salt), served with **antipasti** and canapés.

salcrauto (sahl-KRAU-toh) Sauerkraut. From the German *Sauer kraut.*

sale (SAH-leh) Salt. The name derives from the Latin *sal,* and the Roman god of health, Salus. Salt has been mined since the Neolithic era, first in Europe, but most salt used in Europe today is sea salt. In Italy, it is produced primarily from Mediterranean seawater in salt flats near the coast. Until 1974, salt was a state monopoly in Italy.
  Sale fino is a fine-grain sea salt, used in cooking and at the table. *Sale grosso* is a coarser sea salt, used to flavor cooking water for pasta. *Salata* means salted or brined. *Salsume* means salty.

Salento (sah-LEHN-toh) Red, white, and rosé wines made around the Salento peninsula of Apulia.

Salice Salentino (sah-LEE-cheh sah-lehn-TEE-noh) **DOC** red and rosé wines of Apulia, made from **negroamaro** grapes grown around Salice Salentino.

salino (sah-LEE-noh) "Salt [bread]." Northern bread roll containing rock salt in its crust. Often eaten with sausages and beer. From the Latin *sal* (salt).

salmì, in (een SAHL-mee) Marinated in herbs and wine and cooked into a stew. A cooking method for game. From the French for a roasted game stew in a rich sauce.

salmone (sahl-MOH-neh) Salmon, *Salmo salar.* There are no salmon in the Mediterranean, so the fish must be imported from the North Atlantic.

Not a particularly popular fish in Italian cookery, it is often smoked or cured in a sugar and herb marinade. Fresh, it may be poached or grilled.

salmoriglio   (sahl–moh–REE–l'yoh)   Condiment consisting of olive oil, salt, garlic, oregano, parsley, and lemon juice, typically served with grilled fish or grilled or broiled eggplant, from Calabria and Sicily. Also *sammorigghiu*.

The word refers to *sale* (salt) because original forms of the condiment contained a drop of seawater to provide a taste of salt.

salnitro   (sahl–NEE–troh)   Sodium nitrite, used for preserving meats. From *sale* (salt) and *nitro,* from the French *nitre* (salt of nitric acid).

salpa   (SAHL–pah)   Mediterranean fish with horizontal golden stripes, *Sarpa salpa.* Usually grilled.

salsa   (SAHL–sah)   Sauce. From the Latin *salsus* (salted).

Salsa may be made with a wide variety of ingredients, and, when used on pasta, is interchangeable with **sugo** (but see both **sugo** and **ragù** for further explanation). *Salsa al pomodoro* is tomato sauce. *S. verde* is a green sauce made with vegetables, particularly parsley, and traditionally served with **bollito misto.** *S. aurora* or *s. rubra* is a tomato-tinged dressing resembling Russian dressing. *S. bastarda* (bastard sauce), so called because of its mixed ingredients, is similar to a hollandaise. *S. **picchi–pacchiu*** is a Sicilian sauce made with quickly cooked tomatoes in onion, garlic, and basil. *S. maro* is a Ligurian sauce made with fava beans, mint, and anchovies, commonly served with meat. It is a specialty of the town of San Remo. *S. genovese* is a sauce of Genoa made with parsley, bread crumbs, pine nuts, garlic, olives, anchovies, and boiled egg yolk, usually served with boiled meats. *S. d'agresto* (sour sauce) is a rustic sauce made with unripened grapes, onions, nuts, bread, vinegar, honey, and broth.

SALSA AL POMODORO

¹/₂ cup olive oil
1 garlic clove, crushed
1 onion, diced
2 pounds ripe tomatoes, peeled,
seeded, and chopped

Salt and pepper
10 to 12 fresh basil leaves, washed
and chopped

Heat the olive oil in a saucepan, add the garlic, and sauté until golden. Remove the garlic from the pan. Add the onion and sauté until wilted. Add the tomatoes and salt and pepper to taste. Cover and simmer for 1 hour, stirring occasionally. About 10 minutes before the end of the cooking time, add the basil. Serves 6.

salsicce e facioul d'pane   (sahl-SEE-cheh eh fah-J'YOOL D'PAH-neh)   "Sausage and beans like bread." Sausage and bean casserole, from Abruzzo. The colloquial expression is supposed to indicate that the sausage and beans are as tasty and filling as bread.

salsiccia   (sahl-SEE-ch'yah)   Sausage. From the Late Latin *salsicia*. See also *salame*.

saltare   (sahl-TAH-reh)   To sauté.

saltato alla bandiera   (sahl-TAH-toh AH-lah bahn-dee-YEH-rah)   Sautéed green peppers, red tomatoes, and white onions, whose colors represent those of the Italian flag called the *bandiera*.

saltimbocca   (sahl-teem-BOH-kah)   "Leap in the mouth." Veal *scalloppine* layered with sage leaves and *prosciutto,* then sautéed in butter with white wine or *Marsala.* The dish is most associated with Rome, though food authority Luigi Carnacina contends the dish originally came from Brescia.

SALTIMBOCCA ALLA ROMANA

8 veal scaloppine
Salt and pepper
8 slices prosciutto
8 fresh sage leaves

1 cup flour
2 tablespoons butter
2 tablespoons olive oil
¹/₂ cup dry white wine

Season *scaloppine* with salt and pepper to taste. Place a slice of *prosciutto* and a sage leaf on each *scallopina,* fold in half, securing with toothpicks. Dredge *scaloppine* in flour. Heat the butter and oil in a sauté pan and add *scaloppine.* Brown the meat for about 2 minutes on each side, then reduce the heat and cook for about 4-5 minutes more. Remove the *scaloppine* and keep warm. Deglaze the pan with white wine, scraping up the browned bits and reducing the sauce by half. Remove the toothpicks from the *scaloppine* and place on a serving platter. Pour the sauce over the *scaloppine* and serve. Serves 4.

salto   (SAHL-toh)   Method of cooking by quickly sautéing in oil so that the food "jumps" in the pan. *Risotto al salto* is leftover *risotto* formed into patties and quickly sautéed.

salumi   (sah-LOO-mee)   General term for cured meats, including *salame, prosciutto, coppa,* and other pork products, that are eaten sliced.

salvia (SAHL-vee-ah)   Sage. From the Latin for healthy; sage was often used as a medicinal herb.

Sage, a native plant of the Mediterranean with 500 species, has been used as a flavoring for millenia, and Charlemagne ordered it to be planted throughout the Holy Roman Empire of the Middle Ages.

Salviata is an egg custard flavored with sage, from Tuscany.

sambuco (sahm-BOO-koh)   Elder bush, *Sambucus nigra.* The flowers are used in fritters and soup. They are also used to make *sambuca,* a licorice-flavored Roman liqueur, from Rome, elsewhere called *anisetta.* It is produced principally in Civitavecchia. It is traditional to serve *sambuca con le mosche,* meaning "with flies," referring to the coffee beans floated in the glass.

San Colombano al Lambro (SAHN koh-lohm-BAH-noh ahl LAHM-broh)   *DOC* red wine of Lombardy, made from *croatina, barbera,* and *uva rara* grapes grown around the hills of San Colombano.

sangiovese (sahn-joh-VEH-seh)   Predominant red wine grape of Tuscany, used in making *Chianti, Brunello di Montalcino, Vino Nobile di Montepulciano,* and many other wines. It is considered a grape whose clones, like *sangiovese grosso,* are capable of producing some of the world's greatest red wines. *Sangiovese di Romagna,* also called *sanzves* in the local Emilia-Romagna dialect, is a clone. *S. dei Colli Pesaresi* is a *DOC* red wine from the Marches.

sangue, al (ahl SAHN-gweh)   "Bloody." Very rare, as applied to cooked meat. From the Latin *sanguis.*

sanguinaccio (sahn-gwee-NAH-ch'yoh)   Blood pudding. In southern Italy, a dessert by this name is made with chocolate, sugar, cinnamon, and candied citrus peel. In Sardinia, blood pudding is called *sancele.* From the Latin *sanguinarius* (blood).

San Martino della Battaglia (SAHN mahr-TEE-noh DEH-lah bah-TAH-l'yah)   A white wine made from *tocai friulano* grapes grown around a battleground *(battaglia)* named after Saint Martin. Once exclusively vinified dry, it is now also made in a sweet style.

San Pietro (sahn pee-EH-troh)   "Saint Peter's fish." A cichlid in the genus *Tilapia,* called tilapia in English, though known as John Dory in Great Britain. Throughout Europe it is called Saint Peter's fish because of the biblical story *(Matthew* 17:26–27) in which Christ told Saint Peter that the first fish he would catch would contain a coin with which Peter could pay a local tax. According to a later legend, Peter did catch such a fish, but when the fish cried out in pain from Peter's squeezing it so tightly with his thumb and forefinger, he threw it back into the ocean, leaving the fish with a mark on either side of its body—a round black spot with a yellow halo (called an ocellus) that the species bears to this day. Also *pesce San Pietro.*

San Severo   (sahn SEH-veh-roh)   *DOC* zone of Apulia that produces red, white, and rosé wines from grapes grown around the town of San Severo.

Santa Maddalena   (SAHN-tah mah-dah-LEH-nah)   *DOC* red wine of Trentino–Alto Adige, made from **schiave** grapes in and around the village of Santa Maddelena. Also *St. Magdalener.*

saor, in   (een sah-OHR)   Method of marinating cooked fish in a sweet-and-sour mixture containing onions, raisins, and pine nuts, from Venice. From the Old High German *sur* (sour). See also **scapece.**

SARDELLE IN SAOR

2 pounds sardines	*1 pound onions, sliced*
¹/₂ cup flour	*2 cups red wine vinegar*
1 cup olive oil	*2 tablespoons pine nuts*
Salt	*2 tablespoons raisins*

Gut and remove the bones and heads of the sardines. Wash, pat dry, and dredge the sardines in the flour and shake off the excess. Heat ¹/₂ cup of the oil in a frying pan. When the oil is hot, fry the sardines, drain them on paper towels, salt them, and set them aside. Heat the remaining ¹/₂ cup olive oil in another frying pan and fry the onions over low heat until soft and golden brown. Add the vinegar and cook for a few more minutes to slightly reduce the vinegar. Salt the onion mixture to taste and set aside. In a terra-cotta, glass, or porcelain dish, alternate the sardines and the onion mixture with the pine nuts and the raisins in layers, finishing with an onion layer. Cover, refrigerate, and let rest for 1 to 2 days before eating. Serves 4 to 6.

sapore   (sah-POH-reh)   Flavor. From the Latin *sapidus* (tasty).

saradusu   (sah-rah-DOO-soo)   Sicilian sweet-and-sour almond sauce made with olives, anchovies, and chile pepper, from Sicily. *Saradusu* is usually served with fish. From the Arabic for sweet and sour.

sarago   (sah-RAH-goh)   Bream or porgy, *Sparus pagrus.* In Campania, **pagello.** Larger ones are best baked or grilled, smaller ones are good in soup.

sarde   (SAHR-deh)   Sardine, *Sardinella anchovia.* Small saltwater fish whose fatty flesh makes them excellent for grilling. They are most often packed in oil. A *sardina* is a sardine preserved in oil. *Sardone* are pickled. *Sardelline* are young sardines.

Sardines are widely dispersed throughout the world and swim in every sea but the coldest waters of the Arctic and Antarctic. They are easily harvested because they swim in vast schools, and records indicate they were being fished as early as 495, when fishermen waited for them to swim into shoreside weirs. Today sardines are encircled out at sea by large skeins.

Italian legend has it that the sardine has 24 virtues, but loses one each hour, so that the fish should be cooked within a day of its being caught.

One of the classic dishes of Sicily is *pasta con le sarde*. According to legend the dish was created by an Arab cook for Admiral Euphemius's troops when they invaded Sicily at Mazara del Vallo in 827. In Sicily they also make a dish of pasta with fresh sardines called *alla milanese,* because the Milanese were the first to use fresh, rather than salted, sardines.

Another dish from the same region is a sardine pie called *s. a beccaficcu* (sardines like warblers), so called because rolled, stuffed sardines are propped in the baking dish to look like birds. *S. a scapece* is a Calabrian dish of fried sardines that have been breaded, then dressed with hot oil, vinegar, mint, and garlic.

Sardegna   (sahr–DEH–n'yah)   Sardinia, an island in the Tyhrrenean Sea. This fiercely independent land, always described as rugged and rocky, has a culture as unique as Sicily's and is even less tied to the culinary traditions of mainland Italy. The inhabitants speak a language most Italians have no knowledge of, and these mountain people have maintained their customs despite being conquered over the centuries by Phoenicia, Carthage, Rome, Savoy, and Spain.

The Sardinians love to cook outdoors, whether it's baby lamb or *porceddu* (suckling pig) over an open fire or in a pit or fish grilled at the seashore. The local lobster, **aragosta,** is a specialty of Alghero, and their **burrida** is a hefty fisherman's stew made with eel in an almond–olive oil sauce or a dogfish steak covered with walnuts and bread crumbs. *Arselle* are a local clam.

Sardinian cheeses have a real pungency, including **pecorino sardo,** and their most famous breads are the paper-thin **carta da musica,** or *pane carasau,* and the huge **civraxiu.**

For **pasta** there are little saffron-tinged **gnocchi** called **malloreddus** and **ravioli**-like **culurzones** stuffed with peppers and potato. Another *ravioli* is served for dessert—**seadas,** filled with cheese, then fried and served with honey.

Other sweets include pastries called *ciccioneddas,* filled with cherry preserves; *pabassine,* filled with almonds and raisins; and *tilicas,* filled with marzipan.

The wines of Sardinia, with its 18 **DOC** regions, are not well known beyond the island, and many of the grape varieties show the influence of Spanish domination. Some of the better-known wines are the red *cannonau* and *Monica* and the white *Vernaccia di Oristano* and *Nasco.*

sardenaira   (sar-deh-NAY-rah)   "Sardine (pizza)." A *pizza* made with tomato, anchovies or sardines, olives, and onions; a specialty of Liguria, where it is also called *pissadella.* Similar to the *pissaladière* of Nice.

sarma   (SAHR-mah)   Pickled cabbage rolls stuffed with rice and meat and braised in tomato sauce, a specialty of Istria. The word is of Turkish origin.

sartizzu   (sahr-TEE-t'zoo)   Smoked pork sausage spiced with cinnamon, fennel, and pepper, from Sardinia.

sartù   (sahr-TOO)   Rice *timballo* filled with meatballs and chicken livers, mushrooms, hard-boiled eggs, and melted *mozzarella,* a specialty of Naples. The name was given by French aristocrats who loved the dish and pronounced it *sûrtout*—"above all." See also *riso.*

sasizzeddo   (sah-see-T'ZEH-doh)   Little sausage in Sicilian dialect.

sassella   (sah-SEH-lah)   Considered the best red wine made under the *DOC* zone of Valtellina Superiore. It is 95 percent *nebbiolo.*

Sassicaia   (sah-see-KAI-yah)   Notable red *vino da tavola* of Tuscany first made by Mario Incisa della Rochetta at the Tenuta San Guido. Wines from the 1968 vintage were released in the 1970s. *Sassicaia* is made mostly from *cabernet sauvignon* grapes. The name refers to the parcel of land where the grapes are grown.

Sauresuppe   (saur-SOO-peh)   "Sour soup." Tripe soup with onions, nutmeg, and white wine vinegar, as made in the Tyrol. The word is from the German.

sauvignon   (soh-vee-N'YOHN)   White wine grape now being planted in many regions of northern Italy. Known in Bordeaux as *sauvignon blanc.* The name comes from the French.

savoiardi   (sah-voy-AHR-dee)   "Savoys." Ladyfingers, a specialty of the Valle d'Aosta. Supposedly first made in 1348 by the head chef of Amadeo VI of the House of Savoy. Also *biscotti di Savoia.*

savor   (sah-VOHR)   Mixed autumn fruits cooked in unfermented wine, a specialty of Venice. From the Latin *sapor* (taste).

sbollentare   (s'boh-lehn-TAH-reh)   To scald, as milk. From the Latin *bullire* (to bubble).

sbrisolona   (s'bree-soh-LOH-nah)   "Big, crumbly (cake)." A cornmeal, butter, and almond cake, from Mantua.

scaachi   (SKAH-kee)   Passover *torta* made with layers of matzoh, chopped beef, artichokes, spinach, chile peppers, mushrooms, and eggs, from Rome.

scacciata   (skah-CH'YAH-tah)   Savory pie with a filling of cheese, vegetables, and meat. A sweet version contains *ricotta,* sugar, and coffee.

Scaliere di Rosa del Golfo   (skah-L'YEH-reh dee ROH-sah dell GOHL-foh)   Rosé wine of Apulia based on *negroamaro* and *malvasia nera* grapes grown around Alezio.

scalogno   (skah-LOH-n'yoh)   Scallion or shallot. Used like onion, in sauces, stews, and many other preparations. Caramelized onions are a popular *antipasto.* From the Latin *ascalonia caepa* (onion of Ascalon).

scaloppina   (skah-loh-PEE-nah)   A thin, pounded piece of meat, usually sautéed with a wide variety of ingredients on top. From the French *escalope.*
    The most common dishes made with *scaloppine* are *alla **marsala,*** with Marsala wine, and *al **limone,*** with lemon juice.

scamorza   (skah-MOR-t'zah)   A cow's milk *pasta filata* cheese similar to *mozzarella,* from Abruzzo and Molise, aged about two weeks. It is sometimes smoked. The name refers to a "dunce" because of the cheese's pointed top, but it can be made into many animal shapes.

scampo   (SKAHM-poh)   Prawn, *Nephrops norvegicus.* Almost identical to the langoustine and Dublin Bay prawn. It is a very small lobster but not a shrimp, and it is usually grilled with olive oil and lemon.

scannello   (skah-NEH-loh)   Butcher's term for a beef cut. Rump roast.

scanno   (SKAH-noh)   Ewe's milk cheese made around the town of Scanno in Abruzzo.

scapece, a   (AH skah-PEH-cheh)   Preservation method, mainly for fish but also for some kinds of meat. It is floured and fried, then vinegar and other ingredients are poured over it. *Scapece di Vasto* contains chile peppers and saffron, from Vasto in Abruzzo. In Basilicata, sardines are preserved in vinegar with garlic, parsley, mint, and chile peppers. See also *carpione, in,* and *saor, in.*

scarafuoghi   (skah-rah-F'WOH-gee)   "The remains of the cooking." Pork stew made by cutting the fatty and leftover parts of the pig into pieces and stewing them with chile peppers in a special copper pot, from Calabria. Usually served lukewarm in soft bread rolls. Bits of meat and the fat that is skimmed off the top of the stew make a snack spread called *fresculimita.*

scarcedda (skahr-CHAY-dah)   Easter tart of *ricotta* and hard-boiled eggs, from Basilicata.

scarola (skah-ROH-lah)   Escarole. From the Late Latin *escariola*. See also *indivia*. *Scarola* is used in salads and cooked in soups and as a *contorno*.

scarpaccia (skahr-PAH-ch'yah)   Zucchini tart, from Tuscany.

scarpazzone (skahr-pah-T'ZOH-neh)   An Emilia-Romagna egg custard with spinach, *parmigiano,* and onion. Also *erbazzone.*

scarpetta di Sant'Ilario (skahr-PEH-tah dee SAHN-tee-LAH-ree-oh) "Saint Ilario's shoe." A boot-shape cookie flavored with cinnamon, cloves, nutmeg, and cocoa, from Parma. From the legend that *Sant'Ilario* lost one shoe when he crossed the river into Parma.

scarpetta, la (lah skahr-PEH-tah)   "Little shoe." Method of scooping up the last of the sauce on a dish with a morsel of bread that seemingly scoops it up like a shoe.

scatagghiett (skah-tah-G'YETT)   Fried pastry ribbons soaked in honey, from Apulia.

scaveccio, lo (loh skah-VEH-ch'yoh)   Eel sautéed in olive oil then served with a mixture of vinegar and crushed chile pepper, a specialty of the Maremma region of Tuscany.

scavino (skah-VEE-noh)   Long utensil used to remove marrow from the bone. Also a utensil to carve out balls from fruit like melon.

scelta, al (ahl SHEHL-tah)   "Your choice." A menu phrase indicating that the customer may choose from among several items at a fixed price.

schiacciata (skee-ah-CH'YAH-tah)   "Squashed." Flatbread, usually glossed with olive oil, from Tuscany. *Schiacciata con l'uva* has grapes in the dough. In Modena, it is called *stria*.

In Apulia, the term refers to a large bread loaf weighing about four pounds; since it rises only once, it is rather flat. *S. alla fiorentina* is an orange cake, from Florence.

schiaki sciuka (skee-AH-kee SK'YOO-kah)   Dish of sautéed vegetables and eggs, from Pantelleria, an island off Sicily. The name is of Arab origin and refers to the town of Sciacca to which many Tunisians immigrated.

schiava (skee-AH-vah)   Red wine grape of Trentino–Alto Adige (where it is also called *Vernatsch)* grown in several subvarieties such as *schiava gentile* and *s. grigia*. The name, which means slave and suggests Slavic origins, is also used for several **DOC** wines in Alto-Adige and elsewhere.

schidone   (skee-DOH-neh)   Long skewer or spit. *Schidionata* is meat on a skewer or spit. From the Middle English *skenier.*

schienale   (skee-eh-NAH-leh)   Spinal cord, usually cooked like sweetbreads. Also *filone.*

schile   (SKEE-leh)   Very tiny shrimp that are eaten either raw or quickly fried, from Venice.

schioppettino   (skee-yoh-peh-TEE-noh)   Red wine of Friuli based on *ribolla nera* grapes grown in the **DOC** zone of **Colli Orientali del Friuli.** Though dating in print back to the 13th century, this varietal was left to languish after the phylloxera epidemic of the late 19th century. It was brought back to the region in the province of Udine as of 1978 by the EEC.

schiuma di mare   (sk'YOO-mah dee MAH-reh)   "Sea foam." *Antipasto* of anchovy spawn dressed in lemon, olive oil, and pepper. From the Latin *spuma* (foam) and *mare* (sea).

schiumare   (sk'yoo-MAH-reh)   To skim, as a sauce or broth. From the Latin *spuma* (foam).

schiumoni   (sk'yoo-MOH-nee)   "Big foam." Dessert made of egg whites, sugar, and almonds, from Catania. In Ragusa, it is called *schiumette.* From the Latin *spuma* (foam).

sciabbacceddu   (shah-bah-CHAY-doo)   Deep-fried tiny fish, from Sicily. The word is from *sciabacchiari,* to eat noisily.

sciatre e matre   (SHAH-treh eh MAH-tray)   Eggplant sandwiches made with a *balsamella* sauce, breaded, and fried. Sicilian slang for buttocks, which the sandwiches supposedly resemble.

sciatt   (shee-AHT)   Buckwheat **ravioli** filled with **bitto** cheese and **grappa,** then fried, a specialty of Valtellina. Originally, and still occasionally, the dish was made with a buckwheat batter that surrounded a morsel of the *bitto,* and the word *sciatt* is dialect for "frog," referring to the shape. The *ravioli* are often accompanied by grated horseradish mixed with olive oil.

sciroppo   (shee-ROH-poh)   Syrup. From the Arabic *sharab.*

sciue' sciue'   (SHOO-ay SHOO-ay)   "Quick! Quick!" Quickly made pasta dish of **spaghetti** with a sauce of garlic, chile peppers, olive oil, and cherry tomatoes, from Calabria.

sciule pienne   (SHOO-leh pee-EH-neh)   "Stuffed onions." Onions stuffed with macaroons, bread crumbs, raisins, **parmigiano,** and spices, from Piedmont.

sciumette (shoo-MEH-teh) Meringues poached in cream, often flavored with **pistachio,** from Liguria. From the Latin *spuma* (foam).

sciuscieddu (shoo-SHEH-doo) "Soufflé." Soup containing veal meatballs, which is topped with egg whites that puff up in the last minutes of cooking in the oven, from Sicily.

scodella (skoh-DEH-lah) China or ceramic cup that holds two cups of milk. Also, a soup bowl.

scontrino (skohn-TREE-noh) Receipt received from a cashier at a bar or café when placing an order. The *scontrino* is then brought to a serving counter to have the order filled.

scorfano (skohr-FAH-noh) Scorpion fish, *Scorpaena scrofa. Scorfano rosso,* known in France as *rascasse,* is a basic ingredient of *bouillabaisse.* This brilliant red or orange fish feeds in deep waters. *S. nero* is a black fish that feeds in shallow waters. Both are used to make fish stews in Italy.

scorpacciata (skohr-pah-CH'YAH-tah) "Bellyful." A gluttonous gorge on a seasonal food.

scorza amara (SKOHR-zah ah-MAH-rah) "Bitter [grape] skin." Deep red *frizzante* wines of Emila-Romagna based on *scorza amara* grapes.

scorzanera (skohr-t'zah-NEH-rah) "Black peel." Black salsify. Usually blanched and fried or braised.

scorzetta candita (skohr-T'ZEH-tah kahn-DEE-tah) Candied citrus peel. Used as decoration of desserts and eaten as candy.

scottadito (skoh-tah-DEE-toh) "Burned finger." Grilled baby lamb chops, usually eaten with the fingers, hence the name, originally from Rome.

scottare (skoh-TAH-reh) To sauté in hot fat to make a food golden brown and crisp. From the Middle English *scorch.*

scottiglia (skoh-TEE-l'yah) Mixed stew of game, poultry, and veal with white wine and tomatoes, from Tuscany. Sometimes called **cacciucco di carne.**

scrippelle (skree-PEH-leh) Crepes made from a batter containing chopped parsley, from Abruzzo. They are rolled up and fried, then placed in a soup bowl, sprinkled with grated cheese, and covered with chicken broth. From the Latin *crispus* (crisp). Also *crispelle 'mbusse* and *crispelle 'nfuss.*

scrofa (SKROH-fah) Sow or female pig. From the Latin.

seadas (seh-AH-dahs) Large deep-fried **ravioli** filled with **pecorino** and served with a bitter honey from the *corbezzolo* (strawberry bush), from Sardinia. Also *sebadas.*

secco   (SEH-koh)   Dry, as in wine. From the Latin *siccus.*

secondo   (seh-KOHN-doh)   Second course of a meal, usually referring to the meat or fish course, after the pasta or soup. From the Latin *secundus* (second).

sedanini   (seh-dah-NEE-nee)   "Little celery stalks." One-inch-long *maccheroni* with a slight curvature that makes them resemble celery stalks.

sedano   (seh-DAH-noh)   Celery. Also celery root (celeriac), sometimes called *sedano rapa* or *sedano di Verona.* A plant largely confined to the eastern Mediterranean and Italy until the Renaissance in Europe. The ancient Romans preferred wild to cultivated celery. After the fall of the Empire, cultivation of celery ceased until well into the 16th century. Also *accia* and *appiu.*

   In sedani di Trevi in umido is steamed celery with tomato sauce, from Umbria. Otherwise *sedano* is braised or baked with *parmigiano* or a *balsamella.* It is often used as part of a *soffritto.*

segale   (seh-GAH-leh)   Rye, used in breads and *grissini,* especially in northern Italy.

selvaggio   (sehl-VAH-j'yoh)   Wild, referring to a wild animal or game *(selvaggine)* or to a dish made with wild mushrooms or other forest-grown ingredients. From the Latin *silvaticus* (of the woods). See also *cacciagione.*

semelle   (seh-MEH-leh)   Small bread rolls with a cleft in the top, from Florence.

semi   (SEH-mee)   Seeds. *Semi di finocchio* are fennel seeds; *S. di sesamo* are sesame seeds. *S. di papavero* are poppy seeds, usually black, though white ones are used on some breads. From the Latin *semen* (seed).

semidano   (seh-mee-DAH-noh)   White wine grape of Sardinia, used in making an amber, semisweet wine.

semi di melone   (SEH-mee dee meh-LOH-nee)   "Melon seeds." Very small, seed-shape pasta cooked in soups.

semifreddo   (SEH-mee-FREH-doh)   "Semi-frozen." Usually referring to *dolce al cucchiaio*—a custard or mousse with a slightly softened texture that is eaten with a spoon. From the Latin *semi* (half) and *frigidus* (cold).

   There are four types of *semifreddi:* Custard desserts such as *crema caramella* (caramel custard); cakelike desserts like *tirami sù;* fruit-flavored cream desserts; and desserts containing cheese like *ricotta.*

semisecco   (SEH-mee-SEH-koh)   Half-dry or semisweet, as in wine. From the Latin *semi* (half) and *seccus* (dry).

semolina   (seh-moh-LEE-nah)   Soup made with *semolino.*

semolino   (seh-moh-LEE-noh)   Ground durum wheat used to make *gnocchi,* pasta, bread, and other foods. From the Latin *simila* (wheat flour).

senapa   (SEH-nah-pah)   Mustard. The ancient Romans gathered wild mustard, they chewed the seeds, cooked the leaves, and made a paste from the seeds, which they mixed with *agresto* to make a dressing or sauce. From the Latin **sinapi.**

The three principal varieties of mustard used in Italy today are the dark *(Brassica nigra),* the white *(Sinapsis alba),* and the Indian *(Brassica juncea).*

seppie   (SEH-p'yeh)   Cuttlefish, *Sepia officinalis.* Cephalopod mollusks commonly cooked like squid or octopus. They are sometimes called *calamari* (inkwell) because of the inky body fluid, which is used in a variety of sauces and pastas. The large *seppie* are best found between January and June.

Seppie are the basis for the famous Venetian dish of pasta that incorporates their ink into the dough to give the pasta a purple-gray color and that contains freshly cooked *seppie.* It also goes into making *risotto nero* (black *risotto*). *Seppie in zimino* is a classic dish made with cuttlefish and beet greens, from Liguria. In Abruzzo, *polpi in purgatorio* (octopuses in Purgatory) is actually made with cuttlefish, which is cooked in tomato, garlic, and chile peppers, giving it its name, in Purgatory.

sero   (SEH-roh)   Piemontese form of cottage cheese eaten with *polenta,* from Piedmont. If made with pimento and dried flowers, it is called *salignon.* Also *seras.*

serpentaria   (sehr-pehn-TAH-ree-yah)   Snakeroot, *Dioscorides chrysocoma.* A plant believed to be an antidote to snakebite, hence the name *serpentaria,* which was known to the ancient Romans. But Italians today often use this name for tarragon *(Artemesia dracunculus)* more properly called **dragoncello,** a word which may derive from the Arabic word for the plant, *tarkhun.* In any case, tarragon did not come to Europe from Asia until the late Middle Ages, probably carried back by the Crusaders.

serpentone   (sehr-pehn-TOH-neh)   Sponge cake with almonds and dried fruit in the shape of a serpent, from Umbria. Also *torcolato* or *torcolo.*

servizio compreso   (sehr-VEE-t'zee-yoh kohm-PREH-soh)   Menu term for "service included," usually 10 to 12 percent of the bill. Also *servizio incluso.* It is therefore not necessary to tip the waiter, although a small extra tip called *una mancia* of about 5 percent of the bill might be given for particularly good service. *Servizio non compreso* or *s. non incluso* means the service is not included and the customer is expected to tip the waiter.

setaccio   (seh-TAH-ch'yoh)   Sieve.

seupa di gri   (SOO-pah dee GREE)   "Grain soup." Soup made with barley, onions, potatoes, and salt pork, from Valle d'Aosta.

seupetta di cogne   (soo-PEH-tah dee KOH-n'yeh)   *Risotto* made with *fontina* cheese and stale rye bread, from Valle d'Aosta.

sfince di San Giuseppe   (S'FEEN-cheh dee SAHN joo-SEH-peh) Traditional Sicilian fried puffs filled with *ricotta* and candied fruit, served on the feast of San Giuseppe (March 19). They are sometimes dipped in honey, from Sicily. The dialect word *sfince* is from Arabic *sfang* (fried pastry). See also *zeppole.*

sfincione   (s'feen-T'CHOH-neh)   Thick-crusted *pizza* of Palermo. There are two types. One is topped with tomatoes, anchovies, *caviocavallo* or *mozzarella,* bread crumbs, and oil. The other, called *sfincione di San Vito,* after the convent of San Vito where the nuns created the dish, is made with a filling of sautéed pork, sausage, and *mozzarella* placed between two sheets of *pizza* dough and then baked like a *calzone.*

sfogi in saor   (SFOH-jee een sah-OHR)   Sole cooked in a sweet-and-sour *saor* sauce, from Venice.

sfoglia   (SFOH-l'yah)   "Sheet." Thin sheet, as of *pasta* or pastry. From the Latin *folium* (leaf).

sfogliatelle   (SFOH-l'yah-TEH-leh)   "Little   sheets."   Flaky   pastry wrapped around sweet ingredients like sweetened *ricotta* or *crema pasticcera.* A standard breakfast item in Italy.

sformato   (sfohr-MAH-toh)   A   flan   containing   vegetables,   usually molded in a ring mold and cooked in a water bath. It may also be baked in a springform. *Sformaro di riso* is a rice ring. From the Latin *forma* (form). See also *timballo.*

sfratti   (SFRAH-tee)   "Eviction [sticks]." Cookies shaped like sticks and filled with honey, citrus peel, and nuts. The name refers to the sticks landlords used to drive out unwanted tenants, particularly to drive Jews from their houses. The cookie is traditionally made and served by Jews on Rosh Hashanah.

sfursat   (SFUHR-saht)   "Forced." A process of using semidried grapes to bring the alcohol level of *valtellina* wines up to 14.5 percent. Dialect name from Lombardy. Also *sfurzat* and *sforzato.*

sfuso   (SFOO-soh)   "Loose," referring to a house wine drawn from a large bottle or container and served in a carafe. *Burro fuso* is melted butter.

sgabei (s'gah-BAY)   Cheese-filled fried dough in the shape of long breadsticks, from Liguria.

sgavecio (s'gah-VEH-ch'yoh)   Fried fish pickled in wine, vinegar, onions, and spices, from Liguria. See also *scapece.*

sgombro (S'GOHM-broh)   Mackerel, *Scomber scombrus.* A beautiful, shiny blue fish that develops a strong flavor if not consumed quickly. It is often cooked in a parchment or paper pouch, *al cartoccio.* In Liguria, where the fish is called *lacerto,* it is served with peas and tomato sauce. Also *scombro, pesce turchino* (Turkish fish), and **pesce-cavallo** (horse fish).

sgroppino (s'groh-PEE-noh)   Lemon sorbet whipped with **prosecco** sparkling wine, from Venice.

sguazet, in (een SKWAH-zeh)   Poultry or beef stew, usually containing onion, tomato, bay leaves, rosemary, and wine, from Istria.

sicciolo (SEE-koh-loh)   Cracklings. Also *cicciolo.*

Sicilia (see-CHEE-l'yah)   Sicily, the southern Italian island in the Mediterranean whose historic links to Asia Minor, Greece, and Africa, has had tremendous influence on the locals' food as well as on Italian cooking in general.

The island is sun-drenched, with excellent harbors, inundated with towering mountains, and possessed of wondrous valleys. There is a year-round supply of good seafood, meat, and vegetables, and, despite centuries of foreign domination, Sicilians have made an art of eating and drinking well.

Here **maccheroni** is king and the tomato is queen, the two married in dozens of **pasta** dishes, including the various forms of layered and baked dishes called **timballi.** Owing to the importance influence of Arab food culture, Sicily has a wide range of **cuscus** dishes here called *cuscusu,* many with seafood.

Fruits are abundant and lemon trees are everywhere. Vegetables are plentiful and are used in many nonmeat dishes, including Sicily's famous eggplant and pepper stew called **caponata.** Eggplant is also the basis for **spaghetti alla Norma.** Tuna and swordfish are cut into steaks and grilled; meatballs are an island specialty; and *spaghetti con sarde,* with sardines, is a local favorite.

The best-known cheeses are **pecorino** and **caciocavallo,** and **ricotta** is very rich and creamy here. For dessert there may be the world's most luscious fresh fruit or the famous **cannoli** tubes stuffed with pastry cream or the lavish **cassata,** made with layers of sponge cake, chocolate, **pistachios,** and candied fruit.

Sicily, with 10 **DOC** zones, produces a tremendous amount of wine, some of which is actually shipped to French and German vineyards to bolster their own lighter red wines. The best-known Sicilian wines are sweet, like **Moscato Passito** and **Malvasia** *delle Lipari,* but the most famous is **Marsala.**

sigano (SEE-gah-noh) Rabbitfish, spinefoot, *Siganus rivulatus.* Olive green with golden stripes and sharp spines on the fins, the fish entered the Mediterranean only recently, through the Suez Canal. The stomach meat is the most tender and takes well to most cooking treatments.

sigaretti (see-gah-REH-tee) "Cigarettes." **Maccheroni,** about 1 inch long, shaped like cigarettes.

signorini (see-n'yoh-REE-nee) "Misters." Small fish that are breaded and fried, from Liguria.

simmuledda alla foggiana (see-moo-LEH-dah AH-lah foh-J'YAH-nah) *"Foggia*-style mash." Soup containing fennel, potatoes, and cornmeal, served over a slice of bread, from Foggia.

situla (SEE-too-lah) Wine bucket used for chilling wines.

sivolits (see-voh-LEETS) A *maccheroni* shape from Friuli.

Sizzano (see-T'ZAH-noh) *DOC* red wine of Piedmont, made from **nebbiolo, vespolino,** and **bonarda** grapes grown in the region around Sizzano.

smacafam (SMAH-kah-fahm) "Push away hunger." Buckwheat *polenta* baked with sausage and, sometimes, cheese, from Trentino–Alto Adige. Probably from Vulgar Latin *affamare* (famish).

snocciolatore (SNOH-kee-yoh-lah-TOH-reh) "Cutting out utensil." Utensil used to remove pits or kernels from fruits.

Soave (soh'WAH-veh) *DOC* white wine of the Veneto, made from **garganega** and **trebbiano** *di Soave* grapes. It is a mass-produced wine, made mostly by consortiums, but *Soave Classico,* made around the town of Soave, shows the delicate character of well-made examples. *Recioto di Soave* is a dessert wine of the region, made from semidried grapes.

sobbollire (soh-boh-LEE-reh) To just barely simmer. See also **pippiare.** From the Latin *bullire* (boil) and the suffix *sub-* (under).

soffiello (soh-fee-EH-loh) Soufflé. From the French *soufflé,* and ultimately from the Latin *sufflare* (to blow).

soffocato (soh-foh-KAH-toh) "Suffocated." Venetian term, *sofegao* in dialect, for cooking very slowly with a very small amount of liquid in a covered pan. From the Latin *suffocare* (to choke).

soffritto (soh-FREE-toh) "Under fried." Finely chopped *pancetta,* onion, garlic, parsley, carrot, and celery that is sautéed in olive oil to form the base of a soup, stew, or sauce.

soglia (SOH-l'yah) Name for *semolino* flour used to make *pasta,* from Bologna.

sogliola (soh-L'YOH-lah) Sole. A flatfish with many species within the family Soleidae. It is best simply sautéed or grilled with butter or olive oil.

Solopaca (soh-loh-PAH-kah) *DOC* zone of Campania that produces white wines from a blend of *trebbiano* and *malvasia* grapes and reds from *sangiovese, piedirosso,* and *aglianico* grapes grown in the Calore Valley and named after the town of Solopaca.

sopa caôda (SOH-pah KOW-dah) Pigeon and cabbage soup served with toasted bread, from the Veneto. The dialect expression may mean simply hot soup, but some believe it comes from the verb *covare,* to brood or sit on eggs until they hatch, in reference to the very long time it takes to cook this soup.

soppressa (soh-PREH-sah) "Compressed [pork]." Cured pork shoulder, a *salame* that is a specialty of Treviso.

soppressata (soh-preh-SAH-tah) "Compressed [pork]." *Salame* made from pork meat and fat, flavored with lemon peel and various spices, from the Veneto. It is aged for at least 40 days.

sorbetto (sohr-BEH-toh) Sorbet or sherbet. The word is from the Arab word *sharbia,* which simply meant drink, and was originally associated with the iced fruit drinks of the Middle East. Today, Italians make *sorbetto* with a wide range of flavors, principally fruits but also chocolate.

Sorni (SOHR-nee) *DOC* red wines of Trentino made from *schiava, teroldego,* and *lagrein* grapes and whites from *nosiola* grapes grown around the town of Sorni.

sorprese (sohr-PREH-seh) "Little wonders." Small, ridged *maccheroni* in the shape of a horseshoe.

sorrentina, alla (AH-lah soh-rehn-TEE-nah) "Sorrento style." Usually indicates a sauce of tomato and *mozzarella,* sometimes with eggplant.

sospiri (soh-SPEE-ree) "Sighs." Almond-flavored sweets, from Sardinia. There, *sospiri* also refers to a dish of egg white flakes cooked with myrtle leaves. From the Latin *suspirium.*

sottaceti (soh-tah-CHEH-tee) "In vinegar." Pickled vegetables used as a garnish.

sottobosco   (soh-toh-BOH-skoh)   "In the woods." Different kinds of berries. From the Middle English *bosk.*

sottofiletto   (soh-toh-fee-LEH-toh)   "Above the filet." Short loin of beef, minus the filet. From the Middle French *fil* (thread).

sott'olio   (soh-TOH-l'yoh)   "In oil," meaning preserved in olive oil.

spaccatina   (spah-kah-TEE-nah)   "Little cleft [bread]." Round, clefted loaf of lard bread, from Abruzzo. *Spaccatini* are clefted bread rolls, from Lugano.

spaghetti   (spah-GEH-tee)   "Little strings." Long, thin strands of dried pasta. *Spaghettini* and **vermicelli** are thinner than *spaghetti,* which are usually about ¹/₈ inch in diameter. (See also **capelli d'angelo.**) It is one of the most versatile pastas in Italian cookery, and many regional sauces have traditionally been used with *spaghetti,* including **aglio e olio,** with garlic and olive oil, also called *alla pretinara; alla ciocara,* made with bacon, ham and sausage, from Lazio; **all'amatriciana** (Amatrice style); **cacio e pepe,** a Roman preparation with **pecorino** cheese and black pepper; **alla carbonara;** *alla checca,* also Roman, made with tomatoes, garlic, basil, oil, and fresh **mozzarella; alla norcina,** with a sauce of olive oil, black tuffles, garlic, and anchovies, from Norcia; *alla cavalle-gerra,* with eggs, walnuts, and cream; **alla puttanesca,** and **alla Norma.** In Apulia, *s. alla zappatora* (ditchdiggers' style) is made with copious amounts of garlic and chile peppers. *S. alla Carlofortina* is made with anchovies and fresh tuna, a specialty of the town of Carloforte on the island of San Pietro. In Umbria, *s. alla rancetto* is a specialty of Spoleto, made with **pancetta** and marjoram. *Ciuffiti* is a Calabrian dish of *spaghetti* with a sauce of garlic, olive oil, and chile peppers. In Sicily's Marsala region, *s. al mataroccu* (silly style) is made with tomatoes, garlic, basil, and crushed almonds. In Tuscany's Maremma region, *s. alla maremma* is with garlic, tomato, eggplant, peas, sausage, and cheese.

spalla   (SPAH-lah)   Shoulder of lamb or pork. *Prosciutto di spalla* is cured pork shoulder. *Spalla cotta* is boiled cured pork shoulder.

spanna   (SPAH-nah)   Local name for the **nebbiolo** grape in the Novarra-Vercelli hills of eastern Piedmont. Unclassified wines are often bottled under this name, but 7 **DOC** wines, including **Gattinara,** are made in the region under this name, which is said to refer to either an ancient Roman city named Spina or to Spain *(Spagna).*

spappolare   (spah-poh-LAH-reh)   To mash or crush.

spätzle   (SH'PEHT-z'lee)   Little dumplings. Common in Alto Adige. From German.

speck   (spehk)   Bacon. Boned pork flank, brine- or smoke-cured. *Speck* contains much lean meat. It is a specialty of Alto Adige and commonly made at home. From German meaning lard or bacon.

spezie (SPEH-t'z'yeh)   Spices. From the Late Latin *species.*

spezzatino (speh-t'zah-TEE-noh)   "Broken pieces." Stew, often made with cubed shoulder or shank of veal and cooked in an earthenware pot. *Spezzatino di montone* is lamb stew. *Spezzatini di pollo* is cut-up chicken sautéed and browned, then simmered in a sauce, often including wine.

spianata (spee-ah-NAH-tah)   "Prickly bread." Bread sprinkled with rosemary similar to *focaccia,* from Romagna. It is often stuffed with onions, garlic, cheese, and other fillings. When made with *pancetta,* it is called *crescentina* in Bologna. When brushed with lard and coarse salt, it is called *torta salata.*

spianatoia (spee-ah-nah-TOI-yah)   Large wooden pastry board. Used to make *pasta,* which should never touch marble.

spicchio (SPEE-k'yoh)   Segment, as of orange, apple, or garlic.

spiedo (spee-EH-doh)   Kitchen spit. *Spiedini* are foods that are placed on a *spiedo* and cooked over a fire. *Spiedini alla romana* are slices of bread and *mozzarella* cheese set on a skewer, then fried in oil.

spigola (SPEE-goh-lah)   See *branzino.*

spina, alla (AH-la SPEE-nah)   On tap, as beer in a tavern. The word refers to the plug of a barrel. From the Latin for thorn.

spinaci (spee-NAH-chee)   Spinach. Native to Persia. The word derives from the Arabic *isfanakh,* via the Persian, and the plant was not cultivated outside the Middle East until the late Middle Ages or early Renaissance. It soon became a popular vegetable in Italy. Spinach became so associated with Florence that *alla fiorentina* indicated a dish that included spinach in some form. Caterina de' Medici was responsible for popularizing spinach in France. Today Italians eat spinach in salads, as a cooked vegetable, and in timbales, filled pastas, and savory pies.

spinarolo bruno (spee-nah-ROH-loh BROO-noh)   "Brown, prickly (fish)." Spur dog, *Squalus acanthias,* a spiny shark much appreciated by Venetian cooks, though other Italians find the flesh coarse. It is best stewed. From the Latin *spina* (thorn) and Greek *phryne* (toad).

spongata (spohn-GAH-tah)   Traditional sponge cake soaked with rum and layered with preserves, chocolate, and custard, served at Christmastime, from Emilia-Romagna. In Sicily, a similar cake, of Arab origins, is called *spongarda.* From the Latin *spongia* (sponge).

spremuta (spreh-MOO-tah)   Freshly squeezed fruit juice.

spugnole (spoo-N'YOH-leh)   See *morchella.*

spuma (SPOO-mah)   Mousse. Made by whipping egg whites into a sweet or savory batter and baking it until it puffs up in the oven. From the French, ultimately from the Latin *spuma* (foam).

spumante (spoo-MAHN-teh)   A sparkling wine. The word means foaming. From the Latin *spuma*. See also *Asti Spumante.*

spumone (spoo-MOH-neh)   A molded ice cream confection, usually composed of strawberry, vanilla, and *pistachio* (the red, white, and green colors of the Italian flag), from Naples. From the Latin *spuma* (foam).

spuntatura di maiale (spoon-tah-TOO-rah dee mye-AH-leh)   Tips of pork ribs.

spuntino (spoon-TEE-noh)   Snack, either sweet or savory.

squadro (SKWAH-droh)   See *rana pescatrice.*

squaquerone (skwah-kweh-ROH-neh)   Very soft and tangy fresh cow's milk cheese, from Emilia-Romagna.

Squinzano (skween-ZAH-noh)   *DOC* red wine of Apulia, made from *negroamaro* grapes grown around the town of Squinzano.

stacchjoddi (stah-CH'YOH-dee)   Little flat pasta shapes, about ¹/₂ inch in diameter, from Apulia.

staccio (STAH-ch'yoh)   Very fine strainer.

stagionato (stah-j'yoh-NAH-toh)   "Seasoned." Well aged or hung, as with game. From the Vulgar Latin *staticum* (stand).

stagione, di (dee stah-J'YOH-neh)   "Of the season." Made with ingredients of the current season. From the Vulgar Latin *staticum* (stand).

starna (STAHR-nah)   Gray partridge. See also *pernice.*

steccare (steh-KAH-reh)   To lard meat with seasonings or fat. From the Latin *instigare* (to goad).

stecchi (STEH-kee)   "Sticks." Snacks on skewers. Ingredients like artichokes, truffles, *porcini,* and veal are skewered on olive branches dipped into an infusion of saffron, then breaded, dipped in egg whites, and fried in olive oil. They are a specialty of Genoa, where they used to be sold around the port by sellers of fried foods who were known as *friggitori.* From the Latin *instigare* (to goad).

stelline (steh-LEE-neh)   "Little stars," referring to the shape of this tiny pasta, used in soups. From the Latin *stella* (star).

stiacciata fiorentina (stee-ah-CH'YAH-tah fee-oh-rehn-TEE-nah) "Florentine cookies." Long cookies made with a leavened egg dough containing grated orange peel, from Florence.

stigghiole   (stee-G'YOH-leh)   Grilled lamb intestines or caul–wrapped bunches of lamb innards and vegetables, a Sicilian street food.

stinchetti di morto   (steen-KEH-tee dee MOHR-toh)   "Little bones of a dead man." A bone-shape cookie, from Umbria.

stinco   (STEEN-koh)   Shank. Whole *stinco di ritello* is cooked for a long time with a sauce, like **ossobuco.** The difference is that the latter is often cut crosswise into thick slices while *stinco* is cooked whole, especially in Friuli and the Veneto. *S. di aquello* is lamb shank.

stoccafisso   (stoh-kah-FEE-soh)   Also *stocco.* Air-dried but not salted small cod. In the Veneto it is usually simmered in milk with tomato. *Stocche accomodou* (convenient stockfish) contains several ingredients, usually potatoes, pine nuts, and olives, from Genoa. From a German term meaning "fish as stiff as a stick." See also **pescestocco.**

storione   (stoh-ree-OH-neh)   Sturgeon, *Acipenser sturio.* A good fatty fish, meaty and fine for grilling or broiling. The eggs are processed into caviar. Gelatin is made from the fish's bladder.

storti   (STOHR-tee)   "Twisted [cookies]." Almond and lemon–flavored cookie in a twisted shape, from the Veneto.

straca dent   (STRAH-kah DENT)   "Tired tooth." Meringue dessert of egg whites, sugar, and blanched almonds passed quickly under the flame to give it a golden-brown top, from Emilia-Romagna.

stracchino   (strah-KEE-noh)   Northern Italian cheese made from cow's milk mixed with milk of the night before. **Crescenza, gorgonzola, robiola,** and *taleggio* are all *stracchino* cheeses. The term is Milanese dialect for tired, referring to the condition of the cows when driven to and from their summer pastures.

stracciata   (strah-CH'YAH-tah)   "Little rag." Finely shredded, sautéed lettuce or savory, used as a soup garnish.

stracciatella   (strah-CH'YAH-teh-lah)   "Little rags." A chicken or beef soup to which a paste of egg and cheese is added to make little raglike shreds *(straccetti)* of dough that are cooked in the broth, a specialty of Rome. Also called *stracciatella alla romana* or *minestra mille fanti.*

Stracciatella also refers to chocolate chip ice cream.

STRACCIATELLA ALLA ROMANA

4 eggs	*3 tablespoons chopped parsley*
¹/₂ cup parmigiano	*2 quarts beef or chicken broth*
Salt and pepper	

Beat the eggs with ¹/₄ cup of the **parmigiano,** salt and pepper to taste, and parsley. Bring the broth to a low simmer. Whisk the eggs and dribble them into the soup, which will cook the eggs. Add the rest of the *parmigiano,* blend, and serve immediately. Serves 4 to 6.

---

stracnar (STRAHK-nahr) Homemade pasta squares that pick up a herringbone pattern from a carved board called a *cavarola,* from Apulia. They are usually served with a sauce made of cherry tomatoes, croutons, and anchovies. Also *stracenate.*

stracotto (strah-KOH-toh) "Long-cooked." Pot roast or braised beef, commonly made with sausages and white wine.

strangolapreti (strahn-goh-lah-PREH-tee) "Priest stranglers." Small potato **gnocchi** of Trentino served with tomato sauce, said to be so good that priests would gorge themselves and choke on them. In Romagna, *strozzapreti* are a form of twisted **tagliatelle** whose name means the same as *strangolapreti.* Also *strangolaprievete* in Neapolitan dialect.

strascicare (strah-shee-KAH-reh) To finish cooking pasta with the sauce served with it, usually by briefly cooking it together in a skillet.

strascinati (strah-shee-NAH-tee) Basilicata pasta made of lard and flour made into small sausage-like shapes "dragged" over a tool known as a *cavarola* that gives them a rough macaroni shape. They are commonly sauced with tomato and chile pepper.

strascinato (strah-chee-NAH-toh) Cooking method of southern and central Italy by which vegetables are quickly sautéed—"dragged" through the sauté pan.

strattù (strah-TOO) Concentrated tomato sauce made from tomatoes that have been dried in the sun. From the Latin *centrum* (center).

strega (STREH-gah) "Witch." Yellow, licorice-flavored liqueur actually made from more than 70 herbs. It is 40 percent alcohol. According to legend, it was made by beautiful women who disguised themselves as witches. Probably from the Latin *saga*.

streghe   (STREH-geh)   "Witches." Crunchy crackers, from Bologna.

strichetti   (stree-KEH-tee)   "Pinched." Bow-shaped pasta about 2 inches wide and pinched in the center, like *farfalle,* and containing lemon zest, a specialty of Romagna. In Villa Gaidello, nutmeg and parsley are added to the dough and the pasta is called *stricchettoni.*

stringozzi   (streen-GOH-t'zee)   "Big shoelaces." Handmade thick, sometimes squared-off pasta, a specialty of Spoleto. Commonly served with a spicy tomato sauce flavored with chile pepper flakes. From the Latin *stringere* (to bind tight).

strinu   (stree-NOO)   Beef and pork sausage, usually grilled, from Lombardy.

strucolo   (STROO-koh-loh)   *Strudel* filled with *ricotta,* raisins, and bread crumbs, from Friuli.

strudel   (STROO-dell)   Northern Italian version of the Austrian pastry of the same name. A *ricotta-*and-raisin version is called *strucolo,* from Friuli.

struffoli   (STROO-foh-lee)   Little cookies in the shape of balls fried and coated with honey, traditionally piled together into a pyramid shape, from Naples.

STRUFFOLI

2 cups flour	*Grated zest of ¹/₂ lemon*
2 tablespoons sugar	*Oil for deep-frying*
Pinch of salt	
6 eggs	*TOPPING:*
2 egg yolks	*8 ounces good-quality honey*
3 tablespoons butter, melted and cooled	*4 ounces candied orange rind, finely chopped*

Pour the flour onto a pastry board, add the sugar and the salt and blend. Make a well in this flour mixture and add the eggs, the butter, and the lemon zest. With a wooden spoon start stirring the center, gently incorporating some of the flour as you stir until all the flour is mixed in. Knead the dough until it is smooth. Divide the dough into 6 pieces and roll each piece into a cylinder, ¹/₂ inch in diameter. Cut each cylinder into ¹/₂-inch pieces and set aside on a floured board. Heat the oil and fry a few of the *struffoli* at a time until they are golden. Drain them on paper towels and repeat until all the *struffoli* are fried. Put the honey into a saucepan, bring to a boil, and let simmer until the foam subsides. Add the candied orange rind and *struffoli* and mix until all the *struffoli* are coated with the honey. Place this mixture on a plate and with wet hands shape the *struffoli* into desired shape—round, conical, or flat. Serve at room temperature.

---

strukli   (STROO-klee)   Savory **strudel,** made with potato dough and filled with **ricotta,** from Friuli.

strutto   (STROO-toh)   Rendered pork fat or lard. See also **lardo** and *sugna.*

struzzo   (STROO-t'zoh)   Ostrich, *struthio camelus.* Imported to ancient Rome as a delicacy, from Arabia and Africa, but never a popular meat among Italians.

stufata   (stoo-FAH-tah)   Stuffed or layered. From the Vulgar Latin *stuppare.*

stufato   (stoo-FAH-toh)   Pot roast or stew made from beef, veal, or pork with wine and usually tomatoes in the braising liquid. In Sicily, *stufato nero* is made with rabbit and contains chocolate, which gives it a dark color.

stuzzichini   (stoo-t'zee-KEE-nee)   "Little poked [pastries]." Puff-pastry straws.

suacia   (SWAH-ch'yah)   Scaldfish, *Arnoglossus laterna.* A brown flatfish whose scales and fin are easily rubbed off.

succo di frutta   (SOO-koh dee FROO-tah)   Fruit juice.

succu tundu   (SOO-koo TUHN-doo)   Large couscous cooked in consommé with **ricotta** *salata.* See also *fregola.*

su farru   (soo FAH-roo)   Soup of *farro* cooked in beef broth and sour milk flavored with mint and cheese, from Sardinia. Also *su farri.*

sugna   (SOO-n'yah)   Pork fat, mostly from the back of the pig. From the Latin *sus* (pig).

sugo   (SOO-goh)   "Juice." Both fruit juice and the juices that seep from meats being cooked. Italians may use the terms *sugo* (plural, *sughi*) and **salsa** interchangeably, but some cooks distinguish between the two—without agreeing on what those distinctions are.

In his cookbook *La Scienza in cucina e l'arte di mangiar bene* (1891), Pellegrino Artusi insisted that a *sugo di pomodoro* (tomato sauce) is "simple, i.e., made from tomatoes that are simply cooked and run through a food mill. At the most, you may add a small rib of celery and a few leaves of parsley and basil to tomato *sugo,* if you must." *Salses,* he contended, are accompaniments like green sauce *(salsa verde),* mayonnaise *(maionese),* and tuna sauce *(salsa tonnata)* to other dishes. Yet *sugo di carne,* a sauce made with meat juices (if with beef alone, it is called *sugo di manzo),* was well known among wealthy families of the 19th century, and *sugo finto* (fake sauce) is a common term used by poor people for a **pasta** sauce made to taste like a *sugo di carne* by using the same ingredients, but without the meat. And meat sauces are also termed *salse.* To further complicate matters, the words **ragù,** and in Tuscany, **tocco,** are often used for a meat sauce.

In her book *Ultimate Pasta* (1997), Julia della Croce writes that *salse* may be made from "any number of ingredients," while *sughi* "are simple essences with few ingredients," and **ragù** are "meat-based sauces."

It would appear, however, that the two terms *sugo* and *salsa* are often interchangeable, with *sugo* reserved for a *pasta* sauce while *salsa* may be used to describe sauces that may or may not accompany *pasta.*

Sugo scappato is a winter tomato sauce made with canned tomatoes, while **pummarola** is a summer tomato sauce made with fresh, ripe tomatoes.

SUGO DI CARNE

2 ounces ham fat, sliced into slivers	*2 onions, sliced*
2 ounces fresh pork rind	*1 whole clove*
1 pound beef shank	*1 bay leaf*
2 carrots, chopped	*¹/₄ teaspoon each dried marjoram and*
Salt and pepper	*thyme*
4 strips pancetta	*1 garlic clove, crushed*
¹/₂ pound veal shank	*¹/₄ cup dry red wine*
1 veal knuckle	*2 teaspoons flour*
1¹/₂ tablespoons dried porcini, soaked	*2 teaspoons olive oil*
for 1 hour in warm water and	*1 tomato, peeled, seeded, and chopped*
drained	*1 teaspoon sugar*
1 celery stalk, sliced	*About 8 cups boiling water*

Preheat the oven to 450° F. Place the fat and pork rind in a large heavy-bottomed pot. Cut cavities into the beef shank and insert pieces of one of the carrots, season with salt and pepper to taste, wrap with **pancetta,** and place on top of the fat. Add the veal shank, knuckle, **porcini,** remaining carrot, the celery, onions, and clove. Place the pot in the oven for about 20 minutes, or until the meat begins to brown, stirring occasionally. Remove from the oven and reduce the heat to 300° F. Add the bay leaf, marjoram, and thyme. Add the garlic and red wine. Place the pot on top of the stove and cook over medium heat until the liquid has almost boiled away. Remove from the heat, blend in the flour, and return to the heat, stirring occasionally, for about 3 minutes. Add the tomato and sugar, then enough boiling water to cover the meat. Add salt and pepper to taste, mix well, bring to a boil, and cover the pot. Place in the oven for 4 hours. When done, remove the meat and veal knuckle. Strain the liquid into another pot and place on medium heat to cook until thickened. Skim any fat from surface, as necessary. Serves 8 to 10.

suino (soo'WEE-noh) Swine. Another word for pork, usually as an adjective. From the Latin *sus* (pig).

sultanina (sool-tah-NEE-nah) "Sultans' wives." Golden raisins. The origin of the name refers to the raisins coming to Italy from the sultans' land, Turkey. See also *uva passa.*

superiore (soo-peh-ree-OH-reh) *DOC* wine that meets certain standards higher than the basic requirements, such as higher alcohol or longer aging. From the Latin *supra* (above).

supplì (SOO-plee) "[Telephone] wires." Also *supplì al telefono.* Rice balls filled with *mozzarella* and or other ingredients, such as ground meat, chicken livers, tomatoes, and peas. They are dredged in bread crumbs and fried. The odd Roman name comes from the appearance of the stretched strands of *mozzarella* cheese when it melts.

SUPPLÌ

¹/₂ cup diced mozzarella	*Nutmeg*
1 tablespoon chopped parsley	*4 cups cooked risotto, cold*
¹/₂ cup grated parmigiano	*Flour*
¹/₂ cup diced prosciutto	*1 cup bread crumbs*
4 eggs	*2 cups olive oil*
Salt and pepper	

Mix the **mozzarella,** parsley, **parmigiano,** and **prosciutto** in a large bowl. Beat two of the eggs and add to the mixture. Blend well. Add salt, pepper, and nutmeg to taste.

With moistened hands, form the **risotto** into balls about 2 inches in diameter. With your finger create a deep hole in the center of each ball and fill with the cheese mixture. Close the ball, with additional *risotto* if necessary, then dredge first in flour, then in the remaining beaten eggs, then in bread crumbs. Allow to rest for about 15 minutes. Fry in hot oil until golden brown. Drain on paper towels and serve hot.

surgelato (soor-jeh-LAH-toh)   Frozen, a term required by law to be attached to any restaurant food that is thus treated. From the Latin *gelo.*

suro (SOO-roh)   Scad or horse mackerel, *Trachurus trachurus.* Big-eyed fish with lozenge-shaped scales and manelike upper branch, probably the same fish as the *surico,* found in Calabria fishmarkets. An eastern Atlantic species, *T. picuratus,* sometimes found in the Mediterranean, is called *sugarello pittato.*

susina (soo-SEE-nah)   Plum. Originally imported by the ancient Romans from Damascus, then propagated to produce a wide variety of the fruit.

Plums are eaten fresh, stewed, used as stuffing, baked, and made into ice cream and desserts. **Gnocchi** *di susina* are made with a prune in the middle. See also **prugna.**

Coscia della monaca (nun's thigh) is a colloquialism for a very succulent plum.

suspirus (soo-SPEE-roos)   "Sighs." Walnut-size balls of ground almonds, sugar, and egg whites that are baked and coated with lemon icing, from Sardinia. From the Latin.

su tataliu (SOO tah-tah-L'YOO)   Lamb innards, bacon or ham, and bay leaf, barded with sausage casing, and cooked on a spit, from Sardinia. Also *trattaliu.*

svezzato (s'veh-T'ZAH-toh)   Weaned baby lamb or pig.

sylvaner (seel-VAH-nehr)   White wine grape of Alto Adige. The name is from the French name for this grape (referring to the forest, in Latin, *silva*) grown in Germany and Eastern Europe.

T

tabulon (TAH-b'yoo-lohn) Mule, donkey, or horse stew, a specialty of Novara and in particular of the town of Borgomanero in Piedmont. The dialect word refers to the cutting up of the tough meat with a knife. The ingredients cooked with the meat are traditionally lard, olive oil, bay leaves, cloves, fennel seeds, garlic, and red wine. *Tabulon* is usually served with **polenta.**

tacchino (tah-KEE-noh) Turkey, also known in Venice as *paeta* and *dodino,* in Milan as *pollin. Gallotta* is a female turkey.

The turkey came to Italy from America and garnered its English name because of the mistaken belief that the bird came through the Turkish trade routes, but the Italian word *tacchino* (early on *tacchinotto)* is believed to be a derivation of the French word *tache,* meaning a stain or spot, because of the mottled appearance of the turkey's feathers. Turkeys are eaten in many ways in Italy. *Tacchino in carpione* is first cooked, then marinated with vinegar, oil, and herbs. *T. ripieno* is a turkey stuffed with fruits, nuts, minced veal, salt pork, herbs, and brandy, a tradition of Christmas, from Lombardy. *T. alla storiona* (sturgeon-style turkey) is an elaborate Christmas terrine from Genoa; the name may recall the days when sturgeon was a local delicacy or, as has been suggested, a corruption of the name Styria, a region in southeastern Austria. *Filetti di tacchino alla bolognese* is white turkey meat cooked with ham and grated cheese, baked in the oven, from Bologna. For *t. alla canzanese* the turkey is boned and rubbed with herbs, then simmered with the turkey bones, calf's or pig's feet, carrots, and herbs. When done, the meat is placed in a round bowl, covered with strained broth, refrigerated until a jelly forms, and then unmolded before serving, a specialty of Abruzzo.

taccola (tah-KOH-lah) Snow pea, not commonly seen in Italian cookery. Also *pisello mangiatutto.* The word probably refers to *tacco,* "little shoe heels," which snow peas resemble.

tacconi (tah-KOH-nee) Tuscan pasta cut into 3-inch squares. *Tacconelli* are somewhat smaller, and in Abruzzo they are cut ¹/₂-inch wide and 2 inches long. The word probably refers to *taccole* (little trifles).

tagliatelle (tah-l'yah-TEH-leh) Freshly made pasta ribbons about ¹/₄-inch wide, made with egg, and, if green, with spinach. From the verb *tagliare* (to cut). *Tagliardi* are oblong pasta, about 1-inch wide.

Legend has it that Maestro Zafiramo, Bolognese cook of Giovanni II of Bentivoglio, first served them to and named them after the long, golden hair of Lucrezia Borgia upon her arrival on May 28, 1487, to marry Ferrara's Duke of Este.

The *Accademia Italiana della Cucina* defined *tagliatelle*'s dimensions as 8 mm wide (⁵/₁₆ inch) and .6 mm thick (¹/₃₂ inch), a golden replica of which has been kept, since 1972, in Bologna's city hall. *Taglione,* also called *nidi di taglioni* (nests of cut [pasta]), are slightly thicker.

Tagliatelle are identified with Emilia-Romagna (where they are called *tajadel)* and traditionally made *alla duchessa,* with browned chicken livers, beaten egg yolks, and **parmigiano,** a dish named after the 19th-century Duchess of Parma, Maria Louisa. *Tagliarini* are thinner than *tagliatelle,* and *tagliolini* are thinner still. *Tagliolini colla croccia* (crusty tagliolini), a dish of Italian Jews, is a round casserole dish of *tagliolini* mixed with raisins, meat sauce, chicken fat, and nuts, then baked until crunchy on top. It is sometimes referred to as *ruota di faraone* (Pharoah's wheel), served on Shabbàt B'shallàch to commemorate the Israelites' passage out of Egypt as described in the Bible.

In Piedmont, a form of *tagliatelle* is called *tajarin,* a specialty of the city of Alba, where they are made with white flour and egg yolks and possibly a little oil, but no water. They are commonly served with a **ragù** of liver or simply with butter and cheese.

tagliere (tah-L'YEH-reh) Cutting board. From *tagliare* (to cut).

taglio (TAH-l'yoh) Cut of meat. *Primo taglio* (first cut) would be the best, prime cut of meat; *secondo* (second) and *terzo* (third) would be lesser cuts.

taleggio (tah-LEH-j'yoh) Soft, buttery, mild cow's milk. **DOC** cheese from the Taleggio valley near Bergamo in Lombardy. It is aged about 40 days and consumed as a table cheese. *Taleggio di Monte* (mountain *taleggio)* is made in the Valtellina.

tanuta (tah-NOO-tah) Black bream *(Spondyliosoma cantharus),* adaptable to all forms of fish cookery.

taralli (tah-RAH-lee) "Round [things]." Unsweetened round semolina cookies that are boiled, then baked. They come in various shapes like rings and knots and may be flavored with fennel seeds, peppercorns, or chile peppers.

tarantello   (tah-rahn-TEH-loh)   Spiced tuna *salame* of Taranto.

tarello   (tah-REH-loh)   Wooden stick used to stir *polenta.*

taroco   (tah-ROH-koh)   Blood orange, from Sicily. See also *arancia.*

tartazuga   (tahr-tah-T'ZOO-gah)   Sea turtle. Turtles are not common in Italian cookery, though they may be made into soup or stews. From the Late Latin *tartarucha* (of Tartarus).

tartina   (tahr-TEE-nah)   A savory snack of bread topped with meat, fish, egg, or vegetables. From the Middle French *tart* (tart).

tartra   (TAHR-trah)   Savory custard, from Piedmont.

tartufo   (tahr-TOO-foh)   Truffle, both black, *tartufo nero di norcia* or *invernale (Tuber melanosporum),* and white, *tartufo bianco (Tuber magnatum pico).* From the Latin *terra tuber* (root of the cyclamen).
   More than 10,000 Italian truffle hunters, called *cavatori* (from *cavata,* meaning extraction) collect the expensive fungi. Most truffles are sent to the truffle capital of Europe in the town of Scheggino in Umbria, where the firm of Urbani processes and distributes the truffles to Europe and the rest of the world.
   Black truffles, in season in Italy from December through May, are used principally as a garnish and served fresh. White truffles are more prized in Italy, and they are named after the town of Alba in Piedmont where the best are to be found, although the white truffles of Aqualagna are also prized. The full Latin name of the white truffle, *Tuber magnatum pico,* is derived from the Piedmontese mycologist Vittorio Pico, who first named the fungus. They are in season September through January, and trained dogs are used to sniff them out.
   In Italy, truffles are usually eaten raw, cut into thin slices on a blade called a *tagliatartufo,* shaved over pasta, *risotto,* in salads, and on many other dishes. Owing to their great price, they are used sparingly.
   The word *tartufo* also refers to a Roman dessert created at Tre Scalini restaurant on the Piazza Navona. It is a ball of dark chocolate ice cream with bits of chocolate and a candied sour cherry in the middle.
   Tartufi di cioccolata are chocolates shaped like truffles.

tartufo di mare   (tahr-TOO-foh dee MAH-reh)   "Truffles of the sea." Venus clam, *Venus verrucosa.* Also *tartufolo.* In Venice, it is called *caparozzolo.*

Taurasi   (tau-RAH-zee)   *DOC* red wine of Campania made from *aglianico* grapes from around the village of Taurasi.

taverna   (tah-VEHR-nah)   Tavern. From the Latin *taberna.*

tavogliolo   (tah-voh-L'YOH-loh)   Napkin. *Tavogliolo di carta* is a paper napkin.

tavola   (TAH-voh-lah)   Table. From the Latin *tabula* (board).

tavola calda   (TAH-voh-lah KAHL-dah)   "Hot table." A snack, bar, usu-ally with a counter, serving hot food. *Calda* is from the Latin *caldus*.

tazza   (TAH-t'zah)   Cup. *Tazzina* is a small cup for **espresso**.

tazzelenghe   (TAH-t'zeh-LEHN-gheh)   A Friulian dialect word for *tazzalingua* (tongue-mouth) for a dark red wine of **Colli Orientali**. Also *tace-lenghe*.

tazzine, le   (leh tah-T'ZEE-neh)   "The little cups." Dessert custard made with almonds, egg yolks, sugar, cinnamon, and orange flower water, served in demitasse cups.

tecia   (TEH-ch'yah)   Venetian dialect word for pot.

tegamaccio   (teh-gah-MAH-ch'yoh)   "Sloppy stew." Either of two dishes: a mixed lake-fish stew, usually made with carp, tench, pike, and eel, from Umbria; or a tossed-together compote of vegetables.

tegame   (teh-GAH-meh)   A shallow saucepan usually made of copper or earthenware, with two side handles. A *tegamino* is a smaller version of the same pan.

tegamino alla lodigiana   (teh-gah-MEE-noh AH-lah loh-dee-J'YAH-nah)   Layers of white truffles and **parmigiano** baked in the oven, from Lodi.

teglia   (TEH-l'yah)   Baking pan.

tegole   (TEH-goh-lah)   "Tuiles." Hazelnut cookies so called because of their curved shape. They are a specialty of Valle d'Aosta.

tellina   (teh-LEE-nah)   Cockle, *Cardium edule, Cerastoderma edule, Acantho-cardia echinata,* and others. Usually eaten raw or cooked in a court bouillon.

temolo   (TEH-moh-loh)   Grayling. A freshwater fish in the genus *Thy-mallus* that lives in Lake Como. A troutlike fish that is cooked in much the same way: grilled, sautéed, or poached in a court bouillon.

tempestina   (tehm-peh-STEE-nah)   "Little snowfall." Very small pasta used in soups. From the Latin *tempestas* (storm).

tenerume   (teh-neh-ROO-meh)   Cut of beef consisting of the muscles and tissue at the end of the ribs.

tenuta   (teh-NOO-tah)   Wine estate.

terizzo   (teh-REE-t'zoh)   A red wine of Liguria based on **sangiovese** and **cabernet** grapes.

teroldego   (teh-ROHL-deh-goh)   A grape of Trentino, used in making red and rosé wines. *Teroldego Rotaliano,* made on the Campo Rotaliano plain, is a **DOC** appellation for red and rosé wines.

terre di Ginestra (TEH-reh dee jee-NEH-strah)   A white wine of Sicily made from *catarratto* grapes grown near Palermo.

testa (TEH-stah)   Head of an animal. *Testina* refers to calf's head.

testaroli (teh-stah-ROH-lee)   Pasta cooked like pancakes on stacked earthenware dishes called *testelli,* from Liguria. They are then cut into strips or triangles, quickly boiled, and sauced, usually with *pesto.* Also *testaieu.*

tetouns (teh-TOUNS)   Salt-cured, herbed cow's udder, a specialty of Valle d'Aosta. From Middle High German *zizle* (teat).

the (teh)   Tea. From the Chinese *t'e.* Also *te.*
   In Italy, tea is not nearly as popular as coffee, which preceded it in arriving in Italy by a century. Tea was brought to Europe by the Dutch East India Company in the 17th century.

tiella (tee-EH-lah)   Layered baked dish that may include potatoes and onions, seafood, rice, and/or mushrooms, from Abruzzo and Apulia. Also *taiedda* and *teglia.*

tigelle (tee-GEH-leh)   Fried or grilled yeast dough circles, commonly served with *lardo,* rosemary, and garlic. They are cooked between two terracotta tiles called *tigelle,* from Emilia-Romagna.

Tignanello (tee-n'yah-NEH-loh)   Proprietary name of the Antinori company in Tuscany for a blend of *sangiovese* and about 20 percent *cabernet sauvignon* from the *Tignanello* vineyard, eliminating the white grapes traditional in Tuscan blends. It was also innovative in that *Tignanello* was aged in small oak barrels, called *carati,* rather than the traditional large barrels called *botti.* The first vintage sold was 1971, bottled in 1974, and the wine is only made in excellent years. Since it is an individual wine, it does not carry a *DOC,* but it is often referred to as one of the "Super Tuscan" wines of high quality.

timballo (teem-BAH-loh)   Timbale. A dish, often with pasta or rice, made in a form and unmolded. *Timballini* are small molds. From the Arabic *at-tabl* (the drum).
   The most famous *timballo* is the Sicilian *timballo di anellini,* made with ring-shape dried pasta, *balsamello,* ground beef and chicken, peas, and vegetables, all wrapped in lettuce leaves and baked in a mold. *Timballo di crespelle* is crepes layered with spinach, ground meat, giblets, *mozzarella,* and *parmigiano,* from Abruzzo. See also *sartù.*

timo (TEE-moh)   Thyme. Thyme is native to the Mediterranean, used in Sumeria and Egypt for medicinal purposes, its main usage until well into the Middle Ages, when it grew wild. From the Latin *thymum.*

tinca (TEEN-kah)   Tench, *Tinca tinca.* A freshwater fish in the carp family found in the rivers and lakes of northern Italy. It is most often stuffed and baked or cooked with white wine, tomatoes, and peas. See also *carpa.*

tino (TEE-noh)   Large wooden wine cask that stands vertical rather than horizontal in the aging room.

tirami sù (tee-RAH-mee SOO)   "Pick me up." A rich dessert made of layers of ladyfingers, *mascarpone, espresso,* and chocolate. The dish was created in the 1960s at El Toulà restaurant in Treviso and has since become one of the classic and international Italian desserts.

tirata a mano (tee-RAH-tah ah MAH-noh)   "Stretched by hand." *Pasta* made by hand, not machine.

tocai friulano (toh-KYE free-oo-LAH-noh)   Widely propagated grape of Friuli, also grown in the Veneto and Lombardy, used in making **DOC** white wines. Despite its name, it is related to neither *tokay d'Alsace* nor to the Hungarian *Tokay,* although some experts believe the varietal is related to the *furmint* grape of Tokay in Hungary, imported by Count Ottello di Ariis in 1863 when Hungary ruled Friuli. Others believe the varietal was actually exported from Aquileia *to* Hungary in the 13th century by patriarch Bertoldo di Andechs to King Bela IV. Because of the confusion of the names, however, Friulian viticulturists have agreed to cease using the name *Tocai* in the future.

toç (tohk)   "Mush." Friulian term for soup made with *polenta* and diluted with milk. *Toç de purcit* is pork with *polenta,* white wine, cinnamon, cloves, and other spices.

tocchi (TOH-kee)   "Little pieces." Small morsels or leftovers of food like vegetables or meat added to a soup, pasta, or other preparation.

tocco (TOH-koh)   Sauce used to dress pasta or rice, from Genoa. *Tocco di carne* is made with braised beef or veal, which is eaten separately; *T. di funghi* is made with mushrooms. *Tuccu de nuxe* is made with mashed walnuts, garlic, bread, and, often, a yogurtlike cheese called **prescinseha.** Also *tuccu.*

tofeja (toh-FEH-yah)   Soup made of beans, cornmeal, pork, thyme, rosemary, parsley, garlic, and vegetables, traditionally served at Carnival, especially in Turin. The name refers to the four-handled terra-cotta pot in which it is cooked. Also *stofor.*

toma (TOH-mah)   A smooth, firm, cow's milk cheese, aged between 3 and 18 months, from Lombardy and Piedmont. In Sicily the name refers to fresh ewe's milk curds molded in a basket. Also *tuma.*

Tomini are smaller versions of the cheese, traditionally coated with herbs and marinated in oil, a specialty of Lombardy and Valle d'Aosta.

tomaxelle   (toh-mah-t'SELL)   Braised veal rolls filled with ground meat, mushrooms, potatoes, eggs, and beans, from Liguria. From the Latin *tomaculum,* a kind of cooked sausage.

tonda gentile della Langa   (TOHN-dah jehn-TEE-leh DEH-lah LAHN-gah)   An esteemed hazelnut from the Langhe region of Piedmont. The name means "tender round (nut) of the Langhe."

tondus   (TOHN-doos)   "Round." Large round bread loaf, from Sardinia.

tonnarelli   (TOH-nah-REH-lee)   Homemade egg pasta with squared-off sides, a Roman specialty very similar to **maccheroni alla chitarra** in Abruzzo.

tonno   (TOH-noh)   Tuna, *Thunnus thynnus.* A very large nomadic saltwater fish with firm, rich meat. It is a very popular fish in Sicily, the island to which the tuna swim to spawn. There are countless tuna dishes, especially in Sicily, and the fish may be baked, broiled, or grilled and served with any number of sauces.

Tonno sott'olio is tuna in oil. The underbelly, called *ventresca,* is considered the best part of the fish; it is often canned. The egg sac is made into **bottarga.** See also **bonito.**

tonno di coniglio   (TOH-noh dee koh-NEE-l'yoh)   "Rabbit tuna." Marinated boneless rabbit whose texture is so tender it resembles tuna. It is usually served as an **antipasto.** From Piedmont.

toppe   (TOH-peh)   Tuscan pasta shaped like patches about 3 inches square.

torbato   (tohr-BAH-toh)   A white wine grape of Sardinia, used in making a dry white wine. Probably imported from Spain.

torcetto   (tohr-CHEH-toh)   "Twist." Butter crisp, from Valle d'Aosta.

torciglione   (tohr-chee-L'YOH-neh)   "Big twists." Snake-shaped cookies made with almond paste and coffee beans for eyes.

torcolo   (TOHR-koh-loh)   Sponge cake studded with raisins and candied fruit, from Perugia.

tordi finti   (TOHR-dee FEEN-tee)   "Mock thrushes." Dish of chicken livers, juniper berries, anchovies, **prosciutto,** and sage molded and tied to resemble thrushes. They are sautéed, then simmered in broth and served on slices of toast with the pan drippings.

tordimatti   (tohr-dee-MAH-tee)   "Crazy thrushes." Sienese dish of veal **scaloppine** stuffed with **prosciutto,** sage, juniper berries, and eggs, then wrapped in caul fat, skewered, and baked, from Siena. The name refers to the stuffing, which is the same as commonly used for thrushes, *tordi.*

tordo (TOHR-doh)   Thrush. The best tasting are said to feed on juniper. Also a long dark-green Mediterranean fish, *Labrus turdus.* Usually spit-roasted and often used in soup. *Tordo fischietto* and *tordo nero* are similar species.

torello (toh-REH-loh)   Uncastrated bull, usually slaughtered at two years. From the Latin *taurus.*

toresani allo spiedo (toh-reh-SAH-nee AH-loh spee-EH-doh)   Spit-roasted pigeons basted with a mixture containing basil, rosemary, and juniper berries, from the Veneto.

Torgiano (tohr-J'YAH-noh)   *DOC* zone of Umbria that produces white and red wines, including *Torgiano Rosso Riserva* made from **sangiovese, canaiolo,** *ciliegiolo,* **montepulciano,** and **trebbiano** grapes. The name comes from the tower of the god Janus on the plot of land where the grapes are grown.

torricella (toh-ree-CHEH-lah)   Horn-shell mollusk, *Cerithium vulgatum.* Used in soup.

torrone (toh-ROH-neh)   A nougat candy made of honey, sugar, egg whites, and hazelnuts. It is an ancient sweet of Piedmont, originating in Cremona, with records of its service dating to a banquet held in 1395 in Milan by the Duke Gian Galeazzo Visconti. See also **cubbaita di giuggiulena.**

torta (TOHR-tah)   Cake, either sweet or savory. The *torta* is so essential to the cooking of Parma and its surrounding mountain villages that two—a savory one with spinach, potato, or squash and a sweet one with **ricotta**—may be served at the same meal. From the Middle French *tarte.*

Torta al testo is a flat unleavened Umbrian bread baked on a flat stone called a *testo. T. di fagioli bianchi* (white bean cake) is made with white beans, from Istria. *T. sabbiosa* is a cake with a granular texture, from Venice, and *t. nicoletta,* also from Venice, is a bread pudding named after the city's beggars, who are called *i nicoletti. T. sbrisolona,* made with cornmeal and ground almonds, and flavored with lemon peel; *t. di tagliatelle,* a crunchy cake made with pasta, almonds, and chocolate; and a light sponge cake called *t. di paradiso* are from Lombardy. *T. di mandorle* is made with almonds, chocolate, and **strega** liqueur, from Capri. *T. savoia* is a sponge cake coated with chocolate, from Sicily. *T. nera* is made with chocolate, coffee, crème de cacao, and rum, from Modena.

Cheese-based cakes include *t. coi becchi,* also called *t. co' bischeri,* a sweet-and-savory *torta* made with vegetables, **ricotta,** raisins, and chocolate, with a decorative design that looks like birds' beaks traced on top, from Tuscany. *T. gaudenzio* has alternate layers of **mascarpone** and **gorgonzola.** *T. pasqualina* is an Easter *torta* traditionally made with 33 sheets of paper-thin pastry, representing the years of Christ's life, filled with chard, artichokes, **ricotta,** and hard-boiled eggs, from Liguria. *T. dei fieschi* is made each year on August 14 in the town of Lavagna in Liguria to commemorate the wedding of Count

Opizzo Fieschi to Bianca dei Bianchi in the year 1230. The original cake was said to be 39 feet tall and pieces of it were given to everyone in the town. *T. di farro messisbugo* is made with a saffron-flavored crust, filled with cheese, barley, spices, and grated orange peel, from Ferrara. It was created in the 16th century in the palace kitchen of Cardinal Ippolito d'Este. *T. Barozzi* is a very rich flourless chocolate cake created in 1897 by Eugenio Gollini, a pastry maker in Vignola, a town near Modena, to commemorate the birthday of Renaissance architect and native son Jacopo Barozzi, who invented the spiral staircase. *T. della befana* is a fruit-studded sweet cake with a bean baked in it, for the feast of the Magi. It is traditionally served on a silver crown. Whoever finds the bean wears the crown for the day. According to legend, *la vecchia* Befana refused to acknowledge the Christ child at his birth in Bethlehem and so forever after brought gifts to children on the Epiphany in the hope that she might find Him again.

tortella   (tohr-TEH-lah)   "Little cake." Fritter.

tortelli   (tohr-TEH-lee)   "Little cakes." Fat elongated **ravioli** filled with a variety of ingredients, from **ricotta** and spinach to winter squash.

Tortelli di zucca, which contain yellow squash and crushed almond cookies, are served with butter and **parmigiano.** They are a traditional Christmas dish in Lombardy. *T. di mostarda e castagne,* a traditional autumn dish, is made with dried fruits and chestnuts. *T. di erbette,* filled with Swiss chard and **ricotta,** are served on the feast of *San Giovanni* (June 24), a specialty of Parma. *T. con la coda,* or *turtei* in Piacenza dialect, have pinched ends that resemble little tails.

TORTELLI DI ZUCCA

3 pounds pumpkin, peeled, seeded, and diced	*Salt and pepper*
	Grated nutmeg
4 ounces amaretti cookies, crushed	*Melted butter*
1 cup grated parmigiano	

Preheat the oven to 500 degrees. Bake the pumpkin for about 30 minutes, or until tender. Remove from the oven and puree. Allow to cool, add half the **amaretti** cookies, the **parmigiano,** salt, pepper, and nutmeg to taste, and mix together. Pass the mixture through a sieve. Set aside in a cool place for one day.

Place a small amount of the mixture into **pasta** squares and fold into the shape of large *ravioli,* moistening the edges to seal them. Add the *tortelli* to boiling salted water and cook through for about 3 minutes. Drain and serve with melted butter, the rest of the *amaretti* cookies, and the *parmigiano.* Serves 4 to 6.

tortellini   (tohr-teh-LEE-nee)   "Tiny cakes." Small **pasta** nuggets filled with various ingredients, usually meat or cheese. Bologna and Modena both take credit for the creation of *tortellini,* but both cities agree that the shape is mythically inspired by Venus's navel. In Bologna, *tortellini* are sometimes called *umbilichi sacri* (sacred navels). *Tortellini* are a traditional dish served on Christmas day. In Romagna, *tortellini* are called **cappelletti** (little hats).

  Tortellini alla bolognese, with a **ragù,** is a classic marriage of pasta and sauce, though *tortellini* are also often served with cream *(alla panna). T. alla modenese* are filled with chicken or turkey, **parmigiano,** and grated lemon peel. If baked with a topping of *parmigiano,* the preparation is called *t. gratinati. Tortelloni,* called **cappellacci,** in Ferrara, are large *tortellini.*

  A *pasticcio di tortellini* is baked layered *tortellini, ragù,* and meatballs in a sweet pastry.

tortiera   (tohr-tee-EH-rah)   Casserole, or an Apulian dish prepared in such a casserole with gratinéed cheese or breadcrumbs.

tortiglione   (tohr-tee-L'YOH-neh)   Almond cake.

tortiglioni   (tohr-tee-L'YOH-nee)   Large tube-shaped pasta with spiraled edges. Also *elicoidali.*

tortino   (tohr-TEE-noh)   Vegetable pie.

Toscana   (toh-SKAH-nah)   Tuscany, a region of northeast Italy on the Tyrrhenian Sea. Despite Tuscany's evident beauty, its long history of art, and its current image as an international style-setter, the region's gastronomy is relatively simple and straightforward. Most of its breads contain no salt. Meats and seafood are plainly grilled. **Pollo al mattone,** chicken flattened with a brick, is simply grilled. **Pappa al pomodoro,** a quickly made stew of tomatoes, garlic, olive oil, and day-old bread, is a fashionable item on **trattoria** menus. Nevertheless, Tuscans will proudly remind visitors that it was Caterina de' Medici who brought a highly refined cuisine to France and set the standards for court banqueting in the 16th century. And Tuscany has given Italy many of its favorite dishes, beginning with excellent sausages and **salame** atop **crostini** of toasted bread spread with virgin olive oil. Tuscans eat more salad than most Italians, especially **panzanella** made with tomatoes, basil, cucumbers, onion, and bread mixed with olive oil.

  Pastas can be quite hearty, like **pappardelle** *con la* **lepre,** wide homemade pasta ribbons with a rich hare **ragù. Acquacotta** is a very popular vegetable soup while **cacciucco** is one of Italy's most famous seafood stews.

  Bistecca alla fiorentina is made with Tuscany's famous Chianina beef. **Cibreo** is a sauce or stew of chicken livers, cockscombs, and unlaid chicken eggs. **Stracotto** is braised meat, *trippa alla fiorentina* is one of the richest of Italian tripe dishes.

At the end of a meal, **pinzimonio,** raw vegetables dipped into olive oil, may be served.

Desserts include *castagnaccio,* a chestnut-flour cake with pine nuts and raisins, and **zuccotto,** a chocolate and cream dessert.

Many of Italy's most renowned red wines—**Chianti Classico, Brunello di Montalcino, Carmignano,** and **Vino Nobile di Montepulciano**—are Tuscan. They are made from the **sangiovese** grape and have a **DOCG** designation. Tuscany has 7 **DOC** zones, but there have also been recent attempts by some of the region's most notable producers to make big-bodied red wines of high quality, often with components of **cabernet sauvignon,** that do not fall under the *DOC* regulations, which have taken on the unregulated name "Super Tuscans." The best-known white wine of Tuscany is **Vernaccia di San Gimignano.**

toscana, alla   (AH-lah toh-S'KAH-noh)   "Tuscan style." A dish prepared as they do in Tuscany, often indicating the addition of chicken livers.

toscanelli   (toh-s'kah-NEH-lee)   "Small Tuscans." Small brown beans, from Tuscany. Also *fagiolini all'occhio.*

tostapane   (toh-stah-PAH-neh)   Toaster. From the Late Latin *tostare* (to roast).

tostare   (toh-STAH-reh)   To toast. From the Late Latin *tostare* (to roast). *Tosticchiare* means to brown slightly. *Tost* is a toasted ham and cheese sandwich.

totani   (toh-TAH-nee)   Flying squid, *Todarodes sagittatus.* In Liguria, these squid are nicknamed *siluri* (torpedoes). They are often stuffed with bread crumbs, cheese, and garlic, then cooked with tomatoes.

tozzetti   (toh-T'ZEH-tee)   "Little morsels." Small nut and raisin cookies with a very hard texture, from Tuscany and Venice.

tracena drago   (trah-CHEH-nah DRAH-goh)   "Dragon of Tracena." Weever, *Trachinus draco.* Gray-blue fish with venomous spines that must be cut away. Usually fried or used in soup. *Tracena vipera (T. viperus)* is a smaller species. Other species include *T. raggiata (T. radiatus)* and *t. ragno (T. araneus).*

tramezzino   (tra-meh-T'ZEE-noh)   Small sandwich usually eaten at a bar with an **aperitivo.** The word refers to a filling. See also **panino.**

traminer   (trah-MEE-nehr)   A white wine grape of northern Italy, where the Alto Adige town of Tramin or Termeno gives the varietal its name.

A progenitor of the *Gewürztraminer* white wine grape, *traminer* has a spicy flavor and floral aroma.

trancia   (TRAHN-ch'yah)   A thick slice, usually of fish.

trattoria   (trah-toh-REE-ah)   A local eatery, less elegant than a *ristorante* and usually having a limited, seasonal menu of the cook's specialties. *Trattorie* have traditionally been family operations of modest size and price, though in recent years many *trattorie* have become large and quite fashionable. From the French *traiteur* (to treat), which also referred to a small cookshop.

trebbiano   (treh-bee-AH-noh)   Workhorse white grape found throughout Italy in various degrees of quality. The grape may be named after the river Trebbia in Emilia-Romagna, though some authorities believe it refers to an ancient Roman district of Trebulana in the vicinity of Capua.

Elsewhere in Europe it is called *ugni blanc,* and it is believed to produce more wine than any other variety in the world, accounting for up to a third of Italy's wine production. There are several subvarieties in Italy, including *trebbiano toscano, t. romagnolo, t. giallo,* and *t. di soave. T. toscano* was once a required component of **Chianti,** but it is now added only as an option by modern *Chianti* producers. *T. d'Abruzzo* is now believed to be a varietal called **bombino bianco,** and while producing mostly undistinguished white wines, it is the basis for one of Italy's most renowned white wines, *T. d'Abruzzo* from the firm of Valentini.

tre brodi   (treh BROH-dee)   Broth made from chicken, veal, and beef or pork, a specialty of Cremona. Often **pasta** is served in the broth.

treccia di pane all'uovo   (TREH-ch'yah dee PAH-neh ahl'yoo-OH-voh)   Braided egg bread. Cake with citrus peel baked for special occasions, from Istria.

tre mosche   (TREH MOH-skeh)   "Three flies." Three roasted coffee beans traditionally floated on the top of a glass of **sambuca.**

trenette   (treh-NEH-teh)   "Ribbons." A Ligurian term for thin strips of pasta, usually served with **pesto** in a dish that commonly contains string beans and potatoes (see page 190). Elsewhere the pasta may be called *fettucelle. Trenette a stuffo,* the pasta is served with a bean sauce, a specialty of La Spezia. Also *trinette.*

Trentino–Alto Adige   (trehn-TEE-noh AHL-toh AH-dee-jeh)   Two provinces of Italy located in the extreme northeast, bordering Lombardy and the Veneto to the west and south and Austria to the north. Formally separated into two distinct regions around 1848, the two provinces have much in common. The gastronomy is quite similar, with a good deal of Austrian influence in both food and wine. Many dishes also have picked up Venetian flavors.

As in Venice, **polenta** is preferred to pasta. Dumplings, such as **Spätzle** and **canederli,** are very popular in soups and stews. **Sauresuppe** is made with tripe, onions, herbs, and white vinegar. The region produces an excellent bacon called **Speck** and chamois cooked in vinegar, spices, and sour cream—a dish called **Gemsenfleisch**—is prepared throughout the two provinces.

The best-known cheese of the area is a sharp **Graukäse** and the goat's milk **Ziegenkäse.**

Desserts are rich and mostly derived from Austrian dessert-making, such as *Kastanientorta,* a cake made with pureed chestnuts and **Apfelkuchel.** Special at Christmastime is a fruit cake made with rye flour, called **Zelten.**

Wines are often made from the same grapes as used in Austria, including *Gewürztraminer,* **sylvaner, riesling,** and, especially, **pinot grigio.** There have been modern attempts at developing **chardonnay** and **pinot nero.**

Trentino is also the general name for a large **DOC** zone that makes 20 types of wine, including *Lagrein,* in a red *(rosso* or *Dunkel)* and *rosato* or *Kretzer; Marzemino,* a light red; *Nosiola,* made from a native white grape; and *traminer aromatico,* made with the **traminer** grape, called *Gewürtztraminer* elsewhere in Europe.

Alto Adige produces a small amount of wine, including **cabernet sauvignon, cabernet franc, chardonnay, Müller-Thurgau, pinot grigio, riesling renano,** and **traminer aromatico,** most exported to Austria, Germany, and Switzerland.

trifolato (tree-foh-LAH-toh)   Cooking method in which vegetables are sautéed in olive oil with garlic and parsley, to which a wide variety of other ingredients may afterwards be added.

triglia (TREE-l'yah)   Red mullet, *Mullus surmuletus* and *M. barbatus.* A bony saltwater fish, usually grilled, fried, or broiled; the liver is considered a delicacy. Sometimes referred to as *diti di apostoli* (Apostles' fingers).

Triglie alla genovese is baked red mullet with a sauce of white wine, fennel seeds, capers, and tomato paste, from Liguria. In *t. alla livornese,* the *triglia* is cooked with tomatoes, from Leghorn in Tuscany. *T. all'ebraica* is a dish of the Roman Jews served on Yom Kippur. It is a sweet-and-sour preparation with raisins and pine nuts. Also *trigghia* and *treggh.* See also **cefalo.**

trincas (TREEN-kahs)   Buns flavored with grape must, from Sardinia. In the northern part of the island, they are called *tillicas.*

trionfo di gola (tree-OHN-foh dee GOH-lah)   Triumph of gluttony. Elaborate Sicilian dome-shape cake made with watermelon, **pan di spagna,**

biancomangiare, zuccata, and **pistachios,** and covered with **pasta reale** and candied fruit.

trippa   (TREE-pah)   Tripe. The stomach of the cow is divided into four edible sections: *rumine,* the thick spongy tissue; *reticolo,* the honeycomb part; *centopelle* or *foiolo,* the overlapping strips of tissue; and *ricciolotta,* the fat curly part of the stomach. It must be carefully cleaned before cooking and is sold already cleaned. From the Middle French. Also *foiolo.*

In Florence, *trippa alla fiorentina* is braised with tomato and marjoram, then served on a piece of bread called *lampredotto.* In Pisa, it is served with a green sauce. In Rome, *t. alla romana* is made with tomato and mint. In Milan, tripe is called **büsecca** and prepared in winter as a soup.

Tripe is usually boiled once by butchers before being sold, and in the past the boiling liquid would be given away free to the poor to use to cook their rice in.

trippati   (tree-PAH-tee)   *Frittata* cut into thin strips and served with tomato sauce.

trisa   (TREE-sah)   Porridge made from cornmeal, wheat flour, milk, and butter, from Trentino. In Alto Adige, this is called *mus.*

tritare   (tree-TAH-reh)   To mince. *Trito* is a mixture of chopped vegetables and herbs, similar to a **battuto** and the basis of a **soffritto.**

troccoli   (TROH-koh-lee)   Homemade pasta ribbons cut with a ridged rolling pin called a *troccolo.* The pasta is served with a tomato-and-garlic sauce with **pecorino** and fresh asparagus. A specialty of Foggia in Apulia.

troffiete   (troh-fee-EH-teh)   Ligurian term for **gnocchi** in a squiggle-like shape, often served with a **pesto** sauce. They are always made by hand from flour and water, not with potato. A specialty of the town of Recco in Liguria. Also *troffiete* and *trofie.*

trota   (TROH-tah)   Trout. Freshwater fish, now often farmed. From the Latin *tructa* (a fish with sharp teeth).

The most common species of trout in Italian waters include the brown trout *(Salmo trutta)* and *Trota salmonata,* a brown trout that acquires a rosy tinge because of its primary diet of shrimp. Rainbow trout *(S. gairdneri)* were introduced to Italian mountain streams and lowland lakes from North America. Trout are best pan-fried or grilled, though larger varieties may be poached or baked.

Trota in blu (trout in blue) is a Trentino–Alto Adige rendering of the French *truite au bleu* made by cooking trout in white wine, herbs, and vinegar, which gives the trout a blue color. *T. alla mugnaia* (trout in the style of the miller's wife) is the Italian version of the French preparation *à la meunière,* in which the fish is dusted with flour, salt, and pepper, then sautéed in butter with a dash of lemon juice.

truscello (troo-SHEH-loh) Dish of layered beef meatballs, *ricotta, parmigiano,* and eggs, a specialty of Messina.

tumazzu (too-MAH-tzoo) *Pecorino* cheese from Sicily. Also *tuma.* The dialect word means "hard like a bat," which refers to the consistency of the cheese.

tumbada (toom-BAH-dah) Timbale. Pudding of macaroons and lemon juice, from Sardinia. See also *timballo.*

tummala (TOO-mah-lah) Lavish Sicilian molded rice or pasta dish containing chicken, sausage, veal, and vegetables. The dish is supposedly named after the 11th-century Arab emir of Catania named Ibn-at-Tumnah, though Clifford A. Wright, in his book *Cucina Paradiso* (1992), contends the word may derive from Arabic *tummala,* for a kind of plate.

tuoni e lampo (too-OH-nee eh LAHM-poh) "Thunder and lightning." Southern Italian dish made with leftover pieces of pasta and beans or cabbage. The name may jokingly refer to the gaseous effect on the digestive system. From the Latin *tonitrus* and *lampas* (torch).

tuorlo d'uova (too-OHR-loh D'WOH-vah) Egg yolk.

turbante (toor-BAHN-teh) "Turbans." Puff-pastry shells, like French *vol-au-vent.*

turcinieddhi (toor-chee-N'YEH-dee) "Little rolls." Apulian rolls made of lamb lungs, liver, and heart.

turiddu (too-REE-doo) Christmas biscuit made with flour and *moscato* wine and, sometimes, almonds. The dough is cut into biscuit shapes, then fried in olive oil flavored with cinnamon with almonds, from Calabria. From a Calabrian nickname for "little Salvatore."

turteln (TOOHR-tehln) *Ravioli* made with rye flour, from Trentino–Alto Adige. They are commonly filled with crushed caraway and spinach or with sauerkraut, then fried in lard. *Turteln* boiled and served in broth are called **Krapfen.** The name *turteln* from German supposedly suggests the billing and cooing of birds.

Turtei are made with a filling of Swiss chard, beet tops, and/or spinach, from Parma. In Piacenza, *turtei cu la cua (turtei* with a tail) are filled with *mascarpone, ricotta,* egg yolks, and spinach, and the *ravioli* are twisted at the ends to form a tail.

turtidduzza (toor-tee-DOO-t'zah) "Little pie." Stew of lungs, liver, heart, and intestines of goat or lamb, with tomato sauce, from Sicily.

U

uccelletti di campagna (oo-cheh-LEH-tee dee kahm-PAH-n'yah) "Birds of the country." Thin beef rolls grilled over charcoal, from Rome.

uccelletti scappati (oo-cheh-LEH-tee skah-PAH-tee) "Little birds that got away." Lombardian dish of cubed veal or pork and pieces of liver skewered with *pancetta* and sage, then fried in butter. Their appearance is somewhat like little birds.

uccelletto (oo-cheh-LEH-toh) General term for bird or fowl. *Uccellagione* are feathered game.

uccelletto, all' (ahl oo-cheh-LEH-toh) "Bird style." Diced or julienned beef slices quickly seared in olive oil with sage, then splashed with white wine and served immediately. The name refers to the style in which birds are commonly prepared.

Umbria (OOM-bree-yah) A central, landlocked Italian region with a largely hilly or mountainous terrain and a large central plain that give it the nickname of the "green heart of Italy." The region is a major *pasta* producer, dominated by Perugia, and the city of Norcia is so famous for its pork butchers that the term *alla norcina* usually indicates a recipe including pork. The hills and forest provide abundant game and the lakes and rivers a good supply of freshwater fish like carp, trout, and pike.

Tegamaccio is a stew made of lake fish and white wine.

The cooking is simple, based on seasonal fresh ingredients, such as cardoons and fava beans, as well as lentils. Cheeses tend to be fairly simple and straightforward, like *mozzarella, ricotta,* and *pecorino.*

The wines of Umbria, which has 8 **DOC** zones, are dominated by the international renown of dry **Orvieto,** while refined reds like **Torgiano** have also attained worldwide recognition.

umido, in   (een OO-mee-doh)   Cooking method of slow cooking in a small amount of liquid, usually tomato sauce, often with wine and demiglace.

ungheresi   (oon-gah-REH-see)   "Hungarians." Butter cookies with tips dipped in chocolate glaze. The reason for the name is unclear, perhaps because these cookies were of Hungarian origin.

uova di mare   (oo-OH-vah dee MAH-reh)   Sea eggs, *Microcosmos sulcatus.* Tough-skinned sea creature taken from rocks. The edible part is an egg-yellow interior, which is consumed raw. Also *limone di mare.*

uovo   (oo-OH-voh)   Egg. Italians eat mostly chicken eggs. Eggs are used in pasta, cakes and cookies, custards and sauces. They are also eaten on their own.

Poached eggs are called *uova affogate* or *u. in camicia.* Fried eggs are *u. fritte, u. in padella, u. al tegame, u. affrittellate,* or *occhio di bue.* Soft-boiled eggs are *u. barzotte, u. mollette* or *u. à la coque.* Coddled eggs are *u. nelle tazzine.* Hard-boiled eggs are *u. sode.* Scrambled eggs are *u. stracciate, u. strapazzate,* or *u. rimestate.* Shirred eggs are *u. al piatto al tegamino.* For *u. alla monacale* the yolks of hard-boiled eggs are removed, mixed with a **balsamella,** and put back into the whites. The egg is closed, dipped in egg wash, dredged in bread crumbs, and deep-fried. They are part of a *fritto misto,* from Sicily.

An omelet is called *omeletta,* which is not the same as a *frittata.*

U. non nate are unhatched eggs.

uva   (OO-vah)   "Bunch of grapes," the same meaning as the Latin word. *Un acino d'uva* is a single grape. *Uvaggio* is a mixture or blend of different grapes. A bunch of grapes is also called *grappolo d'uva.*

Although rarely used in cooking, grapes are eaten fresh in Italy. But mostly they are made into wine. No one knows for sure how many different wine grape varieties are grown in Italy, but the figure exceeds two thousand, with about four hundred recommended by viticulturists or approved by government authorities for wine production. See also **DOC, DOCG,** and **vino.**

uva di troia   (OO-vah dee TROI-yah)   "Grape of Troy," from which it supposedly originated before being planted by the Greeks in Apulia. It is now made into a sturdy **DOC** red wine.

uva passa   (OO-vah PAH-sah)   Raisins. Several types are used in Italy, including the muscatlike *Malaga* from Pantelleria, the golden **Sultanina** from Sicily, and the *Zibibbo,* also from Sicily. Dried currants, *panoli,* are also raisins. *Uvetta* is the name of tiny, very sweet raisins similar to currants. From the Latin *uvae passus.*

V

vacca (VAH-kah) Cow. While cows are used principally for their milk, Italians drink very little milk, using it instead to make cream and cheeses. From the Latin.

vaccinara, alla (AH-lah vah-chee-NAH-rah) "Butcher style." Any of a variety of Roman dishes containing oxtails. From *vaccinus* (relating to a cow).

Valdadige (VAHL-DAH-dee-jeh) "Valley of the Adige." *DOC* zone of Alto Adige producing five types of wines, including **Schiava.** Also *Etschtaler.*

Val d'Arbia (VAHL DAHR-bee-yah) *DOC* zone of Tuscany that produces a dry white white and a *vin santo* from **malvasia** and **trebbiano** grapes grown in the Arbia river basin.

Val di Cornia (VAHL dee KOHR-nee-yah) *DOC* zone of Tuscany that produces red, white, and rosé wines from grapes grown on the Cornia hills.

valdostana, alla (AH-lah vahl-doh-STAH-nah) Any of a variety of dishes from the Valle d'Aosta containing the region's *fontina* cheese.

valeriana (vah-leh-ree-AH-neh) Corn salad or mâche, also called lamb's lettuce. *Valerianella* is wild lamb's lettuce. It is traditional to eat *valerianella* after the lamb at Easter dinner. Also *soncino.*

valigini (vah-LEE-jee-nee) "Little suitcases." Cabbage rolls stuffed with meat or vegetables.

Valle d'Aosta (VAHL DOH-stah) Region of northern Italy bordering France and Switzerland. The region has a decided French cast, and both Italian and French are spoken freely. Much is made of the cheeses of the region, which figure in many traditional dishes. *Fontina* is the best known, while *toma* and **robiola** are also gaining an international reputation. Served with a piece of rye bread called *pane nero* and thin slices of chamois **prosciutto** called **mocetta** or pears called **martin sec,** they make a fine lunch. Melt *fontina* over a breaded veal cutlet and you have *costoletta alla valdostana;* stir it into rice and you have *risotto alla valdostana.*

The viticulture of Valle d'Aosta, with 21 **DOC** zones, is modest, though the region uses dozens of grape varieties to produce as many different kinds of wines, the best known of which are *muscat de Chambave* and *blanc de Morgex.*

Valle Isarco (VAH-leh ee-SAHR-koh)   **DOC** zone in Trentino–Alto Adige that produces several German-style white wines, including **Müller-Thurgau, pinot grigio, sylvaner,** *Traminer Aromatico,* and *Veltliner.* Also *Eisack-taler.*

valpolicella (vahl-poh-lee-CHEH-lah)   **DOC** red wine of Veneto, made principally from the *corvina* grape. The wines range from a light red to the robust **amarone della valpolicella.** The **classico** zone produces somewhat less than half the total production.

valtellina (vahl-teh-LEE-nah)   **DOC** zone of Lombardy that produces wine principally from the **nebbiolo** grape, locally called *chiavennasca. Valtellina* and **sfursat** wines are produced in large quantities. Propagation of the varietal only began in the early 19th century. *Valtellina Superiore* is a separate *DOC* zone that makes four reds, named **Grumello,** *Inferno,* **sassella,** and *valgella.*

vaniglia (vah-NEE-l'yah)   Vanilla. Native to Central America, vanilla reached Europe only in the 17th century. It took another century before its use as a flavoring agent—specifically with the better-established chocolate—took hold. From the Spanish *vainilla.*

vapore, al (ahl vah-POH-reh)   Steamed, as in cooking. From the Latin (steam).

vari (VAH-ree)   Assorted. From the Latin *varius.*

vecchia, la (lah VEH-k'yah)   "The old woman." Vegetable and meat gratin, traditionally made by grandmothers, although the term also refers to the older, less tender pieces of meat and poultry used to flavor broth, from Emilia. From the Latin *vetula.*

vecchio (VEH-k'yoh)   "Old." Used to describe long-aged **DOC** wines. *Stravecchio* (very old) is used to describe the longest-aged **Marsalas** and certain spirits. From the Latin *vetula.*

Velletri (veh-LEH-tri)   **DOC** zone of Latium that produces a red and a white wine.

vellutata (veh-loo-TAH-tah)   A soup thickened with egg yolk. From French *velouté* (velvetiness), which is itself from the Vulgar Latin *villutus.*

vendemmia (vehn-DEH-mee-ah)   Grape harvest. Sometimes refers to the specific vintage, which is more commonly called *annata.* From the Latin *vindemia* (vintage).

Veneto (VEH-neh-toh)   The Veneto, a region in northeast Italy located on the Adriatic Sea. Dominated by Venice, this region has for a thousand years been one of the principal ports for bringing in the foods of the Mediterranean. Its own food is, therefore, rich in spices such as cumin, saffron, cinnamon, and the spice mix called curry. Seafood takes up the most significant part of any Venetian cook's repertoire, and *polenta* is usually preferred to *pasta.*

The Veneto is, of course, dominated by the seaside Venice, but the region is rich in vegetables raised around Treviso, which contributes their famous *radicchio,* and the fruit from Verona is known for its sweetness as the base of juices. Olive oil in the Veneto is of very high quality, and the best-known cheese is *Asiago.*

The Adriatic provides the Veneto with abundant seafood, which is cooked in a wide variety of ways, from *pasta* with *seppie* (cuttlefish) to simply grilled *scampi.*

Fegato alla veneziana is a rich mixture of sauteed liver with onions, and *peverade* is a sauce of salami, anchovies and chicken livers. Several dishes of note come from the restaurant called Harry's Bar in Venice, where *carpaccio* (raw, dressed slices of beef) and the *bellini* cocktail (peach juice and *Prosecco*) were created.

For dessert there are numerous cookies and cakes, from the cornmeal yellow *zaletti* to the luscious *tirami sù* and *pandoro* Christmas cake.

The Veneto, with 17 **DOC** zones, is best known for its white wines, including **Soave, Bianco di Custoza,** and the sparkling *prosecco,* which go well with the seafood consumed in the region. Two of its light red wines, *valpolicella* (which may be made into the robust red called *amarone*) and **Bardolino,** are widely exported.

veneziana (veh-neh-t'zee-AH-nah)   "Venetian." A large bun covered with sugar crystals, a specialty of Venice on New Year's Eve.

veneziana, alla (AH-lah veh-neh-t'zee-AH-nah)   A dish cooked as in Venice.

Venezia Giulia (veh-NEH-t'zee-yah JOO-l'yah)   See *Friuli–Venezia Giulia.*

ventaglini (vehn-tah-L'YEE-nee)   "Little fans." Sugar-glazed, butterfly-shape puff pastries like the French *palmiers.* From the Latin *ventilo* (to toss in the air).

ventaglio   (vehn-TAH-l'yoh)   Pilgrim scallop, *Pecten jacobaeus.* From the Latin *ventilo* (to toss in the air).

ventrelle d'agnello di latte   (vehn-TREH-leh d'ahN'YEH-loh dee LAH-teh)   Baby lamb stomach filled with blood, bread, bacon, onions, and spices, sewed up and boiled, from Sardinia.

ventresca   (vehn-TREH-skah)   Belly of tuna fish, preserved in barrels or cans. The word is also an alternative to **pancetta,** pork belly. In Sicily the word *surra* (from Arabic) is also used for the tuna belly. From the Latin *venter* (belly).

verace   (veh-RAH-cheh)   "True." Used in a culinary sense to indicate a genuine food or ingredient as opposed to a substitute. From the Latin *verus* (true).

verdeca   (VEHR-deh-kah)   A grape of Apulia, used in making white wines. Possibly related to Spain's *verdejo* varietal.

verdicchio   (vehr-DEE-k'yoh)   A white grape of the Marches, with a **DOC** zone in Castelli di Jesi and Matelica, used in making dry, **frizzante,** and **spumante** wines. The wine became well known abroad when bottled by the producer Fazi-Battaglia in a green amphora-shape bottle.

verdure   (vehr-DOO-reh)   General term for vegetables, from the Middle French *verd* (green).

verduzzo   (vehr-DOO-t'zoh)   A white grape of Friuli, with six **DOC** zones, and in Treviso in the Veneto. The best wines made from *verduzzo* are from the *DOC* zone of **Colli Orientali del Friuli.** Both dry and sweet versions are made; the best of the sweet is **Ramandolo.**

vermentino   (vehr-mehn-TEE-noh)   Grape of Sardinia, Corsica, and Liguria, used in making **DOC** white wines. It is the predominant white varietal planted in Corsica. *Vermentino di Gallura* and *vermentina di Sardegna,* both from Sardinia, have *DOC* appellations. Also *rollo.*

vermicelli   (vehr-mee-CHEH-lee)   "Little worms." Very thin **spaghetti,** less than $1/10$-inch thick, a term used in southern Italy. From the Latin *vermiculus.* *V. all'abruzzese* is made with *vermicelli,* saffron, zucchini flowers, **pecorino,** onions, and parsley, from Abruzzo. *Viermicedde cu lu baccalà* is *vermicelli* cooked with salt cod and tomatoes, a Christmas Eve specialty of Salerno in Campania.

vermouth   (vehr-MOOTH)   Fortified wine flavored with herbs, once considered a medicinal aid, now drunk as an aperitif. It is generally accepted that the word *vermouth* is derived from the German *Wermut* (wormwood), although some believe it may derive from the German words *Veran* (to raise) and *Mut* (spirit).

While the ancient Romans drank flavored wines, it was not until the 16th century that a Piedmontese named d'Alessio adopted the idea for a fortified medicinal wine flavored with wormwood *(Artemesia absinthum)*. By 1786, the firm of Antonio Benedetto Carpano was commercially producing a drink called *Vermouth*. After wormwood was found to have debilitating effects on the body, it was taken out of formulas for *Vermouth*. Today, *Vermouth* is made with an infusion of a wide variety of herbs, spices, and fruit peels in both white *(bianco)* and red *(rosso)* versions.

vernaccia   (vehr-NAH-ch'yah)   A red grape of the Marches, not related to *vernaccia di San Gimignano,* used in making sparkling or sweet red wines. The word derives from the same roots as "vernacular," meaning indigenous and commonly planted.

vernaccia di Oristano   (vehr-NAH-ch'yah dee oh-ree-STAH-noh) Sardinian grape used to make a sherrylike dessert wine. A *DOC* wine of Sardinia, made from very ripe grapes that produce a high alcohol content, (the *riserva* reaches 15 percent), grown near Oristano.

vernaccia di San Gimignano   (vehr-NAH-ch'yah dee SAHN jee-mee-N'YAH-noh)   *DOC* grape of Tuscany, used in making white wines from grapes grown around the town of San Gimignano.

Vernaccia di Serrapetrona   (vehr-NAH-ch'yah dee seh-rah-peh-TROH-nah)   *DOC* sparkling red wine of the Marches, made from grapes grown around Serrapetrona.

verza   (VEHR-t'zah)   Savoy cabbage. *Verza con salsicce* is savoy cabbage cooked in a casserole with a sweet beef sausage, a dish that originated in the Jewish community of Mantua.

vespaiola   (veh-spye-OH-lah)   A white grape grown in the Veneto. The name derives from the word *vespe* (wasps), supposedly because the insects are so attracted to the grape. Blended with *tocai* and *garganega,* it produces a well-regarded sweet wine called *Torcolato,* made around Breganze.

vespolina   (veh-spoh-LEE-nah)   A red grape of Piedmont, used in making a blending wine.

vestedda   (veh-STEH-dah)   "Little dress." Soft roll topped with sesame seeds that is used for *guastedde,* from Sicily. From the Latin *vestis* (garment).

vezzena   (veh-T'ZEH-nah)   Cow's milk cheese related to *asiago,* made in the hills around Mount Vezzena, in Trentino. Also *veneto* and *venessa.*

vigna   (VEE-n'yah)   Vineyard. Also *vigneto*. From the Latin *vinetor.*

vignarola (vee-n'yah-ROH-lah)   "Vineyard [dish]." A springtime Roman dish made with artichokes, fava beans, new potatoes, peas, and, often, cured pork, sautéed in olive oil.

vimine (VEE-mee-neh)   Straw used to whip cream, often taken from a grape vine.

vin brulé (VEEN broo-LEH)   "Cooked wine." Red wine flavored with cinnamon, sugar, apples, and cloves.

vincisgrassi (veen-chees-GRAH-see)   A *lasagne* containing layers of a sauce with mushrooms, chicken livers, and sausage, a specialty of the Marches. The name derives from the name of a commander of the Austrian army in the mid-19th century Windischgratz, for whom this dish was supposedly created.

In Abruzzo, this dish is known as *pincisgrassi* and is made with little meatballs between the layers.

vino (VEE-noh)   Wine. From the Latin *vinum*. The ancient Greeks called Italy *oenotria,* the "land of trained vines," since, when they colonized it, they found it covered with grapevines propagated by the inhabitants of every region. They brought in their own favorite varieties and planted them in Sicily and southern Italy, including **aglianico, moscato, malvasia,** and *grecanico.*

Though most wine of the pre-Christian era was probably of low quality, made with local grapes, by the time of Imperial Rome, writers like Pliny, in his *Natural History,* commented on the relative quality of one wine over another. The ancient Romans improved the taste of their wines by adding spices like cloves or resin or honey, as well as seawater, which also helped stabilize the wines.

Wines continued to improve as the Romans gained dominance over other European lands, from which they brought back vine cuttings and where they planted their own native Italian vines. As Roman cities grew in importance, so did the quality of wine and the wine trade, so that many of the best vineyards were planted in port cities like Rome and Naples.

After the fall of the empire, many of the Roman grape varieties disappeared and many of the European vineyards declined, but the continuing economic dominance of Italy helped maintain a healthy viticultural industry that drew not only on local vineyards but also on wines brought in from Crete and Greece, carried in large jars called amphoras. Fine wines became a mark of one's wealth, and authors wrote of the delicious wines of Campania, Latium, and the Po Valley. By the 13th century, wine had become Italy's most profitable crop, and the Italians learned how to raise their vines on poles and trellises, which not only allowed the vines to receive the most sun but also allowed the vineyard owners to grow crops beneath the grape vines, a custom called *coltura promiscua*. By the time of the Renaissance, Italians were drinking at least a gallon of wine per week *per capita*.

Ironically, the importance and dominance of Italian viniculture did not keep up with modern winemaking technologies developed in the 17th and 18th centuries, when bottles with corks replaced jars as containers in the rest of Europe. Italian winemakers preferred to sell their wine in bulk, and the reputation of Italian wines declined in the 18th and 19th centuries in favor of French wines. The Italians still clung to old traditions, so that many of the better-known wines were still made in an old, often sweet style, and white wines were often oxidized. Largely this stagnation and decline came as a result of foreign control of Italy and its politics, and it was only after the Unification of Italy in 1861 that Italian viniculture again gained some slow momentum. At that time the preference for drier, better-made wines had its effect on reds like **Barolo, Barbaresco,** and **Chianti,** which began to be made with more care and with better grape varietals that best suited the widely varying terrain and microclimates of individual regions like Campania, Tuscany, Piedmont, and so on.

Then, as in the rest of Europe, Italian vineyards were nearly destroyed by the infestation of phylloxera, an aphid that eats away at the roots of vines. The infestation was first noted in France in 1863, and it was thought that the insect came on vine cuttings from the United States. Phylloxera reached Italy in 1875 and wreaked havoc on the vineyards, and it was only by grafting phylloxera-resistant American vines onto European stocks that the tide was eventually turned in Europe. Today most Italian vines have American grafts, although there are a few, rare vineyards that escaped the infestation and still thrive today.

Nevertheless, the Italian economy and two world wars did little to encourage better winemaking in Italy, and it was not really until the 1960s that a handful of producers like Antinori, Frescobaldi, Ruffino, and Biondi-Santi of Tuscany, Mastroberadino of Campania, Ceretto and Gaja of Piedmont, Bolla of the Veneto, and a few others began upgrading and modernizing their vineyards and facilities to reflect the new technologies of cold fermentation, small barrel production, blending, and bottling that brought about a revolution in Italian winemaking. The *coltura promiscua* of the past was largely stopped, and vineyards were replanted exclusively with grapes. Today only about 5 percent of the vineyard lands have mixed crops. Large cooperatives in Sicily, Sardinia, and elsewhere began to produce better, fresher, more stable wines, and now produce two-thirds of all the wine made in Italy. Traditional red wines like **Barolo, Barbaresco, Brunello di Montalcino, Vino Nobile di Montepulciano,** and **Aglianico del Vulture** are being made to be drunk sooner, rather than after decades of aging. **Chianti,** once known as the "pizza wine" because it seemed fit only to go with pizza, was improved by alteration of its component wine grapes, while white wines like **Soave, Greco di Tufo, Orvieto,** and **Trebbiano d'Abruzzo** are made in a cleaner, fresher style.

The establishment of government regulations called the **DOC** laws in 1966, overseen by Italy's winemakers and enologists, was a much needed attempt to make sure that Italian winemakers adhered to traditions and guidelines specific to their region and to the kinds of wines produced in them, including requirements as to the kinds of grapes allowed to be used, the territory from which the grapes must come, and the label language on the bottles.

The *DOC* laws, which now cover about 250 zones, were superceded by the **DOCG** rules, which sought to guarantee a certain standard of quality for several of Italy's better wines (currently 15). Together the *DOC* and *DOCG* wines make up only about 12 percent of Italian wine production.

Still, the stringency of these laws has restrained winemakers from experimenting with new blends or varietals, lest their wines be labeled nothing better than *vino da tavola* (table wine). Nevertheless, several notable winemakers, principally Tuscan, have produced new wines, including **Sassicaia** and *Solaia,* that rely on their international reputations to sell at high prices, despite lacking a *DOC* or *DOCG* designation. Other Italian winemakers have also begun experimenting with grapes like **cabernet sauvignon** and **chardonnay,** which are better known in France and California than in traditional Italian viniculture.

Today Italian winemaking is as modern as any in the world, and Italy produces an extraordinary range of wine styles, from bone-dry sparkling wines called **spumanti** to sweet dessert wines and spicy **vermouths.**

According to a 1990 census, Italy has 1,200,000 growers of wine grapes who tend 1 million hectares of vines that produce between 650 and 800 million cases of wine annually. The most widely planted varietals (in decreasing order) in Italy are **sangiovese, catarratto, trebbiano toscano, barbera, merlot, negroamaro, montepulciano, trebbiano,** *romagnolo,* **primitivo,** and white **malvasia.** Approximately 340,000 cellars actually produce wine, and about 50,000 of those bottle and sell it.

Italians drink about 15.5 gallons of wine per person per year, an amount that has been steadily declining over the past 20 years. (By comparison, Americans drink about 1.76 gallons per person.)

vino da meditazione   (VEE-noh dah meh-dee-tah-t'zee-OH-neh) "Meditation wine," meaning a wine to sip on its own, without food, for its unique qualities.

vino da tavola   (VEE-noh dah TAH-voh-lah)   "Table wine." A wine that does not pass the requirements for a **DOC** or **DOCG** designation. Nevertheless, some of the most highly regarded wines of Italy, like **Tignanello** and **Sassicaia,** are labeled as *vino da tavola* because they do not fall under the *DOC* or *DOCG* designations for a region. Abbreviated as *vdt*.

vino della casa   (VEE-noh DEH-lah KAH-sah)   House wine. The inexpensive wine offered at restaurants, usually of undefined local varietals. It is inexpensive and is sold in quarter-, half-, and full carafes. Also *vino sfuso*.

Vino Nobile di Montepulciano   (VEE-noh NOH-bee-leh dee MOHN-teh-pool-CH'YAH-noh)   A **DOCG** noble wine, known at least since the Renaissance, made in Tuscany from *prugnolo gentile* grapes (a type of **sangiovese**), often blended with **canaiolo** and *mammolo* grapes grown around the town of Montepulciano. It can age for many years.

vino novello   (VEE-noh noh-VEH-loh)   "New wine." A wine bottled and sold within a year of its vintage, made to compete with France's *Beaujolais nouveau*.

vin santo   (veen SAHN-toh)   "Holy wine." Probably once used to celebrate Mass, this high-alcohol wine (14 to 17 percent) is made in many regions of Italy but is best known in Tuscany. There it is made from **malvasia** and **trebbiano** grapes that are half-dried on racks or hung from rafters (a process called *vinsantaia),* then pressed and placed in small barrels called *caratelli*. The barrels are stored in lofts for three years in order to allow the heat and cold to turn the wine into a golden sherrylike dessert wine, sometimes sweet, sometimes dry. Two **DOC** zones in Tuscany produce *vin santo,* the **Val d'Arbia** and *Colli dell'Etruria Centrale*. Also *vino santo*.

violini di Chiavenna   (vee-oh-LEE-nee dee kee-ah-VEH-nah)   "Violins of Chiavenna." Cured, smoked roe-deer or kid hams made around the Valtellina town of Chiavenna. When cut, they are held under the chin like a violin.

virtù, le   (leh veer-TOO)   "The virtues." A soup traditionally containing 49 ingredients, a specialty of Teramo in Abruzzo. According to legend, seven maidens contributed seven different ingredients each. Supposedly, feeding a woman of virtue such a dish will increase a man's chances of seducing her.

The dish is traditionally made in six different pots containing different kinds of vegetables—fresh spring vegetables in the first; leafy vegetables in the second; pig parts in the third; cured pork, onion, and garlic in the fourth; **pasta** in the fifth; and meatballs in the sixth. These are combined in specified order until everything is united in the seventh pot. A springtime dish, *le virtù* contains peas, fava beans, and spinach, as well as dried legumes.

visciola   (vee-skee-OH-la)   Sour cherry. See also **marasca.**

vite   (VEE-teh)   Vine. From the Latin *vitis. Vitigno* also means vine as well as a grape variety.

vitello   (vee-TEH-loh)   Veal. The best veal is considered to come from a milk-fed calf no older than three months. *Vitellone* is used to describe a calf that has begun to graze. When fully mature, it is called **manzo.** In Sardinia the word *vitella* indicates veal made from heifers. From the Latin *vitulina.*

vitello tonnato   (vee-TEH-loh toh-NAH-toh)   "Veal [made with] tuna." Slices of cold veal in a creamy tuna sauce made with mayonnaise, capers, and anchovies, from Piedmont.

VITELLO TONNATO

2 pounds veal tenderloin
2¹/₂ cups white wine
1 red onion, chopped
¹/₂ celery stalk, chopped
1 small carrot, chopped
1 bay leaf
6 anchovies in oil
2 tablespoons capers

1 hard-boiled egg yolk
Juice of 1 lemon
1 tablespoon white vinegar
7 ounces tuna in oil, drained of oil

GARNISH:
1 lemon, sliced
1 tablespoon capers

Put the veal, white wine, onion, celery, carrot, and bay leaf in a bowl, toss, cover, and let marinate for one day. Transfer the meat and marinade to an oval casserole, bring to a boil, and gently simmer covered for 1¹/₂ hours. Remove from heat and let the meat cool in the liquid for about 1 hour. Remove the meat to a cutting board, discard the bay leaf, and degrease the liquid. Pour the sauce into a blender, add the tuna, anchovies, capers, hard-boiled egg yolk, lemon juice, and vinegar and blend until the sauce is homogeneous and velvety. Cut the meat across the grain in thin slices and arrange them, overlapping each one on a platter. Pour the sauce over the meat, then garnish with the lemon slices as well as the capers. Serve at room temperature. Serves 4.

vongola verace   (VOHN-goh-lah veh-RAH-cheh)   "True clam." Carpet-shell clam, *Venerupis decussata.* Commonly eaten with **linguine** and dressed in a garlic sauce, as in **linguine con vongole.** A smaller species is called *vongola gialla* (golden carpet-shell clam), *V. aurea.* **Tartufo di mare** (truffle of the sea) is a similar clam; and *cappa liscia, Callista chione* is a larger version. Also *vongola nera.*

VQPRD   EEC designation for *Vin de Qualité Produit dans une Région Déter-minée* (from the French for "wines of quality produced in determined re-gions"), applied to Italian **DOC** and **DOCG** wines. Sparkling wines are designated with the abbreviation *VSQPRD.*

vruoccolata   (vr'oo–oh–koh–LAH–tah)   Boiled pig's head with *broccoli neri* (a local dark purple variety), olive oil, and ***pecorino,*** baked in an earthen-ware dish, from Calabria. The word refers to "something made with broccoli."

W

weinsuppe (VYNE-zu-peh)   White wine-based soup from Alto Adige. From the German (wine soup).

würstel (VOOR-stehl)   Frankfurter, produced in northern Italy. From the German.

Z

zabaione (zah-bye-OH-neh)   A dessert made of whipped egg yolks, *Marsala* (sometimes old *Barolo*), and sugar, served either warm or cold, often with strawberries. It is usually prepared in a copper bowl. Also *zabaglione.*

There are several stories as to the name's origin, which seems to be Piedmontese. The most common contends the dessert was originally called *sanbajun,* the Piedmontese pronunciation for San Giovanni di Baylon, patron saint of pastry chefs. Others believe it commemorates Carlo Emanuele I of Savoy or may be derived from the word *sbaglione* (big mistake). Clifford A. Wright, in his book *Cucina Paradiso* (1992), believes the word derives from the Sicilian dialect word *zabbina* (to whip), which in turn comes from Arabic *zabad,* meaning "foam of water and other things."

ZABAIONE

4 egg yolks
¹/₄ cup sugar
¹/₄ cup Marsala

Warm the eggs and sugar in a double boiler over low heat. Whisk briskly until foamy. Add the *Marsala,* drop by drop, and continue beating until the mixture is a soft, creamy consistency and holds its shape. Serves 4.

zafferano (zah-feh-RAH-noh)   Saffron. The stigma and part of the styles of the flower *Crocus sativus.* Though originating in Asia Minor, saffron has long grown wild in Sicily, Abruzzo, and Sardinia, where the best is still cultivated. It was well known to the ancient Romans. Its name derives from Arabic *za' faran,* referring to its yellow color. Saffron's great expense is due to the fact that it takes 100,000 flowers to produce enough stigmas, which must be picked by hand, to be dried into a pound of saffron. It is, therefore, used sparingly, but is an essential ingredient in **risotto alla milanese**.

zaletto (zah-LEH-toh) "Little yellow [cookie]." Venetian cornmeal cookie, usually containing lemon peel or raisins, whose name comes from the yellow color of the cornmeal.

zampone (zahm-POH-neh) A pork sausage stuffed into the skin of a pig's foot, then boiled, a specialty of Modena, dating back at least to the 16th century. Zampone is cooked in a long utensil called a *zamponiera*.

zastoch (ZAH-stohk) Vegetable dish made by sautéing string beans, potatoes, and squash in pork fat with diced onions, from Friuli–Venezia Giulia.

Zelten (ZEHL-ten) Christmas cake made with rye flour, cinnamon, candied fruit, and nuts, from Alto Adige.

zenzero (ZEHN-zeh-roh) Ginger.

zeppole (ZEH-poh-leh) "Zeppelins." Fried puffs, from Naples. They are traditionally made on the feast of *San Giuseppe* (March 19). The name derives from Count Ferdinand von Zeppelin.
See also **bignè** and **sfince di San Giuseppe**.

zerro (ZEH-roh) Picarel, *Spicara smaris.* Often salted, it is a popular fish in Apulia. Also *mennola*.

zibibbo (zee-BEE-boh) Smyrna grape. From the Arabic (raisin).

zicchi (T'ZEE-kee) Breadsticks, from Sardinia.

Ziegenkäse (ZEE-gen-kay-seh) Soft goat's milk cheese, from Trentino–Alto Adige. The word is from the German for goat cheese.

ziminada (zee-mee-NAH-dah) "Stew." Stew of lamb intestines, from Sardinia. Also *sa corda*.

zimino (zee-MEE-noh) Sauce of minced greens, garlic, and oil. It may be used with vegetables or a dressing for fish. *Zimino di ceci* (also *ceci in zimino*) is chickpea soup flavored with browned onions, garlic, greens, tomato, and celery, from Genoa. The term *zimino* also may refer to salt cod or cuttlefish similarly prepared, as in *seppie in zimino*.

zinne di monaca (ZEE-neh dee MOH-nah-kah) "Nun's tits." Plump cakes topped with icing and a maraschino cherry, from Naples.

ziriddu   (zee-REE-doo)   "Child's plaything." Pastries made with honey, from Sicily.

ziti   (ZEE-tee)   "Bridegrooms." A fairly fat *maccheroni,* a specialty of southern Italy, especially Naples. *Zitone, zituane,* and *candele* are somewhat wider versions. Also *zite* and *boccolotti.*

zogghiu   (ZOH-g'yoo)   *Pesto* made with parsley and mint, from Sicily. From the Arabaic *zait,* which means to add oil to food.

zolfini   (zohl-FEE-nee)   Type of Tuscan bean.

zucca   (ZOO-kah)   Although the word *zucca* most commonly is used to mean pumpkin, it is a more general term for gourds and squashes. Old World gourds (Cucurbitaceae) originated in India but came to Europe early on and were well known to the ancient Romans. Pumpkins and squashes, including zucchini, came to Italy from the New World in the 16th century, where they were soon utilized in a wide variety of ways—boiled, fried, stuffed, and as a filling for pasta like *tortelli di zucca. Z. disfatta* is a traditional Yom Kippur dish of Ferrara's Jews made with local squash cooked with onion and citron.

zucca candita   (ZOO-kah kahn-DEE-tah)   "Candied squash." Candied squash, used in cakes and as decoration, often cut into very thin strands called *cappeli d'angelo* (angel's hair), from Sicily.

zucchero   (ZOO-keh-roh)   Sugar. A sugared dish is termed *zuccherato.* From the Arabic *sukkar.*

zucchero filato   (ZOO-keh-roh fee-LAH-toh)   Spun sugar.

zucchina   (zoo-KEE-nah)   Zucchini. The word is an Italian diminutive of *zucca* (gourd). The *zucchine* of southern Italy and Sardinia are usually sweeter than the dark green varieties of the north. The best of both varieties are those of summer, which tend to be smaller.

   Zucchine are used in many ways, simply marinated, stuffed, grilled, baked, and fried.

zuccotto   (zoo-KOH-toh)   "Large pumpkin." Dome-shaped Florentine dessert made with sponge cake soaked in liqueur and filled with custard or whipped cream and chocolate.

zuppa   (ZOO-pah)   Thick soup, as opposed to *minestra* and *brodo,* usually served over slices of bread. Also *zuppa di pane,* which is usually made with water rather than broth. From Middle English *soupe.*

zuppa acida   (ZOO-pah ah-SEE-dah)   "Sour soup." Sauerkraut soup, from Alto Adige.

zuppa alla pavese (ZOO-pah AH-lah pah-VEH-zeh)   Broth poured over fried or toasted bread, raw eggs, and *parmigiano,* from Lombardy. Said to have been created by a peasant to restore the strength and spirits of Francis I after he lost the battle of Pavia in 1525.

ZUPPA ALLA PAVESE

4 tablespoons butter	*4 tablespoons grated parmigiano*
4 thick slices country-style bread	*4 cups beef broth*
8 eggs, at room temperature	

Melt the butter in a sauté pan until foamy. Add the bread slices and sauté until golden on both sides. Place 1 bread slice in each soup bowl and break 2 eggs on top of each bread slice, taking care not to break the yolks. Sprinkle with *parmigiano.* Bring the broth to a boil, then slowly and carefully add to the soup bowls to cover and poach the eggs. Serve immediately. Serves 4.

zuppa all'arentina (ZOO-pah AH-lah-rehn-TEE-nah)   Chicken soup in which chicken is cooked with vegetables, sliced, and cooked with chicken broth until well reduced, then served over slices of bread, from Arezzo.

zuppa alla tarantina (ZOO-pah AH-la tah-rahn-TEE-nah)   Hot pepper and shellfish soup made with eel, cuttlefish, prawns, and grouper with tomatoes, served with toasted garlic bread. It is a specialty of the Bay of Taranto in Apulia.

zuppa alla ueca (ZOO-pah AH-lah W'EH-kah)   Soup made with vegetables, barley, stale rye bread, and *fontina,* from Valle d'Aosta.

zuppa angelica (ZOO-pah ahn-JEH-lee-cah)   "Angel soup." Sponge cake dessert with an egg-and-chocolate cream, from Sicily. From the Middle English *soupe* and the Late Latin *angelus.*

zuppa dei doges (ZOO-pah DAY'yee DOH-jes)   "Doges' soup." Venetian soup containing large fried rice-and-cheese dumplings, from Venice. Named in honor of the one-time ruling Doges of the city.

zuppa della regina (ZOO-pah DEH-lah reh-JEE-nah)   "Queen soup." Chicken soup made with the white meat ground with almonds and bread, served with croutons.

zuppa di aragosta (ZOO-pah DEE ah-rah-GOH-stah)   Lobster soup, a specialty of Trapani in Sicily.

zuppa di Arey   (ZOO-pah dee ah-RAY)   Soup made with milk, walnuts, sugar, cinnamon, breadsticks, egg yolks, nutmeg, and red wine, from the town of Gressoney in Valle d'Aosta.

zuppa di borlotti   (ZOO-pah dee bohr-LOH-tee)   *Borlotti* bean soup cooked in the oven, from Siena.

zuppa di magro   (ZOO-pah dee MAH-groh)   "Lean soup." A fast day soup containing only vegetables, no meat.

zuppa di pesce   (ZOO-pah dee PEH-sheh)   Fish soup. In Friuli, *zuppa di pesce alla gradese* is made with fish of the northern Adriatic, with garlic and vinegar. In Basilicata, *z. di pesce alla Santavenere* is made with fish of the Ionian Sea, with chile peppers and garlic.

zuppa di terlano   (ZOO-pah dee tehr-LAH-noh)   A cream and white wine sauce, from the town of Terlano in Trentino–Alto Adige.

zuppa di verdura   (ZOO-pah dee vehr-DOO-rah)   Vegetable soup.

zuppa inglese   (ZOO-pah een-GLEH-zeh)   Dessert made of sponge cake soaked in liqueur and topped with custard or whipped cream. The name translates literally in Italian as "English soup," and may in fact connote its similarity to English trifle. Others believe it is a dialectical corruption of the verb *inzuppare,* meaning to sop. Also *zuppa all'emiliana.*

ZUPPA INGLESE

4 cups milk	*¹/₂ vanilla bean*
8 eggs, separated	*1 sponge cake*
1 cup confectioners' sugar	*1 cup rum*
¹/₄ cup flour	*¹/₂ cup alchermes*

Warm the milk in a saucepan but do not bring to a boil. In a bowl, beat the egg yolks, 2/3 cup of the sugar, the flour, and vanilla and gradually pour into heated milk. Keep mixing with a wooden spoon until thickened to a custard-like consistency. Remove the vanilla bean.

   Cut the sponge cake horizontally into 3 layers. Take 1 layer and place it in a deep serving dish. Sprinkle with half the rum and some of the **alchermes.** Spread half the custard onto the cake. Cut up the next layer of sponge cake into pieces about 1 inch long and ¹/₂ inch thick. Place on top of the custard, sprinkle with the rest of the rum and *alchermes*, and spread the remaining custard on top. Cover with the third layer of sponge cake.

Whip the egg whites until they form soft peaks and combine with the remaining sugar. Cover the cake with the whipped egg whites and brown under the broiler. Allow to cool and chill in the refrigerator until ready to serve. Serves 6.

---

zuppa sarda (ZOO-pah SAHR-dah)   Soup made of stale bread, *mozzarella,* egg, parsley, and pepper, from Sardinia.

zurrette (zoo-REH-teh)   Sheep's blood pudding mixed with bread crumbs, the lining of the sheep's body cavity, *pecorino,* and mint, from Sardinia. It is either boiled or grilled.

Bibliography

The following bibliography lists mainly the books published in English that I have found most useful in my own research and the most rewarding for anyone interested in Italian food and drink. Most are still in print or easily accessible at the library. The works cited in Italian are also books that might be found or ordered from a good international bookstore such as Rizzoli. In a few cases, the books in Italian may well be out of print, but for the scholar, they are well worth searching out.

Accame, Franco. *Mandilli de saea.* 6th edition. Genoa: De Ferrari Editore, 1990.

Anderson, Burton. *The Simon & Schuster Guide to the Wines of Italy.* NY: Simon & Schuster, 1992.

_____. *The Wine Atlas of Italy.* NY: Simon & Schuster, 1990.

_____. *Vino.* Boston: Little, Brown and Company, 1980.

Andrews, Colman. *Flavors of the Riviera.* NY: Bantam Books, 1996.

Artusi, Pellegrino. *The Art of Eating Well.* Trans. Kyle M. Phillips III. NY: Random House, 1996.

Barr, Nancy Verde. *We Called It Macaroni.* NY: Alfred A. Knopf, 1992.

Bastianich, Lidia and Jay Jacobs. *La Cucina di Lidia.* NY: Doubleday, 1990.

Bergese, Nino. *Mangiare da re.* Milan: Giangiacomo Feltrinelli Editore, 1969.

Bettoja, Jo. *Southern Italian Cooking.* NY: Bantam Books, 1991.

Bissell, Frances. *The Book of Food.* NY: Henry Holt and Company, 1994.

Bittman, Mark. *Fish.* NY: Macmillan Publishing Company, 1994.

Braudel, Fernand. *La Mediterranee et le monde mediterranean a l'epoque de Philippe II,* 2nd rev. ed. Paris: Librarire Armand Colin, 1966.

Bugialli, Giuliano. *Bugialli on Pasta.* NY: Simon & Schuster, 1988.

_____. *Giuliano Bugialli's Classic Techniques of Italian Cooking.* NY: Simon & Schuster, 1982.

_____. *The Fine Art of Italian Cooking.* NY: Times Books, 1989.

_____. *Foods of Tuscany.* NY: Stewart, Tabori & Chang, 1992.

_____. *Foods of Sicily & Sardinia and the Smaller Islands.* NY: Rizzoli, 1996.

Caggiano, Biba. *Trattoria Cooking.* NY: Macmillan Publishing Company, 1992.

Callen, Anna Teresa. *The Wonderful World of Pizzas, Quiches, and Savory Pies.* NY: Crown Publishers, 1981.

Carnacina, Luigi. *Luigi Carnacina's Great Italian Cooking.* NY: Abradale Press.

Carnacina, Luigi and Luigi Veronelli. *La Cucina Rustica Regionale.* 4 Vols. Milan: Biblioteca Universale Rizzoli, 1977.

Carr, Sandy. *The Simon & Schuster Pocket Guide to Cheese.* NY: Simon & Schuster, 1992.

Cipriani, Arrigo. *The Harry's Bar Cookbook.* NY: Bantam Books, 1991.

Coyle, L. Patrick. *The World Encyclopedia of Food.* NY: Facts on File, 1982.

Dalby, Andrew and Sally Grainger. *The Classical Cookbook.* Malibu: J. Paul Getty Museum, 1996.

David, Elizabeth. *Italian Food.* NY: Penguin Books, 1969.

Davidson, Alan. *Mediterranean Seafood,* 2nd edition. London: Penguin Books, 1972.

_____. *Seafood.* NY: Simon & Schuster, 1989.

Del Conte, Anna. *Gastronomy of Italy.* NY: Prentice Hall Press, 1987.

Della Croce, Julia. *Antipasti: The Little Dishes of Italy.* San Francisco: Chronicle Books, 1993.

_____. *Italy: The Vegetarian Table.* San Francisco: Chronicle Books, 1994.

Doglio, Sandro. *Gran Dizionario della Gastornomia del Piemonte.* Asti: Daumiere Editrice, 1990.

Field, Carol. *Celebrating Italy.* NY: William Morrow and Company, 1990.

_____. *In Nonna's Kitchen.* NY: HarperCollins, 1997.

_____. *The Italian Baker.* NY: Harper & Row, 1985.

_____. *Italy in Small Bites.* NY: William Morrow and Company, 1993.

FitzGibbon, Theodora. *The Food of the Western World.* NY: Quadrangle, 1976.

Giusti-Lanham, Hedy. *The Cuisine of Venice & Surrounding Northern Regions.* NY: Barron's, 1978.

Gottardo, Vittorio. *Osti e Tavernieri.* Venice: Supernova, 1996.

Harris, Marvin. *Good to Eat.* NY: Simon & Schuster, 1985.

Harris, Valentina. *Recipes from an Italian Farmhouse.* NY: Simon & Schuster, 1989.

_____. *Valentina's Italian Family* Feast. NY: Simon & Schuster, 1990.

Hazan, Marcella. *The Classic Italian Cookbook.* NY: Harper's Magazine Press, 1962.

_____. *Marcella's Italian Kitchen.* NY: Alfred A. Knopf, 1986.

Jenkins, Nancy Harmon. *Flavors of Puglia.* NY: Broadway Books, 1997.

Jenkins, Steven. *Cheese Primer.* NY: Workman Publishing, 1996.

Johnson, Hugh. *Vintage: The Story of Wine.* NY: 1989.

Kasper, Lynne Rossetto. *The Splendid Table.* NY: William Morrow and Company, 1992.

Kummer, Corby. "Pasta," The Atlantic Monthly. (July, 1986).

Lanza, Anna Tasca. *The Heart of Sicily.* NY: Clarkson Potter, 1993.

La Place, Viana. *Verdura.* NY: William Morrow and Company, 1991.

Lo Monte, Mimmetta. *Mimmetta Lo Monte's Classic Sicilian Cookbook.* NY: Simon & Schuster, 1990.

Luongo, Pino. *A Tuscan in the Kitchen.* NY: Clarkson Potter, 1988.

Machlin, Edda Servi. *The Classic Cuisine of the Italian Jews.* NY: Dodd, Mead & Company, 1981.

Mallo, Beppe. *Calabria e Lucania in Bocca.* Sicily.

Maresca, Tom and Diane Darrow. *La Tavola Italiana*. NY: William Morrow and Company, 1988.

_____. *The Seasons of the Italian Kitchen*. NY: Atlantic Monthly Press, 1994.

May, Tony. *Italian Cuisine*. NY: Italian Wine & Food Institute, 1990.

McClane, A. J. *The Encyclopedia of Fish Cookery*. NY: Holt, Rinehart and Winston, 1977.

Middione, Carlo. *La Vera Cucina*. NY: Simon & Schuster, 1996.

Milioni, Stefano. *Columbus Menu*. NY: Italian Trade Commission.

Montagne, Prosper. *Larousse Gastronomique*. American Edition, ed. Jenifer Harvey Lang. NY: Crown Publishers, 1988.

Ortiz, Elizabeth Lambert. *The Encyclopedia of Herbs, Spices & Flavorings*. NY: Dorling Kindersley, Inc., 1992.

Piccinardi, Antonio and James M. Johnson. *The Gourmet's Tour of Italy*. NY: New York Graphic Society, 1987.

Plotkin, Fred. *Italy for the Gourmet Traveler*. NY: Little Brown and Company, 1996.

_____. *The Authentic Pasta Book*. NY: Simon & Schuster, 1985.

Ratti, Renato. *Conoscere i Vini d'Italia*. Brescia: Edizioni AEB, 1985.

Rigante, Elodia. *Elodia Rigante's Italian Immigrant Cooking*. Cobb, CA: First View Books, 1995.

Robinson, Jancis, ed. *The Oxford Companion to Wine*. NY: Oxford University Press, 1994.

Roden, Claudia. *The Book of Jewish Food*. NY: Alfred A. Knopf, 1996.

Santin, Gino and Anthony Blake. *La Cucina Veneziana*. NY: Prentice Hall Press, 1988.

Schneider, Elizabeth. *Uncommon Fruits & Vegetables*. NY: Harper & Row, Publishers, 1986.

Scicolone, Michele. *A Fresh Taste of Italy*. NY: Broadway Books, 1997.

_____. *The Antipasto Table*. NY: William Morrow and Company, 1991.

_____. *La Dolce Vita*. NY: William Morrow and Company, 1993.

Sidoli, Richard Camillo. *The Cooking of Parma*. NY: Rizzoli, 1996.

Sokolov, Raymond. *Why We Eat What We Eat.* NY: Summit Books, 1991.

Tannahill, Reay. *Food in History.* NY: Crown Publishers, 1988.

Root, Waverly. *Food.* NY: Simon & Schuster, 1980.

_____. *The Food of Italy.* NY: Vintage Books, 1971.

Visser, Margaret. *Much Depends on Dinner.* NY: Grove Press, 1986.

_____. *The Rituals of Dinner.* NY: Grove Weidenfeld, 1991.

Willinger, Faith Heller. *Eating in Italy.* NY: Hearst Books, 1989.

_____. *Red, White & Green.* NY: HarperCollins, 1996.

Tornabene, Danda and Giovanna and Michele Evans. *La Cucina Siciliana di Gangivecchio.* NY: Alfred A. Knopf, 1996.

Toussaint-Samat, Maguelonne. *History of Food.* Trans. Anthea Bell. Cambridge, Mass.: 1992.

Weaver, William Woys. *Heirloom Vegetable Gardening.* NY: Henry Holt and Company, 1997.

Wells, Patricia. *Patricia Wells' Trattoria.* NY: William Morrow and Company, 1993.

Wright, Clifford A. *Cucina Paradiso.* NY: Simon & Schuster, 1992.

Index

The index contains English names of commonly used terms and foods, as well as Italian terms that do not appear as main entries, and recipes.

A

abalone, 168
abbacchio, 5
accia, 237
accirate, 167
acciugata, 10
acciughe sotto sale, 10
acqua minerale, 11
agarico delizioso, 112
aged, 128
aggiadda, 12
aghiotta di pesce spada, 189
agnoli, 13
agnolini, 13
alaustra, 20
albacore tuna, 14
albarola, 76
al cartoccio, 240
alcohol, 14
alcolico, 14
alice, 10
alla trainiera, 65
almond, 145
amberjack, 216
Americano (recipe), 17
anchovy, 10
anciova, 10

andouille, 7
anelletti, 18
anellini, 18
angler fish, 212
anice, 19
anicini, 19
anisetta, 229
annata, 272
anolen, 19
apertif, 20
aphrodisiacs, 12
Apicus, 2
appetizer, 19
appiu, 237
apple, 150
apricot, 14
arabica, 52
arborio, 217, 218
ardaino, 167
ardenti, 187
argentina, 82
aroma, 205
aromatics, 166
arrabiosu, 187
arselle, 80, 231
*Art de la cuisine française au dix-neuvième,
   L* (Carême), 3
artichoke, 62

G

H